THE AMERICAN CIVIL LIBERTIES UNION

and the Making of Modern Liberalism, 1930–1960

JUDY KUTULAS

The

University

of

North

Carolina

Press

Chapel

Hill

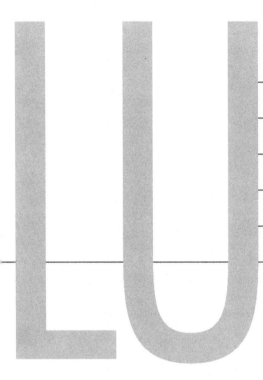

THE
AMERICAN
CIVIL
LIBERTIES
UNION

& the
Making of
Modern
Liberalism
1930–1960

© 2006 The University of North Carolina Press
All rights reserved
Designed and typeset in Arnhem and Futura
by Eric M. Brooks
Manufactured in the United States of America
*This book was published with the assistance of
the Thornton H. Brooks Fund of the University of
North Carolina Press.*
The paper in this book meets the guidelines for
permanence and durability of the Committee on
Production Guidelines for Book Longevity of the
Council on Library Resources.
Library of Congress Cataloging-in-Publication Data
Kutulas, Judy, 1953–
The American Civil Liberties Union and the making
of modern liberalism, 1930–1960 / by Judy Kutulas.
p. cm. Includes bibliographical references and index.
ISBN-13: 978-0-8078-3036-9 (cloth: alk. paper)
ISBN-10: 0-8078-3036-4 (cloth: alk. paper)
1. American Civil Liberties Union—History.
2. Civil rights—United States. I. Title.
JC599.U5K97 2006 323.06'073—dc22 2005036097
cloth   10 09 08 07 06   5 4 3 2 1

To my guys

MICHAEL, ALEX, AND NATE

CONTENTS

ACKNOWLEDGMENTS ix

ABBREVIATIONS xiii

INTRODUCTION 1

1 Becoming Chic
The National ACLU in the 1930s 16

2 Unnecessary Obstacles
ACLU Affiliates in the 1930s 42

3 Holding Us All Together
*The ACLU, the Nazi-Soviet Pact, and
Anticommunism, 1939–1941* 64

4 Losing Our Influence
The National ACLU during World War II 89

5 Sticking Their Necks Out
The Affiliates during World War II 113

6 Nothing Accomplished, Nothing Done
The National ACLU after World War II 136

7 Wedded to Caesar
The Affiliates after World War II 163

8 Mutually Unhappy in Each Other's Company
Crisis and Resolution 189

AFTERWORD 219

APPENDIX 1
*Percentage (and Number) of ACLU National
Board Members, by Occupation* 223

APPENDIX 2
*ACLU Membership Figures, Expenses,
and Income, by Year* 224

NOTES 227

BIBLIOGRAPHY 279

INDEX 293

ACKNOWLEDGMENTS

This project began with a casual e-mail conversation with an old graduate school friend that snowballed into a conference paper, an article, several articles, and this book. At each stage, I received support and assistance from individuals who facilitated it.

An American Council of Learned Societies grant funded my first work on the ACLU. An Associated Colleges of the Midwest fellowship sent me to Chicago. A Fleur Cowles Fellowship took me to the Harry Ransom Humanities Center at the University of Texas at Austin. The Radcliffe Center for Advanced Studies brought me to Boston, where I used the Schlesinger Library, other Harvard libraries, and the Massachusetts Historical Society. St. Olaf College's Faculty Development Grants and special funding from the provost's office have supported the rest of the research, including trips to California and Princeton. Money from the St. Olaf History Department's Kenneth Bjork fund helped defray the costs of photocopying and borrowing microfilm. St. Olaf has been extremely generous in helping me fund this project.

Librarians across the country have been both patient and helpful. I would like to thank the staffs of the Minnesota Historical Society, the State Historical Society of Wisconsin, Special Collections at the University of Chicago, the Chicago Historical Society, the Mudd Library at Princeton University, the Bancroft Library, the California Historical Society, the Harry Ransom Center, the Schlesinger Library, the Harvard Theater Library, the Harvard Law Library, the Harvard Archives, the Massachusetts Historical Society, and Special Collections at the University of California at Los Angeles (UCLA) for their attention and skill. Librarians at the Library of Congress, the Franklin D. Roosevelt Library, Marquette University, the Tamiment Library, the University of California library system, Swarthmore College, Yale University, the Ohio State Supreme Court Law Library, the Southern California Library for Social Studies and Research, Smith College, and the University of Minnesota have been kind enough to share microfilm or photocopied materials with me. Librarians at the University of Washington helped my research proxy, my husband, Michael, accomplish a lot in a little time. Pat Keats and her staff at the California Historical Society deserve a special round of thanks for their kindness the day I wrenched my back. Peter Filardo of the Tamiment Library proved, as always, to be a font of information and advice. An old friend from graduate school, Chip Hixson, nosed around still-being-reorganized papers at UCLA's Special Collections for me. His wife, Carol Hixson, formerly head of cataloging at UCLA, rush processed a microfilm guide that saved me literally hundreds of costly archival hours.

For years I was a fixture at the microfilm readers at Rolvaag Library at St. Olaf College, patiently aided by librarians Bryn Geffert, Kasia Gonnerman, and Mary Sue Lovett. Thanks particularly to interlibrary loan librarian Sarah Leake for getting me four reels of ACLU records every couple of weeks and to Betsy Busa for her wizardry with cranky microfilm readers.

Other individuals have been generous with their time or expertise. One of my best research days ever was the day an audiotape arrived from Leon Despres, Chicago lawyer, former alderman, and civil libertarian. Ann Forwand provided clippings and background information about her father, Ernest Besig. Maurice Isserman sent me photocopies of his files on his uncle, Abe Isserman. Athan Theoharis gave me useful advice on Freedom of Information Act files. Robert Cottrell shared some of his research on Roger Baldwin. Mark Kleinman sent the e-mail that launched the conference paper that launched this. Richard Weiss has gracefully evolved from my graduate school advisor to a supportive friend. Ellen Schrecker has been extremely generous with her time and knowledge of cold war resources and has written more letters of recommendation than anyone should ever have to. Michael Furmanovsky answered e-mail questions about the Southern California left. Jill Watts twice timed her research trips so that we could share the stresses of being on the road.

Working with the University of North Carolina Press has been a delight. Charles Grench was enthusiastic from the start, and his assistant, Katy O'Brien, guided me through the details of the publishing process. Copyeditor Stephanie Wenzel helped me whip the manuscript into shape and is probably dying to edit this particular sentence. Ellen Schrecker and Robert Cottrell both read the manuscript for the press and offered much useful advice. I was lucky to have a good friend, Sarah Entenmann, handle my index.

At St. Olaf College, I have always felt supported by the History Department. My American history colleagues—Jim Farrell, Michael Fitzgerald, Steve Hahn, and Chris Grasso (now at William and Mary)—have modeled a strong commitment to scholarship alongside teaching. Eric Fure-Slocum, the other twentieth-century U.S. historian on my block, has read parts of this manuscript and provided helpful comments. Many thanks to the American Conversations gang for inspiring me to think outside the box. Mary Titus and Carol Holly, my sabbatical support group, have lived through the final push to finish this.

Family and friends helped turn research trips into vacations. Many, many thanks to my parents, John and Alexandra Kutulas, for providing room, board, transportation, and free child care during my swings through California. My sisters and their families, Janet Kutulas and Peter Simcich; Nikki Kutulas and Kim, Kamau, and Kalif Purce; and Sandy, Gus, Christina, Michelle, and Isabella Perez, made being on the road feel like home. Thanks especially to Janet and Peter for planning their wedding around one of my research trips and for putting me up during another. My late father-in-law, William Fitzgerald, an amateur historian, was a great supporter of my work as well as a gracious host during Chicago visits. Thanks also to Rose Fitzgerald, Cheryl and Bill Berriman, Christine Roed, Don Davis, Jackie Braitman, Monte Kugel and Larry Goldstein (and Sky and Dylan), Nancy McCoy, Roberta McCoy, Barbara Boyd, Ryan Boyd, Parke Skelton, and Allison Morgan for making time for me during research visits, for feeding me, and for sometimes driving me around. My husband, Michael Fitzgerald, helped me nurture this project from the start, checking in archives, once calling me from the Chicago Historical Society with a discovery, reading drafts, and listening to about a thousand half-baked ideas. He understands the concept of "academic couple" completely, providing emotional and logistical support along with faith in my abilities. Long before they could read, my sons Alex and Nate learned to pick out their names in the acknowledgments of my first book and made it clear that they expected a second one dedicated to them, which Nate figured would take a few days to write. Okay, so it took a little longer; at long last, here it is.

ABBREVIATIONS

ACLU	American Civil Liberties Union
CCF	Committee for Cultural Freedom
CCLC	Chicago Civil Liberties Committee
CLUM	Civil Liberties Union of Massachusetts
CPUSA	Communist Party of the United States of America
CRC	Civil Rights Congress
ECLC	Emergency Civil Liberties Committee
FBI	Federal Bureau of Investigation
HUAC	House Committee on Un-American Activities
ILD	International Labor Defense
JACL	Japanese American Citizens' League
NAACP	National Association for the Advancement of Colored People
NCACLU	Northern California Branch of the American Civil Liberties Union
NLG	National Lawyers Guild
NLRB	National Labor Relations Board
SCACLU	Southern California Branch of the American Civil Liberties Union
WRA	War Relocation Authority

Note: ACLU branch names have been standardized to the most familiar form.

On the day World War I ended, Roger Baldwin, head of what was to become the American Civil Liberties Union (ACLU), went to prison for violating the Selective Service Act by refusing to register for the draft. Baldwin was thirty-four at the time and not likely to be summoned by his draft board, so his was a symbolic protest against the war and a government that denied dissenters full freedom of expression.[1] Twenty-five years later, this onetime enemy of the people spent the next war not in prison but consulting with representatives of the government he once scorned. Baldwin remained devoted to civil liberties as a calling, but he was not forever doomed thereby to life on society's margins. His work helped transform the ways Americans thought about individual rights, giving him and his colleagues unexpected influence and prestige. "Civil Liberties," noted one of Baldwin's bemused officers in 1939, "are now pretty darn chic."[2] This book examines the ACLU's role in making civil liberties a pivotal liberal value and considers the costs of the organization's journey from the radical fringes to the liberal mainstream.

My work focuses on the years between 1930 and 1960 because during that time the ACLU became institutionalized. Institutionalization is the process by which a movement "loses its non-legitimate character and becomes part of the status quo social order."[3] Outside events first rendered civil liberties chic among liberals. Union leaders quickly learned to take advantage of that popularity, deliberately cultivating liberal respectability, a liberal membership base, a professional operating style, a relationship with liberal administrations, and finally, liberal anticommunism. In making these choices, the organization alienated other supporters, particularly those who formed the national web of branch ACLU offices across the country. Attaining mainstream status likewise angered the Union's traditional opponents, conservatives, who had much to fear from any group that gave liberals power and legitimacy. Pursuing liberal respectability plunged the organization into political partisanships. Institutionalization, thus, was a portentous choice for the organization, one with many consequences, some good and some bad.

The men and women who founded the ACLU were radicals, not liberals, and did not anticipate or necessarily desire that the Union would grow into the organization it became. Some accepted the advantages of liberal sponsorship and access. Others did not. But all could see the opportunities presented by the New Deal. It created a climate where civil liberties could flourish and brought sympathetic public officials and judges into positions of authority. Of course, becoming more of a liberal organization required some fundamental changes in a group created by radicals who never expected to be popular or influential. Between 1930 and 1960, as the organization grew, Union leaders struggled to distinguish between harmless and legitimate alterations and those that might please liberals but violate the group's pledge to defend "everybody."[4]

In general, liberalism and civil libertarianism are harmonious with each other. American liberals, however, became interested in individual rights at a historically specific moment, one when their values did not fully coincide with the Union's traditional mission. Liberals seek to enhance individual lives within a community of competing interests, varying their methods and specific goals over time. New Deal liberals initially equated better lives with more economic equality, counting on the federal government to regulate the free enterprise system. By the late 1930s, economic reform started to lose steam as other governments raised concerns about the consequences of focusing so narrowly on economic equality. Dictators, for example, created state-run economies where everyone was allegedly equal but denied individuals basic freedoms. Liberals retooled, making their program more "rights-based," as Alan Brinkley called it, shifting emphasis "to expand the notion of personal liberty and individual freedom for everyone."[5] Rights-based liberals gravitated toward the ACLU; they made civil liberties chic.

Yet having concluded that dictatorships withheld what liberals regarded as basic human freedoms, they were not entirely comfortable with the apolitical enterprise of protecting everyone's rights. What one attorney called the Union's "poisonous even-handedness," its championing of all dissent, sometimes scared liberals, who imagined situations where extremists using free speech for their own ends might compromise others' free speech.[6] It is the basic dilemma all civil libertarians face, finding balance between individual rights and national security. Not surprisingly, civil libertarians tend to favor the rights, an inclination reinforced by circumstance, since so many of the Union's founders themselves were dissenters with unpopular views. As the group gained credibility, though, some of its advocates shifted their allegiance from the challengers to the status quo. Eventually many accepted the liberal view, that there were circumstances when a minority might threaten democracy with their views. During the years it became institutionalized, the ACLU confronted three serious challenges to its commitment to all dissent, challenges raised by liberals who maintained that certain of the Union's clients advocated dangerous rather than merely unpopular views. Those three challenges were posed by American fascists in the 1930s, Japanese Americans during World War II, and American Communists during the late 1940s and 1950s. At first the organization stuck to its principles. As it joined the liberal mainstream, however, the Union proved more willing to compromise for the sake of influence and popularity.

To modern-day activists and historians, this is a disappointment. The Union started out defiant and unpopular, but it increasingly accepted limits defined by others. By the 1950s it was fully part of the liberal obsession with Communism. In its eagerness to please powerful people, it let go of its "risk, . . . rejection of the status quo and faith in the future," as Mary Sperling McAuliffe noted, to embrace liberals' postwar obsession with "safety and stability." The Union was part of a much larger postwar development, liberal anticommunism, a doctrine whose cornerstones were, as Roger Baldwin's successor once said, "civil liberties, prosperity, and defense."[7] It was complicit in the construction of that ideology, lending its by-then well-burnished reputation to help legitimate the civil liberties compromises necessary for its continued success.

Scholars and activists alike chide the ACLU for being part of the liberal anticommunist mainstream. Even modern ACLU leaders concede that it did not always do its job fully, that it was a "useless organization in the early fifties." Historians recognize the pattern of its reactions. Ellen Schrecker compares the ACLU to the National Association for the Advancement of Colored People (NAACP), Americans for Democratic Action, the American Committee for Cultural Freedom, and similar organizations. These, she argues, "put up little opposition to the . . . big and little violations of civil liberties and political freedom during the early Cold War." McAuliffe sees early potential and later weakness, noting that in the 1930s the ACLU "responded strongly in many highly controversial cases" and seemed "well prepared to resist the pressures of the post–World War II Red Scare." But after the war its leaders started to worry about their "anti-Communist credentials" so obsessively that it manifested "a perceptible wavering and hesitation in cases where civil liberties and the Communist issue intersected."[8] Like most modern liberals, these scholars are disappointed with the ACLU for buckling under pressure to conform.

I, too, am disappointed by the Union's past, but my task here is to explain why an organization committed to defending the rights of all comers fell prey to liberalism's weaknesses and compromised its core values. The answer is complicated, found not just in the Union's pronouncements and positions, but in its internal workings and decision-making processes. As the liberal mindset percolated through the Union's top, leaders desired respectability and government partnership, goals far from its founders' intentions. The more vested the group became in the status quo, the more determined it was to protect its reputation. Yet in order to be effective, the Union had to grow, and growth brought change. The small, centralized, elitist organization of 1930 eventually became a diverse national mass movement. From the grass roots came pressures for the Union to drop its liberal anticommunist pretensions. Some observers see the ACLU's institutionalization as a familiar process, "the natural history of the conservatizing influence of time on an organization."[9] Certainly there is a natural evolution that occurs as a movement ages. It is my contention, however, that what happened to the Union was something more than just a low point in an organizational life cycle. It was an unnatural progression begun by its leaders and reversed by its members.

The Union's founders intended to be our conscience, guarding against the tyranny of the majority. In the beginning, their defense of dissidents was colored by their own identities as rebels, and the organization they created reflected the biases of their heterodox radicalism. Opposed to capitalism, they made it their business to defend its challengers. Their relations with traditional American institutions were adversarial; their tactics were confrontational and included the kind of grand gesture that sent Baldwin to prison. They saw no reason to concern themselves with public relations, education, or recruitment. Had they been liberals, they would have been more hopeful, eager to find a constituency and use it to try to influence government; they would have made better use of the legal system to codify their gains. Of course, had they been liberals in the first years of the twentieth century, their attention would have been elsewhere. Liberals did not oppose Bill of Rights freedoms, but as a social group more privileged than radicals, they had little interest in minority dissent.

The New Deal altered liberals' attitudes about civil liberties, creating a new and increasingly powerful foundation for the ACLU's work. Liberals questioned the capitalist system, flirted with more radical collectivist economic solutions, and became excited by direct action tactics.[10] The Second New Deal, with the National Labor Relations Act, the Works Progress Administration, and Social Security, made them hopeful. Fascism's rise sensitized them to the positive aspects of their own government, chiefly its guarantees of democracy and personal freedom. As Eric Foner noted, "By the eve of World War II, civil liberties had assumed a central place in the New Deal understanding of freedom." By the end of the war, what Brinkley called "reform liberalism" gave way to its rights-based replacement, cautious and individualistic, with "a growing interest in the expansion of rights for individuals and groups."[11] The heretofore small ACLU moved into national prominence.

The People's Front (1935–39) likewise promoted the fusion of civil liberties and liberalism by shifting the national conversation toward shared values. While the New Deal interested liberals in the ACLU, the Front drew civil liberties radicals to liberalism. The People's Front, the American version of the Communist International's Popular Front, constructed a prodemocratic, antifascist coalition. However cynical or temporary, it spotlighted American democracy as the antithesis of fascism.[12] Crucial to that discourse were the rights for which civil libertarians fought: religious tolerance, artistic and creative freedom, free speech, and the ability to disagree without suffering persecution. With Franklin D. Roosevelt's people-oriented Second New Deal remaking American government and the People's Front building new coalitions of freedom-loving people, the ACLU flourished. It attracted hundreds of new supporters. It partnered with a government it respected. Liberals used the ACLU to demonstrate their civil liberties commitments, and the Union used liberals to achieve its agenda.

Respectability changed the Union. Liberals brought their own priorities and prejudices with them. They trusted government. They were practical, accommodating, and scientific. They followed rules. Their definition of national security was elastic. They believed, like Sinclair Lewis, that it (fascism) *could* happen here, so they had little patience for the rights of people like Charles Coughlin and Elizabeth Dilling. They considered World War II an all-out struggle between democracy and fascism, and they fully supported the war effort, including the Roosevelt administration's restrictions on the freedom of war's opponents. Intimidated by the cold war and Republican attacks, they accepted that the American Communist Party was a conspiratorial, violent, and revolutionary organization whose members threatened our way of life. As time went on, the Union bent to the liberal viewpoint, compromising its traditional commitments to dissenters for the good of the country and itself.

Liberalism was not the only influence on the ACLU. Activists who volunteered their time brought more than their politics to the organization. Alan Wald, writing about the 1930s literary left, shows how personal idiosyncrasies, economic situations, sexual preferences, and other elements of identity complicate the otherwise stereotypic assumptions we might make about "Communist artist[s]."[13] His holistic approach reminds us to consider the human element. ACLU activists were products of their times in nonpolitical ways, possessed of uniquely individual personalities. They made friends and enemies. They earned livings. They could be stubborn or cheap or overly critical. To modern eyes, they were sexist, racist, and elitist, all of which generated assumptions about civil liberties just as powerful as their politics. I do not mean to write a group psychohistory, but we must be mindful of the ways individual personalities imprinted the ACLU. Roger Baldwin, as longtime leader, most influenced the organization nationally, but plenty of other volunteers and paid staff members contributed their quirks as well.

Generational differences also affected the ACLU's life cycle. When civil liberties were a peripheral concern, civil libertarians, like Max Weber's first generation of Puritans, had the intense ideological commitment of people who sacrificed for their beliefs. The founding generation's fidelity could never be replicated. Sociologist William Kornhauser argues that advocates of impossible causes identify as outsiders to sustain their devotion.[14] In the early Union, outsider status was crucial, creating a close-knit community of uncompromising purists. The first generation's iconoclasm, however, disguised its connections to the American upper class. Many early civil libertarians had the status markers of the elite: whiteness, maleness, Protestant backgrounds, college educations, university ties, and influential friends. The ACLU did not cover their expenses; corporate law firms, family trusts, or wealthy wives did. If they lived on the ideological margins, theirs were comfortable margins.

The generation of civil libertarians that came of age during the Depression had more hope and less money. As civil liberties became part of the mainstream, members of this second generation were better positioned to profit from their work, both personally and professionally, but their success raised questions about opportunism their elders never faced. The popularity of their cause compensated for their less-elevated personal status. They were more likely to be products of the ordinary middle class: hard working, still privileged to a degree, but outside the traditional elite. They were well-educated, idealistic people scrambling to find good jobs during hard times. By the 1950s, civil liberties was a career—not one that paid as well as corporate law, but one with its own status and professional methodology. Unlike the radicals of the first generation of Union activists, members of the second generation were more commonly self-identified liberals, which bound them to the liberal establishment, the liberal mindset, and ultimately, liberalism's weaknesses. As the ACLU grew, its respectable facade attracted workers who aspired to the advantages its first generation naturally possessed but little exploited.

The professional second generation of liberal civil liberties workers remade the organization according to its own priorities. Jessica Wang and Brett Gary have shown that as individuals conform to professional identities, their communities change. The

ACLU's organizational evolution occurred just as, as C. Wright Mills demonstrated, the New Deal's need for experts and specialists bureaucratized intellectual life. Since then, notes Russell Jacoby, "the habitat, manners, and idiom of intellectuals have been transformed." Public intellectuals rarely survived in a world that valued and rewarded specialization. Volunteers became professionals who met benchmarks and functioned within larger institutions.[15] Professional status brought with it obligation relative to the relatively freer first—amateur—generation. To get paid, professionals needed to follow rules, meet standards, and please superiors. The new generation of ACLU leaders brought important qualities to the organization, such as the research skills of a journalist, the ability of a lawyer to write an amicus brief, and the familiarity of an insider with government agencies. Inevitably, though, these professionals regarded their enterprise differently. They worked to please others while cultivating responsible images. However committed they were to civil liberties as an ideal, they mediated their commitments through professional identities.

Professionalism inclined the next generation of civil liberties workers to seek out relationships with the government and work with its representatives for mutually desired goals. Working with or within the government, as Jessica Wang has shown with atomic scientists, required conformity to government's rules. Civil libertarians functioned outside the federal bureaucracy, but they still had to be respectful of its principles and assumptions if they wanted to serve as its experts. To be partners with the New and Fair Deals meant accepting their limits, as Union officials were always the lesser party in any consultative relationship. The second generation of ACLU activists could not afford to have the first generation's confrontational attitude.

The Union's evolution from a small radical movement to a more conventional liberal organization finally required that its leadership transform. Roger Baldwin was a charismatic leader, the personification of the ACLU and the American embodiment of civil liberties righteousness.[16] His leadership style was functional when the group was small and marginal. It worked less well as the organization professionalized. When Baldwin retired in 1949, it was not just his own restlessness that prompted the decision but his inability to lead a movement on the brink of expansion and restructuring. His successor, Patrick Malin, was a bureaucrat concerned with internal harmony and external appeal.[17] On his watch, the Union became more managerial and employed experts. The holdovers from Baldwin's generation never quite adjusted. Some never stopped longing for the unpredictable, daring, activist organization they remembered. Some saw little value in advising Congress or writing a position paper when they could be on the barricades helping people.

Whatever governance differences existed between the first and second generations, both functioned at a time when the workplace was little regulated by civil notions of legal equality. The Union fell far short of its present commitment to inclusiveness. Its leaders possessed many kinds of provincialism. Old-school ACLU gentlemen were perfectly comfortable ordering around female secretaries. Officers gave wealthy women paper titles and little real influence. The men who ran the office believed that women were instinctively nurturing and emotional, two qualities they did not value in leaders. Similarly, although the ACLU was careful to include African Americans in leadership roles, their expertise was assumed on racial matters only, and they always represented their race. The Union championed racial equality, but its leaders knew few people of color. Those they did know were often far removed by education and wealth from those for whom they purportedly spoke. The Union's leaders were geographically provincial as well as gender and racially biased. They stereotyped westerners as firebrands and assumed the South was inhospitable. Easterners almost to a person, they rarely believed those who functioned outside their immediate milieu could be as smart, fair, or sincerely dedicated to civil liberties as they were.

Organizations are bureaucracies, and bureaucracies are composites of individual values and priorities. The ACLU is no exception. The spillover experiences of its members from churches, political organizations, law firms, boardrooms, and government shaped its day-to-day functions. Institutional histories of the ACLU rarely consider what most interests me about the organization: its bureaucracy and the personalities running it. Legal precedents and civil liberties philosophies are useful categories for assessing the group, but it is also important to know how the office worked. In traditional institutional histories, Roger Baldwin is treated reverentially. Only when biographers write about him do we discover his leadership failures.[18] Under Baldwin, the ACLU national office ran in a disorganized and eccentric fashion. He might have been an innovative thinker, but he was autocratic and slapdash about running the organization with which he was so personally identified. His successors struggled to modernize, streamline, and democratize what had long been a one-man show.

The Union's structure, thus, was always potentially volatile, and while officers spoke often about harmony and fraternity, the organization's institutional reality was tempestuous. Battles punctuated its evolution from radicalism to liberalism. Still, it did ultimately evolve, replacing much of its radical passion with liberal procedures. Its standards and practices were bureaucratized; its officers fell into routines. Yet it failed to evolve voluntarily that classic liberal structure, democratic governance. A handful of leaders made decisions. The first generation governed that way because the group was small and their ownership complete. The second generation of leaders, however, proved to be little more democratic than the first. The more liberal ACLU leaders became, the less they trusted the membership. Despite heading an organization committed to free speech and other elements of personal liberty, Union officers were not interested in introducing those rights into their organization.

Yet, like any other dues-collecting membership group, the ACLU was more than its volunteer leaders and paid staff. Members funded Union work, assuming their dues bought them input should they wish to exercise it. The few who pursued their full franchises quickly learned its leaders were little interested in making the ACLU a membership organization. Excluded from playing active roles in the group, they founded and staffed local civil liberties adjuncts. These branches developed separate organizational identities that challenged the national ACLU. By the 1950s, about fifteen local Union branches of varying size and activity existed. Each designed its own governance, elected its own officers, and until the early 1950s, raised its own funds. Branches varied tremendously. The particularity of the affiliates challenged the national leaders' conceptions of *their* Union as an extension of themselves and their civil liberties beliefs. Despite the best efforts of the New York–based national staff, the branches resisted standardization. The farther into the trenches one descends, the more idiosyncratic and personal the Union appears and the less it conformed to a liberal pattern. Local people, in fact, inhibited and challenged the Union's pursuit of liberal respectability.

Most of the trends that affected the national leadership bypassed local branches. In the hinterlands, civil liberties work neither paid the bills nor enhanced the résumé. Amateurs continued to run most of the affiliates well into the 1950s, shaping them to their politics, preferences, and prejudices. They received little respect for their work. The paid staff and the volunteer board of directors of the national ACLU did not trust them. National leaders found branch leaders troublesome, demanding, costly, childish, a threat to the kind of image the national group cultivated, and occasionally downright subversive. Yet, in the post-Baldwin scheme of things, the affiliates became the fund-raising unit of the ACLU, central to its viability. In existing histories of the Union, the affiliates are rendered much as the national leadership saw them, as adjuncts to the New York office, ideally servile but more realistically on the verge of trouble.

In truth, the affiliates were a vital part of the ACLU. The most unique aspect of the story I am about to tell concerns the ACLU branches and the roles they played in the national organization. The careful balancing of liberalism, professionalism, and nonpartisanship occurred differently in the branches or, often, did not occur at all. There are examples of local groups being entirely too political or, from the perspective of the national office, frustratingly precise about adhering to principle. In the branches, civil liberties work remained much as it always had been, unappreciated and potentially risky. At first, local activists accepted their secondary status in the organization, looking to the national headquarters for direction. Over time, they developed minds of their own and, in some cases, outright cockiness about their rectitude. The first generation of Union leaders took it for granted that the role of local people was to serve the organization as instructed by those who knew best, national leaders. Subsequent generations were allowed no such static hierarchical illusions. But however reasonable affiliates' expectations of democracy might seem to us today, at the time they were generally read as threatening, impudent, and in some instances, naively procommunist. This work is a social history of the whole of the ACLU, one that emphasizes the fractious interaction between those at the bottom and those at the top.

The affiliates were the single biggest counterforce to the larger evolution of civil liberties liberalism. They resisted the standardization and moderation that liberalism required and fought for local control over their work. They challenged the national ACLU to be more thoughtful about its choices. Branch activists humanized civil liberties fights, opposing institutionalization and bureaucracy. Roger Baldwin's experiences with the wartime internment of Japanese Americans, for example, were all academic. He dealt with the precedents of Executive Order 9066 (the legal sanction for wartime internment) and advised the War Relocation Authority (WRA) about internment, but that was as close as he got. Northern California ACLU director Ernest Besig lost his secretary to internment. He toured the war relocation camps and fought with their directors. He met with Fred Korematsu, whose case the national ACLU declined to support, when no other attorney would do so. The experiences, not surprisingly, produced very different attitudes toward the liberal Roosevelt government that set policy. Besig's voice and the voice of others on the ACLU's front lines are not much represented in histories of the ACLU, but their stories are equally valid and add an important dimension to the group's history. Their demands and expectations complicated the organization's path from the margins to the mainstream by questioning the ideological and organizational choices the national ACLU made.

The ACLU's path to liberal respectability and mainstream status, thus, had several dimensions. Leaders had, first, to find ways to harmonize liberalism with civil liberties nonpartisanship and to reverse its early radical reputation. They then altered its bureaucratic structure to reflect its changed identity. A liberal ACLU needed to be professional, adopting the policies and methods of its partners and advocates and building an organization that exuded respectability and competence. But once the Union became a successful and respectable organization, it had, finally, to become a popular one, accommodating to its membership. The first two alterations briefly steered the Union off its course; the third one put it back on track.

My study of the ACLU does not challenge an existing historiography so much as supplement it. Books about the Union are generally partisan in tone. Conservative tracts purport to reveal its "extremist" agenda,[19] while members of the organization celebrate its accomplishments. Neither bias undercuts the accuracy of the events detailed, although my interpretation is closer to the positive accounts than conservatives' attempts at exposure. The first real history of the Union, Charles Markmann's 1965 *The Noblest Cry*, is a little too heroic for modern tastes, written at the high tide of civil rights/civil liberties liberalism. The essays in *The Pulse of Freedom*, published a decade after Markmann's work, are as muted as we might expect from a post-Watergate book. Samuel Walker's massive 1990 history of the ACLU, *In Defense of American Liberties*, is, like the other two, the work of an insider, but it is comprehensive, judicious, and unparalleled in its analysis of the Union's legal work.[20] Alongside it, my work reflects my fascination with the mechanics of organizations and the sometimes petty conflicts of individuals. The ACLU's official history has been more than adequately told. My intention is not to retrace its legal triumphs or failures but to see it as an institution that reveals some insights into the achievements and shortcomings of liberalism and the fundamental contradiction of being popular while protecting the unpopular.

The Union's past also reflects on its present and future. The events of 11 September 2001 have made its mission supremely important. The Union brings a principled and authoritative voice to our modern struggles to find the balance between personal freedom and national security. Anatol Lieven suggests that George W. Bush's post-9/11 policies replaced the "American Creed" of "liberty, constitutionalism, the law, democracy, individualism, and cultural and political egalitarianism"—civil liberties, in short—with a more intolerant nationalism.[21] The ACLU offers a corrective to that mentality—not one everyone willingly accepts or agrees with, but one that challenges us to treat one another with respect and tolerance. History and experience, as well as principles, help guide the group at this critical moment. Nothing about the aftermath of 9/11 is unfamiliar to the organization; it lived through similar challenges in the 1930s, 1940s, and 1950s.

It is traditional for scholars of the ACLU to confess their politics before they begin their narratives. Like so many other historians of the organization, I am not a neutral observer. I am one of its members. I understand the principle of defending the rights of all, but like the liberals I sometimes criticize here, I am not always enthusiastic about the process. I hope this means that I write with sympathy more than judgment about the organization I have studied for so long because I agree with Burt Neuborne, formerly the ACLU's legal director, that the ACLU's job is akin to "taking out the garbage," dirty and unpopular, but "somebody's got to take the garbage out."[22]

BECOMING CHIC

The National ACLU in the 1930s

"In the beginning," remembered ACLU co-founder John Haynes Holmes, "the Union encountered opposition and trouble. Our activities, which we thought to be in the true American tradition, were on the contrary received with alarm, suspicion, and hate."[1] Indeed, the government spied on members, liberals ignored them, and while radicals relied on the ACLU to protect their dissent, they hardly contributed to the group's treasury or prestige. Only in the 1930s did the organization gain an even modestly positive reputation. Outside circumstances handed it opportunities. The Depression, the New Deal, and international developments set in motion social changes that offered the possibility of popularity and influence. Those fortuities, however, came at a cost. The pursuit of respectability challenged the Union organizationally and ideologically. A unity of vision was one of the first casualties of its successes.

The ACLU was part of a larger early twentieth-century reform effort. Industrialization promised better lives but generated inequality and squalor and brought millions of newcomers to America's shores. These changes disturbed confidence in a divinely shaped universe where the meritorious rose to the top. Government as it existed was unequal to the task of addressing modern needs. Instead, a host of competing solutions to social problems emerged, including populism, progressivism, socialism, utopianism, and the Social Gospel movement. Those who founded the ACLU were part of this generation, deeply committed to bringing equality and dignity to the people.

The typical early Union leader came of privilege leavened with service. Roger Baldwin was descended from the Puritans and was raised by prosperous Unitarians in Wellesley, Massachusetts. A Harvard graduate, he chose not to enter his father's leather business. Holmes, who also had Puritan forebearers and a Harvard education, felt "grounded in an abiding sense of the rights of man, [was] moved to pity for the downtrodden and oppressed, [and] taught that only by labor, sacrifice and struggle can liberty be won." Norman Thomas went to Princeton to become a clergyman like his father and grandfather, only to be sidetracked by social reform. One of Baldwin's successors characterized the group's founders as "a group of elitists . . . highly educated." Charles Markmann described them as products of the "intellectual and moral aristocracy." The responsibilities of their status weighed on them. Into their futures, each carried a sense of responsibility for others influenced by an older and more orderly world. Radical politics and World War I added to their felt obligations. Baldwin, working in a St. Louis settlement house, encountered the ideas of Emma Goldman. Thomas joined the Socialist Party, as did Holmes. Like other radicals of their generation, they opposed World War I because it used the poor to defend the economic power of the wealthy.[2]

Early in 1917, the pacifist American Union against Militarism tapped Baldwin to replace its ailing leader, Crystal Eastman. With characteristic eagerness, within it he organized a Bureau for Conscientious Objectors and a Civil Liberties Bureau. Samuel Walker suggests that the war marked a turning point for Baldwin, the moment when he realized that "majority rule and liberty were not necessarily synonymous." The epiphany made him unhappy with the American Union's attempts to work with Woodrow Wilson. His endeavors for conscientious objectors conflicted with its getting-along-with-government strategy, so in October 1917, the National Civil Liberties Bureau became an independent entity.[3]

Ironically, in power Baldwin's first instinct was to seek "access to high places." When "connections of class and privilege" failed him, according to Robert Cottrell, he challenged the system. Soon he was one of the beleaguered conscientious objectors his agency served. His yearlong incarceration affirmed his confusing status as an insider on the outs. The government jailed him, but several officials granted him special privileges. His fellow civil libertarians were as leery of government as Baldwin was, despite their bonds of privilege in a society governed by eastern, educated, well-connected, Protestant white men.[4]

In 1920 the National Civil Liberties Bureau became the American Civil Liberties Union. A board of directors chaired by socialist minister Harry F. Ward nominally ran the group, although codirectors Baldwin and attorney Albert de Silver handled the day-to-day work. Both worked only for expenses, which helped the organization financially. Shortly thereafter, one of Baldwin's St. Louis settlement house colleagues, Lucille Milner, signed on as field secretary. Walter Nelles provided legal expertise. Baldwin had a different approach toward the civil liberties enterprise than did the attorneys, who were eager to establish the field of civil liberties law. He believed in direct action to politicize issues. He did not trust the courts.[5]

Circumstances favored Baldwin's outlook. De Silver died in 1924, leaving Baldwin in charge. The Union's early clients were radicals hounded by a government clearly biased against them. The Union was in no position to influence legal precedents. In 1918 the Bureau of Investigation raided the offices of the Civil Liberties Bureau. The name change to the Civil Liberties Union in 1920 did not affect the government's attitude; it continued to monitor the group. In the 1920s there was little liberal infrastructure to support ACLU work.

Baldwin's strategy was to provoke confrontation, violate existing law, and then make a legal challenge, a method de Silver's legal replacement, Arthur Garfield Hays, also favored. Because clients of the ACLU were primarily radicals, outsiders pigeonholed it as a radical organization or, worse yet, did not even know it existed.[6]

Although Bill of Rights freedoms gained some legal stature during World War I, civil liberties were not a mainstream branch of law. Two wartime cases, *Schenck v. the United States* and *Abrams v. the United States* (both 1919), addressed individuals' rights to free speech and the state's power to limit them. Oliver Wendell Holmes's phrase, "clear and present danger," became the standard for determining when free speech threatened national security, but as Richard Polenberg pointed out, its original intent was "not to protect speech but rather to limit it." Legal realism, a pragmatic approach to law, gained some modest respectability in the 1920s. Legal realists contended that law must evolve, shaped by social conditions. The ACLU was filled with legal realists, including Lloyd K. Garrison, Felix Frankfurter, Zechariah Chafee, and Karl Llewellyn, men who would ultimately influence the practice of law in this country but were not yet the legal establishment. Liberals in the 1920s ranked civil liberties low on their list of priorities, below social need. They believed in government as an instrument of reform; civil libertarians saw the state as a repressive force. The cornerstone of civil liberties theory, the right of individuals to advocate unpopular views, did not immediately commend itself to liberals, who saw the Union's clients, who were ill mannered and demanding, as poor advertisements for change.[7]

The ACLU persevered, slowly gaining ground in the mid-1920s. When J. Edgar Hoover replaced William Burns as head of the Bureau of Investigation, the Union made its peace with the agency.[8] Meanwhile, the Scopes trial brought the Union its first positive publicity. It engaged flamboyant attorney Clarence Darrow to defend John Scopes, who stood accused of violating a Tennessee law against teaching Darwinism. The educated public followed the case, seeing in it a battle between superstition and science. Scopes was not the Union's average client; he was a soft-spoken, middle-class schoolteacher. With none of the baggage that came with defending radicals, the case took "a little of the edge off" the Union's reputation, Baldwin remembered.[9]

Still, the group remained small and dominated by Baldwin. He "was the planner and chief executioner." Every week he "reported to the twenty member board at luncheons, got guidance and went ahead expanding programs and contacts." A Board of Directors officially governed the group, although as Baldwin's biographer noted, Baldwin "never trusted anyone else's leadership."[10] A figurehead National Committee enlisted famous persons unable to be involved in more pressing Union obligations. Yet the group was by no means a national organization. In most states Baldwin located an attorney or two to consult when the need arose. Occasional local branches emerged. Few lasted. The system of affiliation was informal and "run from headquarters" through Baldwin. Until the 1930s, existing members suggested new ones, who were assessed to ensure they were "our sort of person." Exclusivity meant that membership stayed relatively static, reaching barely 2,000 by the end of the 1920s. Money came from left-wing foundations, principally the Garland Fund, and a few generous donors. Some believed that Baldwin deliberately limited the ACLU's size to better control it. Because it remained small, selective, relatively well funded, and centered in New York, it avoided the splits and feuds that so commonly plagued similar organizations.[11]

The Union's officers and staff brought different talents and politics to the group along with their shared commitment to civil liberties. In the 1920s, ACLU boards were heavy with labor and political activists, reflecting the group's implicit radicalism. A roster of early board members reads like a who's who of progressive reformers: Jane Addams, Crystal Eastman, Helen Keller, A. J. Muste, and Oswald Garrison Villard. However radicals also belonged, like Norman Thomas, William Z. Foster, Elizabeth Gurley Flynn, and Rose Schneiderman. ACLU leaders voiced "a great variety of viewpoints,"[12] reflecting an era when the Communist Party of the United States (CPUSA) did not dominate radical politics. While perhaps most members were socialists (though not necessarily Socialists), the

ACLU also had a few Democrats, Republicans, Progressives, and the politically unique. No one questioned anyone else's motives, and even the few Communists in leadership positions coexisted with their Socialist Party rivals. The only group routinely excluded from power were wealthy women, whose offices were titular and whose commitments were, as was customary for the time, assumed to be emotional and simplistic. As Baldwin said of a female colleague, "She was almost blind to the fine shadings, the qualifications, the compromises of the movements she supported." Civil liberties activism offered so few benefits and so many potential costs that the Union's volunteers accepted one another's commitments at face value.[13]

The Depression energized and reoriented the group. Radicalizing liberals saw in the ACLU a righteous cause for their energy, especially when the Union worked for miners, agricultural laborers, and the unemployed. Its priorities suited radicals as well. It represented Bonus Marchers and sent observers to hunger marches in Washington, D.C. Union activists provided legal support for strikers in California and Pennsylvania. An ACLU delegation visited Bell County, Kentucky, where, as in nearby Harlan County, miners had struck. Expecting to document mistreatment by local government, that delegation had "a glorious adventure, which in spite of the attendant danger we enjoyed immensely." If Union volunteers sounded a bit too enthusiastic about fighting injustice, the guilty pleasure they derived was not just because of the intrigue involved. The Depression made them feel needed. "The demands do not let up for practical daily service to radical organizations, strikers, teachers, aliens, and other targets of repression," reported one officer in 1930.[14]

Their energy raised financial challenges. There was more need for civil liberties work, but less money to pay for it. The Union had "depend[ed] too much upon a few large contributors," some of whom were "badly hit by the hard times." Funds invested in the stock market declined, and "receipts have dropped approximately 25 percent this year against last," Baldwin reported late in 1932. Regular contributors wrote mortified notes promising to send a few dollars "as soon as I can get my hands on it." The Board transferred funds "to wipe out deficits." "For the first time in our history," Baldwin confessed in August 1932, "we did not have enough money last week even to pay office salaries."[15]

The ACLU's plight worsened in 1930 when seven CPUSA organizers, convicted of murder following a battle between striking textile workers and local police, jumped bail in Gastonia, North Carolina. Although, as Baldwin carefully explained to the press, the $28,000 forfeited when the organizers fled came from the American Fund for Public Service ("the Civil Liberties Union did not lose a cent," he assured readers of *New Republic*), the Union name appeared in most press reports. The incident hurt the already bad reputation of the Communists, emphasized the ACLU's apparent links with them, and cost a bail fund the Union used regularly about a third of its available moneys. Thereafter, the group refused to provide bail for CPUSA members without adequate guarantees. Angered, the Union's most visible Communist member, William Z. Foster, resigned from its National Committee. Still, the story confirmed the ACLU's reputation as too deeply connected with the Communists, too radical, and financially irresponsible.[16]

Other activities reinforced the group's renegade reputation. The trip into the Kentucky coalfields to investigate alleged mistreatment of striking miners garnered advance publicity as Arthur Garfield Hays traded barbs with the Bell County attorney. But authorities toting guns stopped the delegation from entering the fields. The group filed a damage suit for $100,000; their retreat, however, made "the organization look slightly ridiculous." Baldwin's reputation figured prominently in negative publicity as he was "denounced as a Communist, a red, a slacker, a draft dodger, and a jail bird."[17] While the ACLU did not officially participate in the case of the nine young African American men accused of raping two white women in Scottsboro, Alabama, it was "caught in the middle" between the competing defense teams of the NAACP and the CPUSA. Ultimately, an ACLU-supplied attorney, Walter Pollak, carried two Scottsboro cases to the Supreme Court, where he successfully argued that defendants accused of capital crimes were entitled to legal counsel and got one case remanded on the grounds that Alabama juries excluded African Americans. These important legal precedents, however, occurred long after the Union's frustrating experience mediating between the NAACP and the Communists.[18]

Meanwhile, congressional red hunters eyed the group. The newly formed House Committee on Un-American Activities (HUAC) under Hamilton Fish investigated it in 1930. Baldwin refused to testify "unless I am compelled to do so." The Fish committee did not call him but concluded without his evidence that the ACLU was "closely affiliated with the Communist movement in the United States, and fully 90 percent of its efforts are on behalf of communists." The Fish investigation attracted a lot of press attention, little of it edifying to potential Union members.[19]

If the Union was little known in the 1920s, by the early 1930s its reputation was too often publicized by newspaper editors and conservative organizations. A speaker before the Batavia (Illinois) Kiwanis Club, for example, described it as an enemy of democracy, "boring from within." A Veterans of Foreign Wars member publicly called it "the largest and most active Communist organization" in Cincinnati. A *San Francisco Chronicle* story picked up by the *New York Times* reported that Moscow gold funded California labor strikes through the ACLU. Both the Federal Bureau of Investigation (FBI) and military intelligence considered ACLU membership proof of radicalism. These accusations had their impact. As one San Francisco minister apologized, "I am sorry that the popular conception of what the ACLU may be is so completely and stupidly wrong that we have felt we cannot carry on our movement under your name." The early Depression did little to positively alter the ACLU's circumstances.[20]

In 1931 the group launched a public relations effort to improve its reputation and fill its coffers. Although Baldwin believed that "outsiders" could not understand it, he spent $1,000 on a professional membership campaign that "flop[ped]." For the next few years, the group handled its own modest efforts more successfully. Officers downplayed the Union's reputation. Concerned that it was "too much identified with just one type of civil liberties defense," "radical cases," the organization de-emphasized those efforts and, instead, publicized its splashy free speech and censorship fights.[21]

The group started to put a different face forward in the 1930s because it had better membership prospects than its traditional clients. When Socialists and Communists joined, they invested their spare cash in their parties rather than the ACLU and brought their feuds into the group. An ad in the CPUSA-aligned *Soviet Russia Today* cost the Union $50 and netted only $25 in return. But when liberal theater critic Alexander Woollcott mentioned the ACLU on the radio, the publicity was free, raised nearly $400, and became the basis of successful print ads in the *New Yorker*. Woollcott's topic, censorship, engaged liberals, as did any abuses or exploitations of ordinary people.[22]

The Depression mobilized liberals as never before, and they began to seek suitable organizational options. The CPUSA's intensity scared them, while the Socialist Party lacked potential. The ACLU was a safer way to champion the disenfranchised. Its energy was contagious, and its methods were less intimidating than those of the Communists. "In the old days," Arthur Garfield Hays recalled, "we used to go into the coal fields or over to New Jersey and hold test meetings and get ourselves locked up. We were right in the front lines."[23] Heady engagement for liberals, who could underwrite the Union's Kentucky ventures or be morally outraged by the kidnapping and assaults on ACLU attorneys investigating conditions in California's Central Valley. These dramatic activities offered vicarious connection. They drew people into the ACLU.

For some, writing checks and attending meetings was not enough. Some young liberals sought careers in civil liberties, making the best of Depression-circumscribed opportunities. Higher education and professional school no longer guaranteed a measure of personal success as they once did. The most elite law firms could—and did—discriminate. The corporate career track, moreover, was not as appealing for some as helping people. The New Deal needed bureaucrats to run its programs, assertive young men and women who believed in reform. The ACLU was not as glamorous or secure an employer, but it attracted young liberal attorneys nonetheless. Civil liberties law was nowhere near as lucrative a specialty as corporate law, Roger Baldwin conceded, but it was "an asset in stepping into government service."[24]

These young attorneys started in the affiliates in hungry pursuit of stable civil liberties jobs. They were dedicated but, unlike the Union's founders, hoped their endeavors might provide financial rewards and prestige. Branches could not contain their ambitions; so several asked the national ACLU for jobs, and the most ambitious used the Union as a stepping stone into public service. "For quite some time I have been feeling that the work I am now doing has little, if any, charm for me," wrote one Philadelphia volunteer. His goal was to work for the National Labor Relations Board (NLRB), although others with a "hankering for some place in Washington during the Roosevelt years" settled for less glorious positions. Their ACLU work provided a credential, and Baldwin's recommendations attested to their devotion to civil liberties. Before long, the Union had connections in the Bureau of Indian Affairs, the NLRB, the Interior Department, and the Justice Department.[25]

Perhaps the largest difference between the Union's founders and these newer activists was that the younger men expected to work within the confines of the New Deal, while Baldwin's generation had little faith in government. A 1934 poll of ACLU leaders revealed more registered Socialists than Democrats. Fewer than half voted for Roosevelt in 1932. The Union's radical founders expected the First New Deal would expand repressive federal power and make people complacent. "We have some misguided friends throughout the country," Baldwin noted, "who think that the fight for civil liberties is made less necessary by a presumably liberal administration at Washington. But the record plainly shows that in the months of the New Deal far more issues have arisen than before." The young lawyers the ACLU attracted assumed the New Deal was filled with legal realists who shared their point of view. They saw Union members like Zechariah Chafee and Felix Frankfurter consulting with government. Even Baldwin conceded that the Roosevelt bureaucracy seemed "stacked with our friends." The New Deal forced old-timers to consider the possibilities of partnering with government to advocate for individual rights.[26]

The turning point was the Wagner Labor Relations Act of 1935. ACLU affiliates more quickly grasped the New Deal's civil liberties possibilities. Baldwin's cohort doubted "any scheme at Washington for intervention helpful to labor." They saw the NLRB "as a dangerous, fascist intrusion of government into unions" and were uncomfortable with the power granted it by the Wagner Act. The Board of Directors deemed the bill a threat to rights labor already possessed. The American Federation of Labor, the NLRB, and ACLU branches protested. Directors reluctantly called for an official corporate vote of the Board and National Committee. As one scholar noted, "Baldwin appears to have done everything in his power to weigh the referendum in favor of those opposing the Wagner bill." Despite his interventions, affiliates and the National Committee expressed confidence in the New Deal. Baldwin called the vote inconclusive, but the Board belatedly rescinded its opposition to what had by then become the Wagner Labor Relations Act. The reluctant change was important for two reasons. First, ACLU affiliates successfully pressured the National Board. Second, the Board signaled its grudging willingness to see Roosevelt's New Deal as a potential ally in the fight for civil liberties.[27]

The next year, Union membership, previously growing at a trickle, increased by more than 800 members.[28] The organization's involvement in labor struggles was one reason for its attractiveness, alongside its censorship fights and its support for civil rights. Its work in the Scottsboro cases gave it a higher profile. Its name appeared more commonly in publications liberals read, such as the *New Republic* and the *Nation*. Celebrities like Groucho Marx sent their money. Unlike the first Depression membership boost, the group's post-1935 increase proved to be the beginning of a growth spurt.

Critical to that growth was the misplaced assumption that promoting civil liberties was also antifascist. Antifascism was the most important crusade of the second half of the 1930s. Liberals and radicals shared a strong fear of fascism and a commitment to stopping it. Hitler's rise to power triggered their concern, which then shifted to homegrown leaders whose ideas seemed fascist—Huey Long, Charles Coughlin, and Francis Townsend—and shifted back to international developments during the Spanish Civil War. Where once the left confidently regarded economic equality as the centerpiece of freedom, 1930s fascism, with its efficient state-guided economies, proved that freedom required more than state ownership of the means of production.[29] Radicals and liberals began to talk about the political mechanisms that made people free: the ability to vote, to read newspapers with divergent views, and to advocate for their own beliefs. These were precisely the rights for which the ACLU fought.

Yet civil libertarians believed in extending those same rights to fascists. Liberals opposed censorship but were troubled when fascists asked for the same rights as Communists or Catholics or Democrats. The Union's 1933 campaign to ensure that American Nazi groups had access to public meeting halls raised hackles. What Clarence Darrow called "defending free speech . . . [with] no exception" seemed risky and dangerous, an open invitation for fascists to find more followers. Liberals often "distinguish[ed] between free speech and the use of the Swastika," arguing that fascists did not deserve civil liberties because they would take away those rights should they ever come to power. Fortunately, the ACLU was little called upon to protect right-wing dissent, for inevitably, it was unpopular with its potential membership base.[30]

Most of the time, outsiders forgot about the ACLU's promotion of rights for fascists. Meanwhile, liberals and radicals had a new way of responding to fascism. The Soviet leadership feared being isolated and vulnerable to Hitler, so the Communist International constructed the Popular Front against fascism in 1935. Traditionally, a "united front" brought together disparate elements behind a single cause. This time, the CPUSA proclaimed a People's Front that excluded Socialists and other opponents of the Soviet Union. The People's Front consisted of interlocking organizations, each of which focused on an element of antifascism, such as free speech, intellectual freedom, and collective action, to promote its—and others'—agenda. To enlist large numbers of noncommunists, the Party moderated its line, calling Communism "twentieth century Americanism" and unofficially supporting the Second New Deal. Much of the rhetoric of the People's Front was prodemocratic and rights based. At its most successful (1937), it attracted a broad segment of supporters, and individual front groups functioned with relative autonomy.[31] The ACLU was not a front organization, and its Socialist members vehemently opposed it becoming one. But somehow the civil liberties group seemed more closely attached to the People's Front than it actually was, capitalizing on the tactic's popularity with its potential membership while avoiding its complications.

It was hard for outsiders to tell exactly how entangled in the People's Front the Union was. Roger Baldwin, as always, had the dominant voice in the organization, and he belonged to "almost every United Front organization that there has been since 1920." His close friend, ACLU Chairman of the Board Harry Ward, led—at Baldwin's invitation—the American League against War and Fascism, a front group with a paper membership allegedly in the millions. Both men brought their political enthusiasm to the Union. Their memos and speeches were filled with phrases borrowed from the People's Front. Baldwin even called the ACLU "a 'united front' of persons of very varied political and economic views," technically accurate but misleading nonetheless. Later he coyly conceded that the group gained the "reputation" of seeming to be a front without actually being one, but his actions certainly facilitated any public associations between the Union and the People's Front.[32]

While the Union's critics obsessed about these associations, the group's more invisible links to the New Deal had a more profound impact on the organization. Baldwin, who considered himself "a radical in economics," was initially reluctant to see the federal government as anything other than an adversary. Once he came around to the possibilities of working alongside the Roosevelt administration, he made the necessary adjustments to his organization. Soon, the Union looked different. Many of the "young men recently out of …law school" who did its legal work were New Dealers. These young lawyers positively radiated with urgency and enthusiasm. "We have a situation here where everything we do is of national importance," one Washington, D.C., volunteer boasted. Few Union activists were uncritical Roosevelt supporters, but many felt optimistic about the future with Roosevelt in charge.[33]

No one better epitomized the cooperative attitude between the Union and the New Deal than ACLU counsel Morris Ernst. Ernst joined the Union in 1926. He was Jewish, middle class, and without the cachet of an Ivy League legal education. He was, however, ambitious and found the New Deal a congenial ideological home. Baldwin described him as "a sharp lawyer . . . a negotiator, an operator, a diplomat, if you like, and he enjoyed associations with big shots." Ernst relished working with the powerful, sending memos to Roosevelt and Attorney General Francis Biddle. He was on a first-name basis with labor secretary Frances Perkins and exchanged letters with Harold Ickes, Henry Wallace, and Eleanor Roosevelt. He was the highest-ranking ACLU liberal. He linked the organization with the New Deal.[34]

For a moment in the late 1930s, the Ernst-forged connections between the ACLU and the New Deal and the sly associations between the People's Front and the Union Harry Ward or Baldwin built could coexist. Nowhere was this more evident than in the National Lawyers Guild (NLG), a classic organization of the People's Front era. The NLG grew out of progressive frustration with the American Bar Association. Some credit Roosevelt with the idea of a socially conscious alternative to the Bar Association, a suggestion he allegedly made to Ernst. Certainly he was painfully aware that the existing legal structure limited his liberal agenda, and the conservative Supreme Court ruled unconstitutional most of his First New Deal. Whether or not Roosevelt wanted an alternative to the Bar, Ernst did. He became, as *Time* magazine noted, the guild's "Godfather." He increased its membership from ACLU mailing lists, wrote its constitution, and created its governance process. By 1938 it was as large as the Union, with 5,000 members, including, according to one estimate, about 100 Communists, alongside New Dealers Thurmond Arnold, Nathan Mangold, and Jerome Frank. Osmond

Fraenkel and other ACLU attorneys were active early members, as were ACLU branch leaders in Chicago, Los Angeles, Philadelphia, and San Francisco. The NLG was one of the most successful forums for liberals, progressives, Communists, and civil libertarians.[35]

The Union benefited from the same milieu as the NLG. It no longer assumed that like-minded supporters would find it. It began to court "middle class professional people" as members, explicitly defining its base as liberal.[36] With fewer Communists as clients, it could present itself as a mainstream liberal organization. It publicized its sponsorship of the popular musical *Pins and Needles* as a fund-raiser in several cities. It ran ads in liberal journals. It sought a radio program to espouse civil liberties. By 1939 it was successful enough to be invited to have its own day at the New York World's Fair.[37] Occasionally longtime activists grumbled about the new public relations strategy, but few thought it contrary to the Union's purpose or impartiality.

To please the broadest possible segment of liberals, however, the Union needed to shed its radical identity. "I know you're a Marxist and all that," one friend warned Baldwin, "and I know the argument that civil liberties and economic liberties are all of one piece and are as inseparable as the Trinity. Well, from my point of view that's good theology, but darn poor tactics."[38] Baldwin's politics became a lightning rod for critics, and two comments in particular came back to haunt him. In 1934, at the height of his radicalism, he told *Soviet Russia Today* he was "anti-capitalist and pro-revolutionary." Several months later, in his Harvard reunion book, he declared that "Communism is the goal." Critical commentators and congressional Communist hunters inevitably focused on these quotations in ways that made Baldwin aware of how his personal choices, and those of other members, could threaten the ACLU's respectability.[39]

In the late 1930s the Union cleaned house to present its most moderate and respectable face. Its last radical director was Abraham Isserman, elected in 1935. During the next few years, new Board members included federal judge Dorothy Kenyon, playwright Sidney Howard, the wealthy widow of Albert de Silver, and NAACP attorney Thurgood Marshall. Gone were labor's advocates, so much so that new Communist Party member Elizabeth Gurley Flynn complained.[40] To convey greater political balance, Baldwin wanted to elect "some strong conservatives . . . provided they do not attempt to inject their political or economic beliefs." Two of four Republicans who served on the Board between 1920 and 1960 joined in the late 1930s, businessman Richard Childs and attorney Whitney North Seymour, who regularized his unofficial unpublicized Board status in 1939 because "the dreamers of the Union do not frighten me any more."[41]

What was true of the Board was even more pronounced on "our show window," the National Committee. The National Committee did little, never met, but was "good for letterheads as public relations." Earlier, membership conferred so little status that those who signed on did so with some sincere intention of being actively involved. As the Union pursued a liberal membership base, its choices for committee members reflected that orientation, however little engaged nominees might be. Added in the late 1930s were Newspaper Guild president Heywood Broun, novelist John Dos Passos, and the "former chairman of the National Labor Board," Lloyd K. Garrison. Baldwin desperately wanted Garrison to head the committee so as to "give our organization more weight" by associating it with "persons less tinged with revolutionary propaganda." By the end of the decade, the National Committee appeared prestigious, yet only about half of its members bothered to vote. Instead, they trusted the professionals who, increasingly, ran the organization as they saw fit.[42]

Complimenting the ACLU's new liberal look was its preference for legal remedies over direct action, so different from its early days. While it had always relied on test cases and court challenges, it no longer so commonly waded into controversies to force action. Instead, it lobbied New Deal legislators to change laws. "Prominent personnel with their many contacts" accomplished the most during the New and Fair Deal period, Baldwin later noted. "The New Deal gave us at once a host of sympathetic friends in Washington and reforms long delayed began to come to life. I went to Washington much oftener, with a dozen projects on my calendar, pushing our friends toward our goals." The group at first committed only a volunteer attorney to lobbying but later was "prepared to put up any amount necessary within reason to maintain a Washington office and lobbyist." In December 1937 the Board approved payment of $10 a day for someone to "be in charge of the Union's congressional work" and forwarded to him a list of congressmen who also belonged to the ACLU. Baldwin and his national officers learned the advantages of working from the inside to create pro–civil liberties policies.[43]

The Union's 1938 work opposing New Jersey political boss Frank Hague displayed the new ACLU style. Hague was the mayor of Jersey City, a Democrat, and an opponent of organized labor. The Union used the older tactic of calling meetings to provoke the necessary legal challenge to aid labor organization. Those meetings, though, featured New Deal congressmen and prominent local liberals alongside the usual contingent of radicals and labor organizers. Officers tried to discredit Hague before the attorney general, the head of the Democratic National Committee, and Roosevelt. Ernst wanted to intimidate him with "names like [Harold] Ickes and other important persons, saying that they are staunch supporters of the Union," but his colleagues thought that crossed the line to "devious political methods." It took a court case, finally, to loosen Hague's grip. At every stage the ACLU pressed its big-name connections and worked its public relations machine as hard as it could. The Hague case was the "last big case in which direct action played a part." Thereafter, the Union shifted its focus toward test cases that originated elsewhere.[44]

Campaigns like the one against Hague required resources and professional expertise. During the 1930s the group reshaped its bureaucracy, eliminating its more slipshod and improvised methods. In the late 1920s Baldwin took off on extended adventures, leaving an associate director, Forrest Bailey, to run the office. He proved "[ill] equipped to handle a fighting job," but no one would fire him because he was so dedicated. He stayed on until his health failed and he had to resign.[45] After Bailey left, Lucille Milner took over day-to-day management, although, tellingly, she retained the lesser title of national secretary. She was invisible yet efficient, the perfect female officer for someone as mercurial and sexist as Baldwin. By the end of the 1930s the Union functioned like most other organizations. It standardized its relations with affiliates, stabilized its financial structure, and vested bureaucratic power in the Board of Directors. Ernst and his more left-wing counterpart, Arthur Garfield Hays, advised on cases and oversaw a staff of attorneys. Its more professional look helped reassure the New Deal's civil liberties bureaucrats that the ACLU was no renegade organization, but a team player. Baldwin sometimes exercised his personal latitude to the detriment of professionalism; nevertheless, the group's general profile appeared more organizationally respectable.[46]

Baldwin was not the only weak spot in the Union's shiny new facade. Internal disputes between warring radical factions marred the ACLU's genteel image. Socialists and Communists were both welcome but were expected to check their politics at the door. Most honestly tried to do so; occasionally, though, tempers flared, and angry directors fought turf wars through other issues. The People's Front emboldened both sets of radicals. The CPUSA reached its prewar numeric peak in the late 1930s, but the Socialists dwindled in numbers and influence, especially after an unfortunate fusion with American Trotskyists.[47] Socialists blamed the Communists for many of their woes, arguing that the People's Front bullied and intimidated liberals into defending the Soviet Union lest they be branded red baiters. The People's Front provoked a frightening new intensity to radical rivalries within the ACLU.

While the Communists were the more powerful group outside the Union, the Socialists were more influential inside it. Norman Thomas had been the Socialists' presidential candidate, more publicly identifiable with socialism than Baldwin was with civil liberties. John Haynes Holmes was as committed as Thomas was to the ACLU and socialism. They were outspoken critics of the CPUSA and the front tactic. Communist directors were more circumspect about their affiliations, except Elizabeth Gurley Flynn, who notified her fellow officers after she joined the Party late in the decade. Samuel

Walker identifies Mary Van Kleeck, Abraham Isserman, and Robert Dunn as secret Party members.[48] Their secrecy hindered their effectiveness, whereas Holmes and Thomas pressed their agendas with visible relish. Meanwhile, the People's Front lost momentum, which made some of its noncommunist supporters, progressives, more leery of its commitments. Others, though, stayed the course, including two Union progressives, Corliss Lamont and Harry Ward, who eagerly promoted labor's rights. Baldwin should have held these partisan forces in check, but he had his own causes to promote. As more and more political movements embraced civil liberties, a series of factional fights rocked the Board, increasingly debilitating it.

In 1934, after Communists disrupted a Socialist Party rally in Madison Square Garden, Union directors intervened in the hopes of finally ending the radical rivalry. A Board-appointed committee chastised the Communists for showing up uninvited and the Socialists for being provocative and attacking a CPUSA leader with a chair. Both radical organizations objected, although the Socialists pushed harder than the Communists did. Thomas rebuked the Communists for believing in civil liberties "only in so far as they were of benefit to the Communist movement." Holmes threatened to call "for the retirement of all the members of the Communist Party from our Board of Directors, and for the ending of all work with the Communists." Baldwin talked him out of it, assuring him that there were no Communist directors. But at regular intervals for the next couple of years, Thomas complained anew about the report, until a fellow director finally begged him to give the matter "a decent burial after a lapse of . . . years."[49]

The People's Front aggravated the long-standing Socialist-Communist rivalry, drawing in others. The late 1930s were a time of intellectual flux. Marxist opponents to the People's Front emerged. These anti-Stalinists, as they were called, had modest intellectual respectability; a journal, *Partisan Review*; and a forum, the American Committee for the Defense of Leon Trotsky. Theirs was a minority position, but they put the Communists on the defensive, ideologically and strategically. The People's Front peaked in 1937;

by 1938 and 1939 membership in its component front groups had declined. At the same time, traditional right-wing anticommunism gained visibility, if not credibility. In 1938 Texas congressman Martin Dies launched a series of hearings into un-American activities in the United States that included the New Deal and superficial connections between it and the CPUSA. Anti-Stalinism, the Dies Committee, and other anticommunists chilled the climate. The Roosevelt administration retreated, and the ACLU followed suit.[50]

In consequence, it became less possible for the Union to occupy the free space between the People's Front and liberalism. Conservatives simply assumed that there was no free space, just a clear, unbroken line from the New Deal through the ACLU to the CPUSA. In 1934 the patriotic group America First called on Roosevelt to dismiss twenty-five members of his administration because "they were connected with the American Civil Liberties Union and other subversive groups." Congressman Hamilton Fish, whose HUAC had gone after the group in 1930, alleged that most members of the "brains trust" were ACLU members. A paper in Albany, New York, explained that one of Roosevelt's advisors, Felix Frankfurter, "IS AN ACTIVE MEMBER OF THE COMMUNISTIC AMERICAN CIVIL LIBERTIES UNION" and, therefore, full of "socialist ideas." Secretary of the Interior Harold Ickes's speech at the Union's 1937 annual dinner drew criticism, including from Walter Lippman, who opined that the ACLU's failure to defend the civil liberties of "anyone on the Right" weakened its reputation. Lippman was exactly the kind of public liberal the Union recruited, so his accusation of "partisanship in the defense of the principle of civil liberties" stung. When Fish's successor, Martin Dies, began congressional hearings into un-American activities in 1938, several witnesses made familiar claims about the New Deal, the ACLU, and the Communists. The next year both the appointment of Frank Murphy to the Court of Appeals and the nomination of Frankfurter to the Supreme Court were slowed in part because of their ACLU memberships.[51]

The attacks hurt the Union. HUAC's 74 percent approval rating was much higher than the ACLU's 34 percent or the president's 55 percent. Roosevelt disapproved of Dies but was afraid to challenge him. This put the Union in a difficult position. Pollsters found that the public thought the evidence linking the ACLU to the CPUSA was "plausible," which seemed not to deter its supporters but raised its disapproval rating from 5 to 38 percent. Tacitly acknowledging the Union's potential liability to Roosevelt, in 1939 Baldwin sent some "embarrassing" files away from the office, in case the Dies Committee gained access to the ACLU's secrets. Contained in those files were memos and statements that documented the ACLU's New Deal connections.[52]

Under the circumstances, some Union officers feared the political fallout of being associated with the People's Front. In 1936 the *American Mercury* called the ACLU a Communist front, citing familiar quotations from Baldwin and noting connections between the Union and the American League against War and Fascism. Although Baldwin believed the author, Harold Lord Varney, was a "well-known Fascist propagandist," he worried about "the effect among our friends" should the organization not answer the charges. The Board sued Varney and the *Mercury* for publishing "false and defamatory matter" that had "greatly injured" its reputation. In compensation, editor H. L. Mencken agreed to publish a fairer piece. His article was more judicious, but the front accusation remained. Baldwin tried to keep the essay from appearing. Failing, he got Mencken to agree to publish a Union rejoinder. Baldwin composed it, but several of his fellow directors protested his too-conciliatory tone and gratuitous boast that the organization was so broad-minded as to include on its board Elizabeth Gurley Flynn, "exhibit A—'our only Communist.'" The matter took nearly two years to resolve, and the final result did little for the Union's reputation. "Next time you have to settle a law suit by an article," advised a director with public relations expertise, "for God's sake turn it over to this office."[53]

As time went on, Baldwin and the staff felt increased pressure—most of it self-imposed—to disassociate the ACLU from the People's Front, especially in the Front's last year. The victory of the Spanish fascists over the Front-backed Loyalist government hurt the Front, as did the revelations of the Moscow trials. Certainly Baldwin began to change his politics. Other progressives also wavered, forcing the Communists to assume more active roles in front groups. By early 1939 many fronts looked too much like the Party adjuncts anti-Stalinists described. ACLU Socialists touted the Union's defense of the rights of fascists as proof of nonpartisanship, a claim that horrified rather than impressed liberal members. "I know that it is your boast that you have helped W. R. Hearst and other fascist organizations," wrote one, but "some of us are wondering if . . . [this] is not resulting in too great a promotion of fascism."[54]

The office's eagerness to disassociate the Union from Communism and affirm the group's respectable reputation divided the organization. The staff feared the Dies Committee put the ACLU "in a much worse [public relations] position." Despite an official policy "that no representative of the Union should appear before the Dies Committee except under subpoena," Arthur Garfield Hays solicited "an opportunity to appear before your Committee." When Dies proved unwilling to hear anyone from the Union, Board member Raymond Wise privately approached his counsel. Finally, Baldwin, National Committee chairman Holmes, and treasurer Benjamin Huebsch submitted affidavits to the committee. Baldwin's assured Dies that, while the Union might have fifty Communist members, "we have never elected to our national committee or our board of directors any member of the Communist Party," a lie.[55]

Pressures inside and outside the organization unbalanced its internal dynamic. The staff worried more and more about how the Union looked to the powerful. Board factionalism worsened. Anticommunists, nearly all of whom were Socialists, obsessed about some of the Union's policies, singling out its "partiality in defending labor" as proof that the group was too Communist-influenced. The Union, however, had always been partial to labor; but members were more sensitive now about responses that used to be automatic and unquestioned. So anticommunists began to raise complaints that the Union was "quick as lightning" to protect workers while "slow as death" in its "defense of capital."[56]

Workers' rights became a litmus test, a way Union anticommunists determined which "of our board . . . are not fundamentally interested in civil liberties at all, but only in the questions . . . of [how] civil liberties may now be used for the benefit of labor." Holmes kept track of who did not measure up and threatened to "withdraw" if the ACLU "compromis[ed] its principles in the interest of any one group in the community." Baldwin began to monitor votes, deciding what to put before the Board based on who showed up. He tended to trust the integrity of Holmes and Thomas, even if he disagreed with their politics, so he looked elsewhere to explain the unmistakable Board tension. His candidate was social reformer Mary Van Kleeck, who inserted her "radical views" into ACLU business by "put[ing] up an opposition to every proposal made." His nervousness about how outsiders perceived the group's activities contributed to the overall uneasiness and "lack of agreement" between previously friendly directors.[57]

The simmering conflict came to a head during discussions of a 1937 NLRB cease-and-desist order against Henry Ford for distributing antiunion materials to his workers. Did the NLRB's order limit Ford's speech, or did his status as employer intimidate his workers and, thereby, limit their freedom to join a union? The order suggested the latter. The Union's pro–People's Front faction agreed, citing the clear-and-present-danger standard, while anticommunists insisted Ford's entitlement to free speech was absolute. Partisans of both positions overstepped Union proprieties in their eagerness to prevail. Harry Ward, absent during the early debate, exercised his privilege as chairman of the board to ask "for further consideration" of the matter. Anticommunists, afraid their majority was "exceedingly small," complained when Ward reopened the discussion, although they, too, planned to keep "pushing the matter further." The organization ultimately asked the NLRB to clarify its order by distinguishing "between expressions of opinion and language which is directly coercive" and that which was not. It was not a "mainstream liberal" attitude, Samuel Walker points out, because it did not reflect liberals' absolute faith in New Deal government. But neither was it progressive or pro-Front, for it opposed labor's interests. Divided at the top, the ACLU had trouble making anyone happy.[58]

The Ford case demonstrated how the polarized intellectual climate hampered Union effectiveness. Anti-Stalinism influenced Holmes, Roger Riis, and Norman Thomas, who seem to have adopted its personal, angry, and sometimes vindictive style. They were adversarial, fighting to defeat opponents more than reacting as civil libertarians to individual issues. They learned to threaten, prolong, and expose. They quickly found Baldwin's vulnerability, fear of public resignations that would undermine the Union's reputation, and used it. "If we have to split on this issue," Holmes told Baldwin about the Ford case, "so be it."[59]

Tempers modulated on the ACLU Board but heated up elsewhere. Holmes and Thomas joined the Committee for Cultural Freedom (CCF), a civil liberties organization founded in late 1938. Its organizers, including Sidney Hook (a Union member) and former ACLU public relations officer Eugene Lyons, were disillusioned radicals. This new group was to serve as a rallying point for left opposition to the People's Front. It, too, was provocative and confrontational, with a founding manifesto that directly challenged the Front's rationale, which was that antifascism was a shared venture of democrats. Hook and Lyons wrote that communism and fascism were two forms of the same ideology, "totalitarianism," defined as political dictatorships that scapegoated ethnic minorities, employed secret police forces, and allowed no dissent. Holmes and Thomas, along with Morris Ernst and at least one other Union Board member, endorsed the statement and joined the CCF. They then pressed the Union to adopt a similar affirmation.[60]

At one of the first board meetings of 1939, Ernst introduced a resolution declaring the ACLU "opposed to all totalitarian governments—Fascist, Nazi or Communist" but committed to the rights of people peacefully advocating those philosophies. The timing was deliberate; January was both a month of warm-weather vacations and the end of officers' terms, so meetings were often sparsely attended. The resolution passed, chiefly for its "public opinion" value. A few weeks later, at a better-attended meeting, directors rescinded the measure and voted "not to adopt any formal statement in opposition to any particular theory or form of government" as such actions fell outside the organization's responsibilities. Most directors quickly forgot about the vote, but the anticommunists among them stewed for months over their latest failure.[61]

Ernst introduced a similar antitotalitarian statement at the NLG convention a month later. Defeated as a policy statement, it only found voice in the speech of NLG president Ferdinand Pecora, which the NLG convention then endorsed.[62] As anticommunists escalated the fight, defenders of the People's Front responded. They created a challenge to the CCF, the American Committee for Democracy and Intellectual Freedom.[63] Both organizations purported to defend intellectual freedom. Both argued that "totalitarianism" threatened individual rights, although the Committee for Democracy and Intellectual Freedom defined totalitarianism as fascism alone. Both had civil libertarians as leaders, Hook of the CCF and anthropologist Franz Boas of its rival. Boas's group quickly overtook the CCF numerically. Yet the ACLU had more liberal prestige and clout than either new group. Of course, since it also had members of both groups fighting in its boardroom, it was also more volatile than either group.

When radicals founded the ACLU, their purpose was clear: they protected dissenters. Since their commitment was so abstract at that point, they had not been tested by the realities of politics and ideology. Back then, defending dissent meant defending radicals against a repressive federal government. The Union's first generation did all that it could against that clear target, using confrontation and exposure to force the government to change. But by the late 1930s, the Roosevelt government was not a hostile force. Quite the contrary, it proved to be an ally and partner, whereas the relationship between the ACLU and the radical organizations it once protected was messy and contradictory. Old political categories no longer made sense; new ones overlapped and changed. Civil libertarians were joiners by inclination, participants in the great political and ideological debates of their time. As a variety of different political movements claimed civil liberties as their own cause, the ACLU was pulled into all manner of controversies. Civil liberties were "chic," which made the ACLU's task easier in some ways and far more complicated in others.

The Union made choices and "prospered in the thirties" because of them. Its 1939 annual report "was a chronicle of glad tidings."[64] What mainstreamed it, what doubled its membership and gave it power with New Dealers, was its appeal to American liberals. It offered a safe, responsible, meaningful engagement with issues: fighting censorship, protecting the rights of striking farmworkers, advocating for civil rights, and promoting secularism. But liberalism was at a crossroads in the late 1930s. Some liberals—progressives—joined with the Communists, imagining a very broad coalition that stretched from the left edge of the New Deal to Party head Earl Browder. Others grew increasingly disillusioned with the People's Front. It was clear that the ACLU was only a crisis away from having to address this problem. Still, however beleaguered directors might have felt in 1939, they could also take pride in what they accomplished during a very hard time, how their ACLU had survived the Depression, not just intact, but stronger, larger, and more influential. For better or worse, they had steered their Civil Liberties Union into the liberal mainstream.

UNNECESSARY OBSTACLES

ACLU Affiliates in the 1930s

In 1923 the Southern California branch of the American Civil Liberties Union (SCACLU) became the ACLU's first affiliate. It came into being due to the largesse of novelist Upton Sinclair. Sinclair, long a social activist, read the Bill of Rights to longshoremen striking at the San Pedro harbor. After he was arrested, he pledged a year's salary for a director to organize a local ACLU branch to help monitor the notoriously problematic Los Angeles police force. Fifteen years later the group celebrated its anniversary in high style. There were speeches, dinners, and a commemorative pamphlet written by the group's leader, Dr. Clinton Taft.[1] The SCACLU had good reason to celebrate. Local organizing to advocate for Bill of Rights freedoms was hard work. Being a civil libertarian in an ACLU affiliate in Los Angeles, Cleveland, or Detroit was not like being a national leader. While the New York office courted respectability, liberal prestige, and professionalism, local officers struggled to keep up. It was not just that their treasuries were smaller and their workers unpaid that distinguished them from the Union as a national entity. Rather, affiliate leaders pursued their own versions of success, much to the dismay of the national organization.

The Southern California affiliate was for many years the only stable ACLU local branch. Most affiliates began as it did, because of the determined efforts of one or more individuals in response to some local crisis. In the SCACLU's case, though, Sinclair's financial support enabled the affiliate to build structures that outlasted the immediate crisis. More commonly, after the crisis abated, so, too, did the branch, only to be revived for the next challenge, often by a different group of people.

From the beginning, efforts to create a truly national ACLU were "fragmentary and spasmodic." Although Roger Baldwin and Elizabeth Gurley Flynn undertook a six-week cross-country trip to organize the ACLU in 1920, Baldwin did not really welcome affiliates. The national ACLU's elitist nature, its small size, and the great distance between headquarters and most branches inhibited affiliate growth. Local groups contributed little to the national organization, being separate dues-collecting entities. Individuals in any region of the country could belong to the national ACLU, the local branch, or both, although the latter option cost two annual fees. The structure did not inspire much investment in local branches by national officers.[2]

During the 1920s, little inspired local organization either. Baldwin developed his own web of big-city attorneys to serve as state correspondents. They handled regional problems at his discretion. The arrangements he made in San Francisco suggested how he wanted the Union to function outside New York. Attorney Austin Lewis began his affiliation with the Union's wartime precursor in 1917. After Baldwin spoke in San Francisco in 1926, a local committee emerged expressly to work with the SCACLU to repeal California's Criminal Syndicalism Law. Once the state legislature tabled a repeal bill, financial support and enthusiasm waned, and Lewis went back to being the ACLU's representative in San Francisco.

For his work, he accepted no money, and because his civil liberties cases were an addition to a heavy client load, he pursued nothing beyond what the national office explicitly asked of him. This level of engagement initially suited both the local people and the national office.[3]

But the Depression made local people and the national office more interested in real branches. Even Baldwin advocated their formation, declaring that "the time has come to decentralize our work; to build up local organizations all over the country." Abstract advocacy did not guarantee concrete commitment, however, and local volunteers found it hard to sustain branches on scarce resources. In Madison, Wisconsin, for example, a group of academics organized themselves after Harry Ward came through town, their last official act for several years. Branches that survived replaced their fantasies of paid secretaries, plush offices, and high profiles with hard work, generally accomplished on the fly. New York personnel, insulated from the narrow possibilities of local committees, set the bar high. In 1930 the national office recommended affiliates hold meetings of executive committees of at least five people every month and one or two membership meetings per year. As late as 1936, only six of nine official branches had executive boards, and only four had regular meetings. Most groups "exist informally and do not function excepting when local situations develop." Local people preferred ad hoc arrangements and thought Baldwin's office was unreasonable in its expectations.[4]

Finances were the biggest hindrance to civil liberties work. "We are full of enthusiasm but not full of money," one letter from the Detroit affiliate began. "Our pulse is very weak. . . . Our treasury is empty," wrote the Pennsylvania secretary. Requests for money were incessant and often unreasonable. While it was not a burden for the ACLU to fund one new affiliate, funding three or four at $25 a week (the standard rate in the early 1930s) amounted to nearly a fifth of the organization's annual budget. Some affiliate financial plans were positively fanciful. In Detroit, organizers imagined an annual budget of $5,000, well beyond the range of any affiliate in

1932, and thought it could be raised in Detroit, something Baldwin quickly scotched as "entirely out of the question." While national funding was supposed to be temporary, enabling the branches to generate their own sources of income, weaning them proved difficult. The entire organization existed in a depressed economy with heavy unemployment and other problems. The St. Louis office, for instance, lost its entire treasury in a bank failure. Tough times made local organizing a challenge.[5]

In those few lucky places where the Union invested in local affiliates, there were problems of expectation and control. Baldwin was unrealistic about what paid local secretaries could achieve. He was, by his own admission, "picky" and critical, assuming that everyone had his charisma, energy, and contacts and could quickly put together a functioning organization.[6] In 1930 he targeted Pennsylvania, the site of coal strikes, as a promising ACLU venue. He gave a local organizer two months to build membership and raise funds, and after two months stretched into six, he complained because the local person had only managed to raise half the proposed budget and organized merely four or five subaffiliates. Baldwin criticized him for "lack of planning," "lack of drive," and "too much time spent on travel." The organizer, not surprisingly, told Baldwin to find "someone who will have your confidence." His replacement, Allan Harper, an ambitious Harvard graduate, made a better impression, but Harper was "disappointed" with what he achieved. Unlike his predecessor, though, Baldwin liked him and kept him on for years. Baldwin's administrative weaknesses made the affiliates' jobs harder than they had to be.[7]

The Depression was the primary reason affiliates waxed and waned. Like any other segment of American society, they had their share of hard luck stories. In the summer of 1933, for example, the Boston branch desperately needed money to pay their secretary, whose personal financial situation was likewise dire. In a series of sad letters to the local director, she outlined her plans to sell some jewelry, but when that fell through, she confessed that "I haven't any further resources nor any particularly bright prospects." After

Baldwin "decided *not* to loan us the $100," the director noted, he wrote her a check for $110 from his own account. For the next year, the group lapsed into inactivity, since it had no treasury, no secretary, and no bright prospects of its own.[8]

Sometimes affiliates failed because they had no nurturing environments to support them. This was especially true in the South. The Union could not organize in places like Atlanta, Chattanooga, and Miami. Local activists did not want to be associated with a northern-based institution with a radical reputation. Ira Latimer would become a successful affiliate leader in Chicago, but in Memphis he could not form a branch at Le Moyne College, where he taught. He complained to Baldwin that the college president told him "not [to] be connected in any official way with a local ACLU committee," which, he added, was "true of every other member here."[9] Southern authorities saw the Union as a threat to their traditional way of life. The best the organization could manage was to work informally with local groups, most of which were religious. However, this strategy left large swaths of the country without a civil liberties affiliate directly under the ACLU's auspices.

The South was only the most extreme example of the regionalism and sometimes eccentric localism that thwarted standardization of affiliates, something national officers wanted. America was a more provincial country in the 1930s, and regional differences abounded. Since the Board trusted branches with nothing but local cases, branch officers quickly became adept at handling those, negotiating with quirky sheriffs and learning city and state codes. Such freedom meant that they evolved their own methods, procedures, and rules. They received little guidance until they did something wrong; then they heard from headquarters. Baldwin commonly chided branch leaders for violating the "elementary principle" of nonpartisanship by endorsing candidates. Many assumed that the ACLU defended only the rights of the downtrodden. "I can't conceive of the Union interesting itself on the side of an industrial baron," the Minnesota state correspondent explained.[10] Local volunteers made their decisions with none of the New Yorkers' sense of propriety.

Turf wars, gender stereotypes, and difficult personalities also complicated affiliate organizing. Local efforts to create an affiliate in Seattle hit a snag in the name of Adele Parker-Bennett. She ran the Conciliation Committee, a defense group for striking lumberjacks convicted of murder in Centralia, Washington. Whatever her actual strengths, her male comrades regarded her as a busybody and a leftist partisan. When she volunteered to form a civil liberties branch, they reported her every action to Baldwin. Parker-Bennett actually assessed the Seattle situation in exactly the kind of terms Baldwin wanted to hear, noting that any committee formed must be "harmonious, . . . have a good background of wide acquaintance, . . . [and be composed of] persons of influence." "We cannot rely," she added, "on New York wholly for prestige." Yet Baldwin patronized her, insisting that she let others handle the work so as to "conserve your influence on the Centralia work." Her colleagues excluded her, protested that she "blocked" their efforts to form a committee without her, but conceded that "we haven't found the right person" to lead their group. Ironically, when local Seattle males finally organized their branch, they demonstrated less astuteness than Parker-Bennett about their situation, asking for money the national ACLU could not provide.[11] Such problems seemed trivial to Baldwin, who preferred trusting one local correspondent to sorting out conflicts himself.

For the most part, the affiliates were too widely scattered to pose territorial problems, but the California affiliates squabbled regularly over responsibility. Some of the discord was inadvertently caused by the New York office's unfamiliarity with local geography. Referring cases, the staff might ask the San Francisco group to address something that happened in Bakersfield or the Los Angeles group to monitor Sacramento. When Baldwin asked the Southern California office to handle a lynching case in San Jose, roughly 50 miles south of San Francisco and nearly 400 miles from Los Angeles, the usually placid Austin Lewis grumbled "that the ill fated interference . . . has worked enormous harm." The two busy western affiliates remained wary of each other for years, a reality exacerbated by Baldwin's preference for the Southern California group. In the San Jose instance, for example, the national office paid the salary of the SCACLU attorney.[12] The Northern California ACLU branch (NCACLU) was rightly sensitive of its place in the national hierarchy.

Turf wars were not just a local problem; they also existed between the national organization and the branches. Because affiliate and national ACLU memberships were separate, there was no coordination of recruitment drives. At times, the locals and the national group unknowingly competed for members. A woman the national office appraised as "not a very promising prospect" to give the ACLU money turned out to be keeping the SCACLU solvent by contributing $75 each month. The director of the Southern California group explained how much work he had put into courting this "new angel" and cautioned Baldwin not to "poach on our territory." Baldwin backed off. The conflict, however, was not just financial.[13] Sometimes nationally prominent people in affiliate areas scorned the branches and associated with the national organization because it had higher status. Some sent regular critiques of local activity to Baldwin. Affiliate officers resented their preferences and Baldwin's faith in their assessments. Volunteers quickly realized that in a more respectable ACLU, they would be little more than drones.

National officers had trouble judging local work because they had no clear conception of how it differed from their own contributions. At any level, the ACLU was primarily a volunteer organization, but local work was much more labor intensive. National Board members met for lunch, stayed current on civil liberties projects, and served on committees. Paid staff handled membership matters, publicity, and office work. Affiliate volunteers cut stencils, composed membership solicitations, and maintained mailing lists. They also spent time in the field, researching legislative decisions, organizing meetings, and talking to prisoners, miners, and Communists. When local attorneys took on cases, few had the staff resources that prestigious National Board members had. For regional volunteers, ACLU work was hard, thankless, potentially dangerous, and time consuming.

At their most successful, branches accomplished impressive feats. In 1931 the SCACLU, in tandem with the Communists' International Labor Defense (ILD), took a challenge to a 1919 California law prohibiting the display of red flags to the Supreme Court, where they gained a ruling that still serves as a precedent. Yetta Stromberg, head of a Communist Young Pioneers summer camp outside Los Angeles, had raised the flag, little knowing that she broke a law disallowing displays of "signs, symbols or emblems of opposition to organized government." SCACLU staff attorney John Beardsley argued that flying a red flag was a protected right. The Court concluded that the law was so "vague" as to be "repugnant to the guaranty of liberty contained in the Fourteenth Amendment." The New York office consistently underplayed the case's importance, but for the SCACLU it was a tremendous achievement, typical of their low-key civil liberties work.[14]

As the Stromberg case suggested, affiliate work could have a significant impact. Branches had advantages national officers did not; they were better acquainted with the disenfranchised. Arthur Garfield Hays's much publicized trip to the Kentucky coalfields was a failure, as authorities halted the Union delegation at the border. The SCACLU received less press attention but gained the trust of workers by standing up for organizing efforts in California's Central Valley. SCACLU representatives, supported by a treasury and a paid director, helped protect the Communists' efforts to create the California Agricultural Workers Industrial Union. Often working, as they did in the Stromberg case, with the ILD, they made slow headway in the fields. In the early 1930s, authorities used the Criminal Syndicalism Law to stop unionization efforts, defining them as revolutionary threats. Conditions were always bad for migrant workers but became especially bad during the Depression.[15] Yet few respectable people mustered much concern for the heterodox workforce of Mexicans and Asians, particularly because of the obvious Communist role in organizing efforts. The SCACLU, however, did pay attention and act.

In the spring of 1930, SCACLU director Clinton Taft and staff attorney Leo Gallagher visited the small Central Valley town of Brawley to investigate a lettuce strike after word came that local authorities abused the organizers. Taft and Gallagher volunteered to aid those who had been arrested. In an effort to stop their intervention, the local sheriff "rushed toward him [Taft], grasped him by the throat with both his hands and kicked him viciously." He then ejected both Taft and Gallagher from the jailhouse, denying them access to their clients. Taft was so outraged that he told Baldwin it was "advisable to open an office down there . . . and put someone on the job of mobilizing any liberal sentiment that exists." But while Baldwin paid to get the Union involved in such activities in Pennsylvania, he hesitated before committing to the more volatile California situation, promising aid but naming no amount.[16]

While Taft, Gallagher, and another attorney spent their days in the hot valley towns trying to communicate with Mexican Americans, dodging local authorities, and fearing for their safety, national staff members nagged them to provide the "records and documents in the various bail cases." The office needed their paperwork to pay out bail money. Gallagher was incensed by the lack of appreciation for "those in Southern California who are *working* for civil liberties." "I can't decide," wrote the national secretary of Gallagher, "whether he is to[o] lazy to get the proper papers or really too stupid." Gallagher was neither, but his style was very much like that of the Communists he defended and the ILD, for which he often worked: confrontational and direct. He and Taft sued the Brawley sheriff who mistreated them, and they won.[17] Local civil liberties work was riskier, more intensive, and often more radical than national civil liberties work, but it was also extremely satisfying.

The New Deal made some, but not enough, difference in California. Whatever relief its farm programs provided, landowners, working through the antilabor organization, Associated Farmers, exerted power on sheriffs and judges to thwart organizing efforts. The federal conciliator the NLRB sent, Pellham Glassford, disappointed local volunteers. The Communists pushed on, organizing and calling more strikes. In 1934 Taft dispatched two other attorneys, Gallagher's law partner, A. L. Wirin, and Ernest Besig, to investigate another Brawley strike. Following a local meeting, vigilantes attacked Besig, beat him, and left him with the warning that "this will teach you [to] keep out of [the] Valley." Wirin was "kidnapped, beaten, threatened with death by vigilantes and Legionaires." Few national officers had such adventures, but this time they could augment local efforts with their New Deal contacts. They notified Labor Secretary Frances Perkins, Agriculture Secretary Henry Wallace, and Robert Wagner of the NLRB, urging them to replace Glassford because he displayed such "open hostility to workers." Wirin followed up by meeting with various Washington officials, although he correctly assessed that the government would only commit itself "to minor steps." Still, he reasoned, minor steps "would serve as an introduction to taking . . . more positive and more aggressive action" in the future.[18]

The backgrounds and experiences of Gallagher, Wirin, and Besig caused them to conceptualize their jobs in ways that conflicted with the Union's national vision. Gallagher had chosen the law over the priesthood and had a long history with radical organizations, including the ILD. He was the attorney who finally won alleged bomb-thrower Tom Mooney his freedom. His success cost him a teaching position at Southwestern University Law School. Wirin was Russian born, Harvard educated, and as devoted to the difficult field of labor law as his partner was. Besig had a law degree from Cornell University but ran a Pasadena settlement house for Mexican immigrants. None of the three had family money, connections, or much faith in the federal government, although Wirin aspired to New Deal work. All questioned the national organization's strategy of professionalism, believing that it distanced it from the people who needed their help. They thought respectability weakened the Union, making it "entirely too 'proper' and therefore useless." Local activists wanted to be valued for their contributions to the ACLU and given the tools and autonomy to do their jobs their own way.[19]

Yet, paradoxically, affiliate workers also banked on Union respectability, or at least the money they assumed respectability provided. Despite receiving regular financial statements, they continued to believe headquarters could fund their efforts.[20] Their more aggressive style could be, as Baldwin himself noted, "an asset as well as often a liability," but an asset that required precious financial backing from New York. Wirin was a master of impulsive case pursuit, sometimes far outside the SCACLU's territory. His affiliate could not afford him and expected the national ACLU to cover his costs. In 1935 he rushed to Gallup, New Mexico, to defend striking miners without "the formalities" of securing Board approval, which was necessary since New Mexico was beyond the SCACLU's territory. Baldwin informed his Southern California superior that "we cannot maintain him in New Mexico." Wirin assumed the ACLU could—and would—back him, even though he knew that the national organization scraped by financially. His confidence that Baldwin's officers would underwrite his impulsive ventures never wavered. Neither did his Los Angeles colleagues' sense that his strategy was appropriate because "it *was* very important that he get there as quickly as he could." In the most active affiliates, officers saw themselves as the equals of their national colleagues, eager to take advantage of the organization's strengths.[21]

Such brashness, though, threatened the organization's newfound legitimacy and professionalism. Venturing into union meetings, challenging local sheriffs, employing visibly radical attorneys, and staging protests were the actions of a more radical group than New Yorkers wanted the Union to be. Besig's independence, Wirin's excitability, and Gallagher's radicalism all made some officers nervous. To counteract such unpredictability, the office created rules, regulations, and procedures. Affiliates appreciated any money and support that came with the comparatively prestigious ACLU name, but they disliked the chain of command. Acting on their own initiative earned them members and money. Acting as instructed by headquarters drained their coffers without emotionally engaging local people. Besig's Northern California branch recognized this sooner than any other local and cultivated independence early. In 1935, when most of the other affiliates expected national subsidies, the NCACLU contemplated "the autonomy of the local committee with reference to New York." Its financial capacity was legendary. By 1939 it had more than 600 members and an annual income of approximately $3,600. But from the national office's perspective, its success was a problem, for only a minority of its members also belonged to the national ACLU.[22]

Localism became more controversial during the days of the People's Front. Branches wanted to go their own ways, but Baldwin saw in the Front's expansiveness the opportunity to enlarge his organization. He recommended that local groups link themselves with civil liberties front groups like the ILD, figuring that coordinated efforts would save the national office money while acquainting new volunteers with the ACLU. Local workers often assessed the consequences of shared endeavors differently. In California, for instance, the Communist Party was unusually strong and likely, therefore, to dominate any group effort.[23] Little did Baldwin know that Communists in the San Francisco area intended to capitalize on the NCACLU just as much as he hoped to take advantage of the ILD. Forgetting his own group's sometimes rocky relationship with the ILD, he insisted that the California affiliates work with the Party's premier civil liberties group.

The Southern California branch was quite willing to cooperate with the ILD. The two organizations had worked together before, and each trusted the other's sincerity. The ILD might occasionally disrupt the SCACLU's meetings but made few attempts to absorb, subsume, or dominate the affiliate.[24] Gallagher, who was probably a Communist, helped bridge any gaps between the two groups. In fact, the groups worked together so harmoniously and so often that many thought the SCACLU was "a nest of communists." Potential satellite branches in Riverside and Bakersfield insisted on associating with the national ACLU rather than the Los Angeles group for "tactical reasons." Ironically, even Baldwin interpreted the affiliate's synergy with the ILD as proof that the SCACLU was "infiltrated by Communists and fellow travelers." Yet the style worked for the SCACLU, and during the People's Front's heady middle days, the branch became the Union's great success story.[25]

The NCACLU had a contrary experience with Party fronts. It lacked any mitigating factors to protect it from Party aggression. Baldwin disliked Besig from the start, something local Communists tried to exploit. When the NCACLU revived in 1934 in the wake of the San Francisco General Strike, the Party was at its most militant and eager to squash the potential rival. Later, with the coming of the People's Front, Ella Winter, the widow of Communist journalist Lincoln Steffens and an old friend of Baldwin's, set her sights on the group. "It is obvious to me," Besig reported in 1935, "that the Communist Party does not want us in San Francisco unless they can control our activities."[26]

The political terrain Besig negotiated was inordinately complex—far more complex than national officers realized. Besig and Chester Williams, dispatched from the SCACLU, quickly discovered that the situation in San Francisco was very different from that in Los Angeles. The Bay Area was a hotbed of radical activism. Socialists and Communists were bitter rivals. Soon the Trotskyists arrived with their ILD rival, the Non-Partisan Labor Defense, to fight the Criminal Syndicalism Law, joining the already crowded field. All three factions approached the national office, undercutting the branch's legitimacy. Each sent critical appraisals of the affiliate's conduct. Yet while the Trotskyists and the Socialists confirmed Besig's assessment of the CPUSA's intentions, the Communists boldly asked Baldwin to cede to them the authority that rightfully belonged to the affiliate. "I suggest if you really want me to help and be effective," wrote Winter, "you make me one of your representatives and give me equal powers with Chester and Besig." No one at the ACLU's national headquarters was naive enough to believe everything Winter reported; still, the sheer number of derogatory communiqués eventually took their toll.[27]

Thus while the national office agreed that the branch "should be separate and distinct" from any front group, over time it came to doubt that evaluation and, on and off, sided with the Communists. It was not that Baldwin trusted Winter so much as Besig so little, because Besig "ignor[ed] or oppos[ed] 'New York.'" Winter reported that the NCACLU was full of "insane" and "dangerous" people, which sounded exaggerated to Baldwin but not that improbable. He felt little compunction about working out "terms of cooperation" in New York that he expected the local branch to follow. When Besig and his colleagues offered their own more jaundiced view of the situation, he complained that they ignored "the plan agreed upon."[28]

Baldwin was in no better position to solve the San Francisco branch's problems, as none existed. In 1933 leaders of the Agricultural and Cannery Workers Industrial Union were arrested for violating the Criminal Syndicalism Law. In 1934 they went on trial in Sacramento, part of Besig's territory. At first the ILD represented the accused, all Communists, until one, Norman Mini, defected to the Trotskyists. Thereafter the Non-Partisan Labor Defense represented Mini, and the ILD handled everyone else. Besig tried to coordinate a meaningful defense plan and an equitable distribution of defense funds.[29] These were impossible tasks, but the New York office never appreciated their difficulty and, instead, barraged him with directives and complaints. Soon Besig's local board found the New Yorkers nearly as obstructive as the Communists who tried to dominate them.

Because the national office displayed so little confidence in the NCACLU, local Communists assumed they could safely undermine the group. Winter and other Party activists sent Baldwin long and detailed criticisms. Board member Mary Van Kleeck, a Communist, echoed their attacks. In 1935 and again in 1938 local Communists, only some of whom were NCACLU members, petitioned ACLU headquarters to oust Besig and reorganize the group. These were minority views expressed by people with obvious partisan axes to grind; however, the Board privileged them over Besig's assessments. Baldwin acknowledged that the branch was "autonomous and . . . entirely self-supporting" but reprimanded it so much that Besig expected to see it reorganized. He was at a loss to respond, having been "charged with nonfeasance by certain critics unknown to me." The San Francisco–based branch never relinquished the sense "that the national office has shown an extreme lack of confidence."[30]

The NCACLU's experience was extreme, but its leeriness of front groups was not atypical. While the SCACLU worked with them, most branches steered clear of them, often, like Besig, to protect their autonomy. Most affiliates were willing to consider the organization's policy toward front groups but expected a consistent one. "I wish that you would write down what should be our relation with the ILD and the WDL [Workers Defense League]," the secretary of the Chicago Civil Liberties Committee (CCLC) begged Baldwin. But the office was not to be pinned down, since doing so would likely trigger arguments between anticommunist and pro-Front directors. "We cannot bind ourselves to a policy," the Portland Civil Liberties Union was told. With no consensus at the top over fronts, the branches never received useful guidance from New York.[31]

Advice from headquarters was sporadic, unpredictable, and not always helpful. The national staff expected professional behavior from the affiliates but did not treat them as professionals. They lectured and instructed, impugned their motives, and doubted their judgments. Certainly there were problematic volunteers, but the New Yorkers seemed inherently suspicious of local enthusiasm. Frederick Drew Bond, for example, wanted to form a branch in Hartford. National secretary Lucille Milner actively discouraged him, citing as reasons the absence of local civil liberties issues, Hartford's proximity to New York, and the possibility that it would constitute "a drain . . . on New York's finances." Milner found Bond's eagerness a liability. She thought he would be "a headache." He persisted, and she dispatched a couple of local members to meet him and report back. They called him sincere but "a bit over-enthusiastic." Rather than reassure her, this alarmed her. Another Hartfordite suggested that there was "no harm in trying" to organize a branch, but once Board member Alfred Bingham expressed "some doubts" about Bond, Milner concluded that they should "drop the matter as graciously as can be done" and leave Hartford unorganized.[32]

Bond's enthusiasm, like Besig's, was a risk for an organization that claimed local groups were "independent units" but did not treat them as such. Cooperating with the national ACLU quickly diminished affiliate ardor, especially when the New Yorkers had the financial upper hand. In Washington, D.C., for example, Baldwin promoted Geraldine Van Gerbig, "a woman of large means and great interest," as a volunteer but was skeptical of Maurice Wilsie, the local secretary whose legislative work New York underwrote. Baldwin thought Wilsie was "disorganized, slip-shod, nervous." Van Gerbig, a self-defined novice at civil liberties work, sent Baldwin regular reports about Wilsie's weaknesses, as did other "friends in New York." Once Wilsie learned of the complaints, he offered to resign unless the branch gave him a vote of confidence. They did, so the National Board withdrew his legislative work and the stipend that went with it. As so often was the case, the New Yorkers rallied around Baldwin, but local volunteers backed their own.[33]

To expand the ACLU without ceding control, officers tried to tie local volunteers to the national office via the "subvention," or "subsidy," paying them "one dollar for every three...raised." These workers were supposed to pay for themselves while recruiting national members and raising contributions for New York. Once on site, though, many redirected their energies. Part of the national office's complaint about Wilsie, for example, was that he "concentrated on concrete endeavors with respect to specific civil liberties issues, . . . [and thereby] subordinated efforts toward building up the membership and securing contributions." Even in an era of massive unemployment, the job of ACLU organizer was undesirable. In New Jersey the national ACLU agreed to pay for a part-time person to recruit members during the Boss Hague fight. The first person they hired changed his mind before he started, and the second turned down the position because the office would not guarantee it for two years. Headquarters refused to pay the third organizer because the New Jersey group picked him. The fourth, someone hired in New York—the "brother-in-law of one of our attorneys"—turned out to be "a little too expensive." Three months into the hiring process, there had been four job offers and no work. The Washington, D.C., and New York City affiliates had similar experiences.[34]

As the national ACLU moderated and professionalized, it tried to groom affiliates to be subsidiaries, tractable and helpful. After branches challenged them over the Wagner Act, directors insisted on structure and standardization, subject, of course, to Baldwin's arbitrary whims. Affiliates were not consulted before a Board committee drew up regulations to achieve "greater uniformity," something desired in New York but not elsewhere. Branches saw some of the rules as problems. They found the Board's funding proposal especially alarming. This required them to charge at least $2.00 for joint national and affiliate membership, payable directly to head-quarters in New York, which would then return $1.00 to the local. The arrangement would have made national funding more stable. Affiliates knew, though, that they would be the first to suffer when members could not pay the full amount during "this period of depression." The directive to cooperate "with other organizations engaged in combating repression" (fronts) unnerved many, as it left them with "no judgment" over policy. The branches stopped both proposals, retaining latitude with respect to fronts and separation of membership dues. They did so because directors themselves could not agree on the policies. The growing division at the top made national governance more difficult and local autonomy easier to obtain.[35]

Baldwin, of course, continued to interfere whatever the rules. In the mid-1930s he pressed his enthusiasm for the People's Front onto the branches, sometimes with the encouragement of director Mary Van Kleeck, whose politics and interference he would later decry. In 1936 several affiliates opposed his urgings that they hold joint meetings with Harry Ward's American League against War and Fascism. Such a meeting occurred successfully in New York City, so Baldwin touted Ward's national speaking tour as a way of taking advantage of the league's popularity. Few affiliates were keen on cooperative ventures. The Portland branch called the league "a Communist organization." The Chicago group was nervous about Ward's unwillingness to "draw a clear line of distinction" between his role in the ACLU and the league. The Seattle branch judged a joint meeting bad public relations, noting that "prejudicial public opinion [was] against it." In San Francisco, Besig gave a "flat refusal" because Ward "is sure to drag in the fellow travelers and then we are cooked." In Madison and Los Angeles, jointly sponsored meetings proceeded uneventfully. In more places, though, branches opted for closed Union meetings with Ward or no meetings at all.[36]

Among all the affiliates, the CCLC worried the most about the stigma of connections with the People's Front. Chicago was one of the few places where Socialists and Communists openly competed in the branch. Tired of constant bickering, the local board brought in a new director, Ira Latimer, in 1936. He "qualified because I was neither a Socialist or a Communist," although the CPUSA attempted to enlist him as a member thereafter. Latimer declined, persuaded that the branch's success lay elsewhere. He quickly removed a local Communist workhorse from the local board. "Anything touched by the CP," he explained, "has an unnecessary obstacle to overcome." He was part of a new generation of ACLU local leaders with ambitious organizational agendas that, at the very least, made life harder for Union leaders.[37]

Latimer was eager to capitalize on the Union's growing liberal respectability. He believed that bringing New Dealers into the branch would make it more influential. He worried about the CCLC's reputation. Did the fact that the branch shared an office with the People's Press reflect badly on the group? Would changing its name to the Chicago Civil Rights League make it more palatable to those whose view was currently "unfavorable if not antagonistic"? Latimer's conception of his affiliate was expansive. He wanted to bring in some "new conservative friends" and build connections with "churches, unions and other organizations." These, he predicted, would "protect the steady growth of the Committee and . . . raise more funds for more complete work." Yet Latimer also described himself as "a civil liberties communist, so to speak, in quotes" because "they [the Communists] were for civil liberties."[38] His goals were radical, but his approach was professional, as he posed questions about group perception and functionality, considering how best to impress and recruit a diverse group of local supporters. While his energetic attitude ought to have delighted the New York staff, it annoyed them, for the more professional the CCLC became, the more it wanted, especially financially, from the national ACLU.

Key to Latimer's vision was a full-time civil liberties presence in the office. For personal as well as professional reasons, he schemed to attain the same setup that clearly distinguished the two California affiliates: paid directors, regular newsletters, and staff attorneys. Latimer was, CCLC colleague Leon Despres recalled, a "careerist and . . . an ardent office holder where he thought he could get somewhere." His original appointment to the CCLC was half time, but after he lost his Works Progress Administration, job he contrived to attain full-time status. He succeeded, and his success led to a series of escalating expectations: a bigger office, a membership secretary, a part-time attorney, and a publicity representative. Latimer was, in Baldwin's words, "a good choice as an organizer," but his every letter to headquarters included an idea that would cost money.[39] Local people like Latimer were both the pride and the bane of the national organization, for they built up affiliates so effective as to place too many demands on a national organization unprepared and unwilling to welcome them.

Latimer was but one example of a new generation of local activists who chose the ACLU as a forum for their values and their careers. In contrast to members on the unpaid National Board, Latimer, Besig, or Wirin depended on ACLU branch work for income. Wirin, especially, expected civil liberties work to be financially and emotionally satisfying. He had strong political opinions and an immigrant's raw ambition to succeed. Baldwin thought him "a rare find" but "impulsive" and "wild" when it came to his simultaneous pursuit of money and moral vision. His ardor took him from the Southern California office to the national ACLU to the NLRB (where his ACLU connections got him into trouble) and back to Los Angeles, where he settled in the late 1930s. The national office generally approved of him, although directors were sometimes frustrated by his many detours. But his biggest liability was his constant financial neediness. "Work for the American Civil Liberties Union does not pay in money," Arthur Garfield Hays advised him when Wirin began prolonged negotiations for a national ACLU position. Yet at a time when full-time local directors made about $25 a week and national secretary Lucille Milner earned $75 a month, the SCACLU paid Wirin a monthly retainer of $200 that he augmented with his own practice. "At times," the head of the SCACLU recalled, "[we] had to raise almost as much for Wirin as [for the] director."[40]

In the past the ACLU had not had to contend with many people as demanding as Wirin. So long as civil liberties work was a marginal occupation, nobody expected it to pay. People like Wirin worked hard, revitalizing the Union in ways that brought glory and money to the whole hierarchy. In other ways, though, they unsettled the organization and shifted attention away from New York. Paid local directors were not content merely to follow orders. They wanted to set policy and influence others. People like Wirin or Besig or Latimer, who lacked eastern polish, wealthy fathers, and Ivy League credentials, were unfamiliar personality types to many national officers. Directors could not identify with their ambition and often regarded it as a distasteful partisanship that demeaned the civil liberties enterprise.

Affiliates without paid staffs, though, did not even approach equal footing with the San Francisco, Los Angeles, or Chicago groups. They struggled, rose, and fell on single personalities; remained idiosyncratic; and in the end, also disappointed the national organization. Local civil liberties work attracted two types of people: political activists and ministers. Activists too commonly interjected their politics into their ACLU work, and the ministers tended to be overly cautious. Both frustrated national officers. Branches were also more diverse than headquarters, particularly in their use of female volunteers. Tenacious female secretaries held several groups together, even though Baldwin thought of them as loquacious spinsters with misguided politics. He tried to rein in Bostonian Florence Luscomb's leftism and warned St. Louis's Elizabeth Gilman to confine her group to "civil liberties matter[s]."[41] Some volunteers were problems; however, the national staff almost routinely patronized anyone not paid for their civil liberties work.

But the affiliates were not full of imbeciles and fluttery ladies. Even without paid staffs, they took on an increasing share of the Union's work in the 1930s. Recognizing that they could not engage civil liberties as broadly as did the national organization, affiliate volunteers learned to focus their energies. The Massachusetts affiliate specialized in censorship cases, capitalizing on the traditional "banned-in-Boston" label. Smaller branches concentrated only on emerging issues such as election fraud or police brutality. The West Coast affiliates, principally the two California branches and the one in Seattle, handled labor cases, while the independent allied groups that operated out of the South dealt with race-related civil liberties fights. Local committees learned their limits early. The Detroit branch might have had grandiose schemes in 1931, but by 1937 it had settled into operating a "skeleton committee" that provided legal aid and existed as a more respectable alternative to the Front-linked Conference for Political and Civil Rights.[42] The national organization failed to give the affiliates credit for what they did well, focusing instead on what they failed to do.

By the end of the decade, affiliates suffered from the fallout of New Deal retrenchment and conservative revival. Latimer's obsession with reputation was one reaction, as was Besig's determination to clear his group before HUAC.[43] With HUAC's high approval rating, the Communists exerting more control over front groups after 1937, and anti-Stalinism gaining force, affiliates again struggled to survive. The backlash was sometimes more than local agencies could handle. The national ACLU and local Communists pressured the Boston group to spearhead a public relations challenge to the Massachusetts version of HUAC. The group protested that it was not situated "to perform miracles."[44] Local boards did not experience the factional struggles that increasingly disrupted the national boardroom; however, branches struggled to keep their treasuries out of the red, their volunteers mobilized, and their momentum going.

There is no doubt that ACLU affiliates benefited from outside changes, augmented by their own hard work, in the 1930s. Their record challenged the attitudes at headquarters that they were lazy and ineffective and their officers too amateurish to make a difference. Committed leaders, in particular, made branches active, engaged, and valuable. These local leaders were dedicated civil libertarians of a different stripe. Their identities and careers were bound to the small organizations they helped create, not to the national ACLU and the milieu that supported it. To stay vital, local branches needed local people and local money. Famous speakers from New York might draw a crowd, and loans from the national group helped for a while; but the day-to-day work that followed was what truly mattered. What happened in New York was often neither relevant nor interesting to local activists. Branches had their own loyalties. With time, the dimensions of these differences would become deeper and broader.

HOLDING US ALL TOGETHER

The ACLU, the Nazi-Soviet Pact, and Anticommunism, 1939–1941

In 1968 former ACLU Board member Corliss Lamont published the transcript of the controversial Board hearing of Elizabeth Gurley Flynn conducted twenty-eight years earlier. Flynn stood accused of civil liberties partisanship because she belonged to the Communist Party. Lamont sent Roger Baldwin a copy of the book along with a note that read, "You're a great man but you're not always right and you weren't right in this case." Baldwin's response consisted of three short words: "Yes, I was."[1] For the ACLU, 1940 was a fateful year, one that generated long-standing resentments and started the organization on a long detour. The Nazi-Soviet Pact of August 1939 intensified problems the ACLU already faced, polarizing directors and exacerbating affiliate resentments. During the 1930s the national ACLU united a diverse group of people interested in civil liberties. Anticommunism challenged that diversity as its advocates questioned the sincerity and legitimacy of others' motives. The battles that followed threatened the group's respectability. These were not good days for the ACLU.

The People's Front faced its most formidable challenge in the Nazi-Soviet Pact. The nonaggression treaty between Stalin and Hitler undermined the Front's raison d'être. Perhaps more than any other officer, the pact "shocked" Roger Baldwin, a longtime radical already feeling vulnerable about his past choices. "The archetype fellow traveler," as one historian called him, Baldwin's world fell apart. "I was never so shaken up by anything," he recalled. One of his most valuable personal characteristics was his certainty. His absolute confidence in his opinions gave him the strength to defy convention, just as his commitment to all dissenters helped him steer his Union. Once he faltered, others seized the initiative from him.[2]

Union anticommunists immediately capitalized on his horror. Sidney Hook, anti-Stalinist and irascible cofounder of the CCF, led the charge. At the end of September he notified Baldwin that "I am letting my membership in the Civil Liberties Union lapse." His reason was that two Board members, Lamont and Harry Ward, had signed a public letter that made "slanderous" attacks against himself and the "other distinguished members of the ACLU" who belonged to the CCF. The letter did not mention Hook, the ACLU, or the CCF, and neither Ward nor Lamont appended his Union credentials to his signature. It was one of the dozens of political statements Union members signed every day. What was different about this one was that it contested the CCF's inclusion of communism in its definition of totalitarianism, the central ideological claim of the new anticommunism. Hook demanded to address the Board, and when so denied, he threatened to resign publicly.[3]

Board anticommunists, "largely in sympathy" with Hook, recognized an opportunity to replace Ward as Board chairman, something they had longed to do since the 1938 fight over Henry Ford's rights. The pact left Ward, the enthusiastic Front defender, in a difficult position as the Communists' allegiances changed. Calling Ward "more of a liability than an asset," Norman Thomas and

John Haynes Holmes pressed to rescind his office and complained when the Board failed to move fast enough.[4] In October the Dies Committee on Un-American Activities subpoenaed Ward to answer questions about the American League for Peace and Democracy. His testimony confirmed that Communists, whom he estimated as never more than 12 percent of league members, had unusual power in the group. Their "willingness to do the 'Jimmy Higgins' work," he explained, helped, but so, too, did their ability to intimidate progressives with the prospect of destroying the People's Front. Although he did not mention the ACLU by name, one Union staff member called his testimony "awful."[5]

Consequently, anticommunist directors wanted Ward publicly disassociated from the Union, his powers weakened, or his title withdrawn. Most others continued to think of him as a "firm and fair chairman," but anticommunists warned he was "a serious danger." When the organization launched a fund drive, they demanded that he not sign the appeal letter, "since he is discredited in the minds of the American people." Baldwin signed the letter instead. Anticommunists began talking about Ward to their friends. Soon a small flurry of postcards asking, "Just when is Harry Ward resigning?" arrived in the New York office. Taken by surprise, the Board continued to ignore the ruckus until Thomas made a "vicious" public attack on Ward's Union status in the Socialist press.[6]

The directors were puzzled and disconcerted by the anticommunists' fervor, since Ward's term ended in January. After the fight over Ford, the Board had not functioned as congenially as it once had, but the anticommunists' pressures made the directors anxious and uncomfortable. Some found the whole attack on Ward fabricated, unnerving, and even "nuts." Reluctantly recognizing that the agitation would not go away, on 4 December the Board voted to guarantee Ward's freedom of speech and association, while expressing regret that anyone might confuse his league and Union personae. A few weeks later, the directors reprimanded Thomas for his newspaper exposé's "reckless damage to the repute of the ACLU." Any more loose talk, they warned, would "make his further presence [on the Board] embarrassing." Under ordinary circumstances, a vote of confidence for one faction, coupled with a rebuke of the other, should have settled matters.[7]

The anticommunists, however, seethed. They found the willingness of the directors to forgive Ward but not Thomas inexcusably partisan and proof of Party intimidation. At the same time, they were appalled by their own reactions. "I got stupefied and finally tongue tied," Margaret de Silver explained after the meeting where the directors scolded Thomas, classic symptoms of the "frightful liberal disease of inaction." De Silver expected others to choose the easier path of defending Ward but was disappointed that she lacked the spine to stand up to her fellow directors and force them to act appropriately. "I am not a political or professional person," she told Baldwin, so her only option was to resign, making a symbolic, moral, and personal statement about the ACLU Board. Her attitude was extreme and her actions were frightening, particularly to Baldwin.[8]

Baldwin was used to running the ACLU by his charm and occasional bureaucratic legerdemain, and the intensity of anticommunist sentiment disturbed his easy authority over the organization. Suddenly, he remembered, "emotions arose high enough to threaten disruption." Always the conciliator, he worked to forestall confrontation, juggling agendas depending on who showed up at meetings and hoping "to avoid a fight."[9] But he could not defuse the conflict. The anticommunists stood firm. When they felt their grievances did not get a fair hearing, they took their complaints elsewhere, as Thomas did, or they leaked stories to the anticommunist press, violating directors' tacit discretion about ACLU inner workings. They quickly recognized that they could capitalize on Baldwin's uncertainty. They used Baldwin as a reluctant ally, exploiting his fears about the CPUSA and the Union's reputation and stature.

Baldwin was not quite the anticommunist Holmes, Thomas, or de Silver was. Osmond Fraenkel thought he had "anticommunist fits" rather than their moral invective. ACLU national secretary Lucille Milner felt he "revert[ed]" to his class background and identified with his more Brahmin colleagues.[10] Holmes and Thomas were particularly close to him, with their associations dating back to the Union's founding. He trusted that they looked out for the organization rather than using it for their own political purposes. Baldwin was a situational anticommunist, appreciative of the perspective but more concerned about the damage to the group if well-placed persons resigned. His disappointment with the People's Front after the pact colored his perspective so that he had trouble reading the liberal mood. Liberals drew back from the Soviet Union, but their higher priority was antifascism; they simply let the CPUSA retreat into isolation. Some progressives stuck with the Communists; others also chose antifascism. Even the Roosevelt administration's anticommunism was more political than ideological, a response to the maneuverings of congressmen like Martin Dies. There was a red scare in 1939–40, but its advocates were not especially devoted to civil liberties. Baldwin delayed as long as he possibly could, waiting to see where liberals lined up, hoping that there would not be too large a gap between what the anticommunists demanded and what the organization could legitimately give them.

One looming pressure point was the Union's response to the Dies Committee. In the fall of 1939 Dies started investigating front groups, illegally seizing membership lists. In the past, he had been an easy target, as his methods were irresponsible and his claims lurid. But while anticommunists conceded the committee's misdeeds, they now delighted in its discoveries. "The Committee has been getting the goods on some of our friends and associates," Holmes gloated. "You are so right about . . . history somehow catch[ing] up on people," agreed Ernst. "The Dies Committee has much to its credit," concluded Roger Riis, not the least of which was trapping "our extreme left-wing members" in their own hypocrisy. These were not popular liberal sentiments.[11]

Thus when rumors of a relationship between the committee and the ACLU circulated in the fall of 1939, the primary reaction was outrage. The rumors started after Dies summoned Ward to testify. When questioners asked about Ward's Union activities, Dies cut them off, announcing that "there was not any evidence that the American Civil Liberties Union was a Communist organization."[12]

Coming on the heels of these remarks were reports of meetings between ACLU personnel and Dies staffers a few days before Ward's testimony. Union counsels Morris Ernst and Arthur Garfield Hays met with Dies; the most liberal member of his committee, Jerry Voorhis; and some "New Dealers" (Jerome Frank and Adolf Berle) in Dies's office and again at a cocktail party. Baldwin insisted that the meetings were innocent, that "their only purpose . . . was to convince them [Dies's representatives] that they should hear the Civil Liberties Union in answer to the many charges made [against it]. The meeting was unsuccessful." Yet Ernst told Baldwin that "*I am thoroughly convinced that I was successful* in preventing the hearing from wrapping Ward's testimony, as head of the League, around the neck of the ACLU." He boasted to a decidedly unsympathetic Corliss Lamont that "I have saved the Civil Liberties Union from taking a terrible rap, by seeing Dies." While Ernst exulted, other members cringed at the notion of clandestine meetings with Martin Dies.[13]

Ernst enjoyed hobnobbing with powerful people. He felt none of the other anticommunists' shame or complicity if they failed to act. He reveled in his cocktail party planning. He was "a very political guy, always maneuvering," Lamont recalled. For days afterward, he badgered Jerome Frank with reminders of the meeting. When he read in the papers that Frank had met with Roosevelt, he wondered "if you talked about the cocktail party" and asked that if they had, "Won't you drop me a confidential line?"[14] While it is possible that what led Ernst to believe he had "saved" the ACLU was bringing together New Deal liberals, ACLU staff, and Dies representatives, he probably did more than book the room, order the liquor, and invite the guests. Freedom of Information Act documents show that, around the same time, Ernst "alerted the FBI to the anti-FBI sentiment of some Union members and to plans of some ACLU members to attack the bureau." Indeed, the Freedom of Information Act file of Ernst's fellow Board member Abraham Isserman contains a report that an unnamed informant identified Isserman as a Communist Party member at approximately the same time. It is very possible that Ernst provided information to the FBI or made promises to Dies in exchange for Dies's clearance during the Ward hearing.[15]

We will never know what went on at that cocktail party or the private meeting with Martin Dies a few days before. Yet a number of ACLU volunteers suspected the worst. Lamont believed that "Dies suddenly switched policy toward the ACLU because he was assured at the off-the-record Washington conference that the organization itself would take the necessary steps to 'cleanse' itself of Communists." Isserman thought there had been a "deal" of the kind Lamont suggested.[16] Rumors sprang up almost immediately, especially in the affiliates. Alfred Lewis Baker of Boston heard them, as did Arthur Ackland in the SCACLU. Gardner Jackson of Washington, D.C., learned about the meetings from "a number of newspapermen" and then saw reports of them in print. Everyone seemed to know about the matter, but, as several complained, neither Baldwin nor any other executive had enlightened them officially. Anticommunists quickly jumped on the "miserable slander," blaming it on malcontents or, more sinisterly, Communists. But in truth, most Union members heard about the meeting innocently, from a newspaper story or from another member.[17]

Most scholars believe that there was an informal or tacit deal between Dies and ACLU representatives promising the Union a public "cleansing" if the group got rid of its Communists. Jerold Simmons finds the idea "persuasive" but bureaucratically difficult to manage. Samuel Walker sees it as "fully consistent with Ernst's style" but not Hays's.[18] The timing of events—that Hays, Ernst, and Dies talk one day, and the next day Dies voluntarily interrupts hearings to offer his judgment about the ACLU—lends credence to the notion of some sort of intervention. Certainly Ernst was, as Walker suggests, precisely the kind of person to broker such an arrangement, perhaps implying to Dies that he had authority he did not have or dropping the details of his reports to the FBI into the conversation. It seems unlikely that ACLU officers formally agreed to anything, but whatever implied arrangement existed undoubtedly involved Ernst as a key actor.

The uproar that greeted these developments conveyed to Baldwin the consequences of being too anticommunist. Yet, when appointing a committee to assess Dies's work (an annual Union undertaking), he named a large number of anticommunists. He was not so naive as to think their report would go unchallenged—certainly not when the organization was already riled over alleged deals with Dies. The new committee was provocative, believing it their responsibility "to turn out 'a middle-of-the-road report' that would help lead liberals into a position of 'pragmatic realism'" toward Dies's work. And that was just what they did. "Discount as you will the asinine manner," anticommunist Roger Riis told Baldwin, and "the fact remains that he [Dies] has produced much of value and we need to have that sort of thing produced." Baldwin let the anticommunists hang themselves with a report that treated Dies "a little too fairly."[19]

The report triggered an angry response that allowed Baldwin to stand back while others handled the anticommunists. Hays thought the "'kind' words" and temperate attitude inappropriate. The report "ran contrary to our whole previous position," Lamont complained. The most substantial criticisms came from the Union's New Dealers. They offered an expert's view of Roosevelt's probable response, as they were "on the scene here in Washington" and "possibly in a better position" to know just how inappropriate the report was. They threatened to "publicly withdraw from the ACLU" if it was not rewritten.[20] The response to the report left no doubt as to the Board's post-pact center of gravity.

Presented with the report draft, the Board whittled away at any favorable comments. Although committee members felt the tone "ought to be carefully preserved," the directors forced them to delete their more positive references to Dies. The result was a "hodgepodge," but it was more acceptable than the original had been.[21] But rather than constraining the anticommunists, the greatly edited report had the opposite impact. There was, John Haynes Holmes asserted, a fair report, until "the [procommunist] opposition began its familiar work of 'boring from within,'" a loaded phrase used to describe a Communist tactic. In response, "we liberals did what we usually do—instead of fighting for what we believed in, we sought to make concessions and compromises." Holmes refused to see what happened as an honest assessment of the Board's true position. Instead, he called it a victory for the "radical minority group which follows the party line laid down in Moscow."[22]

Faced with such unyielding stubbornness, Baldwin concluded that his top priority was "hold[ing] us all together." With the Ward business, the Dies report, and ACLU elections all converging, he thought he might find a bureaucratic solution to the Board's differences by separating the factions. "The damage to the Union," he concluded, "if any, will be less this way." His proposal demonstrated which Board bloc scared him more, as he wanted to move nearly all of the leftist faction (Flynn, Isserman, Van Kleeck, and Dunn) off the Board and onto the Committee on Civil Rights in Labor Relations, ceding them control over labor policies. Meanwhile, the anticommunists would stay on the Board, except for Norman Thomas, who had provoked the strongest reaction. Baldwin's plan favored the anticommunists but not enough to suit them, and its bureaucratic nature offended them. Thomas vetoed the arrangement, which required complete agreement from all involved, because "I could not possibly admit that what seems to me to be a very important struggle to preserve the integrity and usefulness of the ACLU was primarily a personal wrangle."[23]

After his least controversial solution failed, Baldwin settled on another: having the ACLU accept the anticommunists' definition of totalitarianism. It would meet the terms of any deal with Martin Dies, and he hoped it would satisfy Thomas, Holmes, and their friends. Baldwin assumed that Ward and friends were either too demoralized to respond or so dedicated as to swallow an unpleasant position. Here his instincts failed him. He seemed not to consider the ideological implications of any statement. He overestimated—or at least oversold—the public relations angle, misjudging the climate. He also failed to anticipate the organizational consequences. As part of the routine election process, he directed the Nominating Committee "to consider the whole question of the Union's personnel in the light of recent discussions." Innocuous as that sounded, he then quietly supplied them with a statement that declared it "inappropriate" for any person on an ACLU governing committee to belong to "any political organization which supports totalitarian dictatorship in any country."[24]

Baldwin hoped "to settle a controversy which threatened to split us," but he begged those who knew of his role to keep quiet because "I don't want to be identified with any of them [Board factions]." The directors rejected his statement, voting to sustain Harry Ward's ruling as chair that it was "outside the [Nominating] Committee's authority" to propose it. At the next meeting, though, opponents could not fully defeat the anticommunists. Their motion that the only membership test the ACLU needed was "complete and consistent support of civil liberties" failed by one vote. The impasse again incited the anticommunists. Holmes pressured Baldwin, while Thomas threatened a group resignation calculated for its public relations impact. Baldwin notified the directors that "five or more members of the National Committee are planning to appeal" their vote against the statement, an infrequently invoked part of the by-laws that allowed the full Board and the National Committee to act on a contested issue. Anticommunists timed their appeal for the Union's annual meeting, collecting all the proxies they could. Thanks to the proxies, they won. Sustained by their victory, they immediately brought the statement before the intimidated Board and got it passed.[25]

Only after the statement passed did Baldwin confront anything more than the immediate practical impact of this 1940 resolution. Until then, he saw it primarily as a way to placate anticommunist directors and stave off any mass resignation of them. Now, as paid head of the organization, he had to explain and justify the measure. Publicly he claimed it marked no change in "the fundamental policy of the Union over the 20 years of its existence," something no one familiar with the Union believed. As directors and National Committee members confirmed the voice vote with mail-in ballots, he received a torrent of complaints about the policy implications of the act. Many thought it violated Union principles. Several caught Baldwin in his lie. Most acrimonious was the mail from affiliates, where there was nearly unanimous disapproval of the resolution.

It was, one affiliate declared, "a bad example" or "a serious change in the policy [that] . . . yield[s] to hysteria or expediency." Some disliked it on principle, while others felt it pandered to anticommunist pressures. The California branches distinguished between what the national organization did and their "more liberal" or "less scared" local groups. Outside the organization, the 1940 resolution hardly stirred a whisper of complaint. Communists denounced it; liberals said little about it. Inside the ACLU, however, the conflict tied up the organization from top to bottom.[26]

In the branches, there was outright shock and surprise as local volunteers discovered that they had so little say in an organization they had always assumed was democratic. Baldwin had his hands full quelling branch rebellions. He advised one affiliate that it was "very unwise" to let their members vote informally about the decision. He warned the NCACLU that it would "look very foolish" if it withdrew from the national organization in protest. It was not just the content of the resolution that offended local boards; it was also their lack of power in the larger Union bureaucracy. When Holmes showed up at local meetings, not to listen to members, but to tell them how to think, volunteers seethed. As one disgruntled Board member later noted, the 1940 resolution "made for bad relations between the national office . . . and the various branches."[27]

Most ACLU members paid their dues and left others to conduct the group's business. But when the Board passed the resolution, it became important to members that they have input into the running of the organization. "It seems to me that this is a matter of policy," one wrote, "which should be settled by the whole membership rather than the officers alone." "We should have all been consulted before they [directors] made their unfortunate decision," another said. Still another reminded the Board that "even the presence of non-communists on the Board of Directors does not democratically enfranchise the rank-and-file." Members discovered that they were expected to defend something over which they had no say and then were forced to live with its consequences.[28]

Always the autocrat, Baldwin dismissed these objections. He knew the branches were "practically unanimous in condemning our resolution" even though "they [local people] understand it pretty well." Rather than hear their objections or allow them to vote on the policy, he thought the staff should tell members "what our policy should be." The only recourse unhappy members had were letters of protest, although Holmes directed the staff to disregard any correspondence from people with "closed minds."[29] When too many letters came in to ignore, Baldwin appointed a committee to screen the correspondence and report back; he assigned an anticommunist, Roger Riis, to be its head. Riis never revealed how many negative letters he saw, but the fact that he divided them into eight separate categories suggests a fair number. His summary to Baldwin was full of conditions: keeping in mind that there were always more anti- than pro- letters, and after discarding eighteen letters written by "dupes," he found the balance "more even than I would have guessed." The 1940 resolution consumed an ever-growing amount of the organization's energies.[30]

Worse yet, anticommunist directors were not satisfied by the measure alone. The same night the 1940 resolution passed, Board members replaced Ward with Holmes as their chair. Accepting the honor, he warned them, "Our conflict is not over." Anticommunists badgered Baldwin for more. They critiqued his public relations efforts, complaining that his pamphlet on the 1940 resolution was too defensive. "I see no earthly reason why we should go so far out of our way to over-paint the opposition," Riis told him. They wanted him to defend the measure as ideology and not just a public relations choice, forcing from him a more anticommunist public statement than he wanted to make. Holmes acknowledged that the "avalanche of correspondence" must be making him "fatigued" and "discouraged"—a rare concession that the numbers were not with the anticommunists—but urged him to stay the course.[31]

Baldwin was going to need strength to handle "certain implications of action," for anticommunists next wanted to remove the one public Communist director, Elizabeth Gurley Flynn. Flynn was a Communist but "quite open and aboveboard," Thomas noted, "in her membership." Her colleagues reelected her nevertheless. She was a model director and, as Arthur Garfield Hays observed, "No one among us had fought more consistently and strenuously for the right of free speech over the years." There were other Board Communists, so we must assume that two things made Flynn vulnerable: she was the only self-identified Communist director and she was female, with a trail of ex-lovers in high places. One was Italian anarchist Carlo Tresca, who in 1940 lived with Margaret de Silver. De Silver continued her husband's donations of $1,200 each year. When she resigned from the Board when it chastised Thomas for speaking ill in public of Ward, she indicated she might rejoin it if the ACLU stopped its "nonsensical shilly-shallying" and dismissed Flynn. If she returned, her donations could "make up perhaps for the loss of the money through changes that she, like the rest of us, wanted," Baldwin told Holmes. Baldwin's motives were, thus, "economic and sexist," as historian Rosalyn Baxandall said. But Tresca was not Flynn's only ex-lover. Baldwin was another, and the two remained friends. Flynn was in a moment of personal crisis in 1940. Her son was dying of cancer, and "it has about used Elizabeth up," Baldwin noted. It is hard to imagine a more distressing scenario for Baldwin than having to sacrifice his old friend and lover to satisfy the anticommunists.[32]

The board, however, needed Baldwin's imprimatur on Flynn's expulsion. Baldwin tried to avoid any direct role in the prosecution. He drafted a resolution against Flynn but induced another—female—director to introduce it, ostensibly to soften the blow. Still, Ernst predicted to Holmes that "the turning point will come when you call on Roger at the meeting to state his position." Flynn stood firm, and the Board scheduled a hearing against her—a hearing postponed two months so she could attend to her dying son. During those months resentment percolated through the organization, and bickering continued at the top. The Board just barely turned back a compromise affirming the 1940 resolution, expressing regret that Flynn was reelected but allowing her to serve out her term. Anticommunists knew that "the feeling is running against expulsion," and the Board seemed "doubtful of the propriety or wisdom of carrying out the intent of the resolution."[33]

Indeed, Baldwin had "doubts . . . as to whether we could ever explain an act of expulsion." Anticommunist directors tried to fortify him, while Holmes threatened resignations should Flynn not be removed. Anticommunists were worried. She was a sympathetic character, and her son's recent death made her more so. Moreover, her "plea is effectively written."[34] The "trial" convened in May 1940. Lacking any precedents, the directors improvised. Holmes presided as chair, giving his faction the advantage. "What fun it was in an intellectual shadow-boxing way," recalled Roger Riis. Others disagreed. The hour grew late and tempers flared. Finally, Holmes sent Flynn from the room, and the directors voted. On the most important charge, that her CPUSA membership made her ineligible for office under the 1940 resolution, the Board deadlocked, and Holmes, as chair, "did what I would not have done," Osmond Fraenkel remembered, casting the deciding vote against her. The vote was more lopsided on the two lesser charges, that she misused her position by discussing Union business in Party journals and newspapers. Having established her guilt, the Board moved on to the question of "'punishment.'" A sympathetic director told Flynn that "Roger pressed very hard for non-ouster, stating quite frankly that to oust you . . . would raise hell with the ACLU for months."[35]

Baldwin's hunch was correct. The problems began even before the directors dispersed. The hearing ended so chaotically that no one remembered to notify Flynn, who had been instructed to wait in the hall for the verdict, and she had to find her own taxi home at 2:00 A.M. In an organization filled with old-fashioned gentlemen, this was a breach of etiquette as well as a final unnecessary betrayal of Baldwin's friend. He tried to make amends to Flynn in a note about their "enduring" friendship, but she ignored him. After months of fighting, the National Committee rendered its opinion, affirming Flynn's ouster by one vote. So demoralizing was the whole experience that Baldwin ordered the trial transcript "kept in a locked drawer" where he never had to see it.[36]

Flynn's defenders doubted that the decision accurately reflected members' opinions, belatedly recognizing that actual Union democracy would have yielded a different result. Their last desperate hope was to deprive the "tiny New York group" of sole authority and reverse the decision. Mary Van Kleeck urged affiliates to "start a movement to end their own disenfranchisement." The directors held the power, though, and whatever their other views, did not favor widening the Union franchise. Most seconded Baldwin's opinion that "policies are pretty democratically determined by a Board of thirty-five members meeting weekly in New York." He let Van Kleeck pursue the matter, confident that it would produce no real power sharing. By wide margins, the directors defeated even the most rudimentary democratic proposals, approving only one small change, allowing larger affiliates to nominate members of the National Committee.[37]

Angry members voted with their feet. Holmes might have felt morally vindicated by Flynn's removal but predicted that the ACLU "may lose 1000 members and $5000.00 in membership dues" because of it. If accurate, those numbers represented about one-fifth of the membership and one-fifth of the operating budget. But we cannot assess the true costs because the record is confused. Only for 1939 and 1940 do multiple sets of membership figures exist: two for 1939 and three for 1940. Those figures vary wildly, from a low of 4,378 to a high of 5,732. It seems possible that the Flynn business so affected membership that Baldwin tried to cover up a substantial decline. Certainly he had to institute austerity controls because "the budget was for the first time very considerably exceeded."[38] Affiliates experienced less quantifiable discomfort but more psychological malaise. Several branches never got over the 1940 resolution and would remind the national office of their displeasure at intervals for years. Much as Baldwin might have wanted to sweep the whole mess under the rug, he could not.

As the premier civil liberties organization in the country and an increasingly prominent liberal voice, the ACLU affected other organizations. Baldwin later claimed that other liberal organizations "followed our example." Certainly the precedent was an important one, as combining fascism and communism under the same totalitarian rubric provided the ideological justification for postwar liberal anticommunism. But while the liberal magazine *Survey Graphic* noted that the NLG, the Teachers Union, the American

Youth Congress, the American Student Union, and the American Artists Congress adopted antitotalitarian statements in imitation of the ACLU, the truth is more muted. Those organizations debated various antitotalitarian statements following the collapse of the People's Front; some adopted resolutions, but none went to the extreme of expelling officers. Many years later, Joseph Freeman, a former publicity agent for the ACLU, concluded that the Flynn matter marked "the turning point in the attitude of *liberals* toward civil liberties." What seemed obvious to him in hindsight, however, was not so obvious at the time. The Union's reaction was extreme.[39]

Liberals neither rushed to defend the ACLU's actions nor condemned them. While they might have mustered some agreement with the definition of totalitarianism, plenty were uncomfortable with Flynn's expulsion. No one in the Roosevelt administration welcomed the antitotalitarian statement either. Even though they were still reeling from the Nazi-Soviet Pact and the messy end of the People's Front, progressives registered their opposition to the Board's actions, sometimes by leaving the organization altogether. One anticommunist officer noted that the ACLU "waxed powerful and successful while it had the left-wing group on the Board" and that its latest actions rendered it "not too popular." Holmes, Thomas, Ernst, and other anticommunists believed they occupied the high moral ground, but many others thought "that the Union is now violating its own fundamental principles." Baldwin claimed that the resolution and the expulsion were necessary to preserve harmony in the ACLU and to improve its reputation. He accomplished neither goal.[40]

Scholars have been rightly critical of the ACLU's actions. Richard Steele believes it "undercut the moral authority of free speech for everyone" with a panicked bureaucratic action that demonstrated "the shallowness of the organization's original commitment." Samuel Walker calls Flynn's purge "a disaster" strategically, politically, and morally, "a breach of principle" that neither sufficiently impressed its critics nor pleased its supporters. Brian Wright thinks that the Flynn trial revealed that the Union "was concentrated on the process of compromise, organizational safety and credibility." Whether or not the 1940 resolution and the Flynn expulsion were morally appropriate actions for anticommunists, they were not morally appropriate actions for a civil liberties organization to take.[41]

Anticommunists optimistically touted the benefits of the Union's new position, sure that there were potential members that could be recruited on the basis of anticommunism. Morris Ernst launched his own private membership drive but was informed by Lucille Milner that his anticommunist pitch was "not keeping within our established line." In the end, he sent the more traditional recruitment form letter to ninety-eight acquaintances. Fifteen people responded, returning $250 in donations, about $15 each. This was considerably more than the Union's $2 membership dues. Ernst's success dovetailed with the staff's plan to approach "higher bracket members" to "increase our budget by $10,000." Among the complaints that got Flynn expelled was the accusation that the organization was replacing its original membership with "many wealthy people." Respectability, ultimately, required a different kind of member. The accompanying public relations push also supported Flynn's observations, as Baldwin downplayed the Union's former radicalism. "The conservatives in the Union's Board of Directors," director Richard Childs proudly boasted, "have always been in the overwhelming majority."[42]

As its membership became wealthier and more moderate, the organization needed the kind of managerial "organizational culture" that reassured professionals. New director Alfred Bingham, who published the liberal magazine *Common Sense*, was immediately critical of how the Board did its work. Too much of the business before the directors, he complained, was of "comparative unimportance." Instead of wasting their time considering the merits of cases, the directors ought to delegate that task to experts and concentrate on "promotion, propaganda, education, and publicity," things that would make the Union bigger and more national in scope. In an efficiently run organization, volunteers worked on expansion and fund-raising and paid professionals handled legal work. The Board considered his plan but resisted any recommendation that ceded their control to paid professionals. Instead, they considered field secretaries to aid affiliates, a Washington activist to confer with government, a publicity committee, and advertisements in liberal journals.[43]

The events of 1940 forced the Union to examine its past and its future. During its prolonged growth spurt, there were occasional practical debates, and a few disgruntled members left; but everyone could see how much bigger and more influential the organization had become. In 1940 it was equally obvious that the group had stumbled badly. While it agonized over internal matters, others tried to seize its initiative. The war in Europe and the Roosevelt era Supreme Court "put First Amendment rights into a 'preferred' position."[44] Protecting democracy, not defeating Soviet totalitarianism, became liberal watchwords. New groups emerged to do that: the National Emergency Committee for Democratic Rights, the American Committee for the Protection of the Foreign Born, the National Federation for Constitutional Liberties, the CCF, Friends of Democracy, and the American Committee for Democracy and Intellectual Freedom. Each, in its own way, challenged the ACLU. As new groups built memberships, organized conferences, and interacted, the ACLU found it more difficult, especially in the wake of the Flynn debacle, to continue as before.

The Board was in "a rut." The Flynn affair was so disconcerting that it triggered an identity crisis. Some directors wanted to reevaluate "the whole business of civil liberties" in anticipation of the coming war, setting up the ACLU to lead an "affirmative crusade" supported by "a more functional, as distinguished from legalistic, conception of freedom." They believed that only a pro-Allied partisanship would "prevent our whole democratic structure from being overthrown by an outside force." As one of the advocates of this position admitted, though, such a "drastic change of policy" would "split . . . the board wide open and . . . result in the complete dissolution of the Union."[45] Liberals were more antifascist than they were anticommunist, but the Union was less driven in 1940 by antifascism than by anticommunism, which put it out of sync with the influential liberal community.

Morris Ernst had his own elaborate vision of tying together all these loose ends, of making the ACLU at once professional, antifascist, anticommunist, and prodemocratic. He wanted it to become an informal branch of the New Deal, a kind of "SEC [Securities and Exchange Commission] for civil liberties," as he told *Liberty* magazine. Its job would be educational, helping people distinguish between legitimate freedom organizations and those with communist or fascist ties. Simplifying this task was his pet project, something he called disclosure. Disclosure would force both fascist and communist organizations to reveal their true agendas. Under his scheme, any public organization would be required to declare its officers and funding sources. Union directors listened politely to his proposal, but many considered disclosure a "quack" remedy. By a close vote, they declined to endorse his plan, seeing anonymity as an implicit component of free speech. He took it elsewhere, making the rounds of liberal organizations and receiving the same polite refusals. He continued to bring similar proposals before the Board and continued to have them dismissed as incompatible with free speech rights. Frustrated, he grew cozier with Dies and Hoover.[46]

Baldwin preferred cosmetic measures to shore up the group's sinking reputation. The National Committee, the most public but least powerful part of the ACLU, needed a new head, and he had strong opinions about who it should be. He did not want a "stuffed shirt" but someone who would "let a Board in New York handle the details"—in other words, someone with good public regard who would defer to him on every matter. The chairmanship of the National Committee tended to reflect the Union's unacknowledged biases. During the 1930s, leaders sought figureheads with connections to the labor movement or the New Deal. In 1940 Baldwin hoped for a lawyer because "an organization whose work is ninety percent legal needs that symbol." As a concession to affiliates, he wanted someone from outside New York, "to give the Union a national symbol and to take some of the 'curse' of the New York atmosphere off of it." Baldwin's ideal figurehead was unwilling to serve. After two attorneys declined the position, he settled for someone outside New York, Edward A. Ross, who taught sociology at the

University of Wisconsin. Ross was willing but turned out to be less pliant than Baldwin hoped. He signed petitions circulated by front groups but otherwise contributed little to the organization, and the staff almost instantly concluded his election was a mistake. Baldwin found it harder and harder to shape the ACLU.[47]

Anticommunists, meanwhile, made it difficult for the group to put the Flynn matter behind them. They fought critics of the 1940 resolution who used their own money to circulate a pamphlet denouncing the measure.[48] In 1941 they blocked director Abraham Isserman's renomination, even though traditionally all willing officers stood for reelection indefinitely. When a curious Board member asked why Isserman's name was not on the list of nominees, he received contradictory answers: that there were "too many lawyers on the Board," that there was "a plan to rotate membership," and finally, that Isserman was "too far left." Belatedly, the directors added his name to the slate, but anticommunists insisted he first guarantee that he did not belong to a "totalitarian" organization. Isserman sent a blistering letter of resignation. He and Elizabeth Gurley Flynn helped found a rival civil liberties organization, the National Federation for Constitutional Liberties. Union anticommunists seemed to have a knack for alienating once-dedicated volunteers.[49]

Barely a month after Isserman resigned, Sidney Hook went after another Union member he thought too sympathetic to the Party. He protested Robert Lynd's election to the Academic Freedom Committee. Lynd belonged to some front groups, and Hook "expressed reservations about Mr. Lynd's disinterestedness." The committee decided to avoid "controversy" and void his election. Word leaked back to Lynd, who heard that the real reason he lost his position was that he had been identified as "some sort of Communist." Baldwin denied it, but Lynd triumphantly traced the story back to reliable ACLU witnesses. Lynd never got satisfaction, and the story circulated for months. Once again Baldwin had to clean up after Union anticommunists.[50]

To outsiders, the group appeared wishy-washy, neither fully anticommunist nor liberal. Flynn, hardly impartial, predicted that directors would find some "technical excuse" to evade their traditional defense of Communists' freedoms. They did not, although the consensus was neither as firm nor as full as before. Baldwin assured Party leader Robert Minor that "the Civil Liberties Union is prepared to assist in any way possible in the maintenance of the civil rights of the Communist Party in these excited days." The group opposed—with some dissenters—the Rapp-Coudert hearings in New York, which hunted for Communists in the public schools. Osmond Fraenkel testified against the Smith Act in Congress; the CPUSA did not oppose this act, but it would later affect them. The ACLU fought to preserve the Party's access to ballots in several states. Yet there were many occasions when protecting Communists' rights seemed more like a burden. When the Dies Committee raided Party offices in Boston, Pittsburgh, and Philadelphia, Baldwin put an attorney onto the case, telling him wistfully, "Inevitably it has to do with Communists . . . but the legal issue is rather interesting." Holmes took to prefacing his defense of Communists with disclaimers. The directors always seemed a little relieved when other groups stepped in to defend the Communist Party. Their new caution, however, was not enough to stop the FBI from confusing their commitments with their politics. Despite Ernst's attempts at ingratiating himself with the bureau, it began gathering information on the ACLU "with a vengeance."[51]

While the national ACLU struggled with post-pact identity problems, the affiliates gained new confidence. Local volunteers used to regard Baldwin and his officers with awe, but after the 1940 resolution, fewer saw them as infallible and more asserted their independence. Locals conducted no Communist hunts on their own boards, which were not covered by the measure in any case. While the national leadership bogged down in internal fights, branches capitalized on the prodemocratic moment. The CCLC helped organize a civil liberties forum at Hull House. The Southern California branch sent its representatives to a freedom conference that included attorneys, academics, and speakers from the NAACP. The Boston group participated in the New England Conference on Civil Liberties. These things tapped into the public mood, pleased the

Roosevelt administration, and made a splash by "present[ing] a broader front of activities and hav[ing] meetings a little out of the ordinary—a trifle sensational—to attract others than the firmly convinced." Affiliates relished the independence the logjam at headquarters afforded them.[52]

Their initiatives often pleased the national staff but could just as easily distress them. The CCLC's sponsorship of a talk by Eleanor Roosevelt impressed them for its newsworthiness, the $782 it brought in for the CCLC treasury, and the 175 members it recruited. But developments in Denver dismayed them. A "government crowd" took over the affiliate "to use the organization for . . . labor purposes principally." No one at headquarters said anything about communism in the Denver affiliate, but it was clear that branches were not convinced that an anticommunist image was any more practical than it was ideologically appropriate. They rushed to defend fronts when the Dies Committee raided offices, seized file cabinets, and demanded membership lists. They prodded national officers to be "a little stronger" in their defense of Communists' rights. They were the activists FBI agents designated "troublemaker[s]." A 1940 bureau report labeled "every person" in the SCACLU "a Communist." Having always resisted standardization, affiliates now resisted a more moderate course.[53]

The "good old bad issue of the Resolution of February 5, 1940," as one Cleveland member called it, symbolized national authority over branches, even though they were not bound to it. Some directors became intensely curious about local members' politics. Baldwin asked the head of the CCLC outright if Communists ran it. "If there are any members of the Communist Party on the Indiana Committee," he wrote one of the few activists in the Hoosier State, "we would like to know." Holmes complained to the SCACLU that Leo Gallagher was a Communist and "worrying us here in the East," so could they please get rid of him? The branch refused, and there was "nothing that our national office can do." When a new affiliate formed in Rockland County, New York, Baldwin sent its secretary a copy of the resolution, conceding that it did not apply to them but hoping "that there will be no political complexion in the committee out of keeping with the spirit of that resolution." Alarmed, a delegation of local women arrived at the office because, as Baldwin noted, "apparently there are quite a number of Communist Party members in Rockland County" and the delegation feared they would not be affiliated. Later, Baldwin asked an underling to check their bylaws to see if they excluded Communists. They did not, which was "awfully trying [to] our patience." Baldwin and the anticommunist directors intimidated the Board into behaving as they wanted it to, but they could not accomplish the same thing with the branches.[54]

Anger in the affiliates over clumsy tampering was occasionally palpable and public. Baldwin denied that "the national office in any way interferes with the policies of the New Jersey branch." However, its proximity to headquarters, its financial dependency, its past association with Abraham Isserman, and the politics of several of its members led to careful scrutiny of the affiliate's business. In 1940 Baldwin "practically forced the retirement" of one of the group's "most effective and useful members" because of "leanings" toward Communism. The next year Baldwin "suggested . . . that . . . the names of two men prominently identified with Communist united fronts should be left off the advisory committee." The two men were engineering professor Walter Rautenstrauch and anthropologist Franz Boas. This time the New Jersey group was less tractable. They informed both men of Baldwin's request. Both wrote angry letters of protest. "I think you are in [a] very small business," Rautenstrauch said, "especially when you suggest . . . that my name be dropped, not openly, but quietly, in a sneaky fashion."[55]

Faced with "trouble with various of our branches," the national office imposed more rules. Baldwin circulated a memo with suggestions for "more effective cooperation between the local committees and the national office." These extended no more responsibility to branches but told them how to be more efficient. Maybe Baldwin should have concerned himself with the efficiency of his own office, for branches regularly complained that they did not get national mailings on time.[56] In 1941 the staff drafted a set of rules to regularize governance, presented them to the Board, and then sent copies to the affiliates. The directors quickly passed them "in the absence of any objection from local committees." Most branches saw nothing wrong with the new regulations, which required them to maintain political neutrality, to take no action on their own except on local issues, and not to contradict the national organization. The directors acknowledged that branches had matured by offering them the tiniest concession imaginable: "the opportunity to express their view . . . without legal force and . . . solely . . . advisory." Local people were not grateful, but angry. The Civil Liberties Union of Massachusetts (CLUM) proved willing to accept the new rules, "provided that the governing bodies of the ACLU were more democratically organized." The SCACLU wanted to be represented on the National Committee, while the Colorado Civil Liberties Union suggested that local affiliate votes "be binding upon the Board." Affiliates accepted what they could not change but wanted more authority. Otherwise they experienced, as the CLUM secretary asserted, "intellectual taxation without representation."[57]

American war preparations replaced debate about democracy with a new set of challenges. Many of the Union's founders were pacifists, at odds with the liberal mainstream they had drawn into their organization in the 1930s. Whose views would prevail? No one disputed the right of Jehovah's Witnesses not to participate in patriotic ceremonies such as saluting the flag.[58] Labor's rights in defense industries caused more controversy. At the Southern California plant of North American Aviation, Communists helped to organize a strike. The government sent in the military to reopen the plant, insisting that defense needs superseded the right to strike. The case asked a lot of the directors, whether they were anticommunist or antifascist, for they needed to put aside their politics and consider only whether "public employees have the right to organize" and strike when there was not yet an official declaration of war. The Board supported the right to strike, but only after prolonged debate.[59] The longtime pacifists were beginning to retire, replaced by businessmen and attorneys who advocated collective security. But it was already clear that antifascism, at least as much as anticommunism, was going to test Union principles.

Confusion about principles was at the heart of the ACLU's problems in 1940 and 1941. In the 1930s, liberals sometimes misunderstood the organization's commitments, but it was not until the end of the decade that Union leaders started to question one another's dedication to civil liberties as a nonpartisan ideal. Back then, the group acted with confidence and dedication. In 1940 and 1941 the Union lacked both confidence and a unity of purpose. Partisanships complicated its mission. The 1940 resolution and the expulsion of Flynn were partisan issues that absorbed considerable organizational energy without producing anything useful. No flood of new members joined the Union, but many existing members became estranged. Baldwin lost some of the easy power he used to have over the group and found himself, instead, catering to factions, balancing competing claims, and explaining unpopular policies. New civil liberties groups stood ready to engage liberals. Even though the Roosevelt administration appeared more committed to civil liberties than ever before, Baldwin could not translate that commitment into greater ACLU influence. Nor could he persuade anyone to whom it mattered that the group had dealt sufficiently with the issue of Communism. The ACLU was not antifascist enough to satisfy liberals, progressive enough to satisfy progressives, or anticommunist enough to satisfy anticommunists.

LOSING OUR INFLUENCE

The National ACLU during World War II

In 1943 the ACLU Board considered adding a new name to its list of counsel: Osmond K. Fraenkel. Fraenkel "has been doing so large a share of our legal work that he ought to be recognized," Roger Baldwin felt. Yet Fraenkel's wartime service was more complicated than Baldwin let on. He worked at Baldwin's discretion and because the group's longtime legal consultant, Morris Ernst, was disgusted by the group's wartime neutrality. Even though he hardly worked for the Union, Ernst did not want Fraenkel to become so official a part of the Union, first because "he was strictly on the communist line and now . . . because he is on the Wheeler [antiwar] line."[1] Baldwin's championing of Fraenkel and Ernst's resistance to him reveal an organization at war with itself. World War I launched the ACLU. World War II threatened to undo it. In the 1930s it benefited greatly from liberal interest and support. Liberals, including Ernst, expected it to legitimate their opinions. Yet the Union's actual business was protecting dissident rights, a commitment a popular war made difficult. World War II rendered the choice between liberal respectability and the organization's traditional agenda particularly stark.

The Union had already used up some of its liberal capital when it took its anticommunist detour after the Nazi-Soviet Pact. While it was otherwise engaged, newer civil liberties groups mobilized. The organization played no direct role in the clemency campaign for CPUSA head Earl Browder. The federal government arrested him for falsifying passport information, an old and politically motivated charge. While the Free Browder Committee rallied liberal public opinion and organized meetings and petitions, the Union concluded that his case involved "no issue of civil liberty." Affiliates wanted to be involved in Browder's defense, but the national office advised them that joining the campaign was "not a wise step at this time." Better, Lucille Milner insisted, to trust the national office, which "is working out plans for assisting in this." Baldwin assigned the group the role of experts "who can handle the delicate negotiations" with government. After "a very pleasant, frank, but unsatisfying talk" with Justice Department officials, however, Arthur Garfield Hays gave up.[2] While the group appeared to have forfeited the lead in shaping liberal opinion on civil liberties, its alternative strategy, working as an insider to influence government policy, proved no more successful. Despite Baldwin's claim that establishing itself as an anticommunist agency would be useful, the Union actually lost ground.

The Union's very first clients, conscientious objectors, fared little better than Browder did at the hands of a cautious Board. As Congress debated a peacetime draft in the summer of 1940, directors voted to take "no position for or against conscription." The Union last affirmed its opposition to a draft in 1937, when war did not seem imminent. In 1940, American involvement seemed more likely; but liberals favored intervention, and more ACLU members supported the coming war than the preceding conflict. With so much pro-Allied sentiment on the Board, Baldwin diverted conscientious objector work to a separate group. Relieved officers left him to deal with the National Committee on Conscientious Objectors, composed of representatives from the ACLU, the Fellowship of Reconciliation, American Quakers, the *Catholic Worker*, the Socialist Party, the Keep America Out of War Congress, and ministers' groups. That method kept the Union's name off antiwar material. Baldwin appointed himself its liaison to the Roosevelt administration, even though Secretary of War Henry Stimson brushed him off, telling him that there was "little practical value" to be obtained from meeting with him.[3] His faith that he could influence federal conscientious objector policy was typical of his attitude overall. He always assumed he was more influential than he turned out to be.

The Union's actions on behalf of conscientious objectors earned it no kudos from liberals and offended some older pacifist members. Franklin Collier Jr., for instance, resigned as a "gesture of protest." Norman Thomas felt the group evaded its responsibility and, worst yet, was too eager to "help the government sugar-coat the pill of conscription . . . no matter what happens by way of exemption to conscientious objectors." Journalist Dwight Macdonald later rightly suggested that "most conscientious objectors think that the Union let them down."[4] But liberals also felt let down, not by any specific draft-related policy so much as by an overall impression, based on the last war, that the Union was filled with pacifists and others who impeded the war effort.

Liberals believed in the war and had confidence in Roosevelt's handling of civil liberties. Their faith owed much to the comparison with the dismal World War I civil liberties picture. Woodrow Wilson had tried to manufacture unanimity where none existed, while Roosevelt benefited from widespread support for the war. Although Roosevelt's administration avoided some of the roundups and persecutions Wilson had allowed, most of the legal mechanisms for managing dissent in 1917 remained in 1941. The government still had an arsenal of techniques both legal and illegal, including sedition laws and a fortified FBI with wide surveillance powers. The result was, according to Richard Steele, an intense "campaign to silence extremist views" with "meager tangible consequences." As Frank Warren noted, "Liberals saw the war in intensely moral and idealistic terms," as a worldwide struggle for democracy. Roosevelt was "essential to liberalism," like his attorney general, Francis Biddle. Because liberals looked on Roosevelt as one of them, someone who believed as they did and could be trusted to do right, they excused his lapses or viewed them as necessary political compromises.[5]

This attitude was rife in the ACLU. Its 1942–43 annual report included a frontispiece quotation from Roosevelt. Inside, much of its first section analyzed the "striking contrast" between the civil liberties situation in the two world wars. Baldwin, writing in the *Nation*, celebrated the Supreme Court and quoted Biddle on civil liberties. The Union's bureaucratic and personnel changes reinforced the new attitude. Directors were younger and liberal; fewer were radicals or pacifists. Most supported the war and the Roosevelt administration. Few questioned Baldwin's assertion that "in war-time . . . relations with federal agencies becomes the primary concern for all of us." Even an old pacifist like John Haynes Holmes rejoiced in the ACLU's "friends in high places." Holmes's faith reflected his pride in the organization he helped to found. "We have educated a whole generation of people," he explained, "and this is now reflected in the attitude of government." By 1944 Baldwin was so convinced of the necessity of working with the government that he asked "to be relieved of all administrative work in the office," to devote more time to work "in the field," by which he meant the offices of the Roosevelt administration.[6]

There were, to be sure, countercurrents within the organization. Some Board members were made nervous by what Thomas called the ACLU's "jollying public officials into a mere tolerant attitude." This spirit, he felt, deviated from "a forthright advocacy of civil liberties as an ideal."[7] Thomas was not the only person to distinguish between an enduring principle and a wartime compromise. Liberals justified temporarily compromising Thomas's ideal by talking about the exigencies of war and the need to be pragmatic. They called themselves "relativists" who temporarily privileged national security over individual rights. Reinhold Niebuhr, a self-described relativist, explained that during wartime "freedom of speech should be withheld from those political groups which intend to destroy liberty." Through war and peace, the ACLU had always taken what Niebuhr called an "absolutist" position on civil liberties, the principle that action, not speech, threatened liberty, which made all speech a protected right. Many Union leaders feared that standing so firmly conjured up unfortunate images of sympathy for the enemy or, at the very least, conveyed an antiwar position. After Niebuhr raised the issue publicly, Baldwin did all he could to avoid associating the Union with the word "absolutist," telling the *Nation's* readers that "all libertarians are 'relativists.'" Liberals remained to be persuaded. So, too, did many directors.[8]

At the height of the controversy over the 1940 resolution, Baldwin claimed that the Board was so divided as to be dysfunctional. Wartime Board factionalism was more widespread and more paralyzing. One faction was relativist in philosophy, willing to make wartime compromises, eager to have the ACLU help shape public opinion and government, and committed to what Brett Gary characterized as "expert-centered national security liberalism." The relativists were an odd fusion of liberals (like Morris Ernst), Republicans (like Whitney North Seymour), and the one leftist who remained on the Board, Corliss Lamont, who shared the CPUSA's zealous devotion to the Allies. The other faction was absolutist, unconcerned with popularity, and not much impressed with the Roosevelt administration. Unlike the factionalism of 1939–40, which directly involved a relatively small number, nearly every director identified with one or the other camp, creating tension each time they met. "It is apparent to the Board, as it must be by now to the outside world," Ernst wrote to Holmes, "that the Union is split by a very close vote on the sole fundamental issue of civil liberties during the war." Actually, the relativist faction was larger, and the National Committee inevitably supported its positions when called on to settle an impasse.[9]

But the absolutists had other kinds of powers, namely the persons of Board chair Holmes, Union lawyers Arthur Garfield Hays and Fraenkel, and Baldwin, although his cooperation with the Roosevelt administration complicated his absolutism. Immediately after Pearl Harbor, Holmes acknowledged that his pacifism was "not popular" and offered to step down. Directors did not often share his politics but thought him "the best chairman" and did not replace him. Holmes proved to be no quieter or more compromising about wartime matters than about the 1940 resolution. He, though, was removed from the ACLU office routine. Hays, who represented the "principle" of civil liberties to Ernst's "practical considerations," handled, along with Fraenkel, the bulk of the organization's wartime cases, regularly fighting with "that damn board." The real power in the ACLU, of course, was Roger Baldwin, and it was Baldwin, combining the absolutist's philosophy with a relativist's trust of the Roosevelt government, who daily struggled to make things happen in ways he considered morally right. And struggle he did, for as Thomas noted, "It used to be axiomatic that nothing was settled in the ACLU until it was settled Roger's way"; but in 1942, "the Board [was] more watchful and insistent."[10]

Baldwin gave the impression of being forthright about his status. He warned his colleagues that there "might be situations in which he would be unable to act in carrying out the Board's orders" and would instead act on his principles "independently." But Baldwin was not forthright. He never clearly distinguished between his actions as a private citizen and as the leader of the ACLU. He was a master at playing the Union bureaucracy. Ernst observed that "the minorities' [sic] domination of the office and the officialdom, plus the assignment of work for lawyers including the signing of letters, writing of briefs, etc." resulted in "an unfair weighing against the majority." The result, he complained, was that "the Union is losing so quickly all of the support which we thought would stick to us." Holmes dismissed his lament as "over-sensitive to public opinion." But the truth was that the ACLU needed more and more members to fund the many wartime cases it undertook.[11]

The ACLU relativists were, as Holmes said, overly sensitive to liberal public opinion but also frustrated by the absolutists' tricks. They carefully laid down policies and made choices only to have "the office and the officialdom" misrepresent them. Even so simple a matter as picking speakers for the annual luncheon, in 1943 broadcast over New York City radio, became a point of contention.

"I think it was very clear ... that a majority of the Board felt that the list of speakers was packed, whether consciously or otherwise, in behalf of the minority," said Ernst. In the 1930s ACLU, Ernst was a power player, but during the war, he grew frustrated with the organization. He enjoyed "assist[ing] government in formulating its policy" but worried that the Union lost its influence because "the officials in Washington never know where we stand." He came close to quitting, feeling that he could "better spend more of my civil liberties time in avenues other than ACLU." As Ernst backed away, absolutists Fraenkel and Hays took over the lion's share of the Union's legal work.[12]

The absolutists, like the anticommunists in 1940, proceeded with a moral righteousness and determination that made compromise difficult. In the fall of 1942 Holmes convened a special meeting to allow directors to air differences. He began by lecturing his colleagues that the ACLU must hew to "principles ... centuries old ... and fixed." Norman Thomas and Baldwin seconded his statement. When it was finally the relativists' turn to speak, their orations lacked the same lofty fervor. "Few spoke on the [philosophical] topics," Fraenkel noted in his diary. Those who adhered to "the functional theory of civil liberties" emphasized wartime conditions, the missed opportunities "to function positively," the organization's shrinking influence with liberals, their "complete lack of confidence in the office administration," and the Board's failure to move with the times. The meeting allowed officers to let off steam, but Holmes allowed no policy recommendations to come out of it, exacerbating the relativists' frustration with absolutist directors who had power but lacked authority.[13]

Absolutists were no happier. Thomas, like Holmes, already felt somewhat estranged from the Union because it took so much effort to induce it—he thought—to act responsibly about Communism. Now here was another "basic betrayal" of principle, and he used a familiar tactic to try to jolt the Board into acting differently, threatening to resign. Holmes organized a luncheon of sympathetic persons "to persuade Norman Thomas not to resign." While they were successful, several, including Holmes and Hays, confessed that they also considered quitting.[14] Their willingness to abandon an enterprise they had so personally nurtured suggests just how alienated they felt. Inducing the organization to stay its course required constant vigilance and intervention. Relativists had the luxury of numbers on their side, and it was hard work holding democracy at bay. Baldwin frequently tipped the balance for them, but relativists learned to use the Union bureaucracy.

The liberal, early 1940s ACLU was already more bureaucratic than its predecessors. It had rules, routines, and specialists. Younger directors, especially, valued its predictability and pattern. Relativists used these bureaucratic tools. The Lawyers' Panel, for instance, brought together "younger" attorneys to review potential cases, match them with appropriate counsel, direct legal research, and make recommendations to the Board.[15] It controlled at least part of the biweekly Board agenda. It limited Hays's and Fraenkel's influence. It blocked some of Baldwin's privilege.

There were other bureaucratic tactics as well. Relativists sought "the widest possible distribution of support" on ACLU committees, balancing representation by race, religion, profession, and region, bringing in new blood more immune to Baldwin's personal charms. In 1944 the Board revised the bylaws to make it easier for opponents of any policy to gain a rehearing and a complete corporate vote. Bylaws, though, could only carry the relativists so far. The real problem lay in the battles themselves, the "motions and substitutes and amendments" that slowed business and produced hodgepodge policies. "One hasty phrase in a motion concocted on the floor," warned Richard Childs, "could queer us for years." Absolutists cared little about "the hazards of losing our influence," but most directors wanted such prestige. The Board banned free-ranging discussion for three months and required, instead, that all debate focus around proposals that would be voted up or down. This inhibited absolutist speeches about principles and focused attention where relativists wanted it, on practical matters.[16]

Until the early 1940s, the Union reacted to civil liberties challenges as they arose. But since many directors no longer trusted those who worked for them, relativists preferred to set policies and treat Baldwin like a manager who would oversee their enactment. Routines, rules, and regulations explicitly challenged his freedom, imposing on him policies he did not like but was forced, as executive director, to execute—policies he, in turn, often diluted, misrepresented, or ignored. The ACLU replaced its leaders' impulsive and emotional engagement with issues with a more studied, careful, detached style. Wartime matters that might have once compelled directors to act now required a more dispassionate examination.

In February 1942, Franklin Roosevelt issued Executive Order 9066. It created military zones along both coasts and gave the military power to remove from those zones anyone deemed a threat to the war effort. Although the order did not single out Japanese Americans and was used against others, Japanese Americans were its primary targets. In issuing the order, Roosevelt succumbed to West Coast anti-Asian sentiment and Caucasian farmers' long-standing commercial jealousies of successful Japanese American farmers. Further pressure from the states adjoining the western military zones (nearly all of California, Oregon, and Washington) led to the decision to intern citizens and noncitizens of Japanese descent in ten camps in the American interior, forcibly holding people because of their ethnicity. The internees suffered massive personal losses as they liquidated homes and businesses for an unknown period of time. The military made no attempts to determine individual loyalty, interning anyone with as little as one-sixteenth Japanese blood. All this occurred without any declaration of martial law, a violation of due process. The legality of the internment program was clearly dubious. Few Americans, however, questioned any of its specifics.[17]

The ACLU did not immediately respond to the unfolding policy. Its slow and disorganized reaction reflected directors' unfamiliarity with the situation and fear of negative publicity. At first the Board issued a Baldwin-drafted protest to the president, expressing concern that Executive Order 9066 was "open to grave questions *on . . . constitutional grounds*." But five relativists disassociated themselves from "any possible constitutional questions" it raised.[18] The New York Board might have been initially unprepared to address this uniquely West Coast challenge; it soon became clear, however, that there was no consensus about the meaning or constitutionality of the government's internment program.

Relativists successfully induced a policy vote to establish guidelines for future Union action. Two options appeared on paper ballots sent to all members of the Board and National Committee. The first stated that internment was unconstitutional without a declaration of martial law. The other conceded government's right to intern citizens without a declaration of martial law but raised issues of fairness, racial bias, and failure to immediately grant individuals an opportunity to prove their loyalty. By a two-to-one vote, leaders decided that internment was legal. Many voiced partisan sentiments with their ballots. "The Union can be of greater practical service in days ahead," wrote one, "if it makes certain concessions to the general consensus of opinion in regard to the 'National Emergency.'"[19]

In voting as they did, Union leaders stood with the eastern liberal establishment. Virtually all persons of Japanese ancestry lived in California, Oregon, or Washington. Most easterners had encountered them only as house servants or gardeners to their California friends. Having much trust in the Roosevelt administration's conduct of the war, they accepted that immediate internment "based on Japanese ancestry" was reasonable. Yet, directors did not fully rubber-stamp Executive Order 9066, as most other liberals did. They articulated qualms about the absence of procedures to distinguish between the loyal and the disloyal and were particularly concerned about racist intent. Once authority for the interned shifted from the army to the WRA, a civilian agency run by New Dealers, directors relaxed a bit, even though the WRA also did not promptly establish methods to determine loyalty and release the loyal. Like other liberals, ACLU relativists had faith that the Roosevelt administration was doing the best it could to be fair.[20]

Neither relativists nor absolutists knew very much about the Japanese American population on the West Coast. A few held stereotyped views of the Japanese, believing early government justifications for internment because, as National Committee chairman

Edward A. Ross, a sociologist by profession, said, "Their [Japanese Americans'] supreme allegiance is . . . to their blood or kin group." Others accepted the WRA's claims that the camps protected Japanese Americans from hostile attacks and would, in the end, move them into the American mainstream. Even Baldwin imagined that internment would foster "a policy of absorption of the Japanese into American life on an individual basis," which was "preferable to their segregation in virtual ghettos on the Pacific Coast." Racial stereotypes often sustained their optimism. Baldwin, for instance, passed on to Osmond Fraenkel a claim by J. Edgar Hoover that the government's decision to authorize work releases from some of the camps was "prompted in part by the demand for domestic servants and agricultural workers." Fraenkel noted the idea in his diary without a single comment. Whether their understandings of internment were "purely legalistic" or part of a liberal worldview, Union directors tended not to think much about Japanese Americans as people.[21]

Relativists and absolutists also shared a commitment to working with the federal government and, especially, the WRA to improve internees' status. The ACLU cultivated ties with the civilian and military personnel involved in the internment program. Alexander Meiklejohn, NCACLU member, National Committee member, and an influential legal scholar, had a personal connection with "Jack [John] McCloy, Assistant Secretary of War, who is one of my best student friends from old Amherst days." Meiklejohn became the Board's intermediary with the government "on internment questions," even after the switch from military to civilian oversight. Baldwin also had WRA connections, becoming "a friend of [Dillon] Myer," who headed the agency. When he wanted something from the WRA, he went right to the top, sometimes siding with Myer against his own affiliates.[22] Baldwin met, on occasion, with fellow ACLU member Attorney General Francis Biddle and Edward Ennis, head of the Justice Department's Enemy Alien Division, who joined the National Board after the war. Baldwin reveled in these meetings, enjoying what he believed was his access to power.

In real terms, though, the meetings had little impact on the circumstances of the internment. Most of the time, ACLU representatives came away from them with stories of how hard the government worked and how many conservative pressures Roosevelt faced. Leaders began to think in terms of limits rather than absolutes, improving what they could not stop altogether. The Union did, on occasion, obtain inside information from the government about upcoming policy changes, but generally, government officials advised patience and urged Union members to keep the authorities informed of any legal challenges the organization was preparing to mount. As Holmes pointed out, the Washington bureaucracy seemed more "sensitive" to "conservative pressure" than anything the ACLU was able to exert. Working with the government on internment kept the ACLU within the liberal mainstream, placated Board relativists, and helped Baldwin feel useful, but all within a context of getting along. Baldwin was disinclined to challenge the Roosevelt administration, and while Meiklejohn claimed that the government "is very favorable to the purposes of the Union, and is eager to cooperate with it," the interaction was not between equals.[23]

With policy mechanisms in place, directors did not have to spend much time discussing internment. They let staff handle the details. But the staff stumbled over specifics, calling the Tule Lake internment camp "Tuna Lake." "I wonder whether you realize that Tule Lake is over 400 miles from San Francisco, and that it is about 900 miles from Los Angeles," one affiliate officer raged after receiving a national office directive to visit the camp. The staff slipped too easily into the colloquial term for the enemy, "Japs," even though the Board voted that the appropriate phrase was "American citizens of Japanese ancestry." That designation itself revealed the organization's tendency to concentrate on the native-born Nisei while ignoring the Japanese-born Issei, who were not eligible for naturalization. Even relativists understood that most of the Japanese Americans posed no security threat, yet a Committee on Seditious Cases reviewed all legal challenges to internment, including test cases for "Japanese Americans of unquestioned loyalty." Unfamiliar with the situation of Japanese Americans and uninterested in becoming more familiar, the ACLU found it easier to coast along-side the Roosevelt administration than to make waves.[24]

Reinforcing the don't-rock-the-boat mentality was the staff's trust of the Japanese American Citizens' League (JACL), a Nisei organiza-tion eschewed by many Japanese Americans. The JACL claimed to welcome internment as a way of demonstrating loyalty, yet few of its officers spent much time in camps, which undercut its already limited credibility. New Yorkers hailed it as a like-minded assimi-lationist liberal organization "with which the Civil Liberties Union has worked in closest cooperation." Some West Coast activists agreed, but more thought the JACL "discredited because it acted as a stooge for the WRA."[25] The JACL supported relativists' fervid belief that internment did not harm innocent people very much. Its assumption that the group spoke for Japanese Americans alien-ated it from the people who most needed its help, dissenters who challenged internment or were not willing to prove their loyalty to a country that imprisoned them.

The same liberal biases that drew the ACLU to the JACL as a like organization also determined its attitudes toward legal challenges. Despite the policy decision that internment was constitutional, the Union was eager to contest its legality on other grounds, at least once the Roosevelt administration encouraged the ACLU to do so. But when the time came to choose cases, the committee that screened them and the Board demonstrated that they were very ner-vous about public opinion. Test cases, Baldwin explained, needed to be "selected with great care," obtained "with the cooperation of the JACL," and cleared through the WRA first. His ideal test case would involve someone with no ties to Japan, an unimpeachable record, and a relative in the military. What he did not anticipate was how hard it would be to find such cases through the channels the ACLU established. The national ACLU was hardly positioned geo-graphically, ideologically, or racially to connect with large numbers of Japanese Americans.[26]

Four Nisei challenged internment policy. Two, Minoru Yasui and Gordon Hirabayashi, deliberately violated aspects of the program—Yasui the curfew and Hirabayashi the evacuation—out of principle.

A third, Fred Korematsu, was apprehended while attempting to evade authorities. NCACLU head Ernest Besig persuaded him to test the legality of internment. Like Yasui and Hirabayashi before him, Korematsu lost his case, but he established "military necessity" as the official rationale for internment. A final challenge once the government determined loyalty came from Mitsuyi Endo. The late 1944 Supreme Court decision in her case resulted in official termination of the program. The Union's policy statement, the government's tips, and directors' biases influenced the group's choices of whether or not to be part of these test cases.

Hirabayashi's case was the most attractive to New Yorkers. The head of the Seattle ACLU described Hirabayashi as "exceptionally intelligent and generally well-balanced." He was also a college student and "a religious conscientious objector to military service." But because Hirabayashi wanted to challenge constitutional issues, Baldwin helped organize and fund a separate defense committee through pacifist channels. Endo's case also seemed ideal. She was a Department of Motor Vehicles clerk who had never been to Japan, was a Christian, and had a brother in the military. Yet the WRA initially told the Union that her case was not very strong, and only after Edward Ennis pressed them did the ACLU pursue it. By then, Endo's exasperated lawyer preferred the NCACLU's counsel to any attorney the New York office might provide. The national office was distinctly uneasy about Korematsu's challenge. Baldwin asked for the particulars on him—"history, attitude, background, connections, and 'patriotism.'" What he learned did not reassure him; Korematsu was engaged to a Caucasian woman and had had plastic surgery to disguise his features. Baldwin reluctantly agreed to support the case, then backed off only to urge involvement again when "officials in Washington" advised him to file an amicus brief. Directors ruled out Yasui's case, despite his promising credentials (son of a Washington State apple grower, attorney, and reserve officer), as he had been employed by the Japanese consulate. The Union's work became increasingly complicated as it tried to placate warring Board factions, the Roosevelt administration, and its officers' biases.[27]

Directors left the details of cases to the staff, and the staff relied on advice and information passed to them by Justice Department representatives Ennis and John Burling. The two officers, in turn, used the Union as a conduit after their superiors forced them to cover up inconsistencies in the government's case. They leaked sensitive material to Baldwin, who enjoyed the inside connection. Ernest Besig, always suspicious of Baldwin, later complained that "Roger used to go the rounds in Washington and meet all these guys and he was more of a government representative than he was an ACLU representative for a while." Legal scholar Peter Irons agrees that Baldwin and his assistant, Cliff Forster, were "in effect, agents of the Justice Department." Thus even the Union's willingness to participate in the Supreme Court cases challenging internment occurred at the urging of Roosevelt's Justice Department confidants. The ACLU did not always protect the civil liberties of Issei and Nisei as vigorously as it might have, but by working with the government and avoiding the constitutionality question, the Union did not antagonize the larger liberal community.[28]

The same could not be said of the Union's policy toward the war's right-wing opponents. Throughout the 1930s a number of homegrown fascist organizations existed with names like the Silver Shirts and the German-American Bund. Elizabeth Dilling, Charles Coughlin, William Dudley Pelley, and Gerald L. K. Smith rallied followers with their anti-Semitic speeches. They opposed the war, often objecting to the British as allies; most admired the Nazis.[29] Guaranteeing their free speech during war, even while accommodating the many caveats the relativists laid down, outraged liberals, who willingly trusted the Roosevelt administration. Board relativists wanted to stand with liberals but found it immensely difficult to buck the Union's traditional commitment to all dissenters.

Even in the abstract, there was no Board consensus about what the wartime standard for determining free speech ought to be. After World War I, the Supreme Court established the clear-and-present-danger guideline, which held that speech could be limited when it posed an obvious public threat. The Roosevelt administration seemed comfortable backing away from that policy. The Union, on the other hand, had not even endorsed the clear-and-present-danger standard, holding out for the more stringent test of action. "The best practical test of the effect of speech of publication," read one ACLU policy memo, "is to be found in acts attempted or committed." Absolutists held that war made no difference. Relativists shared liberals' opinion that war mattered a great deal, rendering even the clear-and-present-danger test irrelevant. Anything posing "a great danger to the Bill of Rights, democracy and the nation" seemed punishable to them. They were at a disadvantage; defending unpopular dissidents was at the heart of the Union's mission.[30]

The Board first confronted the obviously controversial issue in the spring of 1942. After reading an article on Charles Coughlin in the *New Republic*, Attorney General Francis Biddle recommended that the Post Office Department confiscate copies of Coughlin's *Social Justice* pending a hearing to determine whether to rescind its second-class mailing privileges. Baldwin and Morris Ernst met privately with Biddle to discuss reasonable procedures for determining what was seditious literature. Both loved to consult with government, but when the time came to act, Biddle ignored their recommendations and instead gave his directive to confiscate the literature. The Board criticized the actions of the post office as "censorship without trial," but most liberals disagreed. National Committee member Freda Kirchwey publicly resigned, using the pages of her liberal magazine, the *Nation*, as her anti-ACLU pulpit. Others stood with her. "I'm strongly in favor of proper legal action being taken to stop a paper which repeats foreign propaganda," wrote novelist Henry S. Canby. "The Civil Liberties Union is making a serious mistake," warned Ralph Barton Perry, who suggested that "the public" would come to see the group as extreme and unbending. Perry's prediction quickly came true.[31]

What the ACLU called "censorship," the *New Republic* called "muzzling the fascists," an action both "wise and proper." Board relativists sided with the *New Republic*, but that opinion directly challenged a much more established set of Union principles than internment did. And while the Union found areas of common ground with the government on internment and consulted with the

Justice Department about internment cases, it had no such access or influence over the government's policies toward opponents of the war. All this left relativists with little room to maneuver. Ernst declared he had "no stomach for defending" fascists during wartime, but his gut feeling was no match for principle.[32] Like other relativists, he had limited expectations for reconciling his wants with policy. So, rather than try to argue against Union tradition, relativists used another tactic, finding practical ways to evade—on a case-by-case basis—the principle of defending everyone.

Once again, Ernst and others relied on office bureaucracy to contain absolutists bent on defending fascists. They stalled for time and minutely debated cases. They acknowledged abstract claims to free speech but decided others handled specifics well enough so they did not have to be involved. They counted on the rulings of the Committee on Seditious Cases, disproportionately staffed by relativists. Its official role was to screen all wartime cases and recommend action to the Board, although its most common ruling consisted of two words: "no action." It helped counteract the absolutists in the office.[33]

In the summer of 1942, the federal government, under pressure from liberals, indicted a group of otherwise unrelated war opponents on seditious conspiracy charges and brought them to trial in Washington, D.C. No trial occurred in 1942; they were indicted again in 1944 and brought to trial then. The government's case was weak, with no proof of conspiracy or links to the German government. So too was the process dubious; the government held defendants for years at a time and tried them far away from where their alleged crimes took place. Yet all three liberal journals, *PM*, the *Nation*, and the *New Republic*, endorsed the government's actions. The Committee on Seditious Cases reviewed the indictment and reported to the Board that there were some problems with the cases but that everyone was adequately represented, so there was no pressing need for the Union to intervene. The Board eagerly accepted its recommendation. As Baldwin complained, too many Union members abhorred "who they [the accused] are and what they say" to be objective about fairness.[34]

Holmes thought the government's sedition prosecutions would test "whether or not the Union is going to function at all during this war on issues of civil liberty." Baldwin already guessed that the Board would fail this test of its "declared principles" because "in wartime people are not that dispassionate." Directors' disinterest in the accused, he noted, "pretty accurately reflects our membership." The Board narrowly approved the principle that the accused were entitled to free speech, but relativists did everything they could to make sure the Union neither intervened in the case nor appeared to intervene. Doing so required them to construct a series of bureaucratic roadblocks to keep Baldwin, Holmes, and Hays away from the case. A separate Publicity Committee handled all public statements. Unlike internment test cases, which the organization sought, the Committee on Seditious Cases decided as a matter of policy to "deal only with cases which come to us," and even then, the Board agreed "not to appear for the defendant(s) in sedition cases," but only in amicus briefs. Board absolutists felt that "the all out for the war group," as Osmond Fraenkel called them, was "getting out of hand."[35]

It proved beyond even Baldwin's power to hold the liberal pro-war impulse in check. Relativists argued that any ACLU action would be "fruitless," dividing the group and "lead[ing] the public to believe that the Union is supporting the defendants and even, perhaps, their views." Absolutists tried circulating an open letter as individuals protesting the Washington, D.C., conspiracy cases. "So few agreed to sign" that they abandoned the project. At least one who refused said outright that the group would be more effective "if it cooperated with and supported the Department of Justice." What happened next is not clear. Board of Directors minutes—overseen by Baldwin—report a vote in favor of sending an official protest to the government on ACLU letterhead. Several directors challenged that version, so the Board voted again, this time against sending any such letter. Absolutists appealed the decision by calling for a referendum vote. Finally, a year after it started, the Union officially opposed intervening in the Washington, D.C., sedition cases. By the end of the fighting, any remaining trust and amity between Board factions was gone.[36]

Relativists, meanwhile, found their means for modifying the Union's position to accommodate the war in the Seymour resolution, penned by one of the Board's more conservative members, Whitney North Seymour. The measure held that "the American Civil Liberties Union will not participate—except where the fundamentals of due process are denied—in cases where, after investigation, there are grounds for a belief that the defendant is cooperating with or acting on behalf of the enemy." The group would only involve itself in due process matters, honoring some governmental wartime limits on free speech. Baldwin reluctantly accepted the measure because "it kept us together." He persuaded other absolutists to do likewise. But he subverted it, never giving it "the widest possible publicity" the Board directed. He regularly challenged the manner in which it "has been applied," concluding it was "not . . . that happy solution" he envisioned. Norman Thomas felt that he was "fooled into believing" that the measure was elastic and "due process" was a "loose term." The Seymour resolution successfully limited ACLU action. As Fraenkel noted, since any interpretation of the measure rested with a disproportionately relativist Board, "we are never going to find a case which will not be banned by the resolution."[37]

The measure had little impact on what outsiders saw. The ACLU still seemed like it was "always against restrictions of liberty." Baldwin's high-profile actions had a lot to do with the false impression. Although he cautioned officers to carefully separate their politics and their Union work, he never did. He wrote and spoke in ways that encouraged people to assume the ACLU protected the sedition defendants, just as a decade before he had insinuated that the Union was a front. He continued to run the office his way, knowing that a majority of his Board objected. He wrote vague press releases about the Washington, D.C., trial. His Board minutes, as the relativists already knew, were equally vacillating. Even though he realized that "my recommendations don't go far these days with most of the board," Baldwin took advantage of the public's perception of him as the defining force behind the ACLU.[38]

Most directors complained only privately. They had to, for the Board traditionally avoided public airings of dirty laundry. Under the surface unity, though, there was a great deal of resentment, which Baldwin's behavior intensified. He counted on his colleagues' discretion. But the Union's more professional veneer displaced much of the earlier bonhomie, and the fight over Flynn ended the willingness of some directors to tolerate his actions. After months of private grumbling, Corliss Lamont openly complained in an official letter to Board chairman John Haynes Holmes:

> It is appropriate to note . . . the curious coincidence that practically all the office actions to which I have objected have occurred since you and Mr. Baldwin started to disagree with a number of the basic stands of the Board majority following the entrance of the United States into the Second World War. Another curious coincidence is that all of these clerical, secretarial, ocular, lapse-of-memory and extra curriculum errors in general have been made in a direction opposite or unfavorable to policies of the Board of Directors.

Lamont singled out one particularly egregious example. Circular letters signed by Baldwin, on ACLU letterhead and mailed from the ACLU office, urged the president to commute Max Stephan's death sentence. Stephan had sheltered an escaped German pilot and was convicted of treason. The Board had already voted to take no action on the case. Baldwin claimed the use of ACLU letterhead was a clerical error by a secretary that was possibly compounded by his own "mistake in judgment" in signing a letter he thought made it clear "that the Union was not involved."[39]

Baldwin was unrepentant about his actions, which have to be judged deliberate. Given the Union's wartime polarization, he knew he should not ask Union secretaries to do his personal work. When he signed the letter typed by the secretary, he must have noticed the ACLU letterhead, so different from his own personal stationery. "How the error occurred we do not know," he told one member; but he did know and was perfectly willing to brazen it out, even though his allies agreed that the letter gave "the impression that the Union was unofficially sponsoring the petition." When instructed to send out retractions, he asked an ACLU secretary on ACLU time to do so. His retractions explained that "I acted in my personal capacity in soliciting signatures" without also explicitly denying the Union's involvement. Lamont caught him in the act of falsifying the ACLU's position.[40]

So clear was the complaint that even Holmes thought it "not perhaps without reason." Unfortunately, still smarting from perceived slights over the Flynn matter, which he later recalled resulted in Baldwin "barring [him] from [tennis] court and beach" near the Baldwins' and the Lamonts' summer cottages, Lamont raised his complaint officially. This violated Board etiquette. Absolutists successfully appealed to their colleagues' sense of propriety in maintaining the public image that everybody got along. Directors did not act against Baldwin but agreed that in future, any complaint against an officer should be handled privately. Baldwin felt "the air has been considerably cleared"; still, the affair was "something in the nature of a crisis."[41]

The Stephan affair was not, as Baldwin characterized it, "one isolated instance in over twenty years." It fully reflected his style. He never imagined that the Union's newfound professionalism applied to him. He continued to ask ACLU secretaries to do his personal work. He was "a control freak," according to one, and generally managed to get his way on everything from the wording of a press release to an ACLU policy. But World War II made control harder. Disgruntled officers scrutinized his activities. Secretaries came and went. He was always a hard and stingy employer ("a helluva slave driver, picky, etc," in his own characterization). The war gave staff members better job options. The number of former Union employees, one commentator dryly noted, could "man a fair-sized battle ship." One of them explained that "worthy-cause organizations are always lousy employers, but . . . Baldwin was by far the worst." In the six-month period surrounding the Stephan matter, the period when the debates about the sedition cases raged, twenty-three secretaries resigned or were fired, suggesting that the Union offered a horrid work environment. The tension between relativists and absolutists poisoned office relationships as well as relationships between Board members.[42]

In 1944 the office situation worsened. Lucille Milner, the ACLU's longtime organizational secretary, was in a position to witness Baldwin's intrusions firsthand. Hers was a job requiring great tact as she smoothed any feathers Baldwin ruffled. She and Baldwin were old friends and colleagues. Robert Cottrell, Baldwin's biographer, says they had also been lovers and that Milner had a long-standing crush on Baldwin, which helps explain her loyalty. As the one staff relativist, though, she lost respect for him and he for her. Nothing she did satisfied Baldwin. He scrutinized her behavior and complained that she was "so immersed in winning the war that she'd pass up all civil liberties for the duration." Against Baldwin's judgment but with the Board's approval, she increased her hours during the war, which increased the friction between them. She refused to work on his conscientious objectors cases. He complained she did not get her work done. She resented the way he monitored everything she did. "It is inhuman the way you check up on my time," she told him. Yet while Baldwin spied, judged, and reprimanded her, he and Holmes misused "the facilities, the stationery, the connections and the prestige of the Civil Liberties Union."[43]

Milner was a scapegoat for Baldwin's wartime frustrations. He enjoyed working with government representatives on civil liberties matters but found no similar satisfaction in his own boardroom. As Milner later remembered, he loved "the glory of the job and the fuss that was made over him," two aspects missing during wartime. During earlier periods of personal stress, he turned over the day-to-day operation of the ACLU to others, and that is what he said he wanted to do as the war wound down. He planned "to withdraw from all routine responsibilities as soon as possible" and bring in someone from outside to cover those details. No ACLU officer imagined a woman in that job. Thus Milner was a lame duck, as the group could not afford both a national secretary and an associate director, "but we can't let the jeopardy of her position influence us." When notified of the group's future plans, she promptly quit.[44] The promised reorganization never took place. After the war Baldwin was away from the Union for long periods of time, but no successor-in-waiting was hired. He was not ready to let go of the ACLU, but neither was Milner the source of the trouble in the New York office, as most officers already knew.

Baldwin could no longer run the Union the way he wanted it run. The group lost momentum during World War II, just as it lost liberal stature. Only in 1945 did it grow. In 1943 it lost about 500 members (down 10 percent from the year before) and its income stayed even, which during an inflationary period signaled a loss of purchasing power. Because Baldwin's financial formula was to spend no more than the organization took in, the group had limited ability to finance test cases. It was no wonder the office situation was so tense. The stressed staff had to work miracles on a budget of next to nothing. Attacks on the Union grew and sprang from a wider variety of sources. Conservatives kept up their traditional accusations, arguing that the ACLU served the communists. Liberals called it passé. In a world where pragmatism increasingly represented a liberal ideal, the kind of civil liberties most interested Americans thought the ACLU practiced—absolutist, principled, and politically neutral—no longer seemed to work. Instead, the Union seemed extremist and so concerned for the rights of a few undeserving dissidents that it had lost perspective.

Baldwin attempted to compensate for the group's sagging wartime popularity by developing influence with government, a strategy with very limited success. Certainly the ACLU had members who were also members of Roosevelt's inner circles. The relationship, however, was one-sided. The government could do without the ACLU's advice, but Baldwin needed to feel mastery over some part of his environment as his domination of the Union lessened. He truly enjoyed meeting with Justice Department officials and writing "confidential memos," but he had little real impact on policy, especially on matters of wide disagreement, like the Washington, D.C., trials. His work as an insider, moreover, blunted the organization's assertiveness. Increasingly, Baldwin took his cues from others, developing perhaps too much respect for government and too much faith that it shared the ACLU's principles undiluted by political need. "The success of the war," as David Plotke has noted, "enhanced the political legitimacy of the Democratic leadership." The ACLU gained more access to power but forfeited its fearless attitude. It was already primed to function in a postwar liberal world shaped by corporate ideals such as getting along.[45]

In order to reconcile its directors' divided loyalties, the Union "went through the legal forms" during the war, Dwight Macdonald later wrote, but without "aggressiveness and enthusiasm" for its work.[46] Its fights over Elizabeth Gurley Flynn might have paralyzed the group, but at least they revealed passion and commitment. During the war, it often seemed that there were only compromises—over internment, over fascists' civil liberties, and even over office policy. A newer generation of leaders started to challenge the authority of the founding generation. New members were not entirely comfortable with the wartime Union, but neither were their elders, who barely recognized an organization so careful about upsetting government or so precise about the wording of its policy papers. The Union became more bureaucratized. Bureaucracy impressed liberals and facilitated cooperation with the government. It enabled the Board to carry on despite directors' conflicts. But it also diminished civil libertarians' ardor, making them more professional and less willing to take risks. There would be fewer and fewer Roger Baldwins—fewer crusaders—as the Union aged. As they faded, managers came to the fore. By the end of World War II, the ACLU was poised to become a very different organization than it had been.

5

STICKING THEIR NECKS OUT

The Affiliates during World War II

In the summer of 1944 Roger Baldwin took a much-needed vacation at Martha's Vineyard. While Baldwin lazed on the beach with his wife and daughter, Ernest Besig climbed into his car and, using precious gasoline rations, drove several hundred miles to the Tule Lake internment camp, where the WRA held some Japanese Americans without charges in a stockade. After two days of interviews, the camp director decided Besig was disrupting the routine. He contacted Baldwin, and Baldwin authorized him to expel the NCACLU leader. Security guards escorted Besig to his car, which had been parked in a guarded lot, and he discovered his gas tank had been filled with salt.[1] The incident encapsulates the wartime differences between the national ACLU and the branches. National officers acted cautiously, avoided harm, and worked with government officials to smooth the sharper edges of the government's wartime civil liberties compromises. Affiliates handled the problems of individuals who challenged those compromises. The Board's wartime paralysis both helped and hindered branches, but more importantly, it provided them with the space in which to develop their own organizational personalities. While the national ACLU struggled, the affiliates became assertive and, in their own ways, professional.

The 1940 resolution and the Flynn purge released branches from many of their feelings of subordination. In the larger affiliates, officers began to sit in judgment of the National Board, scrutinizing and criticizing. Many times they felt at odds with decisions made in New York, but beyond expressing their disapproval at regular intervals, they could do little to influence those who made decisions for the group. Even the one small concession the Board granted them, the right to suggest nominees for the National Committee, was an illusion. Branch officers took the policy seriously, yet none of their nominees ever appeared on election slates. Only several years later did they learn why. The Nominating Committee "made . . . a test of appearance in *Who's Who*," Baldwin explained, "to make identification of our personnel more easy with newspapers, magazine writers, etc." Branch people found "a certain element of grim humor" in this; however, the futility of making nominations "which are year after year ignored" irritated them. "It could be worse," Besig mused, "the day may come when one's name has to appear in the Social Register to be a member of the National Committee."[2]

Such impertinence worried the staff, who knew that during wartime the ACLU would come under increased scrutiny. Absolutists and relativists alike expected branches to be subservient and behave professionally. Baldwin stressed cooperation with the federal government, labor groups, and the NAACP. He instructed branches to work with "the most influential liberals in the community" and cautioned them to pay careful heed to their reputations. Affiliates felt these recommendations put them in a subordinate position. More rules followed a few months later in order to assure that the organization had "a uniform national policy in dealing with federal issues." Branches were instructed "to take no action without consulting the national office."[3]

Local activists balked. They wanted a real voice in the organization, "actual representation" rather than the fiction of it. In 1942 directors rejected change, declining to give voting privileges to all members and affirming their power to make nominations. The branches gained only advisory consultative roles, promises that "sound . . . very nice," Besig noted, "but . . . do not seem to be worth the paper they are written on." Besig knew that, especially in his case, officers would ignore his opinions and suggestions. His frustration put him first among several local leaders who advocated for "an actual, not an advisory, vote."[4]

At the same time the Board denied branches any official role in ACLU governance, the war situation required them to make more judgments on their own. The setup encouraged independence. National leaders dallied for months before they established a policy toward internment; the West Coast affiliates needed to act before Japanese Americans sold goods and moved to camps. Baldwin badgered them to find a suitable case to test the constitutionality of the evacuation. The NCACLU did, that of Fred Korematsu, but the relativist-led revolt did not allow for constitutional challenges to internment. The Board ordered Besig to end his group's involvement in the case. He refused. "We cannot in good conscience at this late date withdraw our support after telling him [Korematsu] we would carry the case to the United States Supreme Court," he explained. Division at headquarters aided his rebellion. Lucille Milner, who as executive secretary handled everyday interactions with affiliates, was a relativist and was "affronted" by his choices. But absolutist Osmond Fraenkel, who assigned the bulk of the Union's wartime legal work, judged the differences between the NCACLU's Korematsu brief and the national ACLU's position "very unimportant." Staff attorney Cliff Forster also read the brief and concluded that "I don't believe that the points . . . raise[d] go outside the limits laid down by our Board." Forster coached Besig on how to handle Milner, "but leave me out [of it]," he begged. Besig felt his allegiance lay with the internees, not ACLU headquarters, especially since the absolutist-relativist split made pleasing the New Yorkers impossible.[5]

Baldwin might have been an ally to the NCACLU, but with his

authority eroding elsewhere, he could not risk Besig's impudence. "In a national organization," he instructed, "it is necessary to have some one center controlling both national policies and their application. . . . Control must lie somewhere." Even though split in other ways, the National Board was not divided on the question of its authority over the branch. It supported Baldwin all the way. The branch, however, refused to accept any limits, offering excuses, linguistic challenges, and countersuggestions. "Without autonomy," the local leaders argued, affiliates "become mere agencies of a Board three thousand miles away." Although Alexander Meiklejohn, who knew the New Yorkers well, advised Besig that directors "are a tough crowd to fight and there is little to be gained by slugging it out," Besig persisted and won.[6]

While the national leadership struggled to follow the government's cues and changed their policy with each appeal, the NCACLU confidently carried the Korematsu case to the Supreme Court. Only when the Justice Department "insist[ed] we file a brief *amicus*" with the Court did the national ACLU act. By that point, Korematsu's NCACLU attorney, Wayne Collins, resented the Union's sudden interest and refused to share his court time with its legal representatives. Besig and Collins would have been more resentful if they had known the real reason the national ACLU wanted to contribute to the case. The Justice Department deemed Collins's work weak, and its officers worried that "the case might be lost due to the poor job Collins has done." The case was lost but was a landmark decision nonetheless. As Meiklejohn noted, the San Francisco group redeemed itself as "shrewd and accurate." The NCACLU directly challenged the national office's sovereignty, acting on a matter it regarded as within its jurisdiction and expertise.[7]

When national officers considered internment, they saw potentially thorny policy questions; when the West Coast affiliates considered the practice, they saw people in need, and their passion spilled over into their actions. In his capacity as California's commissioner of immigration and housing, the SCACLU's Carey McWilliams thought he knew about living conditions in the makeshift temporary internment facilities erected on fairgrounds and racetracks. But visiting friends in one of these camps was "an extraordinary experience." Another SCACLU member also visited and remembered that he "just wanted to cry. . . . It was bad enough to see people behind these barbed-wire fences, but when you saw someone you really knew, it drove it home even more."[8] Local people confronted what East Coasters almost deliberately tried to avoid seeing: the human costs of internment. Board members viewed internment as an extension of their own wartime experiences. They lived with rationing, children in the military, and occasional blackouts. They imagined that internment was, like their disruptions, tolerable, if more demanding. Since they did not have to watch friends and acquaintances quit their jobs, sell their possessions, or grapple with persistent racial discrimination, easterners could not easily understand what was happening. Those who knew individuals whose lives were uprooted and whose loyalty was impugned simply because of their race were not inclined to believe the idea of "military necessity."

At a time when there was considerable anti-Japanese hysteria on the West Coast, members of the local affiliates displayed sympathy and sensitivity for the internees. Fred Korematsu recalled that Besig approached him in jail after seeing a headline that read, "Jap Spy Arrested." "It floored me," he noted, "because at the time racial prejudice was pretty strong . . . [and] he was sticking his neck out for me." Besig would remain a loyal friend to Korematsu, bringing him sunglasses to shield him from photographers' bright lights; breaking the news to him that his Caucasian fiancée, Ida Boitano, probably would not marry him; and comforting him when he left the camp and confronted discrimination. In exchange, Korematsu sent Besig regular letters and his $2 NCACLU membership fee. Mary Farquharson of the Seattle Civil Liberties Union developed a similar relationship with a number of internees from Washington State, sending them letters and treats and keeping them informed about "Gordie's" (Gordon Hirabayashi's) case. Personal contact with internees made local activists intimately aware of a wartime program directors preferred to keep on an impersonal national scale.[9]

The westerners anticipated that, for once, geography was on their side and that they would be the experts about internment. Instead, Baldwin's staff relied on the guidance of friendly federal authorities, whose opinions carried weight among national officers disinclined to trust one another. Local boards could not hope to compete, as NCACLU board chair Edward Parsons explained, because they could not "join you in your consultations with the powers that be in Washington." The national office's reliance on "confidential cooperation in Washington," Meiklejohn explained, "tends to leave a local branch uninformed about matters which may be, in large measure, within its control." The strategy inadvertently privileged some affiliates over others. Farquharson was a member of the Washington State legislature and the pacifist Fellowship of Reconciliation, so she had access to several useful networks. The SCACLU had A. L. Wirin, a longtime Washington wheeler-dealer. The arrangement hurt the NCACLU the most, since it had no connections and disapproved of the tactic of consulting officials. "Our National Office," Besig concluded, "relies too heavily upon the opinion of its friends within the government."[10]

The NCACLU's wartime refusal to follow the national office's directives brought the branch to the brink of expulsion. It defied the New York office over the Korematsu case and other matters, ignoring all rebukes. By 1943 everyone expected a "showdown" between the "(quasi-outlaw) Northern California Branch" and the ACLU proper. The Board outlined its expectations to the affiliate, an arrangement Besig characterized as "knuckle down or face expulsion." Since, as Parsons said, the Board could not "go on dealing with us as if we were children," Besig predicted "we'll be disaffiliated."[11] Expulsion was the logical alternative. Besig questioned policy, publicized disputes, and behaved in a manner the Board did not tolerate elsewhere. Yet, when the smoke cleared in 1943 and even when the controversy was revived in 1944, the affiliate never fully accepted the national office's authority and was still not expelled.

The NCACLU could safely assert its independence without punishment because disaffiliating it would cause public relations repercussions. Its members were vociferous and loyal. Sympathetic forces within the Justice Department counted on its legal challenges to internment, even if they thought them sometimes ineffective. Japanese Americans trusted the affiliate far more than the national organization or any of the other West Coast affiliates. Rather than confront the larger meaning of the San Francisco revolt, officers defined it as a Besig tantrum. "We are never going to enjoy right relations with the California group as long as Besig is in the picture," National Board chair John Haynes Holmes explained.[12] Holmes's solution, thus, was to ignore Besig and work with his technical superior, local board chair Edward Parsons. But Besig was paid to handle ACLU work, while Parsons was a busy Episcopalian bishop. This slowed negotiations immensely without yielding any better result. While Holmes might have hoped the ministerial connections between himself and Parsons would make for a better working relation, Parsons shared Besig's conviction that affiliates ought to act as they thought best. He was no more tractable than Besig was.

Besig and Parsons more spectacularly clashed with headquarters over the Seymour resolution limiting the Union's participation in war-related cases to "due process." Parsons asserted that the measure was partisan, its purpose "to back the war in every respect." Besig called it "cowardly." "The Northern California branch wants to take cases forbidden by the October 19 [Seymour] resolution," Baldwin warned Holmes in 1943. Baldwin and Holmes opposed the measure themselves, yet they gave Besig no satisfaction. Alexander Meiklejohn, by contrast, supported the war more than either New Yorker did, but he sided with his fellow San Franciscans, even while serving as a key Union negotiator with the Roosevelt government. "I noted with glee the difference with New York," he told Besig. Norman Thomas, too, enjoyed the show. "All my sympathies are with you," he wrote.[13]

Division in New York complicated the situation. Baldwin left Whitney North Seymour to defend his resolution. The Board followed with terms for continued affiliation. The NCACLU agreed, but only with "some reservations" and conditions of its own. Parsons deftly sidestepped the New Yorkers' threats of disaffiliation. "We will just go ahead and do our job and let questions come up about specific cases, not about the policy in general," he said; then if a difference of opinion occurred, the Board could "repudiate it without firing us from the Union." Faced with such determination, directors either had to proceed with their threat or ignore it. The Board ignored it. The controversy had barely settled when the affiliate again evaded the Seymour resolution and accepted an "emergency" case involving accused German sympathizers. Directors did not discipline the branch, and the branch continued to make its own choices.[14]

The San Franciscans also challenged and sometimes undermined the national ACLU's strategy of working from the inside to influence governmental policies. Baldwin assumed that the WRA under Dillon S. Myer was an agency where a New Deal frame of mind prevailed, which, in general, was true. He trusted that the internees were well treated and that their civil liberties, such as they could be, were respected. All he knew about the camps, though, was filtered through well-meaning Caucasian bureaucrats or JACL leaders.[15] Baldwin monitored internment by looking at the intent of the government. Besig visited the camps and received letters of protest from inmates. He saw another side: how the system treated dissenters.

As federal policy changed, the differences grew. Early in 1943, partly in order to draft Nisei men, the government administered loyalty questionnaires. Those who refused to swear fidelity to the United States found themselves relocated to Tule Lake, in the extreme northeast corner of California, Besig's territory. Tule Lake also housed loyal Japanese Americans, but the camp segregated the allegedly disloyal and imposed more restrictions on them. Some of those interned at Tule Lake were *Kibei*, American-born, Japanese-educated young men who were militantly pro-Japanese. In late 1943, camp inmates staged a strike after a truck carrying internee workers overturned and one person died. They submitted a list of demands that included the removal of the camp director. Military authorities assumed control over the segregated sections of the camp and stockaded twenty of the alleged leaders without holding hearings or filing charges against them.[16]

Besig and his counsel protested. Baldwin accepted WRA assurances that "Tule Lake is not being used as a disciplinary center." Besig wanted to see for himself. Baldwin consulted Myer and then asked Besig to delay his trip. Besig declined, aghast that the ACLU had "more or less joined forces with the War Relocation Authority." Lacking official blessing, he decided "to reach the same goal in a less convenient way," which is how he found himself at Tule Lake that hot July day. At first the visit proceeded smoothly, although Besig disliked the guards who listened to every interview. But camp officials called Baldwin, who recommended that they "invite him [Besig] to leave." Two security officers escorted him off the premises. When he started his car, he discovered the salt in his gas tank, probably the work of "one of the Internal Security boys . . . because we had been inquiring into their wielding of baseball bats against the heads of some of the segregees." Baldwin feared that Besig undermined his personal relationship with internment officials. He apologized to Secretary of the Interior Harold Ickes and promised that in future no one from the ACLU would visit a camp without his (Baldwin's) written permission.[17]

In New York, Besig's concerns seemed less important than getting along with Washington officials, not upsetting the Board, or not interrupting Baldwin's vacation. If Myer thought it reasonable to hold "segregees" indefinitely without charges, then Baldwin trusted that it was so. Besig believed the prisoners' claims of brutality, which were later confirmed by evidence. He lacked confidence in a group of Ivy Leaguers besotted by their government connections and an office that had to be reminded not to use the word "Jap." The NCACLU pursued its clients' needs. NCACLU attorney Wayne Collins threatened habeas corpus proceedings. The Board wanted to check with the WRA first. Collins acted without waiting for permission, obtaining the release of the stockaded men. Ironically, when it was all over, directors blandly conveyed their thanks to the affiliate for a job well done.[18]

The release of the prisoners did not end the wrangling. Collins's work forced the government to file charges against the stockaded men. Before committing to their defense, Baldwin called Myer to get "the 'green light'" and then asked A. L. Wirin to handle their case. The office preferred him, claiming he was "more expert in these matters," meaning that he better understood the national perspective, had connections to the JACL, and had worked before cooperatively with government agencies. He was the better choice from the "point of view of law and public relations." Collins seemed a maverick to headquarters, but he knew the case better and already had the defendants' trust and respect. Wirin, moreover, was reluctant to undertake the Tule Lake defenses, having other work to do and knowing that traveling from one end of California to the other in the middle of the war would be difficult. Besides, he wanted "to avoid a head on collision with the Northern California Committee." Baldwin's assignment was punitive; he was punishing Besig and Collins for being too assertive. What he failed to understand was that a slap on the wrist did not intimidate the Northern Californians, whose group identity did not depend on what Baldwin thought of them.[19]

Baldwin's privileging of the SCACLU over the NCACLU, moreover, did not turn Wirin into a cooperative ally. In July 1944, Congress amended the Nationality Act of 1940 to enable citizens dwelling in the United States to renounce their citizenship during wartime. Like Executive Order 9066, its wording singled out no ethnicity, but it was aimed at Japanese Americans. The government hoped the act would facilitate the removal of disloyal persons after the war. No one expected many people to use it, perhaps only a few *Kibei*. But some 5,589—one-fourteenth of the Nisei population—did. At Tule Lake seven of ten citizens over the age of eighteen renounced their citizenship. Their reasons were complex. Some honored requests from fearful Issei parents who anticipated being deported after the war and wanted to keep their families together. The anti-American *Kibei* gangs at Tule Lake allegedly harassed young men to forswear loyalty to Japan. But for most, the experience of internment, of being treated as an enemy alien without the rights of citizenship, caused them to lose faith in the United States. The government was shocked by the response and tightened renunciation procedures, but at the end of the war, there were still about 5,500 persons who had changed their minds and wanted to stay.[20]

When the renunciations began, the Board voted that there were no civil liberties issues involved, at least partly "to avoid putting the Department of Justice 'on the spot.'" But as the war wound down, the Justice Department claimed "no authority or discretion in the matter," which removed the obstacle of staying on its good side. Lacking precedents, the Board made a safe bureaucratic decision about renunciation, forming a committee to investigate. The committee advised opposing deportation except in the case of proven enemy aliens and recommended test cases—cases that would logically come from Tule Lake. Instead of asking Besig and Collins to pursue them, the office asked Wirin. It took Wirin the better part of a year to find some that were "reasonably satisfactory from a 'public relations' point of view." He delayed his test cases even longer at the recommendation of the JACL, which feared they would jeopardize a California ballot proposition to negate the Alien Land Law. The national ACLU wanted to help, but its accommodation of the government and determination to exclude Besig slowed its reactions.[21]

Besig and Collins felt no such restraint. Besig briefly tried to follow the protocol, asking Baldwin to intervene in some cases with the Justice Department because "you know Ed Ennis personally." But he privately doubted that the government would treat the renunciants fairly. Collins, meanwhile, visited some of those in danger of being deported and was disturbed by the "barbarism . . . practiced by governmental agencies." Besig and Collins concluded that while test cases could yield a precedent, in the meantime too many people might be deported. Acting "technically independent" of the NCACLU, Collins began soliciting individual renunciant cases, and Besig, while maintaining the technicality of independence, referred cases to him. Collins was wildly successful. The renunciants recognized his deep commitment to seeing justice done, even to the extent that he undertook only what other cases he needed to survive. Tule Lakers had a generally positive image of the NCACLU (as one said, it had "supported us ever since 1942"), while they were less impressed with the national organization, Wirin's JACL ties, or the impersonal idea of test cases.[22]

The national ACLU was not pleased by Collins's actions, and

Wirin thought the individual cases might interfere with his tests. After learning of Collins's work, though, he saw the advantage of proceeding individually. "As I get older and acquire greater financial obligations . . . I want to earn what money I can and the Tule Lake cases seem to offer an opportunity for fair compensation." Wirin was as sincerely committed to civil liberties as any of the New York directors were, but his work for the ACLU was not a pro bono effort handled on the side of a lucrative practice. Collins charged $100 per renunciant case, "but it's between Collins and renunciants how little some pay," Besig explained. Wirin charged $250 per case, on top of the "$4000 a year he earned handling cases for the Southern California branch." Even though "a lot of the Caucasians are encouraging the persons to join up with Wirin" and the WRA gave him preferential access to potential clients, Collins seemed the better deal to virtually all the renunciants.[23]

The national ACLU favored Wirin without providing him with the support he wanted. Besig and Parsons refused to interfere with Collins's work. Collins amassed clients by the score while criticizing the ACLU, its national officers, and especially Wirin. The Board could do nothing since Collins's work was independent, so Wirin took matters into his own hands. He threatened to sue Collins for lost revenues totaling $75,000 and to report him to the California Bar Association. The New Yorkers thought these actions just as unprofessional as Collins's individual cases. Profiting from civil liberties work seemed unseemly to them. When Wirin submitted a $2,500 bill, the Board refused to pay, and one officer implied it was padded. Wirin's situation was hard for New Yorkers to fathom. While Arthur Garfield Hays imagined that he made a lot of money "from civil liberties cases which came to him because of his connection with the Union," ACLU connections generally limited local attorneys' practices to low-paying left-wing clients. Wirin's wartime SCACLU casework required him to defend war opponents, which offended his other client, the Congress of Industrial Organizations. He resigned as its counsel once the SCACLU agreed to pay him an annual salary.[24] National officers tolerated one another's wartime politics yet demanded full obedience of affiliate workers. They had trouble seeing them as people with loyalties of their own, regional commitments, and their own needs as human beings.

Directors responded punitively to Wirin, just as they had to Besig and Collins. To avoid further protests and "confusion as to whether he was acting for us or for private clients," they decided that no attorney paid by the ACLU or its branches could undertake private civil liberties cases "except with the consent of the directing committee to which he is responsible." Since the renunciant cases were national ACLU business, Wirin was not allowed to profit from them so long as he acted for the Union in the test cases. Collins acted outside the Union hierarchy and continued to take cases, a lesson not lost on Wirin. It was information that would prove handy during the cold war.[25]

In the meantime, the westerners developed expertise the National Board needed, making them indispensable, if unreliable. Renunciation was a subject both Wirin and Collins mastered as a legal specialty. Wirin successfully stopped the wholesale deportation of individuals with a test case and reinstated their citizenship, but each claimant had to go through a separate administrative hearing to reverse the renunciation process. Collins devoted the next twenty years to assisting in roughly 3,000 administrative hearings to regain citizenship for his Japanese American clients. In so doing, he made arguments sure to distress national officers, about the psychological impact of internment, the devastating impact of living in camps, and "any [other] God damn issue that is possible." "It is not the function of the Union," Besig noted, "to shield its friends in the War Relocation Authority and the Justice Department." Wirin and Besig better understood the boundaries of ACLU affiliation by the end of the war, while national officers seemed to have learned little about branches, failing even to recognize how much they counted on the affiliates' excellent work.[26]

As the San Francisco group pushed limits, gained experience, and developed expertise, it became the linchpin in a growing affiliate revolt. Across the country, branches complained about various wartime policies, but officers refused to see a pattern. "No other branch . . . takes this [rebellious] attitude," Baldwin insisted. Yet the NCACLU's scrutiny of national policies inspired other branches to examine and question directors' choices. After learning that the San Francisco branch had protested the Seymour resolution, for example, the Los Angeles board put a discussion of the measure on its agenda. They voted not to challenge it, warning, though, that in future "local committees should be consulted first and given larger autonomy." The Iowa Civil Liberties Union wondered if "local branches [were] consulted" about this matter that could "come back to plague us." The Erie County, New York, group was astonished to learn that nineteen board members passed something that affected "thousands of members." Large or small, eastern or western, branches wanted more influence, not just about the Seymour resolution but about other matters as well. Ultimately, officers had to concede that Besig's frustrations were "shared . . . by others."[27]

All four "'strong' local branches" chafed at national control. The CLUM did not contest national policy like the San Francisco branch did, but it was equally mutinous about autonomy. "There was a very strong feeling," reported its chair in 1942, "that we should not be expected to agree in advance to policies in which we do not explicitly share in the making." The next year, it sent a list of procedural recommendations to the national organization. Bostonians thought the Union should "broaden and democratize," giving locals voting privileges and the right to designate one member each to the Board. Resentment simmered over both style and substance.[28]

Branches without paid staffs were less assertive, but they also sometimes complained that the national office was too domineering. In 1942 the Denver affiliate protested when Baldwin "unjustifiably" supported defeated local officers and appointed a state correspondent "behind our backs and without consulting us." Committed volunteers resigned in protest, and Lucille Milner could find no one willing to reorganize the branch. Baldwin tried to force out Cleveland's "fellow traveler chairman, Russell Chase" so the ACLU could "disassociate" itself from his politics. He asked a local member of the National Committee to handle the details, irritating Cleveland affiliate volunteers who had "been much closer to and far more active in the local committee." Once outsiders reorganized the group, it became "nothing more than this executive committee . . . with occasional bulletins to our members," doing little work. The Erie County group protested instructions from on high "without adequate membership participation in the decisions" and complained about the New Yorkers' propensity to seek out "only those cases that can be won, and that tend to enhance the Union's prestige."[29]

After several years of discontented rumblings, Alexander Meiklejohn privately polled local leaders and found considerable disaffection with *the present form of organization*," especially the office's "working relations with the local committees" and the fact that the leadership "is a purely New York local group." At the Union's 1944 annual meeting, he presented an NCACLU-drafted petition for branch "representation" endorsed by the SCACLU, the CLUM, and the CCLC. Directors did what they often did with affiliate matters, referring it to a committee to be appointed by Board chairman John Haynes Holmes. In the meantime, they invited each affiliate to designate a consultant "to serve, in fact, if not in name, on the Board of Directors."[30]

Holmes acted slowly on the matter, talking to Baldwin and waiting several months to appoint the committee. The logical head of any such committee was Meiklejohn as instigator of the petition. Baldwin, though, wanted someone more pliant, someone "here in the city, and therefore in close contact with the office." Yet by insisting that the committee have the "constant advice, help and energy of Roger Baldwin," Holmes practically guaranteed it would not satisfy local groups. While the committee slowly went about its business, the most quarrelsome of the newly designated consultants, Besig, did not receive mailings he should have; naturally, he took that as a deliberate slight. Meanwhile, the committee Baldwin expected to dominate suggested democratic reforms he would never tolerate, proposing that the membership elect the National Committee and ten of thirty-five directors and that each affiliate should get a nonvoting liaison to the Board. It also suggested that affiliates consult the Board on national issues and "abide by its decision."[31]

Directors approved of creating "uniformity throughout the country on national policies," but not democracy. They turned down the proposals for extending the vote, arguing that "no substantial objections have been voiced to the present system," an amazing contention considering all the years of affiliate protests. A full corporate vote (Board, National Committee, and "advisory" input from affiliates) confirmed the decision two to one. The affiliates were unhappy with the result but had no power in a system where "about 100 members in a membership of 6,000 members or more" voted. In the group's 1944 annual report, Baldwin described what happened as the affiliates seeking "closer cooperation" with the national office.[32]

The Board thus forestalled any Union democratization and, instead, used the war as justification for claiming more authority over affiliates. Yet as Besig's affiliate constantly demonstrated, any authority the national organization obtained depended on the affiliates' willingness to cede it. Short of expelling a branch, the Board had no real enforcement powers. The NCACLU preferred to be part of the Union but certainly considered disaffiliation when relations grew strained. Directors threatened it with disaffiliation without ever following through. They needed the branch. It was actually a paragon of affiliate achievement: large, full of committed volunteers, well respected by local people, and perhaps most important, self-supporting. The officers of the Northern California group stood behind Besig whatever he did. There was no evidence of internal dissent or malfeasance that the Board could use against the affiliate. To expel it over differences, such as the Seymour resolution or the Korematsu case, was to invite revived debate between the Board's wartime factions and public scrutiny of the Union's wartime policies, neither of which the organization desired. The same qualities that made the NCACLU a successful organization also made it a bad branch in the ACLU system as it existed. And it was not the only affiliate developing a mind and personality of its own.

The CLUM did not exist in the same constant state of friction with the national ACLU as the NCACLU did, but it, too, contemplated breaking from headquarters and fighting its own fights. While the San Franciscans deplored the New Yorkers' tenderness toward the federal government, the Bostonians were pro-war and wanted the Union to lean more in that direction, too. Chairman Albert Sprague Coolidge was very open about his position, declaring that "I do not wish ever to find myself committed, as spokesman of the Civil Liberties Union, to the defense of those who are in my opinion making war against democracy." Yet Coolidge was the lesser of two evils to New Yorkers. His second-in-command, Florence Luscomb, seemed to Baldwin, "unconsciously swayed toward [Communist] partisanship." He tolerated her to a point, but when she invited Harry Ward to speak at the annual CLUM meeting, he pressed Coolidge to intervene. Coolidge refused. Baldwin could not directly accuse Luscomb "when the evidence is so circumstantial and . . . no admitted [Communist] Party member is involved." Besides, the 1940 resolution did not apply to the branches, so she was free to belong to any other group she so desired. All he could do to "check this [left-wing] tendency" was support Coolidge and live with his pro-war attitude.[33]

Most branches complained during the war, and two at least contemplated breaking free of the national ACLU; only one, finally, had to be cut loose: the CCLC. Generally affiliates performed useful work, brought the organization prestige, and seemed to satisfy local people, however willful their leaders were. The Chicago situation was different, and at the center of its differences was its executive secretary, Ira Latimer. Latimer was an ordained Baptist minister. He had taught sociology in China and at a historically black college in Memphis. In Chicago he first worked at a radio station known as the "Voice of Labor." He was, in short, dedicated to the downtrodden. While Baldwin and others at headquarters could relate to his devotion, they could not understand his ambition. Like Wirin, he was self-made. He wanted, one observer noted, "to be a big man." While Wirin used his New Deal and labor connections to build a law practice, Latimer reluctantly chose the CPUSA as his pathway to success. Local Communists began pressuring him to join, Latimer told the Subversive Activities Control Board, from the moment he took over in Chicago. In 1944 the pressure became "so continuous and so irritating" that he joined, to "get [William] Patterson [identified in testimony as 'Vice-President of the Communist Party of

Illinois'] off my neck." Latimer thought the CPUSA offered both a useful vehicle for helping others and a career with "the possibility of an advance."[34]

Latimer would have preferred to work with the ACLU, but officers never treated him with respect and brushed off his many ideas and suggestions. Once he joined the Party, he knew his days with the ACLU were numbered. He evaded handling local sedition cases, which raised questions at headquarters, especially with absolutists eager to circumvent relativists' restrictions on such matters. The national staff asked him for reports on local cases. He stalled lest he be asked to intervene on the defendants' behalf. He explained that court transcripts cost too much for the branch to obtain; that there was no quorum and, therefore, no opinion from his board; and that his volunteer attorneys were too busy to handle appeals. Finally, he reported that his branch believed these were not civil liberties cases. Baldwin got more irritated with each excuse, at last urging that "if your committee does not want you to get information," Latimer should just say so and the New York office could make other arrangements.[35]

Latimer evaded acting on other sedition cases as well. The CCLC "voted . . . not to enter the case of Mrs. Elizabeth Dilling and two other Chicagoans." The local board debated the issue for six weeks, leaving Latimer to break the tie vote against defending her. The CCLC would not defend German-American Bundists because Latimer had a "vigorous personal opposition to do anything in behalf of civil liberties for 'fascists.'" He found nothing legally relevant in the case of the Minneapolis Trotskyists charged with violating the Smith Act. The national organization obtained an attorney for Clyde Summers, who was deemed unfit to practice law by the Illinois State Bar because he was a religious pacifist and a conscientious objector, since the CCLC manifested a "total lack of interest in the issues of the C.O.s." There was opposition within the Chicago group to several of these decisions, but Latimer held the power and few felt so strongly as to risk the public embarrassment of defending Bundists, Trotskyists, or Dilling. The CCLC "passed the same resolution which the ACLU adopted [Seymour]," which Latimer characterized as a necessary countermeasure to bad publicity and "protests to the ACLU by its Jewish contributors." Although the CCLC's counsel opposed it, Latimer suggested that it was a "necessary guidepost in time of war."[36]

By 1943 nearly everything Latimer did disappointed the national office, but what most alarmed headquarters was how divided Chicagoans appeared. In other branches, pro-Communist factions functioned harmoniously enough that Baldwin could not induce anyone local to address their existence. This was not true in Chicago. Disgruntled members complained that Latimer shifted the group's responsibilities, amending its bylaws in 1943 so as to pursue "charitable and educational" work. Since Latimer worked to help build the Civil Rights Congress (CRC), a new Party front devoted to civil rights, he shifted his energies in that direction, doing work the Union usually left to the NAACP. By 1943 between a third and a half of the CCLC's activities concerned "Negro Rights." Members began to complain. "I can find practically no civil liberties subjects" on the agenda, one said. By 1944 the CCLC board authorized Latimer "to devote his entire time to the many aspects of the problem of racial tension in Chicago," a vote justified with a quotation from Baldwin that these were "the major and almost the only civil liberties issues and problem in the country today."[37]

By the fall of 1944, what the *Chicago Times* called a "small but spectacular feud" prompted resignations, combustibility, and discord in the CCLC. The New York office received a torrent of complaints. Most critics blamed Latimer for creating a personal fiefdom "made up mainly of 'yes' men for the secretary [Latimer]." He "played a partisan game," one declared. The CCLC appeared to be in freefall, although Latimer and an ever-shifting group of activists soldiered on. Beneath the familiar story of small-group dysfunction, the New Yorkers learned of something more sinister. "I have long been convinced that the issue is really the issue of the attempted control by infiltration of Communists and fellow traveler elements," Chicagoan John Lapp reported; "Ira Latimer has followed the line ever since I have known him." Not surprisingly, Lapp's letter attracted the Board's attention. While Baldwin regarded the NCACLU and the

CLUM as salvageable organizations, he recognized that "the group in control [in Chicago] will not withdraw." The office feared that the Chicago affiliate was in imminent danger of being overtaken by the Communists.[38]

While the New York staff suspected a takeover attempt, they were not sure what to do next. Until they figured out how to respond, they preferred to keep the story quiet, but Latimer wanted publicity for his accomplishments. One of the foremost African American papers in the country, the *Chicago Defender*, lauded the CCLC for its racial program and chided the national organization for failing to support it. The story said nothing about Latimer's politics, suggesting that the real problem was that headquarters had too little concern for racial discrimination. Another *Defender* story quoted his threat that if the CCLC was disaffiliated, it "might appeal to the Civil Liberties committees in a number of the larger cities of the nation to resign in protest." Latimer carefully set himself up so that any parting of the ways with the ACLU would not hurt his reputation or his future endeavors.[39]

Indeed, he claimed that copies of the *Defender's* laudatory editorial reached CCLC members by "clerical error." The Chicago office secretary called Baldwin personally to assure him that Latimer could not have sent the copies because he was quarantined with scarlet fever. The Board began proceedings against the Chicago group. Latimer and the chairman of the group, Philip Wain, continued to insist that what had happened was a power struggle where the losers appealed to the home office. Wain responded to Baldwin's inquiries with barely veiled hostility, demanding to know the names of those who complained about the affiliate. The CCLC finally saved the national office the trouble of disaffiliating it by leaving in April 1945. Until the end, the Communist accusations stayed out of the press so that what happened looked like a wartime disagreement over strategy. Both opponents wanted the CCLC's civil liberties reputation, but neither wanted the word "Communist" associated with its work.[40]

When the CCLC left the ACLU family, it took with it most Chicago area civil libertarians. Those without faith in Latimer had long since left, but not everyone who remained was a Communist, a fact that confounded national officers. At the point of separation, the CCLC had about 2,000 members and enough income to pay three fund-raisers, a fully functioning structure destined for the CRC. By the time the CRC was up and running, however, Latimer had serious qualms about working with the Party, and the CCLC never fused into the CRC. By 1946 its fortunes had ebbed a bit, but its prestige and activity level—mainly due to the energetic Latimer—still worried the national ACLU and the ACLU's Chicago replacement branch. Latimer's continued success irritated Baldwin, who wanted to take advantage of it. In 1947 he made overtures to Latimer, telling him that "a merger is desirable" in Chicago. What he meant was that Latimer should turn over the CCLC to the ACLU. Whatever his cur-rent politics, Baldwin was not ready to rehabilitate him because he was "a most undependable character, without principle. . . . He ought to get a job in some other field and turn over his lists to us. He does not belong in civil liberties." But Latimer did belong in the field. He earned a law degree and continued to handle civil liber-ties and civil rights cases through the CCLC, at least until his past caught up with him during the McCarthy era. He proved that local groups could function independently, even without the stature of the national ACLU.[41]

The ACLU, meanwhile, rushed to minimize the consequences of the break. The national office oversaw the creation of a new Chi-cago branch. In the shadow of the larger CCLC, the Chicago divi-sion of the ACLU needed a "substantially different" arrangement with headquarters, especially financially. Its dependencies made a distinct identity hard to establish. Its leaders were so quick to distance themselves from the CCLC and so determined to create internal mechanisms to "prevent . . . infiltration" by the Commu-nists that they had almost no affirmative program. To outsiders, it seemed "an emasculated organization with no guts," its board "weak" and its profile bland. A number of local activists hedged their bets, stayed in the CCLC, and joined the new ACLU affiliate, even though Union headquarters told them the CCLC "is an out and out Communist organization."[42] The experience was so overlaid with controversial politics that no one noticed another lesson to be drawn from the new Chicago Division ACLU: that the national organization could not create successful affiliates. Latimer, whatever the New York Board thought of him, was popular in Chicago because he worked hard, and many local people took his civil liberties commitments at face value rather than judge him on his loyalty to ACLU headquarters. Affiliates built from the bottom up, not the top down, and local activists did not presume to question one another's motives. Thus they were incompatible with the national organization, which never trusted or respected most of the branch personnel.

While the rebellious behavior of big branches like those in San Francisco or Chicago consumed considerable national energy at an already trying time, the smaller problems of smaller branches merely annoyed overworked staffers in New York. They assumed that foolish local workers could no more stay organized than they could handle wartime challenges. Each time the St. Paul branch revived, the national office responded not with encouragement but with exasperation. In 1942 an FBI agent visited and asked for membership lists. A frantic local activist refused but then became "frankly worried about the matter. It does not seem to me that in times like these we should set ourselves against the FBI." Baldwin contacted the FBI, happily accepting the bureau's explanation that the matter was "a 'tempest in a teapot.'" The next year another St. Paul volunteer wrote to New York, implying some kind of potential takeover by Communists, a word that usually had an impact at headquarters, but not when the stakes were so small. Baldwin left the problem to Lucille Milner to sort out. In 1945 the St. Paul branch again fought to keep outsiders at bay and "struggl[ed] with constitution and by-laws which would enable this group to conform to the national rules and regulations." Just how small could an affiliate be? they wondered, which finally prompted Milner to wonder why there even needed to be an affiliate in St. Paul. Milner's annoyed question suggested how low a priority branch building was at the conflict-wracked ACLU headquarters.[43]

By the end of the war, the national ACLU's relations with its affiliates were in disarray. Branches rejected some of the national organization's policies, most of its methods, and especially its attitude. Local activists worked hard during the war and earned little respect in return. Directors complained about inaction but did not reward initiative. The overburdened staff took out their resentments on local workers. Roger Baldwin, struggling to hold control in New York, exerted his lost authority over the branches. Yet lacking sufficient money or unity on war-related cases, the national ACLU had to rely on its branches to accomplish some of its work. Branch officers enjoyed the increased responsibility but hated the extra restrictions. Minus the deep cleavages that slowed their national counterpart, local boards moved with confidence and determination. It is hardly surprising that so many frustrated national officers resented their unity and accomplishments.

During the war, the largest affiliates outgrew the New Yorkers' condescending attitude. They demonstrated the means and ability to handle big wartime cases. War challenged them. In the 1930s, only local controversies kept them active. During the war years, without much encouragement, many became functional and cohesive units. Their identities depended little on the national ACLU. "I think that your Board," Edward Parsons told Holmes and Baldwin in 1943, "must make up its mind whether it really values the work that we are trying to do out here . . . more than it does the assertion of authority."[44] The war weakened the national organization's sense of purpose and forward momentum, but it had quite the opposite impact on the branches.

NOTHING ACCOMPLISHED, NOTHING DONE

The National ACLU after World War II

In 1947 Roger Baldwin met with J. Parnell Thomas, head of HUAC, to make sure the committee would raise no objections if Baldwin accepted Douglas MacArthur's invitation to consult on civil liberties in postwar Japan. The Communist Party press leaked the story, which came as news to many directors. The story reported how one Board member claimed to know all about the meeting, while another, Corliss Lamont, was "openly incredulous" to learn that Baldwin talked to Thomas. The story generated a crisis at ACLU headquarters. Was it worth fighting with the Communists or better to ignore the story? Was it a problem that some Board members knew about the meeting and others did not? And was Lamont's reaction reason, as one director said, for the Union to "dispense with him?"[1] Gone were the days when the ACLU directors were comfortable with difference. A chilly politeness settled over the postwar boardroom, leaving the organization ill-served during yet another period of crisis. Without consensus, it was very difficult for the organization to move forward.

The Union's postwar agenda was straightforward and daunting: aid African Americans and organized labor and help new governments in defeated countries shape their civil liberties policies.[2] Gone, directors hoped, were the crippling wartime differences between absolutists and relativists. Peace offered the hope of mending fences internally and with the Union's liberal constituency. No sooner had the war ended, though, than the perennially thorny matter of free speech rights for fascists again brought the Union some bad publicity. In 1946 Gerald L. K. Smith went on a national speaking tour, relying on the ACLU to protect his access to public halls. It was not a popular action, and the fact that "you [the ACLU] seem so proud of it" irritated a lot of American liberals. Baldwin met with Smith to discuss strategy. "This isn't true, is it?" one shocked member asked. He understood "the principle" of protecting everyone's rights but wished the Union would not "go out of its way" for Smith. Others saw no reason why the Union had to help distasteful people, and one veteran said that he could not belong to an organization that "aid[ed] Fascist groups." Several other members resigned as well.[3]

Union refugees had any number of rival options, demonstrating that civil liberties remained "chic," even if no two groups seemed to define them exactly the same way. Among the competitors was a new generation of fronts such as the Mobilization for Democracy and the CRC, groups with no obligation to defend fascists. ACLU directors had good reason to be concerned about their influence, for the CPUSA reached its numerical peak during the war, and immediately afterward there was no hint that it would decline quickly. Their obsession with one front, the CRC, however, bordered on irrationality. The CRC fused three older fronts: the ILD, the National Negro Congress, and the National Federation for Constitutional Liberties. It emphasized civil rights, something the Union generally left to the NAACP, so some ACLU officers were already sensitive about its mission. Adding to their concerns, four of the CRC's founders were also four of the ACLU's most famous dropouts: Elizabeth Gurley Flynn, Harry Ward, Leo Gallagher, and Ira Latimer. The ACLU staff gathered information about the CRC with the zeal of spies. They sent observers to its founding convention and composed "confidential report[s]" about members. They contacted ACLU members who joined it, warning them that it was "embarrassing" for them to be "identified with a movement which takes a contrary view of civil liberties."[4]

While the CRC clearly vexed the national office, some members wondered what all the fuss was about. Arthur Schlesinger examined material Roger Baldwin sent him about the group and found "no evidence . . . that the Congress is operating on different principles from those of the ACLU." Baldwin dispatched a series of letters to joint ACLU and CRC members warning them about the CRC's Communist connections. The warning convinced some, but not all, to resign from the new front. Carey McWilliams, whom Baldwin characterized as "one of the best in the country" on racial matters, saw no contradiction to serving on the ACLU's National Committee and similar CRC boards. Charles Houston, by contrast, chose the CRC over the ACLU, which left the Union without one of its most visible African American leaders, another kind of embarrassment. Expecting—finally—to have more influence, Union directors were disappointed when others did not agree with their point of view.[5]

The Union's point of view, though, was confused. It had been a long time since the ACLU held a single perspective on civil liberties. In the late 1930s, the Union had mingled New Dealism with a pro-Front attitude. During the war years, it struggled to accommodate relativist and absolutist factions. The postwar divisions appeared milder, as the dominant boardroom force was anticommunism. Its champions included John Haynes Holmes, Norman Thomas, William L. White, Morris Ernst, Varian Fry, and Merlyn Pitzele. Its advocates ran a political gamut. Holmes and Thomas were socialists; the others ranged from liberal Ernst to legal director Clifford Forster, whom Baldwin described as "very right wing." But anticommunism was not so simple a force as it initially appeared.[6]

In the Union, as in the country, there were two versions of anticommunism. The more powerful was liberal, epitomized by Ernst.

The Union's liberal anticommunists "attempted to temper liberalism with Cold War 'realism.'" It was a quick and easy jump from liberals' wartime compromises of fascists' civil liberties to postwar anticommunism. Already conditioned to see fascists as a threat to America's way of life, liberals transferred their fears onto another group of "totalitarians" during the cold war: Communists. The ACLU served the liberal anticommunist ideology by providing legitimacy for its civil liberties compromises and helping it define its boundaries. Thus, liberal anticommunists had some clout. The ACLU's other anticommunist faction was not so influential. Its members were angry and suspicious and less cautious about observing legal niceties, since they believed that the Communists had already infiltrated American institutions. In the ACLU, Norman Thomas was their leader. The postwar ACLU Board was overwhelmingly anticommunist, but not all anticommunism was the same. The liberal anticommunist Board majority and the extreme anticommunist minority did not always get along.[7]

The presence of neither faction at the top reflected who was in the Union's ranks. Postwar membership grew slowly, and while there was a large jump in annual income between 1944 and 1945 (from $35,133 to $50,132), the money leveled off thereafter. The Union's membership was changing. Some liberals left during wartime, unhappy with the group's civil liberties absolutism. Others let their memberships lapse after the war. In many cases what motivated them was fear. It was safer to avoid potentially embarrassing entanglements with a group with a seemingly radical past, especially since groups like the American Legion raised a regular fuss about the Union's politics. Progressives, those onetime noncommunist supporters of the People's Front, were perhaps better recruitment possibilities, sharing a commitment to dissenters' rights and having long since signed all the petitions that might come back to haunt them. But the anticommunists at headquarters continued to market the organization toward liberals and seemed uninterested in recruiting those who were more left wing. The same attitudes did not prevail in the branches, which eagerly recruited and welcomed a more politically diverse membership. Officers suspected that the complexion of the organization they so zealously guarded was changing and sometimes acted to introduce correctives, but they tended to live in a state of denial about what the Union's grass roots had become.

Baldwin's administrative skills were unequal to these postwar complications. During wartime, he taxed his staff's patience. After the war, working conditions did not improve. The Union paid so badly that it had trouble attracting decent help. If the wages did not drive off employees, then Baldwin did. One secretary thought he was "a totally authoritarian person" used to getting his way. He was so frugal that staff strikes threatened. Holmes had to negotiate around Baldwin, ostensibly "to protect and preserve Roger's morale," but really to keep him from antagonizing workers. Samuel Walker noted that he "never liked mundane administrative work" and was incapable of running the type of organization the Union was becoming. Ernst recalled that while Baldwin was dictatorial, he ran the ACLU so well "that no one minded." That might have been true in the 1930s, but younger directors lacked personal loyalty to him and were more aware of his bureaucratic failings. Affiliate leaders resented his abuses of power. He could no longer skate by on his charm. At Douglas MacArthur's invitation, he served as civil liberties consultant to Japan and Korea early in 1947. The next year the Department of War invited him to tour Germany.[8]

With its dominant personality in the office only intermittently, the group had no one to shepherd it through the challenging array of postwar civil liberties matters or broker compromises between competing anticommunist factions. To those used to working in the business world, the ACLU boardroom was a frustration or, as former Federal Communications Commission head James L. Fly thought, chaos. "I am more than casually concerned with the procedure at our Board of Directors meetings," he told Holmes in 1946. "There is no advance agenda and virtually no information circulated prior to meetings." Fly raised the same complaints the next year, since nothing changed, but this time he added that the staff was overworked and underpaid. "Whatever it costs to cure this situation we ought to meet head on," he advised. By 1949 even cofounder Holmes saw the flaws. The Board was divided, so whenever controversy arose, "we pass it over to a committee for consideration and report" and then "tear it [the report] to pieces and either lay the whole business on the table or order it back for further consideration." The frustration of "nothing accomplished, nothing done" lowered morale and gave outsiders the impression that the Union waffled about important matters.[9]

Rather than tackle the differences head-on, Baldwin tried bureaucratic remedies. In 1947 the Board and National Committee refreshed itself with younger nominees because "we have too many over 70."[10] Younger members did not easily tolerate his style. Bureaucratic remedies—not that there were many of them—also did not get to the heart of the problem. Strong anticommunist directors put pressure on the organization to be more publicly anticommunist. Baldwin sympathized with them and, more importantly, feared their extremism and believed their occasional resignation threats. So he continued to avoid conflict, passing it on to committees, editing and re-editing statements of policy, and accomplishing little.

The Board could not agree, for example, on a consistent policy on the rights of Communist teachers. Several state legislatures banned them from the classroom, and many investigated teachers' politics. Most of the ACLU's Academic Freedom Committee did not believe CPUSA membership automatically constituted unfitness to be a teacher. Norman Thomas did, though, and his intransigence encumbered the Union. While attending only two of six committee meetings, he still managed to reject virtually any statement the committee produced. He peppered directors with statements, proposals, and referenda. In response, the committee composed interim statement after interim statement, disappointing members, who complained about "the more ardent anti-Communists on the Board" and the Union's "retreat" on Communist teachers. Finally, the Union's publicity director suggested that the Academic Freedom Committee should pull itself together, take a stand, and stick with it.[11]

The Union's response to President Harry Truman's Loyalty Program was similarly disordered. Intimidated by the Republican congress, Truman announced early in 1947 that the government would assess the loyalty of all federal employees. The program lacked, as historian Alonzo Hamby noted, "elementary procedural safeguards," which should have generated a prompt and critical Union response. Instead, directors appointed a committee to examine the program's provisions. The committee made suggestions to improve the program endorsed by the Board and sent to the attorney general. When affiliates weighed in with their consultative opinions, the NCACLU suggested that the organization should "come out far more vigorously against the President's order" rather than offer correctives to a flawed program. The committee redrafted its statement without incorporating the branch's suggestion. Still, a different configuration of directors voting on a different day turned it down. Frustrated, the committee composed four policy alternatives from which directors and the National Committee might pick. No sooner had the office tallied those votes than the Northern and Southern California groups complained that they had not been asked for their preferences. This precipitated another round of voting and new alternatives. It took the ACLU more than a year to establish its official policy on the Loyalty Program. Seven months later, the Board redrafted it. Ironically, all the bickering was over details, for as Baldwin later recalled, "We did not, as we should have, challenge the concept of 'loyalty.'"[12]

Morris Ernst's draft memo on loyalty confirmed that liberal anticommunists considered the Loyalty Program "unfortunate but necessary." "The President's order," he wrote, ". . . was an important and valuable stop-gap to prevent disastrous hysterical legislation contemplated by the Republicans." Ernst wanted to influence government, which meant following its lead. He forwarded a copy of his memo to the Justice Department, asking "if you think I am screwy on any angles" and telling his contact to "let Tom [Clark, Truman's attorney general] know that if I can be helpful . . . he should not hesitate to call on me." The ACLU tried to work with Clark to protect the rights of those investigated, via directors with government connections. James L. Fly got Clark to "agree . . . to consider" modifications to the program. Onetime Justice Department officer Edward Ennis accompanied Clark to a meeting with the assistant director of the FBI to discuss "procedure to be followed in loyalty investigations."[13] During World War II, working with government reflected faith in Roosevelt's goals and the lofty ideal of making the world a better place. In the late 1940s, Union leaders let go of that idealism so that they could prevent the worst from happening. It was a choice symptomatic of the Union's less confrontational, pragmatic liberal style.

No longer did ACLU attorneys head out into the streets to challenge laws; during the loyalty debates, they wanted to be impartial civil liberties experts. They saw themselves on the side of the government, pressing to improve policies others worked out and then educating the public about their necessity. Some also wanted to advise individuals called before the loyalty boards. Baldwin considered opening a branch office in Washington, D.C., to deal exclusively with loyalty appeals. Legal director Cliff Forster lobbied hard for an office, a full-time secretary, a telephone, and a typewriter, all for $35 a week, and assured the Board that this setup could handle up to 200 loyalty-related complaints and appeals. But while Forster considered such work "our main function," federal employees seemed reluctant to consult with an organization that already accepted the necessity of loyalty screenings. The ACLU did, however, establish itself as an expert of sorts. Asked by one official of the American Russian Institute how his agency came to be placed on the government's list of subversive organizations, Attorney General Clark is said to have explained that "Roger Baldwin tells us" which groups deserved such designations and which did not.[14]

The ACLU's response to the contempt of Congress charges against the Hollywood Ten was also hesitant and confused. The Ten were screenwriters and directors subpoenaed by HUAC to answer questions about their affiliations and colleagues. One by one, they declined to tell the committee whether or not they were Communists, citing their First Amendment right to free associations. After the Ten received contempt citations, the Board consulted its Lawyers Committee, which divided over what to do. Two members recommended intervention, since HUAC "had not established the relevance of the question to the inquiry," but the third, Ernst, opposed joining the fight. The Board approved the "general principle" of the majority report but wanted expert information from the lawyers first. Several months later, directors finally voted to file an amicus brief, a decisive action that lasted all of a minute as seven already-mustered votes forced a referendum. Eventually the Union filed the brief, but the decision-making process was so slow and reluctant that the organization squandered its influence.[15]

The same timidity characterized the Union's reaction to the postwar trials of Communist Party leaders charged under the Smith Act. The Smith Act made it a crime to teach or advocate the overthrow of the government. When Congress passed it in 1940, a Union representative testified against it, arguing that it violated the Supreme Court's own clear-and-present-danger standard. During the war, the Union filed an amicus brief on behalf of the Trotskyists first charged under the law, again arguing that the government failed to prove that their doctrine posed a clear and present danger. After the war, as the government used the act against Communist leaders, the Union maintained its opposition to the act in theory but reacted "somewhat evasively" to the actual cases. It did nothing following the first round of trials (1948), "because no valid civil liberties issue is involved." The second round (1951) brought a close vote rejecting a motion to ask the attorney general "not to bring any further prosecutions under the Smith Act." Nervous about how it might appear if the Union defended Communists and challenged the Justice Department and the Supreme Court, directors instructed the staff "not to issue any statements." The staff consulted the liberal anticommunist organization Americans for Democratic Action, perhaps checking to see how the Union's nonposition measured up. The organization's officers advised them that it was "more realistic" to work to limit the Smith Act than to try to repeal it. Reassured that they fit into the liberal mainstream, officers did little more for Communist defendants. When the Court finally struck down the act in the 1957 Yates case, the ACLU filed an amicus brief, but the SCACLU's A. L. Wirin, acting privately, argued the case. Directors could not even agree that Party picketing outside the courtroom was a form of free speech. Congress contemplated outlawing the picketing, and the Board deadlocked, forcing the issue to a referendum that resulted in a corporate position in support of penalties for picketing. The Union's stance on the Smith Act trials was neither consistent nor strong.[16]

In other cases involving Communists, directors were equally noncommittal. Despite many legal irregularities, the Board maintained there were no civil liberties issues involved in the trial of Julius and Ethel Rosenberg, Party members convicted in 1951 of passing atomic secrets to the Soviets. Even after the Rosenbergs' counsel specifically asked the Union to support the commutation of the couple's death sentences, directors refused to get involved. One staff member explained that there was no evidence that they were treated unequally, since there had never been a crime "comparable to the vastness and scale" of theirs. Pressure from the Chicago, Cleveland, and Southern California branches produced a report but no action. The left-wing press criticized the Union's silence, and affiliates wanted the Board to act. The Chicago Division inquired whether it had "the authority to take a stand contrary to national policy," while the New Haven affiliate went ahead and petitioned Truman "to commute the death sentence." The Board belatedly concluded that its silence was a public relations problem, so it publicly explained its inaction and privately scolded affiliates for acting on their own. But what the Board thought of as "not . . . appeas[ing] critics or volunteer[ing] a position demanded by many pressures brought to bear to get us to condemn the trial" others saw as being afraid to stand behind its principles.[17]

In instance after instance the Union failed to articulate a clear civil liberties line. It went back and forth on the deportation of Australian-born union leader and presumed Communist Harry Bridges. It took "no action" on the government's denial of a passport to Paul Robeson and concluded that a passport "is not an inalienable right." The Union joined other liberals in opposing the Mundt-Nixon bill, which required registration of all Communists and barred them from government employment, although Ernst noted that it "wisely adopts the basic philosophy of publicity and disclosure."[18] Directors fought for three months over the emergency detention provisions in the 1950 McCarran Act. Edward Ennis warned his fellow directors to be careful before settling on a policy. They could oppose a "theoretically defensible program," he said, or "work for its practical improvement." The Board tried to do both, although its willingness "to work with the appropriate governmental bodies to secure harmony" between security and civil liberties sometimes obscured its opposition to the law. The debate over whether Communists' "secret advocacy" constituted a clear and present danger was so convoluted that trained attorney Elmer Rice could make no sense of it. The first generation of ACLU officers tilted at windmills. The second generation seemed more concerned about being realistic and fitting into the liberal mainstream.[19]

Even when the Union had a consensus issue, officers' sense that anticommunism was a realistic response to the modern world muddled its position. The Board unanimously agreed that the Mundt-Nixon bill was unconstitutional. Director Walter Gellhorn recommended that the group mount "an active, aggressive campaign to mobilize public sentiment" against it. Ernst, however, argued "that the ACLU does not merely come out against the bill. We must admit that there is a problem facing the nation." He characterized the bill's authors, Richard Nixon and Karl Mundt, positively, as individuals who "have no evil purposes and are honest and genuinely concerned with the communist problem." Equally obsequious to Republicans and Democrats, he kept up a chatty correspondence with Nixon and offered him the use of his Nantucket house. Cliff Forster believed that working with Nixon would make a bad bill better. Nixon, he explained, "is not a completely unreasonable fellow" and just needed to be jollied along. Forster thought Ernst "the one to do it." Ultimately, the Union played its preferred role as expert, sending its officers to Congress to testify against the bill. Osmond Fraenkel spoke before the Senate Judiciary Committee, and Ernst and Arthur Garfield Hays testified before HUAC. There Hays got into a public tangle with Nixon, who asked him to reconcile the ACLU's opposition to the bill with its 1940 resolution. "We thought people who were on the board should have the same ideas we had," Hays explained, to which Nixon replied, "that is the way we feel."[20]

Some Board members also advocated not the abolition of HUAC but for Union influence "from the inside" to make its methods fairer. Ernst talked to Nixon, and Holmes requested an informal meeting "for a discussion on or off-the-record." Ernst circulated proposed guidelines the committee might follow, but Hays objected to their basic tolerance of committee methods. Another ACLU attorney thought current HUAC practices too outrageous to be reformed, "simply inconceivable." The Board dropped the matter, but HUAC approached the group the next year to see if it wanted to consult on methods. The idea "that the procedures of the Committee be IMPROVED—to make it MORE effective" outraged one member. "I consider it highly significant that the ACLU Administration has conspicuously refrained from presenting this . . . to the actual membership for voting."[21]

The Union's "very equivocal positions" disappointed members. Many disliked its reactive approach, with its "apparent lack of campaigns and cases undertaken by the ACLU on its own initiative." Members felt disengaged as experts worked invisibly within the halls of government. During the postwar years, the Union avoided the direct action of its early days or the big constitutional challenges of the war years. Instead of defining civil liberties law, it worked to refine it with amicus curae briefs, many of which were debated for months. Baldwin noted the change of strategy from "direct challenges" to "the higher courts and the necessary legal work in them." One of his successors, Aryeh Neier, thought the change of tactics related to the Board's divisions, focusing directors on specific "procedural" questions and glossing over broader philosophical differences. The 1953 annual report boasted of the Union's new style, applauding its amicus briefs, its coordination with the government, and its "general education of public opinion."[22]

Yet the style was not affirmative so much as defensive, a classically liberal anticommunist response. Directors reacted to the "retreat of reputed civil libertarians" with panic, scrambling to follow rather than lead the crowd. "We are seeing this more and more on our own Board," a staff member noted.[23] Government became more specialized. The cold war required compartmentalization and secrecy. The ACLU could not keep up. Never had the partnership between the ACLU and the federal bureaucracy been an equal one. Now the scales tipped even more in the government's favor. Union officers concluded that they could have more impact if they were realistic about what the group could achieve, accepting the government's limits. To the lawyers, businessmen, and other corporate professionals who now peopled the ACLU's national boards, getting along made sense. But the strategy was unsatisfying to the Union's membership, who relished dramatic challenges and clear-cut positions. Many complained that "the American Civil Liberties Union has lost its guts." Between 1949 and 1950, there was a 10 percent membership turnover, unexpected enough to merit Board comment.[24]

One disgruntled civil libertarian suggested that the group's membership fluctuations might be related to its "failure to keep members 'sold.'" Members did seem to miss the days when the Union acted quickly and decisively, leading rather than following the government's cues. Many wearied of the Board's anticommunist obsession. They got tired of the staff's constant reiteration of the 1940 resolution. They were not impressed that in 1950 the office began to include mention of "our opposition to Communism" on legal briefs. "I feel the ACLU is losing ground," one member explained. Some thought such statements were unseemly coming from a civil liberties organization, but Norman Thomas insisted that "there is nothing gratuitous in our insisting that we are not communists." To many Union members, though, there *was* something unseemly about so much anticommunism.[25]

To answer such complaints and to be more proactive, in 1952 the Board commissioned a book "to be written by Merle Miller" investigating blacklisting. Blacklisting of entertainment industry personnel followed HUAC's 1947 Hollywood hearings. The movie studios and radio and television production companies would not employ anyone identified as a current or past member of the CPUSA. The idea for the book emerged from Board discussions about actress Jean Muir, who had been dropped from her role in the television series *The Aldrich Family* because of her past associations. Directors thought the matter "a troublesome business that is likely to spread." Opposing censorship had always been a popular position with members, so the undertaking offered the potential for the Union to reclaim a more assertive role. As finally published, *The Judges and the Judged* disappointed many directors, who thought its tone "too staccato" and its presentation "unorganized." Still, the Union released it with fanfare, hoping to capitalize on liberal distaste for stifling creative endeavors.[26]

Instead, the book plunged the group into more controversy by dividing anticommunist factions. Extreme anticommunist director Merlyn Pitzele wrote a critical review of the book in the anticommunist journal the *New Leader*; the review mentioned the ACLU twenty-two times and the book only eight. "It is," Corliss Lamont concluded, "an attack not on Miller but on us." Liberal anticommunists put a premium on decorum and getting along, but Pitzele had other priorities. "The flavor of this book was unmistakable," he told a member of the American Legion, so he felt no obligation to abide by the policy of not speaking ill of the Union publicly, a policy formally established, ironically, after Elizabeth Gurley Flynn took her organizational complaints to the *New Masses*. Pitzele's "press rampage" got the Board's attention. Directors convened the "longest board meeting (daytime) I ever attended," Pitzele noted, and censured him for making "grossly improper" attacks on the group. He offered only a halfhearted apology, saying he was "genuinely sorry to confront honored and respected colleagues" but would take nothing back until proven "substantively" wrong. He remained unrepentant, telling Norman Thomas that "I have learned [from the experience] to be more persistent within the ACLU."[27]

Directors followed up Pitzele's accusations but found that only a few "had some merit." Overall, they were "satisfied that the contents and conclusions of the book . . . are not the product of bias or design." They asked Miller to correct his errors and voted to continue sponsoring the book. But afraid that others would challenge the organization for not being anticommunist enough, directors discouraged the staff from promoting the work. Having spent time and money to produce what they imagined would be a landmark text, Board members lacked the conviction to stand behind it. This the Union's publicist called "public relations at its most inept," a defense that "would not settle anyone's doubts." The Pitzele matter finally broke through the Union's illusion of consensus, as extreme anticommunists, like Pitzele, learned to be more persistent.[28]

A few months later, strong anticommunist Board members forced the organization to endorse Pitzele as they did Miller. Both men faced reelection in 1953. Miller rarely attended meetings, and the Nominating Committee did not recommend renewing his nomination. After Pitzele's attack, however, directors decided to do so and renominated him by a single vote. Miller was reelected, but Pitzele was "just over the line," thirteenth in contention for twelve positions. Thomas lobbied hard to keep him on the Board. He had, Thomas argued, "contacts with important groups . . . in our American community" that were politically useful, and to drop him at that point would give the book fight "inflated importance." The Board grudgingly expanded to accommodate him, even though some directors thought it was a capitulation, "a mistake . . . motivated largely by fear that there would be blasts in the *New Leader* if MP were not elected." Already a public relations disaster, the Pitzele matter also made the ACLU boardroom a more contentious place.[29]

Pitzele was not a popular director, and his aggressiveness made consensus all the more difficult to find. He lacked the liberal anticommunists' discretion. While other directors tiptoed carefully around him, he showed no such restraint around the last remaining leftist on the Board, Corliss Lamont. Lamont was "a strange case," a non-Communist whose politics were still pro-Soviet. As Baldwin noted, "We have never been able to nail him down to a violation of our principles," although not from lack of trying. "We have even gone so far as to seek information from experts on Communist affiliation [the FBI, according to Lamont]," one staff member explained, "and we have been reassured that Corliss Lamont is not a member of the Communist Party." Yet Lamont's very presence tormented strong anticommunist directors.[30]

He "left a bad taste in many mouths" and seemed, thereby, to detract from the Union's reputation. Some tried repeatedly to use the 1940 resolution against him. Other directors, though, judged him by his long commitment to civil liberties and not his left-wing politics. John Haynes Holmes, for instance, was "unwilling to have Corliss singled out" on suspicion of pro-Communist partisanship. When the 1948 Nominating Committee asked Lamont and no one else "about his status under the Resolution," Holmes met with him, and he "demonstrated in detail that he did not come within the terms of the 1940 Resolution." Lamont received the second-highest number of votes that year among nominees for two-year terms, which suggests that his reputation was not as tarnished by his politics as Pitzele's was. Still, Lamont's detractors conceded nothing. They "have hurled personal, provocative and sometimes insulting remarks in my direction at Board meetings," he complained. Such behaviors "increase[d] tension and waste[d] the time of the Board."[31]

The reaction to Lamont revealed the transitional nature of the ACLU board. He was part of the older generation, whereas Pitzele had joined the Board only after the war. Holmes and Lamont had a shared history, one that gave Holmes a good sense of his commitment to the Union. They had lived through disagreements and survived; they expected to do so again. Newer directors had no such personal histories and could only judge one another—and their elders—by their politics, especially once the Board became so formal and polite. The 1940 resolution, Lamont pointed out, encouraged that sort of judgment by providing a standard that overwhelmed other, more personal considerations.[32] One of the reasons Holmes found it easy to tolerate Lamont was that they were both emotional and moralistic. Neither fit in so well in a boardroom increasingly dominated by detachment and professionalism. They felt their politics without any concerns for image or reputation.

The same was true of Pitzele and the other strong anticommunists. They rejected the liberal anticommunist behavior code, believing that any failure to stand up for one's belief was a capitulation to the Communists. Already driven to act, their minority status on the ACLU Board made provocative action and constant pressure necessary. There was no other way to break through the inoffensive liberal anticommunist facade. Intimidation and a knack for working the system were their strong suits. Norman Thomas knew just when to threaten to resign, how best to quietly slip a piece of private boardroom business to the anticommunist press, and how many times one could safely reopen a closed matter. He and Holmes benefited, like Lamont did, from their status as longtime officers with more prestige than younger directors. Their methods, however, were a vestige of older radical politics and, particularly, old Socialist-Communist fights and inimical to the Board's current working style.

Younger directors preferred a formal boardroom. There were no more cozy meetings at Norman Thomas's house with luncheon served by Mrs. Thomas.[33] Professionals did not confront one another directly. Polite directors avoided confrontation or debated symbolic small matters. They appointed committees to deal with disputed matters. Those committees broke controversy into manageable pieces, as reports or statements whose wording could be debated, approved, or sent back to be rewritten. Referenda allowed nervous directors to gain reinforcement from the notoriously uncommitted National Committee, which rubber-stamped most of their work. But with directors conditioned to expect so much bureaucracy, extreme anticommunists with no actual majority could prevail, at least temporarily. All it took was persistence and the right attendance pattern at a Monday meeting. Creating discomfort and planting just a hint of doubt served strong anticommunists well. By the spring of 1947, the Board had to add meetings and postpone agenda items. By December, corrections to minutes took up half a page. Someone scrutinized every vote, forcing reevaluation of nearly every important matter. Finally, in despair, Baldwin created a Policy Committee "in place of the many special Board committees recently appointed."[34] But the Policy Committee could only expedite matters so much and could not erase the conflict masked by the bureaucracy.

Baldwin foundered in the less personal, conflict-ridden ACLU. He himself might subscribe to the dominant anticommunist ideology but not to the new liberal working style. He preferred the Union "small, elite, just large enough to finance the operations that [the] Board was interested in," Eason Monroe of the SCACLU recalled. Although directors "adored" him, they trusted him less and less. World War II was a turning point for him, a moment when he lost the respect of at least some of his colleagues. Once he lost that admiration, his management flaws—his "short leash and tight budget"—became more obvious.[35] He did not agree with affirmative liberal plans to enroll more members, spend more money, or popularize civil liberties still further. Since Baldwin lacked legal training, professionals took over many of the most compelling aspects of his job, leaving him to oversee routine, which bored him. While he was in Japan, Korea, and Germany, the Union managed without him. He returned expecting to resume his leadership role but found the Board less accepting of his style and that he himself was less patient with the bureaucracy.

Inertia reigned at headquarters. The Union was neither one kind of organization nor the other. Baldwin refused to consider changes, and directors were afraid to, preferring the precarious status quo to open battles. Yet in the postwar world, any organization that aspired to influence liberal power brokers needed money and members. Under Baldwin, the Union lacked the resources other liberal groups had. Both the NAACP and Americans for Democratic Action had many more affiliates, much larger memberships, and bigger budgets. The Union had branches, but officers saw them as liabilities rather than assets. Branch officers were certainly amenable to contributing more. Most, in fact, already believed they did a lot of the civil liberties grunt work without any recognition or appreciation for their efforts. Affiliates were as open to change as directors were closed. They wanted more than the advisory vote granted them in 1944, especially since it was "sometimes overlooked," Edward Allen of the Iowa Civil Liberties Union noted; sometimes "totally disregarded," A. A. Heist seconded; and according to Ernest Besig, often circumvented.[36]

Affiliates pressed their agenda after the staff proved Allen's, Heist's, and Besig's complaints by forgetting to consult the branches on three 1947 policy statements. Baldwin acknowledged that it was the office's fault but revealed that there was no process in place "for the mechanical handling of notices to consultants." Considering how restive local boards were by this point, he might have been contrite about the lapse, but he was positively brazen, intimating that it was up to local boards to ask to be consulted. He continued to insist that "local committees are *advising* and carry weight in close votes." His reaction was so cavalier that he united the two often-feuding California branches to confront the national ACLU over governance.[37]

Besig of the NCACLU and Heist of the SCACLU called for a conference to "reconsider the Union's organization and its By Laws." They envisioned a constitution-drafting body; Baldwin permitted a "Quaker style" meeting with no formal voting. Besig recognized that he was being conned. "I get the impression," he wrote Baldwin, ". . . that the Conference is being held to satisfy critics of the California branches, but that it will be run in such a fashion that little, if anything, of importance can be discussed." Baldwin, meanwhile, told another local officer that the Union was incorporated in the state of New York and "I don't think under the law we could provide for control by local affiliates." The proposed conference allotted one session to affiliate relations, which Besig regarded as "wasting my time." "Apparently," he concluded, "the national office doesn't have to[o] strong a desire to settle some of the differences between us." Six weeks before the meeting was to take place, the office canceled it.[38]

At stake was nothing less than the Union's postwar program. The Board was anticommunist; most branches were not, and directors were willing to do almost anything to keep "the mavericks . . . [from] revers[ing] their policy." Frightened by the prospect of losing authority and control, they resurrected the 1940 resolution. When a group from Queens, New York, petitioned for affiliation in 1948, the Board extended the measure to all new branches and asked existing ones about their "acceptance of the principle." Directors explained that "the current debate on the rights of Communists has necessarily raised the question of the Civil Liberties Union's relation to Communism. Some critics still identify us as special pleaders because of alleged sympathy with Communists." But it was not really public relations that motivated directors so much as their need to superimpose their authority on the "divergent policies of locals."[39]

The smaller affiliates saw no sinister intent in directors' action. "We had assumed that the 1940 Resolution . . . applied to our Branch," reported Alfred Lee of Detroit, whose affiliate cast its advisory votes approving the idea. The Pittsburgh branch did likewise, save for two votes, one from someone "generally reputed to be a member of the Communist Party." "No one has ever tried to infiltrate us," noted the secretary of the Erie County, New York, affiliate, which puzzled over the matter before approving it. The Chicago Division already had an informal policy blocking Communists, although the affiliate worried about formalizing it. The unofficial Atlanta group voted twelve to eleven in favor, hardly a ringing endorsement, but enough to put it in the yes column. Only four affiliates rejected the 1940 resolution, but they included the three biggest—the CLUM, the NCACLU, and the SCACLU—and in each case the opposition was substantial. The Board noted their disapproval but "agreed that any departure from [the Resolution] . . . in the future by an affiliate or its officers shall be grounds for action by the national body in order to maintain through the Union's organization a common standard." This was *imposing . . . [the Resolution] upon our affiliates.*"[40]

The larger affiliates, unlike the smaller ones, raised as much fuss as they could. "Do Roger and the national office want to get hung up on an acrimonious and fruitless debate concerning the resolution of February 5, 1940?" Besig wondered. Apparently they did. At the 1949 annual meeting, affiliates proposed an alternative from the floor, "mak[ing] anyone eligible for office who believed in civil liberties for all." Holmes was "riled" and "Baldwin spoke strongly against it from the public relations point of view." Officers defeated it, and the 1940 resolution became policy in the branches as well as in the national ACLU. "I suspect," Osmond Fraenkel noted wryly, "the affiliates will continue to disregard it."[41]

With some of the affiliates near open rebellion, the Board divided. Since Baldwin exerted only minimal bureaucratic energy, pretending all was well in the ACLU finally became impossible. In 1948 the Board established a committee to examine "the scope of the Union's future activities . . . [and] finances." Baldwin immediately tried to set some parameters for it, ruling out expansion and dismissing affiliate complaints. The committee ignored his resistance, although it offered mainly safe recommendations, such as more staff, more "legislative matters," and more attention to public relations—changes that would turn the ACLU into "a coordinator of civil liberties activities." Yet the committee conceded that these ideas were nothing more than dreams because there was no way to raise sufficient cash to fund them. The budget, a little more than $51,000 in 1948, needed to expand "by about $20,000 if our organization is to live and grow." The committee recommended against turning to the branches for help because the Union "cannot itself become a mass organization . . . or even a moderately large organization" without "compromising its principles and diluting its actions." A "decentralized" network of affiliates required too much "supervision and encouragement." About the only concrete recommendation the committee made was to remove the most immediate obstacle to whatever lay ahead. "Roger Baldwin," their report advised, "should be entirely relieved from (indeed, should be strictly excluded from) executive responsibilities."[42]

Baldwin's departure offered at least the fantasy of endless possibilities but would create "a serious crisis" financially. He took no salary, just expenses, and even though the Board had begun to budget for his replacement, the ACLU did not have the funds necessary to pay someone without another income. Baldwin, moreover, expected to continue to bring home enough money in some figurehead capacity to feel independent of his wealthy wife, which meant that any salary for someone new would have to come on top of what he continued to draw. Morris Ernst wanted to offer his successor $20,000, but Holmes reminded him that a large salary did not guarantee a good leader or someone who would turn the ACLU into "the big popular movement which you visualize." But creating some version of a bigger, more popular movement was precisely what liberal anticommunist directors had in mind, so long as the affiliates had no power and Baldwin was not at its helm.[43]

Still, removing someone so closely associated with civil liberties from office was painful, especially since Baldwin "staged a filibuster . . . trying to stave off the inevitable." He meant a lot to his colleagues, and his departure was bound to unsettle the group. A committee interviewed several candidates but reached "an impasse." Finally the organization settled on their fourth choice, Patrick Murphy Malin, an economist who, like Baldwin, had a wealthy wife. A pacifist and an easterner, Malin was reassuringly familiar to the Union's older elite, but he nicely suited the younger generation's agenda as well. Baldwin thought him "more given to conciliation and compromise than I." Certainly his sense "that he is a servant of the Board and that his responsibility is to carry out its directives" represented a very different leadership style. Malin's strength was Baldwin's weakness: he could plan, routinize, and delegate. He was "an organization man." The difference in the Union was immediate. Within a month after Malin arrived, the office was "washed, painted, some rooms have been rearranged and we really look quite decent." But, "the change is not all physical." Malin had staff members send out Board agendas on time. He did not yell at secretaries. Collective bargaining with the staff was "no longer . . . a shattering experience." One year after Baldwin left, Holmes resigned as Board chair, and directors replaced him with Ernest Angell, a Republican who belonged to both the American Legion and the American Bar Association and served on a New York state loyalty review board. Suddenly, the ACLU had a new leadership.[44]

The new man at the ACLU's helm did not have the prevailing New York attitude about the affiliates. He could not afford to; he needed to get along with them. He lacked Baldwin's authority, and the branches recognized his weakness. When asked to name a representative to a Board-appointed committee to consider reforming affiliate relations, they picked the most stubborn person possible.

"Besig was their spokesman," complained the unlucky committee chair. "He is sharp and crude and frankly was trying to get as much as he could." It was quickly apparent that branches and directors were miles apart in their thinking. Affiliates wanted "a basic change in working relations"; directors preferred the status quo. They politely refrained from criticizing Malin but recoiled from what he set in motion. Baldwin, predictably, found the very idea that affiliates vote "quite unrealistic." Holmes, still chairman of the Board, canceled the old committee and appointed a new one—one without an affiliate voice. At its head he put businessman Richard Childs, whose cautious opinion was that the Union "make no constitutional change we could not undo."[45]

Childs's committee ignored Malin's intentions and honored Holmes's request that they "not make any sacrifice of the prestige and authority of the National body in deference to our local groups." They recommended and the Board approved a measure that "from time to time" directors would invite some affiliates "to name a designated number of its members . . . as additional members of the National Committee." Affiliates in California, Iowa, Chicago, upstate New York, and St. Louis protested that the measures were not enough, would cause "tension and friction," and could be "withdrawn in any year." Finally conceding that they had not been fair, directors suggested that local representatives tell them what they wanted. Deliberately meeting far from New York, in Des Moines, affiliate representatives proposed giving branches two votes each on policy matters, initiatives, and referenda, and they asked for a national organizer to work with them and for national conferences. The Board accepted these demands in theory but moved very slowly to establish the new voting procedure.[46]

Unlike Baldwin, Malin truly believed in "building a national organization." He confessed that while the branches might see him as "a slippery anti-affiliate operator, . . . to practically everybody on the national Board I am an idealistic pro-affiliate martyr!" His interest was sincere, but his object was to bring not just the affiliates but their treasuries into the ACLU's orbit. If directors wanted to dream of a big, influential, powerful ACLU, here was the way to finance it.

Malin proposed eliminating the separate membership system and financially integrating the branches into the national ACLU. Every affiliate member would pay a single membership fee divided between the national and local organizations. His goal was to create "a sense of unity in one organization rather than bastard off-shoots which just happened."[47]

Malin remade affiliate relations, just as he repainted headquarters and reorganized the staff. Armed with a bequest, he sidestepped the Board and in 1951 launched an "experimental program on membership and affiliates" designed to broaden the Union and give affiliates more influence. He designated a single staff member, George Rundquist, as field secretary and designed an elaborate formula to give branches electoral power. When the Board learned of the plan, "there was much acrimony" but little they could do. Board minutes from the period show, however, that directors always identified the plan as Malin's, and the Union's annual report emphasized its experimental nature.[48] In one final dramatic move, the Board waited until the affiliate representatives left the constitutional convention to insert the "sleeping dog" of the 1940 resolution into the new bylaws. Malin blustered; but while the Board claimed to feel "terribly unhappy about the disagreement," they would not take back their action. Affiliate boards from Boston to Los Angeles sent their protests, expressing anger, shock, and betrayal. The resolution, they insisted, highlighted that "we are a timid organization" while expressing a demeaning "affiliates be damned" attitude.[49]

Although launched with plenty of ill feelings on both sides, Malin's experimental program had some immediate successes. Between 1950 and 1953, ACLU membership more than doubled, although much of that was paper growth that occurred as affiliates integrated. Six small new affiliates joined between 1951 and 1953. Income grew, too, from $68,460 in 1950 to $182,839 in 1953. Of course a big, truly national organization also consumed more money. By 1953 the ACLU was spending $210,200, which paid for salaries for more staff members, more publicity, and more activities. A report to the Board said it all; between 1950 and 1955 the Union would spend "more than the total expenditure of the thirty years from 1920 through 1949." Malin dug deep into reserves to expand the group, which forced him to shift his energies to fundraising. Baldwin, watching at a distance, was horrified that the Union had become obsessed with "getting more members, more money, and more staff." He worried that "Pat has let things get out of hand."[50]

One of the more expensive items in the Malin budget was an office in Washington, D.C., to facilitate ACLU legislative influence. Funding it was a "deliberate choice" that took money away from other parts of the Union, particularly "increased litigation." In 1950 the office opened, staffed by Irving Ferman. Ferman's strategy was to establish "working relationships with critically placed personnel and officials in both the legislative and executive branches of government"—"'lunching' relationships" that would give the Union influence. Among those with whom Ferman networked were some individuals, such as Joseph McCarthy, who "could never wisely be reported even to the Board of Directors," according to Morris Ernst. Ernst introduced Ferman to Louis B. Nichols of the FBI. Fervently anticommunist, Ferman believed that "it was largely the responsibility of my office to maintain the contact with the Bureau." Malin must have concurred, but even he did not realize just how much information about the ACLU's inner workings Ferman supplied to J. Edgar Hoover's men; at least once, Ferman advised the FBI to respond to Union protests of bureau excesses by "be[ing] very firm with Malin." A 1977 ACLU report examining the extent to which Freedom of Information Act files revealed connections between the Union and the FBI identified Ferman as "the most intensive, extensive, and secretive" contact in the group.[51]

Ferman's office was not popular, and his work received "considerable criticism." To an older member like Holmes, he symbolized the unwise expansion of the ACLU and an "unprofitable business" at that. Most branch officers thought the whole strategy was wrong. The anticommunist liberals at the Union's helm, though, tolerated Ferman because he represented part of their organizational vision. As the Union lost its radical edge, and as it competed in an "overspecialized" field, many of its leaders wanted to be partners with government and serve as liberals' civil liberties experts.[52] Ferman believed these enterprises gave the Union influence with powerful people and made it equal partners with the federal bureaucracy. He thought the government valued the ACLU's recommendations, but he did not consider what it cost the group to play by the government's rules. He trusted the FBI and the federal bureaucracy. Few at headquarters had as much faith in the FBI as Ferman did, but his attitude of respectability and of getting along and working within parameters others set was indicative of the newer generation of Union leaders.

Ferman's efforts alienated many grassroots civil libertarians. To them Ferman symbolized liberal capitulation. One suggested that the ACLU, along with Americans for Democratic Action and other postwar liberal groups, should "bear their share of the responsibility" for the loyalty crusade. Without them "none of these things [loyalty tests, teacher loyalty oaths, investigating committees] would have been able to wrap themselves in the respectability they have enjoyed." While some members complained that the group was not anticommunist enough, more lamented its weaknesses.[53] Their voices became increasingly powerful as Malin's program slowly shifted the balance between branches and headquarters. As timid liberals left the national organization, more assertive new recruits entered it through the branches. The Southern California affiliate, the most radical of all the locals, brought in the largest share of new members. They altered the Union's composition and created a basic inconsistency. The liberal anticommunist Board wanted the ACLU to become a civil liberties partner with government, working through established channels, advising federal bureaucrats, and influencing policy. But the members who might make that partnership a possibility did not share the directors' dream. The ACLU was on a collision course with itself.

Virtually anyone looking at the Union during this period has noted its weakness. Samuel Walker argues that to some degree its reputation is undeserved, the result of internally generated bad press, from "the ACLU's own affiliates, especially Northern and Southern California," and from Corliss Lamont and other Union dissidents. Walker is right in noting that a lot of criticism against the organization came from the inside and that, for all its public relations efforts, "the ACLU never told its own story very well."[54] Yet the very fact that the Union had to explain itself so much suggests a fundamental disunity about the group's purpose. After World War II, the organization made a choice based on its leaders' beliefs. That choice was liberal anticommunism. In making that choice, Union leaders hoped to hold and gain influence with government, a strategy that yielded no great benefits. The ACLU was never anticommunist enough to satisfy its critics and yet too anticommunist to rally substantial numbers of progressives from front groups. Its methods, moreover, were out of sync with its membership, which was increasingly recruited through affiliates, where a different outlook prevailed. Recognizing that the status quo did not work, Baldwin's successor, Patrick Malin, tried to bring democracy to the organization without likewise changing its postwar philosophy. Soon the inconsistencies of these efforts would become all too obvious.

7

WEDDED TO CAESAR

The Affiliates after World War II

In 1947 the Seattle branch of the ACLU, dormant since the end of World War II, revived. By 1949 it had a small cadre of "fine people who know each other well." A few years later the group outgrew its "almost secret fraternal society" and sought a "more democratic" structure. Reformers acknowledged "the possible danger of allowing Communist membership" but seemed little intimidated by the prospect. The Seattle branch's history is not typical of ACLU branches because no two were alike. As a smaller branch, it experienced contractions and revivals larger branches avoided. Its leadership was quirky and unique. What was typical about the Seattle branch, however, was its growth after World War II and its desire to bring more people into the work of defending dissidents' rights. Despite its temporary setbacks, the group had a history, including a variety of wartime experiences that gave its members confidence and commitment. The vigor and enthusiasm that emanated from the branches made affiliate workers unhappy with the places accorded them in the national ACLU, just as most disagreed with the national program of liberal respectability and anticommunism.[1]

The affiliate growth spurt leveled off during wartime but increased thereafter. Although branches still emerged and faded, there was a larger stable core of groups after the war. The two largest were in California, and together they had nearly half the total affiliate membership. The Chicago Division ACLU that replaced the disaffiliated CCLC started out small but by 1951 had displaced the CLUM as the third-largest branch with a membership of 1,400. The CLUM, the Philadelphia ACLU branch, and the Cleveland group had 600 to 700 members each; the dozen or so smallest groups had 30 to 50 active members.[2] Despite attempts at standardization, each branch was singular, with members loyal to the local entity rather than to the national ACLU. In the two large California branches, local identity reigned. Seventy-two percent of all NCACLU members and 56 percent of SCACLU members were not national members. Branches neither looked nor acted like the parent body they were supposed to serve.

Chief among the differences was politics. The national ACLU put down its roots among liberals. Affiliates also welcomed liberals, but liberals backed away from engagement during the McCarthy era, eager as they were to avoid Communist associations. So branches recruited elsewhere, often from the ranks of left-wing progressives. Progressives proved a valuable membership base; they were assertive, engaged, and unafraid of authority. Their politics were very different from the liberal anticommunism that prevailed at headquarters. Affiliates often defined themselves by what they were not, and often what they were not was like the national ACLU. Decades of bad encounters with headquarters tended to make them adversarial in attitude. Many times, their local identities involved heavy doses of superiority over the timid, disengaged anticommunist New Yorkers.

They also resisted the pressure to standardize and bureaucratize that national officers regarded as the hallmarks of liberal organizations. Ann Ray of the Seattle branch called it "the disease of all organizations." "It's a form of senility, perhaps," she explained, "as they grow older and stronger. Anyway, the primary purpose for which they were organized becomes relegated to second and third place and the need to preserve themselves as institutions becomes the primary interest."[3] Branch officers thought headquarters were far too obsessed with perpetuating the organization as it was, too concerned with reputation and image, and too little infused with the spirit and passion of civil liberties as a vocation. They did not want their organizations to become similarly institutionalized.

The national ACLU strategy, liberal anticommunism, had little appeal at the grass roots. The cautious, slow, cool, professional image national officers cultivated did not engage local members or keep volunteers enthusiastic for long periods of time. Local volunteers had no access to the Justice Department, so they did not concern themselves with discussions about how it could do its job better. The national office's more roundabout legislative strategy and amicus briefs frustrated them. Policy debates were fine, but affiliates felt a certain amount of urgency to act. The national ACLU dealt in principles and policies, but the branches continued to defend people.[4]

The more assertive attitude was also a function of the realities of local civil liberties work. In all the affiliates combined, there were only three or four paid directors and even fewer attorneys on regular retainers. Everyone else worked as a volunteer. The postwar climate being what it was, local volunteers had to be bold to persevere— bolder, often, than hesitant liberals. Their willingness to be publicly identified as working alongside or for Communist clients distinguished them from the anticommunist directors, who defended Communists but made elaborate claims about how wonderfully fair-minded they must be to do so. The difference created extraordinary tensions between branches and the office. The national office no longer so readily doled out money, which removed one powerful incentive for branches to cooperate. Instead, local boards toiled to raise their own cash, circumventing nervous liberals and appealing to their more progressive colleagues. Those branches that continued to take money from the national office, especially the new Chicago Division and the New York City group, may have been more like the national ACLU, but they foundered because they failed to inspire enough willing volunteers.

The Chicago Division demonstrated the problems of taking too much support from New York. Formed by the national ACLU and peopled with disgruntled members of the disaffiliated CCLC, it too often accepted moral guidance and financial backing from headquarters. The national office supplied it with an emergency loan of $250 in November 1946, followed by $1,000 the next month and $500 the month after that. Its rival, the CCLC, had a paid director, an office, a secretary, and a fifteen-year reputation for fighting for civil liberties. The Chicago Division wanted those things, too, even though a salary for its secretary was "the main drain" on its coffers. The Chicagoans believed there were "vastly superior resources" to be had from New York, especially if they played up the rivalry with the CCLC. The national office initially obliged but eventually wearied of the group's inability to generate its own funds, which, indeed, reflected its slowness in establishing itself. Finally, the office instructed the Chicago Division to learn to live within its budget, observe business procedures, and "carry its own load."[5]

The national office contributed to the Chicago group's difficulties. Chicago was the scene of the only CPUSA takeover of a branch, so Baldwin preferred to keep the new group "part of the national setup and not just a local affiliate." He was extremely directive; it never occurred to him that local people might have a better grasp of their situation and needs. His concern for appearances dominated his relations with the new group. He worried that Ira Latimer's CCLC was so effective and the new ACLU branch so weak that others got "the impression that CCLC is the Chicago branch of the ACLU." Instead of helping the branch gain confidence and improve its weak image, he let it think he worked with Latimer to achieve "an agreement as to a division of labor in handling the Chicago field," scaring the new group to act. Baldwin had no serious intention of working with Latimer, but he made the new branch feel like it existed only to show up the CCLC.[6]

As Baldwin's tactics in Chicago demonstrated, he was not very patient with affiliate personnel and had little appreciation for their work. Consequently, many branch workers felt abused and demeaned by the people from whom they expected useful guidance. The staff, as Sonia Osler of the Maryland branch noted, "has a tendency to badger the affiliates too much. There is constant complaining and criticism." Local volunteers heard little praise, even though officers were not shy about using their exploits for public relations purposes. Behind his back, Baldwin boasted of Ernest Besig's achievements, noting he "forged ahead to create in the whole Bay Area and throughout Northern California, a respect for the integrity of the Union in its disinterested championship of rights for everybody." But to his face, the national office treated Besig like a child to be humored. "Sometime soon," Pat Malin instructed a New York staff member, "in casual tones, compliment Besig on new letterhead format." Such treatment was hard on affiliate morale and would have been harder still had local activists not found their gratification elsewhere.[7]

Affiliate workers were not impressed by the national Union's postwar strategy and often criticized the national office for being timid and obsequious. The secretary of the CLUM, for instance, raised a ruckus after Baldwin told another local officer to sever his association with the CRC. "I have been cross at the ACLU and Roger ever since his letter came," she told her colleague. She lectured Baldwin about the importance of allowing officers their "full civil rights." "If it embarrasses you to have the 'distinguished head' of one of its local committees sponsor certain dinners, we can always disaffiliate and save you that embarrassment," she threatened and then promptly sent the CRC a contribution.[8]

Affiliates resented most national interference in their work, but particularly that which was anticommunist in intent. Staff members kept a mental list of affiliates that seemed a little too radical and scrutinized their every action. The Boston-based branch was high on that list, so the office kept a close eye on one member of the CLUM executive board, a woman named Mrs. Faxon, whose husband had been identified as a Communist by professional witness

Herbert Philbrick. The staff member demanded the "full facts" on her "for the protection of the Union." He was "relieved" to learn she was not eligible for reelection, assuming her guilt by association and never bothering to ask if she had been a useful member. "We do not keep any sort of blacklist," staff member Herbert Monte Levy assured a member of the Boston group, "but off the record," he denounced Florence Luscomb's politics for causing "much tribulation to us." Luscomb fought hard to hold onto a leadership position in the branch despite pressure from the New Yorkers. "Keep[ing] the [local] organization wedded to Caesar," as she put it, required either great tolerance or skill at circumventing the national office's anticommunism.[9]

Branches noted that the "Red Hunt . . . is making it increasingly difficult to line up new members," as the SCACLU reported, but most learned to compensate. Most stayed with the older direct action tactics, preferring them to the New York office's disengaged liberal anticommunism. The strategy proved successful in many cities. In the late 1940s the ACLU added only a few hundred new members annually. Most branches did proportionally better. The national staff grumbled that they did "all the work" of recruitment (sending out pamphlets, for example) while the branches got all the benefit. Yet often the national organization's postwar profile made the work of recruitment harder, and not just because the group seemed "*too* conservative" to "some members." While the Union hesitated to act on behalf of Communists, rival groups such as the CRC or the more prestigious Emergency Civil Liberties Committee (ECLC) stepped in, and these groups competed with branches as well as the national ACLU. As the Denver branch reported, "There aren't enough people lying around loose to carry on . . . [multiple] organizational drives at the same time." Affiliates disagreed with much of the Union's postwar strategy. Going their own way enabled them to compensate for their inability to control what kind of image the parent body projected.[10]

Respectability, the centerpiece of the national ACLU's identity, did not excite local people. "Prestige," declared the CLUM's Betty Sanger, "isn't always associated with principle." Florence Luscomb agreed. "The 'respectable,'" she complained, "are too lazy and indifferent to take the initiative themselves, and when others start something then cannot cooperate because it is not in 'respectable' hands." Branch workers knew that they rarely enlisted nationally renowned local people, who preferred to lend their names to the less demanding national ACLU. This they thought was a good thing, the source of branch superiority. As A. A. Heist of the SCACLU noted, the National Committee was "very well loaded with 'Who's Who' personalities," but local boards, "by nature of their day to day work . . . come to close grips with civil liberties issues." Affiliates valued the same renegade qualities the national staff found undesirable. Their self-images did not easily reconcile with the careful, detached national ACLU. Their loyalty was no longer automatic. "If the ACLU provides intelligent and vigorous and bitterly needed direction," Luscomb opined, ". . . I will *thankfully and devotedly* follow its leadership. If the ACLU falls down on its job, I intend to fight with every bit of knowledge . . . which I have gained." But whether affiliates agreed or disagreed with New York, they all knew that New York sat in judgment of their methods and personnel.[11]

Such judgment sometimes undermined the last vestiges of trust between branches and Roger Baldwin. In 1946 he pressed affiliates to protect Gerald L. K. Smith's access to public facilities during a speaking tour. This was his crusade, supported by anticommunists eager to prove that the Union did not just defend Communists' free speech. Neither liberals nor progressives found the cause compelling or the Union's demonstration of nonpartisanship attractive. Affiliates, so dependent on volunteer labor, rarely dispatched Baldwin's directives to his satisfaction, something he made extremely clear to them. The St. Louis group "did all that we could to convert the community to a real civil liberties stand on the question of Smith." At one meeting, a representative took the stage before Smith and read a statement declaring him "100 percent wrong." Baldwin lectured the St. Louis group about the importance of excluding political commentary from their work, including a gratuitous comment about the Communists' "totalitarian principles." Then he apologized to Smith for his affiliate's behavior. Nothing

Baldwin did persuaded already dubious branch workers that this was an enterprise noble enough to justify the costs they incurred.[12]

The Chicago Division also found itself in the spotlight because of Smith. "We do not want to dictate your activities," Baldwin told its head, "but it is pretty clear that Smith should be aided." Smith obtained his meeting place, but outside a mob armed with "ice picks, knives, some guns . . . bottles, stones, bricks, etc." confronted him, led by none other than Ira Latimer. When Smith and a colleague were arrested, the Chicago Division appointed two attorneys to defend them—attorneys Smith found "very timid and coerced." Once again, Baldwin apologized to him, explaining that the affiliate was new and "not yet well organized," and that one of the attorneys was running for Congress "and is therefore very cautious." Affiliate officers decided not to pursue Smith's appeal. One local attorney declared that "anything they do to Smith is not bad enough for him and that we should not lift a finger for him."[13]

The rivalry between the old and new Chicago organizations complicated the situation. Latimer filed a complaint that resulted in the arrest of Smith and Father Arthur Terminello, a suspended Catholic priest who joined Smith on the stage and gave an angry anti-Semitic speech. The city charged both men with breach of the peace. Only Terminello came to trial. The new branch found this awkward, since their civil liberties rival seemed to have the more popular position. Defending Terminello's right to anti-Semitic speech was principled, but it was also organizational suicide; Latimer would exploit the case to the cclc's benefit. The branch wanted the whole matter "buried." The National Board also voted to take "no action" itself, yet Baldwin pressured the branch to work on Terminello's behalf. It finally agreed to aid him at the appeals level. In 1948 the case reached the Supreme Court, where the national organization joined the Chicago Division in Terminello's defense. The Court reversed his conviction, articulating the value of dissent in a free society. Landmark though the decision was, it did not seem so in its early local stages, when newspapers emphasized that Terminello was an unpleasant fellow with anti-Semitic views. The national organization may have reaped some benefit from the Supreme Court case, which focused more attention on the free speech element of the case. When locals defended Smith, though, the fascist element was front and center.[14]

The Southern California branch also struggled with Smith, with members manifesting such a variety of responses that the National Board was kept busy for weeks. A. L. Wirin helped him obtain his hall, possibly only the acceptable alternative as far as Baldwin was concerned, but then picketed his speech. Carey McWilliams organized a "C.P. front set up primarily to fight Smith," the Mobilization for Democracy. Inside the hall, meanwhile, Smith "introduced a surprise guest . . . Clinton J. Taft, head of the [Southern California branch of the] Civil Liberties Union." Taft offered "A Tribute to Gerald L. K. Smith," lauding his courage in handling public opposition. Elsewhere, he maintained that Smith was "not anti-Semitic or anti-Negro." Having dispatched its duty to make sure Smith got his hall, the SCACLU exercised little control over its members' private opinions.[15]

The National Board "disavow[ed]" Taft's remarks and reprimanded him for advertising his ACLU credentials at a partisan political meeting. His service to the SCACLU was drawing to a close, and the branch sped up his departure. Taft suspected that he received unequal treatment because of the kind of partisanship he expressed. McWilliams got "tender solicitude," Taft complained, while he got "slapped down swiftly." While that was true in Los Angeles, in New York the Board mustered no more tolerance for McWilliams than for Taft. The Board wanted the Angelenos to ask McWilliams to resign because the Smith matter was "a 'hot' [issue]" and "our position is perfectly clear." The Los Angeles board refused. Only one member complained about McWilliams, Taft's replacement told Baldwin, whereas a lot of local members objected to Taft. McWilliams was contrite, he added, and the whole matter had been blown out of proportion. Local people saw no reason to press him about his politics, so he stayed on their board. While anticommunist national officers defended Smith's free speech, in part to distance themselves from the Communists, the SCACLU remained convinced that it was better to be associated with left-wing rather than right-wing clients.[16]

McWilliams further antagonized national officers by sponsoring the local affiliate of the CRC. "I do not think that our integrity is improved," Baldwin advised, "by having associated with us persons who face in two directions at the same time." McWilliams explained that his motives were pure and that the CRC sometimes had "a far more realistic point of view than the ACLU," an opinion that resonated in several branches. He volunteered to resign if his "presence . . . is . . . embarrassing"; but while anticommunist directors were "prepared to set upon Mr. McWilliams' suggestion," it was the SCACLU's choice, and it preferred to let the "matter go practically unnoticed." Local officers urged the staff to "trust our judgment," which, of course, they did not. McWilliams only left the ACLU on his own terms.[17]

McWilliams did not scare the SCACLU, as members knew him to be a longtime advocate for the disenfranchised. They were inspired rather than embarrassed by his presence in their group. They had more difficulty when Morris Ernst came to town to speak because "none of the Hollywood groups [that headquarters was eager to recruit] seems to want to cooperate in sponsoring" what the SCACLU's director characterized as the "witch hunting which has developed . . . within the National Board." "We are not so greatly frightened by being called a Communist Front organization," he explained, adding that the Angelenos used a report by California's Tenney Committee, the state's version of HUAC, calling them a front organization as a recruitment device. "I credit our increased receipts," he noted, "to the reaction which it produced."[18]

The SCACLU was the most radical of the affiliates, but others shared its sentiments. They objected to the national ACLU's postwar posture, complaining that the Union had "abandon[ed] its role of militant, effective leadership at the very time when these are most bitterly needed if American liberty is to survive." In nearly all the branches, activists remonstrated "that the ACLU is adjusting its social action sails too much to the political climate" or "had become timid." Ernest Besig thought "that the Union is security minded instead of everlastingly emphasizing the need for freedom." "I am concerned," said the head of the Chicago Division, ". . . at the number of times that I find myself writing letters expressing irritation with the New York office." Aryeh Neier, who joined the national staff in 1963, recalled that "the affiliate directors, especially, were outspoken in their criticism of the national ACLU's failure to provide leadership in the battles against the loyalty investigations and purges." Florence Luscomb found the "lack of harmony" between her branch and headquarters "deplorable" but illuminating. "The fact that the same situation exists between the ACLU and every one of its more vigorous and effective affiliates," she suggested, "surely indicates something."[19]

What it indicated was that branches fought to imprint their own views on the national organization, challenging its liberal anticommunism whenever and wherever they could. Both California affiliates were "opposed to the President's Loyalty Order and loyalty tests *on principle*," Besig explained, "while the Board is not." Neither thought the group should work with the Justice Department to establish screening safeguards. The San Franciscans wanted to "seek its [the Loyalty Act's] repeal because it violates the fundamental principles of the Bill of Rights." Taft's Los Angeles successor, A. A. Heist, likened the Board's position on the Loyalty Program to its too-timid reaction to internment. "Instead of hitting an essential and recognizable wrong in a way that really counts," he explained, the ACLU, "thrash[ed] . . . around with academic questions." Heist and Besig fought back, hoping to rekindle some of the Union's prewar spirit, an effort both recognized required organizational democracy.[20]

Both California affiliates lodged formal protests against the Union's academic freedom policy. Directors believed that campus authorities could limit the free speech rights of any organization "moving materially under false pretenses as to its objectives." The California boards felt it was "the *actions* of the group" that mattered. Wirin argued that the Board's stance "deviate[s] from the traditional policy of the Union of opposition to censorship over opinion." The national office seemed surprised, but after what it described as "considerable discussion," directors reaffirmed their original pronouncement and preemptively declared "this would not be a referendum." The California affiliates also objected to the organization's decision to accept peacetime compulsory military training "if proved necessary to national security." "I never expected to live to see the day when the National Board of Directors would take such an action," Heist wrote to Baldwin. In this one instance, the California groups prevailed on appeal. A 1951 Union poll revealed deep cleavages between the national leadership and all of the affiliates. The National Committee, Board, and branches agreed on only one issue: the right of Communists to join unions. On the other three matters—the right of unions to exclude Communists as officers, the exclusion of Communists as permanent immigrants, and the denial of naturalization to Communists—the Board and National Committee voted against the Communists' rights and the affiliates voted for them. Grassroots activists were commonly less anticommunist than the national officers were but could not prevail under the system as it existed.[21]

Local workers understood that the Union's hesitation "when Communists are involved" would probably not survive in a more democratic structure. Heist blamed the "fossilized" Board for this "ridiculous situation" that was "inconsistent with the principles for which we stand." John Haynes Holmes visited his affiliate and confirmed that there was widespread "dissatisfaction with . . . the national body, due to a desire for greater consultation and independence." However, as they did with Besig, officers preferred to see the problem as Heist rather than the system. The staff complained that he would occasionally "go . . . off the reservation" and offer inappropriate political opinions, writing about foreign affairs in the SCACLU's *Open Forum* or acting "a little careless about how his name was associated with groups or causes which were suspect of leftist domination."[22]

Heist was impervious to the New Yorkers' criticisms. When Baldwin scolded him that a SCACLU statement in the *People's World*, the West Coast organ of the CPUSA, welcoming the Dean of Canterbury was "quite outside our function," he was not contrite. "Serves you right!" he replied. "Why do you read the *People's World* and so lose your peace of mind?" The SCACLU seemed unconcerned as well, even when a wealthy investor threatened to deal "a heavy blow" to its treasury. Heist resigned, but the Southern California board unanimously invited him to continue, which he did until late 1951. While the national office regarded him as something of an eccentric, "vague and naive," his local colleagues admired his assertiveness. In California, "where we perhaps lead in the matter of paddling our own canoe," his committee thought him an asset, not a liability.[23]

Paddling one's own canoe, though, was not the same as steering the bigger national ship. Heist and Besig wanted to help steer the ship. Both thought that democratization would give the ACLU some spine. Heist, however, doubted that radical changes were possible in the near future.

> It looks to me as if the New York board is carefully avoiding the organization of branches because it realizes that in the end, it would mean some loss of control. Meanwhile, the cause has suffered beyond any need. I am not at all sure that we can start anything new in this line as long as Roger is in command. After all, it is his baby and he is enjoying the sort of limelight that he has had the last couple of years when he found himself in the good graces of officials at Washington, whom he ought to be fighting as he did in his earlier and more vigorous years.[24]

Heist and Besig began the conversation about reforming governance. In 1948 they drew in other branches. The CLUM declared itself "completely with you about the democratization of the ACLU." The Seattle affiliate found the SCACLU a little too Communist-connected for its taste, but Heist's suggestion "that members of Branch boards should help formulate policies" seemed "plausible on the surface at any rate."[25]

After the Board failed to consult affiliates over the Loyalty Program, the California groups pushed for change. Besig protested the policy; Heist proposed that "we should change our whole set-up."

"I think you would agree," Baldwin coolly replied, "that this would be a departure which we could hardly consider." But Heist was willing to consider it. Although Baldwin claimed that "the Board would be always governed by any strong dissent expressed by them [affiliates]," local leaders knew that their access to directors was erratic at best. They wanted democratization of the Union.[26]

Brimming with resentments, they approached the 1949 annual ACLU meeting prepared to ask for fundamental change. They came away relatively satisfied after directors agreed to a committee to re-examine governance and included several affiliate spokespeople on the group. They should, perhaps, have noted that when the committee presented its recommendations, two of three Board representatives filed their own minority report. Still, both the majority and minority reports advocated giving larger branches an official vote of some kind. The Board accepted the principle "that the affiliates are entitled to an effective voice in the formulation of policies," but in practice Board members wanted that voice confined to the opportunity, at directors' discretion, to name members to the National Committee. As Board minutes understated, the branches expressed "general opposition to the proposal as not meeting the need for effective representation."[27]

Concluding that their only hope lay in meeting "without any interference from the Board," affiliate representatives convened in Des Moines in 1950. They drew up a wish list of measures that would better suit their needs. They asked for two votes per branch, a national organizer to help their efforts, more ACLU participation at the trial stage, all rulings and policies published, and regular national conferences. Even as the Board considered the "basic proposals" that came from Des Moines, branches realized one was a mistake. The two votes per affiliate misrepresented the balance of power. Small groups got as much voice as large groups and because "we have this totally undemocratic procedure of giving an automatic proxy to all of the National Committee and National Board members," as Heist noted, affiliates would gain only 30 of 140 votes, or "well under one-fourth." The branches had been too modest.[28]

When Patrick Malin replaced Roger Baldwin as the ACLU's executive director, he signaled his intention to change the structure of the organization. Using a $25,000 bequest, he immediately hired a field secretary, George Rundquist. Rundquist's job was to integrate the affiliates into the Union, fusing their treasuries and memberships. Malin's motives were several. As an economist, he saw the necessity of a stable treasury supported by funds raised around the country. As a liberal anticommunist, he was disturbed by the branches' disregard for decorum and their willingness to associate with radicals and iconoclasts. He believed that integrating branches into the national organization would help subsume their more radical politics. As a modern manager, he wanted his organization to maximize its influence, something more possible with greater numbers of members. As the ACLU's steward, he believed it was in the best interest of the organization to bring the affiliates into line with the national ACLU, lest they be seduced away by some other civil liberties group.

Affiliate officers wanted a voice but were less sure about integration into the national organization. They had many qualms about the New Yorkers' anticommunism and feared being used. The Massachusetts and Southern California groups inquired if they would have to endorse the 1940 resolution. The SCACLU also asked about finances, requesting a "detailed plan . . . to know the mechanics of our mutual arrangements." In both California affiliates, the large number of local members who did not also belong to the national ACLU posed a problem. Besig would not even entertain the prospect of integrating with the national organization. He suspected that the only reason the New York office wanted affiliates fused was to make the national organization stronger and the locals weaker. He was even more dubious of the "50-50 sharing of income" that was a part of the plan, concluding that it was "a means of collecting money for you," he told the national office. The other affiliates ultimately integrated their finances and memberships, but the NCACLU refused.[29]

Since directors seemed so resistant, Malin went ahead on his own, calling the result "experimental." What he proposed took the Des Moines formula of two votes per branch further. The entire ACLU membership would elect the National Committee, previously elected by the Board and itself. Affiliates got no direct representation on the Board, but they gained a vote, weighed according to a proportional formula, alongside officers. The National Committee's and the Board's votes were determined by dividing the total membership by the number of National Committee and Board members. Each affiliate board received a proportion of the votes calculated according to the number of affiliate members divided by the number on its board. When Malin devised the formula, the Board and National Committee had 17,500 votes to the affiliates' 5,000. But as affiliates grew disproportionately to the national group, they gained power. The Board greeted the program "prepared by the Director [Malin]" with little enthusiasm. Handed a fait accompli, it could do nothing but invite branch representatives to consult about the specifics of the program in New York in the spring of 1951.[30]

Affiliate representatives left New York believing that the ACLU had taken "a step toward a more effective national organization." That opinion did not last very long. As soon as the representatives departed, the Board added an amendment to the new bylaws created in their presence—the 1940 resolution, "to which nearly all of the affiliates have again and again made objections." Since "not a voice . . . was raised for such inclusion," local representatives "naturally assumed that nothing would be inserted" into the rules after they left. New field secretary George Rundquist tried to smooth ruffled feathers, assuring angry local boards that they saw only a "tentative . . . 'office draft'" of the changes, but he finally admitted that "the Board would not repeal the 1940 Resolution."[31]

Directors had little interest in sharing power. Both anticommunist factions feared that broadening the franchise ceded control to untrustworthy people. By adding the 1940 resolution to the bylaws, they reclaimed their authority. Another clause, which was inserted, the branches were told, because New York law governing corporations mandated it, gave the Board veto power over anything enacted by the full corporation. Section 10(d) of the new bylaws read, "The Board of Directors shall act in accordance with the majority recommendations of a biennial conference . . . and the majority vote on a referendum, *except where it believes there are vitally important reasons for not doing so.*" Contrary to what the office told the branches, the attorneys the Union consulted were not clear that state law required the provision. Malin counseled patience to the too-eager affiliates, reminding them that two years before, they "had almost no voice at all in the national organization." Directors, he noted, were "little . . . educated to think in terms of a national organization" and were still gun-shy after some "bitter" experiences with affiliates.[32]

The new bylaws and power-sharing mechanisms did not immediately change the balance of power. But if branches were disappointed, their faster growth rates meant that they would quickly attain a majority of votes. In one four-month period in 1953, membership campaigns coordinated through headquarters in the by-then integrated Southern California, Chicago, Wisconsin, and St. Louis branches brought in 2,200 new members and their dues, carefully divided between the national and local treasuries. The Union grew phenomenally during this period, yet the political complexion of its new members pleased local branches more than headquarters.[33]

No affiliate grew faster and larger than the Southern California branch. By the late 1950s it represented 10 percent of total Union membership and generated considerable income for the national ACLU. Its successes challenged national officers' belief that it was necessary to be liberal and anticommunist to remain viable in the postwar arena. The Los Angeles group's reputation as "considerably influenced by the Communist Party line" did not adversely affect its function, and neither did its more assertive policies toward Communists' free speech rights limit its membership potential. Heist's successor, Eason Monroe, came to the SCACLU from San Francisco State College, where he was fired for refusing to sign a loyalty oath. He was not afraid of making the local branch into a mass organization and did so, in part, by earning the respect of left-wing elements. A 1949 report by the California Un-American Activities Committee (the Tenney Committee), singled out the Southern California group as the most radical branch. As Dorothy Ray Healey, one of three Los Angeles Communists A. L. Wirin defended for violating the Smith Act, noted, "it [SCACLU] was a very different organization than the national ACLU, where someone like Morris Ernst was actually informing on other ACLU members to his great friend J. Edgar Hoover. The leaders of the Los Angeles ACLU were probably the kind of people that Ernst was informing on." While the national ACLU pursued a policy of respectable anticommunism, the SCACLU led the affiliates in opposing McCarthyism.[34]

As Heist threatened, the SCACLU used the Tenney Committee pro-Communist brand as "a badge of honor" when recruiting and "broke all records of new members enrolled"—33 percent higher in 1948 than the year before. It had a local radio program, and TV producers inquired about dramatizing its censorship cases, much to the envy of the National Board. The SCACLU tended to enter cases sooner than the ACLU did, at the trial stage rather than filing amicus briefs during appeals. The Southern Californians helped organize a national fight to abolish HUAC. When the Board proved unwilling to challenge HUAC, SCACLU activists created a separate group to fight it and sought endorsement not from the Union but from the ECLC. Meanwhile, the SCACLU continued to oppose HUAC despite the New Yorkers' nervousness. By the late 1950s, it inspired other branches to circulate anti-HUAC petitions, at least until the national office directed them to stop. It was not until 1960, when the Union operated under a more democratized system, that the organization voted to make HUAC's abolition "a prime order of business."[35]

Like the SCACLU, other branches proved more willing than the national ACLU to stand up for the victims of the cold war, whatever their politics. The NCACLU was also "somewhat more radical . . . than the National Board," explained one of its members. It was considerably more effective than Irving Ferman's heavily self-promoted Washington office was in providing aid for employees called before loyalty boards, filing some fifty cases. It filed its own amicus brief on the Smith Act trials. Northern California officers challenged the legality of the loyalty oath at the University of California and the Tenney Committee. The group actively challenged

HUAC long before the New Yorkers did. Between February 1947 and February 1949, the NCACLU objected to national ACLU policies vis-à-vis Communists' rights fourteen times.[36]

The smaller affiliates had fewer resources than either California branch, but they generally shared a disdain for anticommunism. The CLUM lobbied to support loyalty test cases directors rejected. The Chicago Division criticized the national office's weak stand on HUAC's Hollywood hearings. The Maryland Civil Liberties Committee wanted to support Owen Lattimore, an Asian specialist at Johns Hopkins University charged with perjury before congressional committees. The Board delayed the Marylanders' urgent request and finally denied it, but others took up their cause. Ed Meyerding, the Chicago Division's executive secretary, scolded that "from where we sit it looks to us as if the Maryland branch has been rather shabbily dealt with." He wondered why staff members were so secretive about the whole process, telling the Maryland affiliate they "could not reveal the reasons for ACLU not entering the case." Malin finally had to visit Baltimore to justify the Board's choices. In the 1930s, the national office had often complained about affiliates' unprofessional behavior. In the 1950s, affiliates expressed disappointment over how bureaucratic, ingrown, and stodgy the national ACLU had become.[37]

The trial, sentencing, and execution of Julius and Ethel Rosenberg left branches wanting to do more. The Union's official policy was that there were no civil liberties issues involved, a stand it declined to publicize. Branches felt the "unprecedented" death penalty merited further discussion. The Chicago, Cleveland, and Southern California groups urged "that our national officers make an immediate study of the [Rosenberg] case and recommend such action through the affiliates as will seem warranted by a study of the trial." The New Haven Civil Liberties Council, already suspect to national officers because of its reluctance to add the 1940 resolution to its constitution, got tired of waiting and petitioned Truman on its own "to commute the death sentence of Julius and Ethel Rosenberg." It gave its action so much publicity that the Board was compelled to explain itself publicly. Directors took the opportunity to remind all the branches that affiliates did not act on national matters "without consultation with or authorization from the national office," but branch workers found that when consultation failed, defiance was an effective backup strategy. The defiant strategy, coupled with the branches' generally more left-wing politics, led to repeated clashes as anticommunist directors tried to impose their beliefs on others.[38]

The Boston branch suffered through repeated cycles of interference. John Haynes Holmes complained that one CLUM leader was "a rather easy mark for our unscrupulous Communists and Fellow Traveler friends." Baldwin thought another "so partisan on the left . . . [that] you are going to have trouble." George Rundquist passed along the criticism of a disillusioned Bostonian who said he would not join the CLUM so long as progressive activist Florence Luscomb remained associated with it, "as he is embarrassed by the activities of this woman." Assertive Boston personnel gave as good as they got, especially secretary Betty Sanger, who regularly rebutted Baldwin and the office staff. The staff thought her insolence and her progressive views were related and felt that both justified their interference.[39]

Whenever a branch deviated from or challenged policy, the ready explanation at headquarters was Communist sympathies. Such opinions needed to be uprooted, but since local boards were rarely willing to do the job, staff members tried hard to enhance the power of local people who shared their politics and purge those who did not. In 1951 the national office sided with moderates in a CLUM dispute and tried to prevent the group from challenging a legislative committee investigating loyalty. At the same time, staffers saw an opportunity to weaken Luscomb until "she has no power."[40] In Boston and in other cities, anticommunists learned they could appeal to like-minded New Yorkers to intervene on their behalf. In Seattle, Ann Ray worked "on getting rid of the local boys," even though "I can't prove and won't attempt to prove they are Communists." She sent their names to Norman Thomas, who, in turn, informed his fellow directors, at least one local board member, and Patrick Malin. Malin contacted the head of the branch, but she wanted to handle the matter herself. He lectured her that it was his "non-transferable responsibility of guaranteeing the integrity of all the Union's staffs and governing bodies and we explore to the utmost every hint of failure and see to it that remedial action is taken as required." Her branch's solution was faster and simpler: it dropped Ray from its board.[41]

However interested the office claimed to be in constructing a national organization, its fear that the branches would let Communist infidels overrun the ACLU limited expansion plans. The staff preferred no organization to a potentially suspect or difficult one. In 1952 a couple of people in Portland, Oregon, enlisted George Rundquist's help to prevent people with "ulterior purposes in mind" from reviving the branch. Without investigating, Rundquist honored the request. Several years later his successor, Jeff Fuller, continued to rejoice that the still-nonexistent Portland branch had avoided a "left-wing capture." In New Mexico, Fuller's organizing efforts ended when his local contacts informed him that two individuals on his list were "suspected out here of being members of the Communist Party." Anticommunism at the top inhibited grassroots growth.[42]

So, too, did the Board's anticommunism create unnecessary problems for affiliates. In 1952 Norman Thomas upset the Detroit branch on the flimsiest of suspicions. Local anticommunist Eleanor Wolf did not belong to the affiliate, but she told her boss that she thought its chairman, Edgar Wahlberg, a Methodist minister, might be a fellow traveler. Her boss sent a copy of her letter to Thomas, and Thomas passed it to staff member Herbert Levy, who alerted Malin. With each relay of information, Wahlberg's fellow-traveling credentials grew without any substantiation. The national ACLU could not confirm any specifics, and locals seemed uninterested in Wahlberg's political perspective. Nothing happened until about eight months later when, at a Socialist Party function, Thomas found the Detroit branch under attack. Rather than defend it, he named Wahlberg as a Party sympathizer or outright Communist. Wahlberg was furious, as was Wolf, who heard her privately expressed concerns stated as truth in public. Malin assured her that the ACLU was not responsible, but he was forced to backtrack when Thomas confessed. "It was Norman, after all!" he finally admitted. Anticommunists in the New York office expressed no pride in the burgeoning branches. Instead, they snooped and pried into their local business. Communism became a convenient scapegoat, one that could swiftly undermine any affiliate's legitimacy.[43]

The national office's suspicion of the Detroit branch did not end there either, since, Rundquist explained, "we had been told that the Communists had been ordered to infiltrate into the Union, and that with a key city such as Detroit we could anticipate Commie 'interest' in the Union." It is likely that the FBI supplied this information. Both Irving Ferman and Herbert Levy had "friendly" bureau contacts and ran local names by the FBI to see if they were Party members.[44] So alerted, the national organization continued to scrutinize Wahlberg along with the Detroit group's executive secretary, Kathleen Lowrie. Jeff Fuller warned Wahlberg that the national office would not recognize his branch as the new Michigan state affiliate so long as Lowrie ran the office. But the branch reelected him and Lowrie, who helped support the local organization financially and continued to serve, although in a position that was "mostly title, with less responsibility." As late as 1957, disgruntled local residents still tried to use Thomas as their conduit to change an affiliate they thought "look[ed] like the CP grouping," and the national office remained confident that the information it had "in hand" on the problematic nature of the Detroit group was not politically motivated.[45]

The staff also acted much too quickly after they received an "anonymous accusation that nine members of the MCLC [Maryland Civil Liberties Committee] Board are Communist Party members" that Levy later said came from a Board member. Levy, who had a reputation for acting hastily and making errors, immediately contacted the FBI and then asked the staff for more information. Fuller was sure the branch was clean, as it had incorporated the 1940 resolution into its bylaws and did not "cooperate with possible left-wing groups." It was, he concluded, "one of our most conservative and anti-Communist branches." It turned out that the Board member had "confused [the Maryland affiliate] with another organization," but Levy's eagerness to investigate unleashed the FBI on the local branch. National officers so little trusted affiliates that they felt little compunction about informing on them.[46]

In fact, several officers relied on the FBI to tell them about branch personnel; the FBI based its judgments on measures the ACLU did not officially countenance, such as associations and memberships. Morris Ernst obtained "secret information" about one Denver officer, Rod Holmgren, from the bureau. Holmgren belonged to the Mine, Mill and Smelter Workers Union, which the Congress of Industrial Organizations had expelled because the union was Communist-dominated. Anticommunist officers seem to have accepted his likely guilt by association, but they had few mechanisms for removing him. All they could do was urge local members to ascertain whether or not he came under the provisions of the 1940 resolution and act accordingly. It is not clear whether or not Holmgren's colleagues ever asked him, but he remained in office for several more years. Whatever his affiliations, his work apparently pleased Denverites. After he left the local board, the national office expressed hope that "the caliber of its [the Denver group's] personnel can be improved." Whoever replaced him, though, also did not meet the national office's standards, as the staff continued to rely on FBI information, even after acknowledging that some of what they got turned out to be wrong. National officers did not drop the matter until persuaded that the "danger of CP infiltration" had passed.[47]

Many frustrated affiliate activists often found it easier to circumvent the national ACLU's anticommunist obsession by turning elsewhere for support for their cases. Carey McWilliams was not the only branch member who also belonged to the CRC. The CRC, however, did have limited appeal because it was so clearly identified as a Party front. A more popular alternative for branch workers stymied by the Union's many anticommunist mechanisms was to work with the ECLC, founded in 1951 by people who "were generally sympathetic to the ACLU but who decided that it wasn't sufficiently protecting the rights of American citizens." At headquarters, officers regarded it with suspicion, considering it "at least strongly influenced by communists," even though it never appeared on the attorney general's list of subversive organizations. Officers spied on the ECLC, circulating reports about its activities and expressing concern about its work. They feared that it would steal their branches. Affiliates, however, willingly cooperated with the group. Carey McWilliams helped organize it. John Paul Jones of the New York City affiliate spoke at its testimonial dinner for Corliss Lamont. The SCACLU cooperated with its efforts to abolish HUAC. And the Seattle board sponsored a speech by ECLC activist Harvey O'Connor. To local people, there was no inconsistency in belonging to both groups and counting on the ECLC "to move quickly," something the Union seemed "temperamentally [un]suited" to do.[48]

The staff constantly watched the branches for signs that they were about to shift their allegiance elsewhere—to the CRC, to the ECLC, or straight to the CPUSA. Such unease suggests that staff members understood that local volunteers were dissatisfied with the postwar ACLU and not especially loyal to it. To some extent, they were right. Affiliate workers were loyal to civil liberties but believed there were many different ways to fight for them. If the Union stumbled, they were comfortable with other organizations picking up the slack. They did not see in the ECLC a rival that existed only to plunder or embarrass the ACLU, which is precisely how anticommunist directors regarded it. Local people saw an organization with a different style. When they received warnings from New Yorkers to mind their associations and honor their Union commitments, it reminded them that national officers did not consider them equals but interlopers poised to destroy "their" organization.

Affiliate personnel had no idea just how far officers were willing to go to protect "their" Union. In 1977 the organization obtained its government intelligence files allowed under the Freedom of Information Act. The records revealed that several well-placed staff members and officers had passed information about the branches to the government. Irving Ferman and Herbert Levy, whose jobs were unconnected to the branches, supplied the FBI with considerable information about the affiliates, including local board minutes from the Seattle, California, Pennsylvania, Denver, Oregon, and Chicago groups. Levy later justified their actions, arguing that "to enlist the aid of the FBI whenever we could do so in support of civil liberties" was useful to the ACLU and to civil liberties. Moreover, Ferman argued, working with the FBI was part of a deliberate public relations effort. Even were that true, to violate a branch's civil liberties to protect the ACLU's reputation and to assume that the New Yorkers alone were capable of making such a choice demonstrates just how much the Union bureaucracy and the staff's autocratic mindset supported anticommunism. Levy and Ferman used FBI contacts and information to buttress their own authority and keep the branches subservient. In one instance, Ferman cited an affiliate's criticism of himself as proof of someone's Communist leanings.[49]

Except for the case of the CCLC, the CPUSA never tried to infiltrate a branch. After 1946 it was too busy fighting for its own life to think of subsuming civil liberties groups. The assumption that the Party sought to do so spoke to officers' pride in their organization and their belief that it would be a tantalizing prize for the Communists to obtain. "There have been press reports that the Commies and pro-Commies have been ordered to infiltrate the ACLU," Rundquist reported in 1952. "This is not surprising. I wouldn't expect the Communists to ignore us." Yet this conviction put the Union at war with itself, for affiliates were not afraid of being associated with their Communist clients. The office staff's trust, moreover, was misplaced. However much information Union officials leaked to the FBI about branches' activities and however much they curried favor with Hoover and Nichols, the government agency still regarded the Union as "nothing but a front for the Communists," according to one internal bureau memo. The same mindset that made the FBI a better ally than an affiliate helped rationalize the organization's hierarchical structure, too. Whether called Communist sympathizers or advocates of internal democracy, there was no room in the organization for people with different opinions.[50]

National officers did not recognize or reward the postwar achievements of the affiliates, but the branches' postwar record contrasts strikingly with that of the national ACLU. While the ACLU steered a moderate course that required compromises, local groups up-held civil liberties ideals with more purity and vigor. "In my book," Rundquist told Ernest Besig, "the affiliates have more nearly held to a truly civil liberties position . . . than the national board." While the Board of Directors debated and refined policies, branches tackled an increasing share of the Union's real work: loyalty appeals, teacher oath cases, and Smith Act trials. Their commitments appealed to enough local people that their organizations grew disproportionately large. In 1956 the branches brought in more than $329,000, nearly all of the Union's $343,500 budget, a greater than 14 percent increase over the year before. Once affiliates officially fused their memberships with the national ACLU, the organization's complexion changed, for the branches contained many more progressives unashamed of their past—and sometimes present—Communist connections. Branches diluted the anticommunist presence in the Union, but not on the Board of Directors in New York.[51]

Branches also saved the organization from total collapse. Patrick Malin's expansion nearly toppled the whole ACLU financial edifice, and the leadership's forays into anticommunism weakened the Union's reputation and function. As the branches prospered, the national office gained regular access to their treasuries. Local activists were not content to let New York have their money; they wanted recognition that "our time and effort" counted too.[52] They wanted the ACLU to be a genuinely democratic national organization. Once Malin replaced Baldwin and introduced the rudimentary mechanisms of democracy into the ACLU's organizational structure, it was only a matter of time before the flourishing affiliates gained real influence. It was a prospect so daunting to the ACLU's leaders that they did everything in their power to prevent that day from coming. But it was a moment that, to affiliate leaders, could not come too soon.

MUTUALLY UNHAPPY IN
EACH OTHER'S COMPANY

Crisis and Resolution

In the summer of 2004, the ACLU's Board discussed director Anthony Romero's careful compromise over federal "watch lists," the names of suspected terrorists the government began keeping after 9/11. In order to accept money from the Combined Federal Campaign, the federal employees' charities program, Romero signed a pledge that the Union would not "knowingly employ individuals" or donate funds to organizations on the list. Although he claimed that he skirted the "knowingly" part of the pledge by never checking the watch lists, some directors protested. "We would never terminate or kick off board members or staff members because of their associational rights," one declared. "We've made those mistakes in the past." Most *New York Times* readers of this story likely did not know what those mistakes were, but the paper reiterated the story of the 1940 resolution and the expulsion of Elizabeth Gurley Flynn. Time may pass, but the ACLU still occasionally revisits its anticommunist past.[1]

From the late 1930s until the mid-1950s, civil libertarians engaged in a prolonged conversation about the goals and methods of the ACLU. Directors wanted it to set the example for responsible anticommunism by showing that it was possible to honor individual rights and still protect national security. Affiliate members tended to believe anticommunism violated the group's long-standing commitments to free speech and free associations. These different goals shaped different operating styles: the Board was detached and expert-centered with an amicus-based legal strategy, while the branches were more confrontational and direct. But branches dealt only with local matters. Directors held the power nationally, and they kept the Union anticommunist and disengaged. When Patrick Malin launched his democratization program, though, he altered the balance of power in the organization enough to trigger a series of battles that determined the Union's function and future.

The very idea of organizational democracy was a hard concept for many Union officers, whose mission was protecting dissenters against the tyranny of the majority. Baldwin's generation was "a group of elitists," a civil liberties "vanguard" who thought they knew best. Anticommunism reinforced their prejudices. Some directors believed that a broader movement invited Communist takeover attempts. Open democracy also threatened the careful fiction of organizational harmony that directors had evolved, what John Haynes Holmes boasted was "no sharp cleavage in our Board between hard and fast groups, either left or right." It was a myth that defined Union governance, shaping the excruciatingly slow grind of decisions through committees, drafts, and more committees. "Mutual suspicion," one director claimed, kept attendance high.[2] The method allowed for the continued function of an extreme anticommunist faction, even though it was a minority bloc. As branches gained more power, the members of that bloc recognized that their capacity to impose themselves on a Board too polite to challenge them directly would fade. They found themselves at a crossroads.

Norman Thomas, William L. White, Whitney North Seymour,

William Fitelson, and Merlyn Pitzele had the most to fear from de-mocratization. They could intimidate their fellow officers, but not the officers who ran the largest branches—a fact for which they had a sinister explanation: "officers and directors of some of the branches are under Communist discipline." Staff believed that assessment, too, or at least found Communism as good an expla-nation as any for affiliate assertiveness. "I have been reading the *Daily Worker* for the past four years," noted field secretary George Rundquist in 1952, "and I am convinced that the Communists are attempting to infiltrate into every organization of good repute which deals with civil rights." Traditionally, the Board's dominion reassured those who did not trust the local affiliates and gave the staff but one master to follow. As the ACLU became "a more nor-mal organization," directors' "loss of control" drove a strong anti-communist revolt that undid the careful balancing of forces at the Union's top.[3]

Extreme anticommunists demanded reassurance that Commu-nists could not so easily infiltrate and take over the Union. First they extended the 1940 resolution to cover all branch officers. Next, they wanted the ACLU to broadcast its "opposition to Communism" on relevant legal briefs and publicity releases. Liberal anticommunist directors tolerated these measures, seeing them as politically nec-essary to stay in the liberal mainstream. Branches resisted. "This business of opening and closing any statement of liberal opinion with a declaration that we do not admit Communists to our gov-erning bodies seems to me the cheapest sort of catering to public hysteria," A. A. Heist complained. The branches' disregard for the mechanics of anticommunism alarmed Thomas, Pitzele, and the rest of the strong anticommunist bloc.[4]

A national anticommunist subculture nurtured their fears. Al-though a functional liberal anticommunism pervaded government, extreme anticommunism tended to be more isolated and less prac-tical. It was intense, completely overwhelming its advocates' other values and associations. In such a hothouse atmosphere, attacks on the Union as too close to the Communist Party, a staple of conser-vative ideology, seemed more threatening. Strong anticommunists both feared for the Union's survival and half-believed what conservatives said about the organization. In 1952 the charges seemed to escalate. First came Pitzele's scathing commentary on *The Judges and the Judged*. Then came accusations in the *New Leader* that two Union officers made "an astounding demonstration of bias in favor of Communists" at a public debate. That summer, the American Legion passed a resolution demanding that Congress investigate the ACLU. HUAC also seemed interested in the group. Was all this merely a failure of the "public relations angle" or evidence that the Union's current policies on Communism "are not adequate"?[5]

Extreme anticommunists wanted to alter conservatives' perceptions and halt any infiltration in the branches. Drawing on precedents already established, Norman Thomas argued that the Union ought to extend the 1940 resolution to the membership. "It isn't logical," he explained, "to require of officers what is not required of members." The Membership and Affiliates Committee refused to be engaged by the larger issue, arguing that the suggestion was impractical. "The office is in no position to check on the possible totalitarian associations of the ACLU's thousands of members," it rationalized. Instead, the Board fashioned a guideline calculated to discourage Communist infiltration but that required no policing: "The ACLU needs and welcomes the support of all whose devotion to civil liberties is unqualified by Communist, Fascist, KKK, or other totalitarian leanings." Displaying the statement "on membership cards and on promotional material" seemed reasonable to liberal anticommunists, who concentrated on the perceived public relations value of it and downplayed both the ideological and structural problems it was bound to create.[6]

Pushing on, Thomas and his colleagues asked for what directors had long avoided: a theoretical debate about the nature of communism and its relationship to civil liberties and national security. Patrick Malin scheduled a special meeting in January 1953 and earmarked one ninety-minute period for discussion. The ensuing debate lasted months, prolonged at every step by a full-court press of inflammatory anticommunist tactics. The efforts of Thomas and his allies were relentless and occasionally ruthless. They leaked information to the press and flouted Board rules. Other Union business ground to a halt. Regular biweekly lunchtime meetings stretched to four and five hours. By February, directors could only get through one agenda item per meeting. By April, they met weekly. Malin was swamped with proposals that changed from meeting to meeting and existed in multiple versions. His workload grew, yet he had no time for the fund-raising duties that were increasingly necessary to keep the Union afloat. The group ended 1952 having spent more than expected. Spring brought traditionally lean months. and in April the Board gave Malin permission to sell off some bonds and seek a loan.[7]

What the extreme anticommunists wanted was "a dispassionate and up-to-date statement of the ACLU's position with respect to communism." Such a statement was necessary, they claimed, because there was a "serious and main division of opinion and action of Board members." With a policy in place, the organization could then consider "various pertinent issues," such as whether Communists could be teachers or government employees or could plead the Fifth Amendment. The debate turned on what the Party was. If it was political, like the Democratic or the Republican party, then its members were entitled to the same rights and privileges Democrats or Republicans enjoyed. But strong anticommunists believed that "the Communist Party is not a political party at all." William Fitelson explained that it was "an organization operating conspiratorially in the service of a foreign government and that it is engaged in patently criminal activities." If the Party was not "a legitimate political party" but part of a foreign conspiracy, then it threatened America's national security, and its members were entitled only to limited civil liberties.[8]

On 17 March 1953, the Board devoted its entire meeting to discussing the Communist Party. Anticommunists came prepared. Merlyn Pitzele quickly moved that the CPUSA "is an organization operating conspiratorially in the service of a foreign government and is a real danger to civil liberties." After considerable debate, several defeated substitute statements, and a fight about whether one strong anticommunist who had to leave could give his proxy to another, the Board deadlocked and created a committee to draft a policy statement for later consideration. Strong anticommunists proposed six suggested versions. What the Board finally approved was a compromise. It described the Party as "distinctively and essentially characterized both by extreme anti-democratic doctrine or practice and unqualified obedience to the government of the Soviet Union," but it stopped short of calling it a conspiracy. Strong anticommunists offered eight motions to toughen up the text. Each was defeated.[9]

By the spring, the Board had texts of three policy statements that focused months of discussion. The first was its definition of the CPUSA, which included the claim that "it is not a violation of . . . civil liberties . . . to take into account a person's voluntary choice of association when it is functionally relevant to a particular judgment." The second statement reasserted teachers' freedom of thought but, paradoxically, noted that Communists lacked the capacity for the "free and unbiased pursuit of truth" necessary for teaching. It also opined that United Nations employees representing the United States should be subject to the same loyalty provisions as all federal employees. The third statement suggested that invoking the Fifth Amendment offered no "protection against any consequence," since it was perfectly legitimate to ask about one's association "concerning Communist or other totalitarian associations." Each statement made distinctions between the rights of Communists and those who were not. Against the context of an already irresolute postwar reputation, these would make the Union considerably more anticommunist than it already was.[10]

Liberal anticommunists accepted the three statements as a practical necessity. Many believed them crucial for postwar operations, "an attempt to end a heated controversy growing out of attacks on the Union as pro-Communist." No one seems to have asked why the Union needed statements at all, forgetting that in the past they had not quieted disagreement but prolonged it. By 1953, McCarthyism had done enough damage that Union liberals understood what could happen to them if they bucked the anticommunist tide—that they might be singled out for attack and have their past associations and opinions scrutinized. Osmond Fraenkel voted against the statements but "didn't feel strongly" enough to fight for their defeat. Corliss Lamont did but thought it futile, since "Pat Malin will not lift a finger" to stop the strong anticommunists anyway. Directors long conditioned to avoid open conflict put aside their personal objections for the good of the organization. Some remembered the Flynn fight, the wartime conflicts, and the Pitzele matter. Each had weakened the Union and made enemies of friends. They had little stomach for "another long, bitter personal battle." They were, in short, intimidated by extreme anticommunists, who seemed perfectly capable of McCarthy-like witch hunts. Lamont believed that it was "fatigue, boredom and [the] feeling on [the] part of many directors [that] this [was the] only way to make non-stop talkers cease and desist" that led to the approval of the statements.[11]

Directors felt nervous enough about the statements to call them "old business" that did not require endorsement through the new Union democracy. Instead they circulated their work for "the *advice* of the corporation members," accompanied by Malin's citation of the relevant section of the Union's bylaws allowing them to do so. Lamont was the only director who objected. He asked to have his opposition recorded, which he then explained in a six-page letter to all voting members. He sent it at his own expense, violating no Union rule, but the office copy bore testimony to what the anticommunist staff thought, with comments such as "ugh," "awful," and "silly" scrawled in the margins.[12]

Affiliates did not need Lamont's letter to convince them to protest the Board's action. Ernest Besig immediately asked for a referendum. Malin claimed his was "the only official reply from an affiliate to date." This was technically true, but it hardly indicated widespread endorsement. The CLUM reminded the office that the statements could only become official ACLU policy "with the participation of all members of the corporation." The Iowa branch urged alternative statements. The newly revived affiliate in Madison, Wisconsin, sent an angry letter protesting "such disastrous policies." Lamont also phoned Besig "to express the hope that there will be a movement among the affiliates to secure a referendum." Within several weeks of his call, the Board could no longer pretend that only the long-estranged San Francisco group was unhappy. The SCACLU, the CLUM, the Iowa affiliate, and several Board and National Committee members asked for a referendum. Strong anticommunists had no choice but to put their imperfect work before a democracy they despised.[13]

Officers recognized that this was an "important moment," the first controversial matter to come before the newly enfranchised affiliates. So insular was the New York atmosphere that many had no clear sense of the likely outcome. Osmond Fraenkel, for example, assessed the likelihood of a defeat as "slim." But no one took any unnecessary chances. Board chair Ernest Angell violated Union practice by sending a letter with the ballots. In it, he advocated for the approval of the three statements, stressing the expertise that had gone into preparing them, how they had "commanded the intensive attention of the Board over a period of six months." He reminded affiliates that a "no" vote "would inevitably carry implications." He also emphasized that this was the single best product likely to come from divided directors: "If these statements are rejected, I despair of the Board being able to reach any more generally satisfactory substitution." Lamont missed the meeting where directors authorized the letter, and the high-handedness of it offended him. He cabled the affiliates that it was "improper for [the] chairman in [his] official capacity . . . to influence corporation vote in this manner." Lamont urged them to "protest to [the] office."[14]

Lamont had spent years challenging anticommunist shenanigans. A proud advocate of "the militant tradition of the Civil Liberties Union," he identified with the Communists whose rights were about to be compromised. Anticommunists challenged his every reelection. He alone had to answer questions about whether or not the 1940 resolution applied to him. One Board member believed that he served only through a "special dispensation." Others accused him of using the ACLU to protect his own rights. In 1953 he faced a subpoena from Joseph McCarthy, and his colleagues "hemmed and hawed over my legal case" before voting not to take a stand. After he contacted affiliates about the vote for the three statements, Malin damned him for undermining his authority, and the Board threatened censure, forcing him to express regret at his "mistake."[15]

His "mistake" likely had no impact on the process, since most branches opposed the statements and voted against them when given the opportunity. As one member of the Seattle affiliate observed, "The Civil Liberties Union is in the control of self-appointed and anointed gods. . . . We are mutually unhappy in each other's company." Only three small groups endorsed the statements: the central Ohio branch, the Detroit affiliate, and the newly organized Minnesota group. They did so because they were worried about the "issue dividing the Union," because they took Angell's warning seriously, or "out of respect for the judgment of the majority of the Board." In the end, 73 percent of the Board favored the statements, 66 percent of voting National Committee members did, but only 5 percent of affiliate votes were cast in favor of the statements. There were enough affiliate votes against the statements to triumph.[16]

The vote put Malin in a difficult position. Personally he favored the statements and regarded them as protection from conservative attacks and necessary for continued Board harmony. He also thought they might enhance the group's popularity and, thereby, ease fund-raising, although in the short term they were keeping him from cultivating likely prospects. He who always craved "the board's approval" had incurred its wrath to bring the branches into the electoral process, and now the branches betrayed him. While liberal anticommunist directors might learn to live with the outcome, extreme anticommunists would not. Several made "very hot-headed" resignation threats. Having already devoted "an unconscionable amount of time" to the statements, Malin was expected to reconcile the irreconcilable.[17]

He forestalled the inevitable showdown by promising to "obtain full and exact information from all affiliates." Besig thought the point was to "beat . . . the bushes for non-voting national board and committee members" to change the results. But Malin found his votes elsewhere, at the Chicago Division. Its report described participation as "very small." So perhaps figuring that the branch had an intimate knowledge of Communist connivance thanks to Ira Latimer, he "called the Chicago Division requesting that a phone ballot be taken." The local director dutifully called members who had not voted and asked for their responses, and the result shifted 2,550 Chicago votes into the affirmative column, enough, just barely, to change the outcome.[18]

The reversal barely satisfied anticommunists and laid bare "the absurdity of Malin's procedure." It was, Besig commented "just about the zaniest and rawest thing I have ever seen perpetuated.... It certainly shakes my confidence in the integrity of the board and the administrative staff as well." National Committeeman Alexander Meiklejohn felt the reversal "a fatal mistake."[19] Electoral tinkering made several directors nervous, although only Lamont acted, having nothing left to lose. The Nominating Committee had not included him on their slate; he would soon be free of "that grueling battle at the Civil Liberties Union." Blaming Malin for "the extraordinary procedure of attempting to alter the ballot totals," he phoned the Chicago branch "to question the legality of the telephone balloting." The Chicago Division heard his complaint, found it valid, and elected to report their first tally "as the official vote." What one affiliate director called "the wandering Chicago vote" once again put the three statements—and Malin's integrity—in doubt.[20]

"I am unspeakably outraged . . . at the suggestion that I acted illegally," Malin declared in an emotional letter to the Board. He felt attacked from all sides, the victim of Lamont's misplaced wrath ("me, who has been his chief protector," he marveled) and the scapegoat when the votes did not break the anticommunists' way. Personally wounded, he regrouped, pushed back the date of the upcoming corporation conference, doubtless hoping to postpone the moment when directors and angry affiliate representatives confronted one another. Stressed to the point of illness, he took two weeks' vacation in Florida.[21]

Lamont's phone call overrode what little chumminess remained on the Board. Until then, several old-timers had fought to keep him actively involved in the organization, feeling bonds stronger than politics. John Haynes Holmes was "so fond of the man personally that I can't seem to keep this consideration out of my mind." Holmes was not present the evening a small group of older Board members quietly met to talk about the Nominating Committee's snub of Lamont. He was, they thought, "a useful member" who deserved to be renominated. Their prestige prevailed, and the Board added his name to the roster of nominees. But once he phoned the Chicago affiliate, Lamont became "expendable." Strong anticommunists demanded his nomination be rescinded. "He jeopardizes our prestige," threatened William L. White. Whitney North Seymour resigned, which directors took as "serious, especially as it may be followed by others." They voted to retract his nomination. Lamont switched his loyalties and his generous donations to the Union's postwar rival, the ECLC. Thus his alienation from the organization he had served for such a long time proved, as Holmes noted, "costly" in more ways than one. His departure "forebodes no good for the independence of the Board from right wing pressure," predicted Fraenkel.[22]

Most directors believed the statements necessary to stanch the attacks against the organization and considered the affiliates' vote against them unfortunate, evidence that they lacked the maturity to vote responsibly. The strong anticommunists argued more sinisterly that "this strange 'democracy'" had invited infiltration. White thought that the referendum proved that "these 'affiliates' are now either infiltrated or controlled by Communists or fellow-travelers." Thomas concluded that "the process of interpenetration by communists and fellow-travelers" was well under way.[23] But whether convinced that there were Communists in the branches or merely peeved that unruly locals overrode their authority, directors were united in thinking the vote reversal could not go unanswered. "The boys in New York want to win very badly," Besig observed. Drawing on section 10(d) of the bylaws, which allowed them to override a corporate vote when they deemed it necessary, directors voted to "neither accept nor reject the referendum votes as binding" and authorized Malin to redraft and resubmit them, altering their "form, but not . . . the[ir] substance." Until statements acceptable to everyone could be found, the Board would "exercise . . . its residual power" and treat the three statements as "in essence the policy of the Union." After noting the Board's action "overriding . . . the majority," one National Committee member wondered, "Why have voting members or even a Corporation?"[24]

Leaders clearly understood that they had overstepped propriety, for they schemed to cloak their action "in vagueness and uncertainty," voting not to notify the corporation of it. It did not take long, though, for members to find out what happened and express indignation at the process and the result. "I join you in resenting Norman's suggestion that the ACLU is infiltrated with Communists merely because the branches opposed the three statements," one local leader told another. "I cannot, in good conscience, support an organization devoted to the preservation of democracy," wrote a Virginia member, "if such organization does not follow democratic principles in its own action." National Committeeman Robert Lynd warned that "enough general uneasiness" prevailed in the ranks that anything the Board did "evokes understandable speculation."[25]

Malin dutifully rewrote the three statements and sent them on to the newest part of Union democracy, its first biennial conference, an opportunity for directors, National Committee members, and affiliate representatives to discuss and recommend policy to the Board. The assembled group quickly dismissed his work and passed a single declaration instead, one that "clearly does not take the place of the old [measures]." Written by National Committeeman Frank Graham, it asserted the Union's traditional opposition to "guilt by association, judgment by accusation, the invasion of the privacy of personal opinions and beliefs and the confusion of dissent with disloyalty." It said nothing about the nature of the CPUSA. Anticommunists proposed amendments and counterstatements, but each was defeated. Osmond Fraenkel came away believing the proceedings a success, "reestablishing friendly feelings" between the affiliates and the Board. "Whether it will have permanent results," he continued, "remains to be seen."[26]

Delegates felt they had delivered "a shot in the arm best administered by the concerted action of the affiliates." The biennial conference marked their first chance to challenge "serious defects in the present organization." Although anticommunist directors defeated their attempt to excise the 1940 resolution from the bylaws, they recommended that the Board remove section 10(d), make some "language changes," and establish a fixed schedule of future conferences. They asked for "a larger vote" and a committee "to consider establishment of a convention system to run the organization," one that would replace directors' authority with "some combination of periodic inclusive meetings with interim respective action by national and local boards." "The affiliated groups have come of age," the CLUM noted, "and are therefore entitled to a larger say in national policy matters."[27]

The biennial convention completely unnerved extreme anticommunists, who had trouble believing that the motives of the affiliates were sincere. The "device of democratic election" was precisely how "a well-disciplined minority . . . might . . . easily gain control over the whole Union," James L. Fly explained. Not only was the "field mechanism . . . rigged against us," but the Communists' "tricky procedures and beguiling arguments" duped liberals into tolerating a process not in their best interests. Adding to their concerns was the ECLC, which had gained from its recent association with Corliss Lamont. The New Yorkers regarded it as an "open rival of the ACLU," one that seemed to be wooing the disenchanted branches. Norman Thomas heard rumors that Lamont recruited for the organization by attacking the Union. This seemed like still more proof that the Communists were on the brink of destroying the ACLU. Strong anticommunists decided that this was when they needed to make their final stand, "come hell or high water." Thomas called on his colleagues to reclaim "the power of the Board." Fly urged "disaffiliat[ing]" branches and accepting "some loss to the treasury" to once again possess ascendancy over the affiliates and security of mind.[28]

Thomas and Morris Ernst composed a new statement about the nature of the CPUSA. It was stronger than the statement already passed by the Board, outright asserting that the Party was "part of an international conspiratorial movement which seeks universal power." The statement said nothing about how this "sharp" difference from other political parties might affect the individual rights the Graham statement guaranteed to all. It lacked other clarifying elements as well, such as what would happen if directors adopted it, and whether it would function forever or merely until some compromise could be effected. In fact, it exhorted directors to "reassert" their power over the corporation. It was inflammatory, a final angry retort after what strong anticommunists regarded as their humiliating treatment at the biennial conference.[29]

Malin's recent vacation to Florida must have seemed a dim memory. This time, however, it was not the branches that upset him but the strong anticommunists. Their act, he knew, would inflame the affiliates just when the organization desperately needed their dues. He was afraid that this most recent action was so outrageous that it could easily provoke a split. In the end, as a bureaucrat and a manager, he proved less willing than Baldwin to tolerate extremist intimidation. Yet, true to the liberal anticommunist style, he did not confront Thomas and friends directly. Instead, when he sent out copies of the resolution, he added his own commentary, gently planting the idea that he had been bullied by his more conservative officers. In case that failed to get across his message that things had gotten out of hand, he warned of the "disaster which would occur if our *uniquely comprehensive civil liberties organization* should become two or more organizations. The Emergency Civil Liberties Committee is waiting eagerly to pick up the pieces."[30]

Thomas's resolution and Malin's warning aroused very different responses among directors. Anticommunist William L. White was unmoved by the threats and utterly convinced that without the statement, the Union was "headed toward disaster." "Our recent practice of bowing meekly" left affiliates ripe for picking by the CPUSA. "As maybe they already have," he added ominously. John Finerty, by contrast, was appalled by the anticommunists' "blackmail." Yet when the Board discussed the statement, Finerty was absent, as were several others who might have voted against it. Rather than risk open conflict, directors once again passed it on, endorsing the statement and attaching amendments that made it temporary, to be superseded by a more permanent statement worked out by a corporate committee. They had momentarily humored Thomas and his anticommunist friends and left it to others to slap their wrists.[31]

Affiliates learned of these actions from stories leaked to the press. At first Besig thought it was a mistake, "a colossal boner" by some reporter. But he waited in vain for a retraction and finally communicated his branch's resolution "protesting strongly the action of the Board. . . . We are shocked, amazed and disturbed by this breach of faith and confidence." Other resolutions followed from Seattle, New York City, and Hartford. "It makes me feel like a fool to have given valuable time and money to go to New York to help persuade the board to withdraw these three acts and for them then as soon as we are all safely back home [to] reenact and give to the press the essence of one of them," Howard Beale told Besig. Several who protested indicated that the action had "destroyed that sense of unity, understanding and feeling of co-partnership created by the Conference." Few blamed Malin; most blamed "the Fitelsons, the Thomases, the Frys, Flys, Kerneys, the Barnes, Whites, etc.," the active anticommunist directors. Most thought them so obsessed "with communism [that you] have somewhat lost your perspective." Local boards also objected to "undemocratic By-Laws and voting procedures" that gave the Board the power "to do as they pleased."[32]

While the *Nation* hailed the Graham statement as a sign of Union vitality, the conservative press celebrated the Thomas resolution. The *New York World Telegram* called it "a strong anti-Red stand," while the *New York Post* declared that the "ACLU Board blast[ed] Communism." Both stories named the few directors who voted against the statement, something not even Board minutes revealed. This was the latest in a series of anticommunist leaks to the press dating back to Harry Ward's tenure as chairman of the Board. They challenged the professional image of a respectable, harmonious board and sometimes forced controversies. Malin, like Baldwin before him, usually ignored the slips, preferring to avoid investigating and reprimanding officers. The previous year, however, the Public

Relations Committee had concluded that the leaks harmed the group and in this particular case, naming people who resisted the anticommunist assault potentially exposed them to attacks. Malin was "much upset." He lectured the Board about the "damage," telling directors they were "duty-bound" to report what they knew and threatening the "possible removal" of any officer "who may be guilty." Directors, apparently, preferred not to inflame extreme anticommunists, so they had a "pointless and soul searching" discussion. Still, Malin put the extreme anticommunists on notice, a message they understood. While publicly confident that the new committee would produce a measure similar to his own, Thomas privately acknowledged that the probability of a "very satisfactory statement" was "quite dubious." For that, he blamed Malin's compulsion "to conciliate the affiliates."[33]

And there was much to conciliate. Members were angry. "Let the ACLU make liberty its business, not security," wrote one. "The views of the ACLU are those of its membership," said another, "and that it is from its members that the ACLU draws its strength." The "breaking of the faith" outraged affiliates enough that Malin had to respond. Membership had boomed, reflecting the integration of affiliates into the national organization. But even with the addition of affiliate treasuries, a membership campaign launched in the midst of the controversy had a "slow start," and growth leveled off alarmingly in 1954, down from more than 30 percent the year before to less than 7 percent. Affiliates were in no mood to recruit, and Malin knew he dare not keep a higher percentage of the dues they did bring in. He cut staff salaries instead, including his own. He also delivered to the Board "a little lecture on our responsibility for finances," surely designed to remind them that their choices carried financial consequences. Malin the administrator recognized that he could no longer afford to humor the extreme anticommunists.[34]

Administrative reality, the most compelling reason to liberal anticommunists, dictated changing direction. Appointing the committee to draft new policy statements, Malin named only Thomas to "represent . . . his point of view." The group met several times, accomplishing a lot "with . . . unanimity." Thomas held out for a strong statement on communism, but when no one agreed with him, he had little choice but to let the committee proceed. The result better reflected affiliate rather than anticommunist views. Anticommunists halfheartedly proposed amendments, but the Board defeated them. In some branches volunteers still did not see the necessity of any statements at all, but enough tolerated them to avoid another set of votes. The Union quietly accepted the result and moved on. The organization would never be quite so anticommunist again. But what Samuel Walker called the "struggle for the soul of the ACLU" simply shifted fronts.[35]

Financial need rather than anything more fundamental drove the Union to rein in strong anticommunists. Malin's expansion program was expensive, and members responded negatively to the three anticommunist statements. By the summer of 1954 the Union faced a "cash problem" too enormous to solve by cutting salaries. It required affiliate money, so Malin had no choice but to reassess "unilaterally and without consultation" 10 percent more than each affiliate had already negotiated for 1954. One strong anticommunist director advocated cutting funds to affiliates "to the bone, but Malin objected to that." The combination of the duns and the electoral monkey business greatly angered affiliate officers. "For the national office to take $2 out of every $3 of income," grumbled Ernest Besig, seemed "indefensible." His group, being independent, was not directly affected, but all the other branches were.[36] Like the extreme anticommunists a few months before, the affiliates had reached their moment of truth, the time when they either succeeded in becoming full partners in a national ACLU or considered cutting their losses.

Branches recognized that the fight over the "locus of control" was about "politics" as well as who had power, about the need to create an "atmosphere of respectability" that had become more important than "principle." In the fall of 1954 Malin learned the full extent of their dissatisfaction when a copy of a letter circulating among branches accidentally landed on his desk. Its author was the Chicago Division's Ed Meyerding. Its tone was impatient and critical. "The national organization," Meyerding wrote, "has been consuming a great deal of money and has been producing relatively little." Its obvious failures made "considerable decentralization" a logical choice and staff "appreciation and respect for the affiliates" a necessity. Branches needed a larger percentage of what they brought into the organization to fund their own work. If things did not change, perhaps, hinted Meyerding, it was time to think about "break[ing] up the structure of the ACLU . . . [and joining] a new and competing organization," a reference to the ECLC. Malin immediately understood that the situation was dire. "A number of affiliates (not just Ernie Besig) apparently have . . . many [more] doubts than we have understood," he warned his officers. Devastated, his first instinct was either to resign or to scrap the affiliate system. The Board, by contrast, simply referred the complaints to a committee, expressing confidence that it could handle the brewing rebellion.[37]

Malin hurriedly called a conference to talk about finances, since he saw them as the most pressing affiliate complaint, but he failed to deliver the kind of wide-ranging discussion branch representatives desired. The officer who presided "was authoritarian and even discriminatory." Still, branch delegates stood their ground. They only accepted the national office's financial proposals until a fairer plan could be worked out. They expressed their dissatisfaction with the national bureaucracy by commissioning a study of "the actual operating practices and costs of the national office." Directors refused to be engaged with further reforms and counted on Malin to protect their interests. Malin and his staff found themselves unhappily in charge of a governance system that pleased nobody.[38]

The organizational study confirmed that the system as it existed did not work. The report called national efforts at recruiting members "notably unsuccessful" and observed that affiliates produced more new members than headquarters did. Although the study did not attribute this gap to contrasting styles and policies, it nevertheless confirmed what many had long suspected: that liberal anticommunism was not as compelling a reason for joining the ACLU as the more traditional, forthright defense of everyone branches espoused. The report confirmed other branch opinions as well by asserting that national governance required a legitimately national board of directors, including branch representatives. "This proposal would eliminate a considerable amount of affiliate dissatisfaction and would improve the links binding together the national office and the affiliates," the report concluded. The management consultants also critiqued methods at headquarters, a uniquely painful attack on a staff that prided itself on being professional. The report said there was no "formal structure" for broadening power, and office procedures were sloppy and inconsistent. Investigators got straight at the basic problem with the current Union operating system: it was adversarial and affiliates could gain their share of power only "by the relinquishment of Board prerogatives."[39]

Branches saw themselves paying for an expansion that gave them secondary status. Some doubted Malin's claims of repeated financial crisis, concluding that they were asked to pay up every time "the national board has been overspending." Most thought the group spent money foolishly, on public relations and amicus briefs rather than on actual cases. Financial integration required trust and cooperation that did not exist. Branches sent their money to New York, where the staff doled it out after subtracting the cost of "services from the national office," costs that seemed exorbitant to the branches and ridiculously cheap to the staff. Each affiliate negotiated for a separate percentage of its take, a procedure that ideally allowed for flexibility and special circumstances but often became "a system of begging which we find distasteful." As much as 80 percent of what a branch raised could remain in New York's coffers, funding goals, a Maryland activist noted, "you regard as the best interests of the ACLU" but that often seemed to "ride rough-shod over branches."[40]

The dispute went deeper than money, circling back to the different political perspectives. Affiliates disliked the national ACLU's anticommunist reputation and believed it hindered their collection efforts. They thought they could raise more money standing on their own policies. Their members, they asserted, preferred writing checks to their local branches—branches whose policies they knew and trusted. The staff, meanwhile, equated undisciplined politics with undisciplined work habits, assuming that the too-tolerant branch workers were also lazy. Few, they believed, "even approach the national office in operating efficiency." Despite evidence to the contrary, they still suspected that branches' politics hurt the organization. Financial integration did not meet anyone's needs very well, and it took the organization longer than expected to rebuild surpluses Malin drained to expand the group. Finances remained a constant source of irritation, something that made the Board's centralized power harder for the affiliates to tolerate.[41]

Under Malin, the staff played an expanded role in the organization, but one that trapped them between directors' autocratic expectations and affiliate demands. Baldwin had been hard on paid ACLU workers. Directors, while generally more polite than he was, took their cues from him, treating the staff as their personal assistants. Malin treated them as professionals. He introduced order and organization at headquarters. He made real efforts to build staff camaraderie, such as organizing Christmas parties and performing in staff skits. Of course, he also cut their salaries on occasion; still, most felt valued by him. Directors tended to see the staff as Malin's men. One of the few opinions they and affiliate officers shared was that the paid staff did a poor job. The management study confirmed their suspicions that the office was "far from a model of efficiency." Malin rushed to his staff's defense, telling the Board that the "moral" of the story was not that the office was inefficient but that it was "being asked to do too much" with too little. All of this was true, but more important still was the confusion that settled in at the top. Since Malin succeeded Baldwin and the Union had democratized, nobody "knows or has any idea where the Union is headed and what we ought to do," one worker explained. And nobody knew whom they served—Malin, directors, or the branches.[42]

Malin also struggled to establish himself as Baldwin's successor, fighting both directors who did not want a too-dominant administrator and branches trying to seize more power. He remained a relative unknown, the replacement for someone whose very name was synonymous with civil liberties. Baldwin knew nothing of organizational models or office dynamics. He ran the ACLU as he saw fit. While he did not always triumph, it was not for lack of trying. Even in retirement, he would call the staff nearly every day and "bark out a series of orders." Malin thought of himself as a more conventional manager responsible for "policy application" once others determined what policy should be. Directors, though, expected him to be "an agent of the Board" who would protect their interests and power. Affiliate leaders, too, figured Malin served the Board, which made him their opponent. Malin realized only late in the battle over the anticommunist statements that no one looked out for him. He and the staff faced what seemed an impossible task, reconciling branches and directors with fundamentally different attitudes about civil liberties and different expectations about governance.[43]

As the organization approached another round of reform, the staff panicked, fearing that no one believed in or appreciated their expertise. In 1954 directors reluctantly agreed to accept a constitutional committee to draft new bylaws. As 1954 turned into 1955 and then 1956, no committee materialized. No committee could, until the staff provided its "analysis and recommendations," a responsibility Malin claimed for them because of their "unique position from which to survey the ACLU and its needs." Yet as staff members considered how the parts of the Union whole fit together, they anticipated enormous future problems. Directors were unrealistic, imagining a modern national organization could be run like a small club. Affiliates were unruly, on the verge of financial mutiny, and many seemed to harbor the politically problematic. Adding to the office panic, Malin learned that HUAC was about to release a critical report on the ACLU. In response to all the pressure, as the 1956 biennial conference convened, Malin dropped a "bombshell," a staff recommendation that the ACLU "abandon . . . the affiliate system." In its place, he suggested a centralized organization run "with the cooperation of regional, state and local advisory committees wherever they can be set-up."[44]

As it turned out, Malin had so little authority in the ACLU that no one took this "emotional outburst, wholly unjustified" very seriously. The Board blandly gave him "a vote of confidence" and thanked the staff for all their hard work.[45] Directors were reluctantly coming around to the idea of a national organization. As the extreme anticommunists either retired or resigned, younger, more corporate-minded directors replaced them. Even older officers conceded that the old model Union no longer worked. "The growth of the affiliates makes a total concentration of power in the national Board obsolete," Osmond Fraenkel noted. In 1956, directors, the National Committee, and affiliates embraced a new compromise constitution. This established the biennial conferences as the bodies to set long-range goals and policies. Directors would handle matters between conferences, troubleshooting as necessary. It represented a victory for affiliates. They still did not have an equal voice in the organization; however, they gained considerably more power than they had before.[46]

Financial disputes took longer to settle, being more complex. It was difficult enough to design an equitable system for distributing money between branches and headquarters, but one size did not fit all. Smaller branches had different needs and money-raising potential than larger ones with paid staffs. Working out arrangements that slighted neither category of affiliates took time. Ultimately, to preserve the flexibility of the old system, the organization created a joint finance committee composed of national and local representatives. It studied the budget, allocated money, and made other financial decisions, taking from Malin the power to recalculate percentages affiliates paid the national ACLU. Once branches gained more power over money matters, finances stabilized and there was more predictability and less conflict. By the end of the 1950s, affiliates brought in 90 percent of all ACLU income, giving them more authority than ever before.[47]

The Board grudgingly accepted the affiliates and the organizational shifts that gave local officers more authority. Older directors like Morris Ernst may have preferred the ACLU before it was "federalized," but newer "all youngish" directors replaced them and knew no other way for the organization to be.[48] Directors, though, were disengaged from the ACLU's work relative to the staff. The staff continued to resist democratization, afraid that it left them vulnerable. As the 1956 bylaws decentralized Union authority, vesting more of it in unpredictable national conventions, Malin, accompanied by

Irving Ferman, visited the FBI in search of information about the political complexion of "his twenty-three affiliates."[49] By 1956 the worst of the anticommunist excesses were over. What did Malin expect to accomplish by consulting the FBI?

Malin's visit demonstrated that liberal anticommunism was a style as well as a political ideology. Late in 1955 the ACLU received an advance copy of a HUAC report on the Union. Its origin may well have been the FBI, whose leaders were convinced that certain affiliates were subversive. The report gave the "top echelon" of the group a clean bill of health, noting that the "prominent Americans" who comprised the Union's national leadership were not "disloyal, subversive, or even questionable." The report indicted "the rank-and-file membership," however, for being so "carefree" that they left themselves vulnerable "when the Communist Party is looking around for any available organization that it can infiltrate or take over for its own sinister purposes." HUAC advised that "closer scrutiny on the part of the rank-and-file membership is necessary." In response, Malin mustered page after page of newspaper editorials and laudatory statements from public officials, emphasizing the national ACLU's mainstream credentials and respectable reputation. But the branches were harder to justify. By visiting FBI headquarters, Malin performed a symbolic act, the equivalent of publicly naming names of presumed Communists. He quietly acknowledged the FBI's right to spy on the ACLU, hoping that the FBI would assure HUAC that the Union was clean. Malin's act was both liberal and anticommunist, frightened, desperate, and eager to please. He did what he thought he had to do to protect the ACLU.[50]

Whether or not Malin and Ferman's FBI call made a difference is unclear; however, HUAC never released the problematic report, and Malin believed another crisis was averted as a result. His style was reactive, typical of liberals who by the early 1950s felt reduced in their prospects and caught between flighty progressives and unscrupulous extreme anticommunists. His ACLU moved from crisis to crisis, unable to be anything more than defensive in response to the "shifting, amorphous political world" outside his boardroom. "Our business," explained one leader, "is putting out fires," and there were still plenty of fires to put out in the late 1950s. Although McCarthyism declined, there were debates about loyalty, security, and Communism. In 1960 the group suffered another membership decline because of its defense of the free speech of American fascist George Lincoln Rockwell. In 1963 it was in the news again when the press discovered that Lee Harvey Oswald, John Kennedy's assumed assassin, had attended an ACLU meeting and sent in dues and a membership application. In the 1950s, despite the affiliates' best efforts, the liberal anticommunist ACLU could do little to help set an assertive civil liberties agenda.[51]

Liberal anticommunism lingered on in the ACLU, but outside events finally expanded the sense of possibilities for sometimes-timid directors. Under Chief Justice Earl Warren, the Supreme Court revolutionized the field of civil liberties law. This "explosion of rights" engaged the Union, which helped argue cases to expand First Amendment rights, eliminate censorship, make clear distinctions between church and state, and define the rights of the accused.[52] Such matters were the ACLU's bread and butter, consensus issues shared by everyone from the newest volunteer in the smallest affiliate to Malin himself. Still, because the rights revolution was a top-down event led by the Supreme Court, Union leaders did not need to rethink their reactive strategy, governance, or even finances. Amicus briefs remained, one legal director recalled, roughly 85 percent of its legal work in the early 1960s. In 1960 a committee reported to the biennial convention that "organizational change would create more problems than it would solve." Two years later, another financial crisis forced yet another round of cutbacks at headquarters. The ACLU continued to struggle with its identity, even as it felt clearer about its mission.[53]

While a variety of issues reengaged the ACLU, the civil rights movement really pulled it out of its anticommunist lethargy. The Union had always left racial matters to the NAACP, but what happened in the South galvanized the membership far too much to leave the work to others. In 1955 the Board, appalled by the verdict in the Emmett Till case, promised to "form a chapter in the South." A year later, that promise remained unfulfilled because of budgetary considerations. Morris Ernst sat on Harry Truman's Civil Rights Committee, and Thurgood Marshall credited the Union for "beat[ing] into my head the need for an uncompromising attitude" on *Brown v. Board of Education* (for which the Union filed an amicus brief); but these actions, the work of a professional, detached, liberal organization, were not enough to satisfy members' yearning to be part of a movement.[54]

The Board acted too slowly. It debated the finer points of the 1957 Civil Rights Act, finally taking "a definite stand." It produced a pamphlet, *Race Bias in Housing*. It had a "very technical" debate about school desegregation in Little Rock, Arkansas. Its early contributions to the civil rights movement were "largely paper." Local volunteers wanted the ACLU to provide "all aid short of war," as one said at the 1964 biennial conference. They proposed sending "a contingent to march under its [ACLU] banner," at the March on Washington, but as Osmond Fraenkel noted, such things were "not customary." They wanted the Union to "endorse and support" demonstrations and protests. As Morris Ernst noted, "Energy . . . has substantially evaporated in the Board of Directors" as the affiliates took over the "excitement" of "go[ing] down to do the job."[55]

The momentum was finally with the affiliates. Personnel changes facilitated a more engaged style. Irving Ferman left the Washington, D.C., office in 1959. His replacement, former NCACLU staff attorney Lawrence Speiser, was an "improvement," Fraenkel thought, over the very anticommunist Ferman. The FBI, however, was not happy, having lost their best conduit of information about the organization. Agents actually warned another anticommunist staff member, Herbert Levy, about Speiser's politics. But the Union kept him on, and under his leadership, the Washington office engaged in fewer lobbying lunches and more casework. In 1958 Norman Thomas and Richard Childs, two of the most vociferous anticommunist directors, retired. Socialist Mel Wulf signed on as the Union's legal director in 1962 and quickly reversed its amicus strategy. About the same time Wulf joined the staff, Patrick Malin left, replaced by John de Pemberton. Morris Ernst remained on the Board but was of "declining influence" by the early 1960s. As "the 'elders'" declined in number and power, the organizational style of the liberal anticommunist generation slowly faded.[56]

The change was not, however, quite fast enough to suit the next generation of civil libertarians in the branches, who were eager to contribute to the civil rights movement. In 1964 the affiliate-dominated biennial conference directed the group to "concentrate more of its efforts in the South," creating the Southern Regional Office. To pay for it, delegates approved their first million-dollar budget. Affiliates volunteered to help cover the additional costs of the program; directors, Osmond Fraenkel recalled, "didn't also contribute" to the effort. Pemberton invited Alabama attorney Charles Morgan to run the office. Morgan was energetic and respected by movement leaders. As an outsider, he quickly assessed the leadership weaknesses of the Board, noting it was "dominated by members from the Manhattan Stockade. . . . Some had served for decades. Their meetings were frequent and friendly, like Lion's Club luncheons." That was soon to change. The "tight-knit, clubby" Board lost its "monopoly power" in 1964. A "cumbersome" new system replaced it, grafting two annual plenary sessions of affiliate representatives onto the existing system; directors continued to meet—and intervene—in the interim. Officers recognized that anticommunism was an irrelevant perspective, but they were loath to give up all of the privileges accorded them at the height of Union anticommunism. Affiliates continued to associate greater democracy with greater effectiveness.[57]

Morgan, Wulf, and Pemberton quickly assembled the Lawyers' Constitutional Defense Committee representing the ACLU, the NAACP, the Congress of Racial Equality, and the American Jewish Congress, modeling the group on a SCACLU coalition. After the Student Nonviolent Coordinating Committee announced its plans for Freedom Summer, the defense committee recruited nearly 500 volunteer lawyers in a week. Morgan launched a series of lawsuits in the South, challenging the segregation system. "It was," Wulf recalled, "a very romantic period" that energized and engaged members.[58]

Civil rights and, later, the war in Vietnam raised a new set of questions about the Union's purpose. Pemberton spelled them out to the 1968 biennial convention, noting that the group was divided between "traditionalists" and "militants" who conceptualized the organization differently—divisions that loosely coincided with another set, "nationals" and "affiliates." The Board continued to believe in propriety, dispassionate expertise, and the ACLU as a vanguard movement that could reason with and work with liberal government. The ACLU, Patrick Malin once reminded affiliates, is "not a defense organization." The next generation, however, wanted the ACLU to become a defense organization for protesters and those who challenged liberal government, a "mass movement" capable of helping lots of people. During the 1960s and 1970s there would be numerous battles over "subjects . . . which us old timers have not thought raised civil liberties issues," Osmond Fraenkel noted, "but some of the younger people felt otherwise."[59]

In 1967 Morgan defended Army doctor Howard Levy at his court-martial. Levy refused to instruct Special Forces officers, calling them "killers of . . . women and children." Morgan's unsuccessful defense quickly took the Union into matters such as war crimes and the conduct of the war. Morgan recalled that "some of the ACLU's cold war liberals" thoroughly disapproved of the venture, thinking that "direct representation," rather than an amicus brief, left the Union vulnerable to accusations of partisanship.[60] The next year Mel Wulf volunteered to defend Dr. Benjamin Spock and other Massachusetts antiwar activists charged with conspiracy to disrupt the draft. The Board overrode him, concluding that an amicus brief "could best stress the civil liberties issues and let ACLU be neutral on the war issues." Affiliates did not want to be neutral about the war, and the newest bylaws gave them greater freedom to direct the organization as they thought appropriate. The CLUM took the cases until the biennial conference met. There branches succeeded in rescinding the group's traditional opposition to civil disobedience, reversing the New Yorkers' decision and leaving them to wonder "whether the national Board is any longer in control." The Spock decision collapsed yet another governance experiment. A single eighty-person board consisting of affiliate representatives and thirty at-large directors assumed control. Under the greater affiliate influence, the Union "broaden[ed] . . . its mandate." Two years later, in a "virtual coup by his fellow directors of the large affiliates," the organization replaced Pemberton with New York City ACLU head Aryeh Neier.[61]

Malin and Pemberton were managers; Neier wanted to be something more. He got the Union involved as never before. He established storefront offices in inner cities to aid new clients. He found the money to fund paid staffs in nearly all of the affiliates and used grants to pay for special projects. Expanding into the educational realm, he oversaw the production of a series of ACLU handbooks that informed individuals of their rights. Handling "more free speech cases than at any time previously," the Union grew to 140,000 in 1970. Its new style appalled the few old liberals still around to observe the change. "I am disturbed as to the extent that the ACLU is getting into active party politics," Morris Ernst noted in 1973. In 1974, after three hours of affiliate-initiated debate, the Union voted to call for Richard Nixon's impeachment. Ernst thought the "pleasure in its [ACLU's] campaigns against Nixon" misplaced. For "want of supervision and barristers," he concluded, the Union "flounder[ed]." Yet the impeachment call, skillfully touted in advertisements, ballooned ACLU membership to 275,000 in 1974.[62]

The ACLU eagerly shed the last bits of its liberal anticommunist past. New leaders resisted the protocols of an earlier era. Wulf recalls simply ignoring the practice of "denouncing the Communist party in all cases involving it" and "denounced the forty resolution whenever I could." In 1967 the directors replaced the much-despised measure with a pledge of "unequivocal commitment to the objects of the Union."[63] In 1976, prodded by the affiliates, the group rescinded Elizabeth Gurley Flynn's expulsion, much to the old guard's distress. The few remaining directors who remembered her long hearing saw "no useful purpose being served by our beating our breasts about this in public." "You can't change history," Osmond Fraenkel explained, but younger leaders wanted to distance the modern Union from its anticommunist past. Baldwin warned about bad publicity and "the risk of being charged with opening the door now to Communists," a concern younger leaders knew to be irrelevant. Baldwin, meanwhile, won the Medal of Freedom for being a "national resource" in "the field of civil liberties."[64]

Yet the excesses of the old ACLU style came back to haunt the organization in the 1970s. It was embarrassed when documents revealed that five of its officers passed information to the FBI. Records obtained through the Freedom of Information Act in 1977 showed that Irving Ferman passed so much information that he "served as an informer." Neier quickly moved to quiet the furor by conceding the group's past guilt, further distinguishing the old liberal anticommunist style from the Union's newer activist phase. But the new style had its own problems. Many of the new members flowing in during the war and the Watergate controversy were single-issue members. They understood the ideal of defending everybody but applied a "utilitarian calculus" to determine how far they were willing to go along with that promise. This calculus balanced a hierarchy of individual rights against a reckoning of costs. Defending everyone was the ideal, but as always, members were less enthusiastic about defending some than others. After the war in Vietnam ended, there were no truly popular figures for the ACLU to defend. At the same time, the other element of the utilitarian calculus shifted as Earl Warren retired and Ronald Reagan defeated Jimmy Carter in 1980. By then, liberals, "long the principal source of ACLU strength," were "in terrible disarray."[65]

The cost of defending civil liberties skyrocketed in 1978, when the ACLU fought to obtain for American Nazis the right to march in the heavily Jewish community of Skokie, Illinois. Five hundred people picketed the Union's New York headquarters in protest. Approximately 30,000 people, roughly 15 percent of its membership, resigned, which put the organization down about a half-million dollars.[66] The Union bounced back financially but lost momentum with its defenses of prisoners, mental patients, and AIDS patients, causes the larger public regarded as extreme. During the 1988 election, Republican nominee George H. W. Bush capitalized on that impression and attacked his Democratic opponent, Michael Dukakis, as a "card-carrying member of the ACLU" who was, by association, concerned only with the rights of a lunatic few. While the charge did little for Dukakis, it helped reverse the group's fortunes once again. Nervous officers commissioned a poll to ascertain the cost of Bush's accusations. It revealed that nearly half of all Americans had a favorable image of the organization. The Union actually gained members by urging people to become "card-carrying members of the ACLU." Twenty years later, its website boasted the same phrase.[67]

While much has changed about the ACLU since it was founded, some things remain the same. Its initial mission was to defend every American's civil liberties. It has faltered sometimes, falling short of this goal, struggling to define the best methods to accomplish what it needs to do. Despite its professed nonpartisanship, how people see the ACLU is entirely partisan. To some it is a symbol of extremism; to others it looks out for the underdog. Nobody accuses it of being a Communist organization anymore, but it is regularly condemned for having the attributes of a Communist organization, for being godless and unpatriotic or, more recently, for contributing to the proliferation of "activist" judges on our courts. What was true long ago remains true today: the biggest challenges the Union faces come when it defends the rights of people its members find abhorrent. "Defending everybody," as Dwight Macdonald long ago observed, also means "offending somebody."[68] Between 1930 and 1960 the ACLU learned how to survive offending somebody in order to defend everybody. It was a costly lesson, but one that has contributed to the strength, clarity, and success the ACLU has today.

AFTERWORD

On 5 September 2001, Anthony Romero succeeded Ira Glasser as the ACLU's executive director. Six days later, terrorists attacked targets in New York and Washington, D.C. Three days after that, the Reverend Jerry Falwell declared that "the American Civil Liberties Union...had so weakened the United States spiritually that the nation was left exposed to Tuesday's terrorist attacks."[1] The next month, Congress passed the USA PATRIOT Act (Patriot Act), which gave law enforcement broad information-gathering and surveillance powers. The Union suddenly faced one of the biggest challenges of its lifetime. Or was it merely business as usual?

The events of 11 September 2001 altered the terrain of civil liberties, producing, as the *New York Times* suggested, "a sea change in attitudes."[2] Terrorism scares people, with its intensity, its randomness, and its violence. In exchange for some measure of security, Americans seem willing to accept compromises of their personal liberties. The Patriot Act, which gave the government easier recourse to wiretapping and access to records held by third parties (such as libraries and doctors), passed Congress by very wide margins and with bipartisan support. Travelers willingly remove their shoes and surrender their manicure scissors before boarding flights. They open their bags at museums and subway entrances and tolerate security cameras in a variety of public spaces. Each small sacrifice does not seem big enough to justify fussing about the loss of freedom. It is like World War II or the cold war all over again, only with different villains. As the ACLU long ago discovered, Americans are civil liberties relativists, particularly willing to relinquish someone else's freedom for their own peace of mind.

The Union's response to the challenges of 9/11, by contrast, has been more forceful and principled than its response to either World War II or the cold war. Its methods today benefit from lessons learned in the past. Its strategy builds on the foundation of professionalism laid beginning in the 1930s. ACLU representatives challenged provisions of the Patriot Act in court and testified before Congress against its renewal. The Union represented Muslims removed from planes and forced the processing of suspected terrorists held without charges at Guantanamo Bay, an eerie parallel to what the Northern California affiliate did at Tule Lake during World War II. There was even internal debate and minor controversy over the watch lists of suspected terrorists Romero tried to finesse. In the wake of this minor scandal, the organization spearheaded a campaign to eliminate the requirement that any nonprofit organization accepting money from federal charity programs check its employees against those lists. In past times, such zeal for protecting dissident rights triggered liberal outrage. Perhaps it still would have had a liberal been in the White House when the first plane hit the Twin Towers. ACLU officers, however, like to believe that it is not politics so much as a greater liberal appreciation of civil liberties—much of it due to the Union's many educational efforts—that makes the difference. Liberals may not appreciate all it does, but they see the ACLU as a necessary part of the process, providing some of those checks and balances on which our government is based. There has been no drop-off for the organization in polls. In fact, membership has actually grown since 9/11. More Americans than ever seem to understand the Union's nonpartisan mission. It has become the professional, respected institution earlier generations of leaders wanted.[3]

Professionalism, though, has not been the panacea for all the organization's problems. Certainly attaining the status of a mainstream institution has not insulated the group from criticism. While conservatives have done little second-guessing of the Union's efforts on behalf of individual liberty during a time when we are obsessed with national security, they associate its professionalism with extremism in more conventional ways, as a failure to appreciate American values and traditions. They believe it pursues a radical agenda with ruthless precision, promoting secularism and relativism. The ACLU, Jerry Falwell's infamous post-9/11 accusation implied, is too tolerant of difference and too willing to accommodate dangerous dissenters. It is the thousands of smaller bread-and-butter cases the Union undertakes in its opposition to school prayer, its suits to remove Ten Commandment monuments from courthouses, and its defenses of gay marriages and abortion rights—the civil liberties business as usual—that raise conservative hackles. Professionalism has made the organization no less vulnerable to government attack either. The FBI used the Patriot Act to collect thousands of pages of information about it and other civil rights and environmental groups.[4] Professionalism made the Union more efficient, but not more popular.

Thus, in response to crisis, Romero has sought to "put a human face" on ACLU efforts, drawing not on the Union's professional heritage but on the other aspect of its history, its grassroots engagement. The organization he inherited was top-heavy with lawyers and gun-shy after the 1988 election campaign. Romero responded with the kind of higher profile effort that would have impressed Ernest Besig. He launched a "Keep America Safe and Free" campaign, used a College Freedom Tour to attract a new generation to the cause, and staged an ACLU Freedom Concert headlined by Robin Williams to garner publicity for the organization.[5] Once again seeking to make civil liberties chic, the group has enlisted celebrities such as Tim Robbins and Jake Gyllenhaal in print ads. On the Union's website, visitors can order an array of instructive CD-ROMs, buy a video history of the organization, and order mugs and baseball caps emblazoned with the ACLU's logo. Today the ACLU's budget exceeds $10 million a year, a figure that would have amazed and terrified its founders.

The Union is still not a popular mass organization and probably never will be, and this is a source of both pride and frustration for its leaders. Its approval rating is no higher than it was in the 1930s, and while it can muster a few high-profile conservatives to attest to its nonpartisanship, its membership base remains liberal at a point in America's history when liberal no longer describes either a numerical majority or political power.[6] So despite all the ACLU baseball caps and celebrities at its rallies, the group faces the same contradictory challenges it did in 1930, balancing professionalism with popularity, and principle with practicality. Not everyone understands the ACLU's mission; not everyone has to. The ACLU exists, Romero explains, because "we aren't finished" perfecting our "American experiment."[7] So the ACLU, too, keeps perfecting itself, learning from its mistakes and building on its successes, understanding that the organization, like the cause it serves, is always a work in progress.

APPENDIX 1

Percentage (and Number) of ACLU National Board Members, by Occupation

	Attorney	Academic	Social Worker	Journalist	Publisher	Philan-thropist	Laborer	Clergy	Business-person	Activist
1925 (15)	13 (2)	13 (2)	0	0	7 (1)	20 (3)	20 (3)	20 (3)	0	7 (1)
1930 (13)	23 (3)	8 (1)	0	0	8 (1)	0	23 (3)	23 (3)	0	15 (2)
1935 (24)	37.5 (9)	8.3 (2)	8.3 (2)	8.3 (2)	4 (1)	4 (1)	8.3 (2)	13 (3)	0	8.3 (2)
1940 (30)	40 (12)	7 (2)	10 (3)	17 (5)	3 (1)	3 (1)	7 (2)	7 (2)	3 (1)	3 (1)
1945 (33)	48.5 (16)	12 (4)	6 (2)	15 (5)	3 (1)	0	0	9.5 (3)	3 (1)	3 (1)
1950 (34)	47 (16)	12 (4)	0	20 (7)	6 (2)	3 (1)	0	6 (2)	3 (1)	3 (1)
1955 (32)	46 (13)	6 (2)	0	29 (9)	9 (3)	0	0	9 (3)	3 (1)	3 (1)
1959 (31)	52 (16)	3 (1)	0	29 (9)	3 (1)	0	0	6.5 (2)	0	6.5 (2)

APPENDIX 2

ACLU Membership Figures, Expenses, and Income, by Year

Year	Number of Members[a,b]	Expenses ($)	Total Income ($)
1921	Not listed	21,224	20,264
1922	Not listed	27,925	27,382
1923	1,567	25,912	25,556
1924	1,685	18,133	18,709
1925	1,919	18,769	20,305
1926	2,022	19,189	19,893
1927	No report	No report	No report
1927–28	2,300	19,120	23,182
1929	2,188	21,567	26,791
1930	2,336	19,962	29,533
1931	2,750	24,809	25,199
1932	3,600	25,314	24,299
1933	2,500	20,489	19,689
1934	2,718	17,927	19,418
1935	2,700	19,797	18,410
1936	3,530	21,057	22,999
1937	4,338	20,914	23,607
1938	4,990	25,186	26,404
1939	5,378 or 4,378[c]	25,403	25,600
1940	5,732 or 4,532 or 5,272	27,343	29,507
1941	5,453	27,691	28,844
1942	5,560	29,031	30,622
1943	4,900	27,310	30,796
1944	5,040	30,383	35,133
1945	6,086	40,393	50,132
1946	6,749	46,002	52,433
1947	7,293	47,235	53,459
1948	7,619	51,361	59,403
1949	8,148	57,946	66,854

Year	Number of Members[a,b]	Expenses ($)	Total Income ($)
1950	9,355	67,818	68,460
1951[d]	12,247	124,316	116,087
1952	15,548	158,764	174,174
1953	21,284	210,200	182,839
1954	28,000	265,261	254,218
1955	29,903	282,716	278,253
1956	35,096	343,556	358,353
1957	37,944	367,950	381,165
1958	40,000	380,003	376,889
1959	41,687	410,437	405,868

[a] Called contributors until 1933.

[b] All figures from ACLU annual reports.

[c] Annual Reports carried figures for previous and subsequent years as well as current year. In 1939 and 1940, different reports cited different sets of figures.

[d] 1951 marks the beginning of the program to integrate affiliate membership and finances into the national ACLU, which accounts for some of the expansion.

NOTES

ABBREVIATIONS USED IN THE NOTES

In addition to the abbreviations used in the text, the following appear in
the notes.

ACLU Board series

American Civil Liberties Union Board Papers, microfilm edition. Glen
Rock, N.J.: Microfilming Corporation of America, 1976. Originals at the
Seeley G. Mudd Manuscript Library, Princeton University, Princeton,
N.J.

ACLU papers

American Civil Liberties Union papers, Seeley G. Mudd Manuscript
Library, Princeton University, Princeton, N.J. Microfilm version
published by Scholarly Resources, Wilmington, Del., 1996. Originals
are listed by box numbers; microfilm, by reel numbers. Because more
and more of the papers are being microfilmed, some of my citations
refer to hard copy that is now accessible on microfilm.

AGH

Arthur Garfield Hays papers, Seeley G. Mudd Manuscript Library,
Princeton University, Princeton, N.J.

AJM

Alexander J. Meiklejohn papers, State Historical Society of Wisconsin,
Madison

BH

Benjamin Huebsch papers, Library of Congress, Washington, D.C.

CLUM papers

Civil Liberties Union of Massachusetts papers, Massachusetts
Historical Society, Boston

ELP

Edward Lambe Parsons papers, Bancroft Library, University of
California, Berkeley

IACLU

American Civil Liberties Union Branch of Illinois papers, University of
Chicago, Chicago, Ill.

IL

Ira Latimer papers, Chicago Historical Society, Chicago, Ill.

JHH

John Haynes Holmes papers, Library of Congress, Washington, D.C.

JL

Joseph Lash papers, Franklin D. Roosevelt Library, Hyde Park, N.Y.

MLE

Morris Ernst papers, Harry Ransom Humanities Research Center, University of Texas, Austin

MP

Merlyn Pitzele papers, State Historical Society of Wisconsin, Madison

NCACLU papers

Northern California Branch of the American Civil Liberties Union papers, California Historical Society, San Francisco

NT

Norman Thomas papers, Astor and Lennox Collection, New York Public Library, New York, N.Y. (microfilm)

OKF

Osmond K. Fraenkel diaries, Seeley G. Mudd Manuscript Library, Princeton University, Princeton, N.J.

RNB

Roger Nash Baldwin papers, Seeley G. Mudd Manuscript Library, Princeton University, Princeton, N.J.

RWR

Roger William Riis papers, Library of Congress, Washington, D.C.

SCACLU·papers

Southern California Branch of the American Civil Liberties Union papers, Special Collections, Charles E. Young Library, University of California, Los Angeles

INTRODUCTION

1 See Lamson, *Baldwin*, 86–114, and Cottrell, *Baldwin*, chaps. 7–8.

2 Roger Riis to Baldwin, 4 May 1939, RWR, ACLU files.

3 Roche and Sachs, "Bureaucrat and Enthusiast," 379.

4 "Defending everybody" is widely used to describe the ACLU's mission; the phrase appeared in a 1953 New Yorker article by Dwight Macdonald and, more recently, in Garey, *Defending Everybody*.

5 Brinkley, *End of Reform*, 10.

6 Quotation is from an NLG spokesman as cited in Garey, *Defending Everybody*, 13.

7 Quotations are from McAuliffe, *Crisis on the Left*, 147, and Patrick Malin, speech at 1960 biennial conference, 21 April; see conference agenda, ACLU Board series, reel 29.

8 Mel Wulf in James, *People's Lawyers*, 26; Schrecker, *Many Are the Crimes*, 411; McAuliffe, *Crisis on the Left*, 89, 90, 91.

9 Mel Wulf in James, *People's Lawyers*, 30.

10 Warren, *Liberals and Communism*, chap. 2.

11 Quotations are from Foner, *Story of American Freedom*, 216, and Brinkley, *End of Reform*, 269. Similar economic arguments may be found in Skocpol, "Legacies of New Deal Liberalism," 87, and Milkis, "Roosevelt," 32.

12 On the Front, see Pells, *Radical Visions*, chap. 7, and Kutulas, *Long War*, chap. 3.

13 Wald, *Exiles from a Future Time*, 1–8.

14 Weber, *Protestant Ethic*; Kornhauser, "Social Bases of Political Commitment."

15 Wang, *American Science in an Age of Anxiety*; Gary, *Nervous Liberals*; Mills, *White Collar*; Jacoby, *Last Intellectuals* (quotation from 6).

16 I borrow the term and idea from Max Weber; see his *Theory of Social and Economic Organization*, 360.

17 The concept comes from Roche and Sachs, "Bureaucrat and Enthusiast," 374.

18 Cottrell, *Baldwin*, chap. 20. Compare with Walker, *In Defense*, 203–6.

19 Quotation from Donohue, *Twilight*, xiii. See also McIlhany, *ACLU on Trial*; Donohue, *Politics of the American Civil Liberties Union*; and Grant, *Trial and Error*.

20 Markmann, *Noblest Cry*; Reitman, *Pulse of Freedom*; Walker, *In Defense*.

21 Lieven, *America Right or Wrong*, 5.

22 As cited in Garey, *Defending Everybody*, 14.

CHAPTER 1

1 Draft statement on the ACLU, January 1950, JHH, container 182.

2 Quotations are from Holmes's writings file, n.d., for *Survey Graphic*, JHH, container 182; Norman Dorsen as cited in Garey, *Defending Everybody*, 135; and Markmann, *Noblest Cry*, 15. Cottrell, *Baldwin*, notes that the ACLU's founders were "overwhelmingly members of the American upper crust" (122). On the religious roots of some of this generation, see Crunden, *Ministers of Reform*. On Baldwin's radicalization, see Cottrell, *Baldwin*, 22–45, and Lamson, *Baldwin*, 30–66.

3 Walker, *In Defense*, 21. See also Johnson, *Challenge*, 10–24.

4 Quotations are from Baldwin, *Reminiscences*, 53, and Cottrell, "Baldwin," 87. For background, see Johnson, *Challenge*, 1–84, and Lamson, *Baldwin*, 96–114.

5 For a list of early leaders, see original ACLU letterhead in Chafee papers, Harvard Archives, box 3. For more on the early ACLU, see Murphy, *World War I*, 240–44.

6 See Gentry, *Hoover*, 137, on government surveillance, and Baldwin, *Reminiscences*, 168–79, on strategy.

7 Quotation is from Polenberg, *Fighting Faiths*, 213. On "clear and present danger," see Graber, *Transforming*, 107–8; on legal realism, see Purcell, *Crisis of Democratic Theory*, 74–94. On progressive era liberals, see Murphy, *World War I*, 175, and Graber, *Transforming*, 2, 11, 76–79.

8 See Gentry, *Hoover*, 137–42, and Powers, *Secrecy and Power*, 148.

9 Baldwin in conversation with Alan Westin, 22 November 1978, ACLU papers, box 206. On the case, see Walker, *In Defense*, 72–77.

10 Quotations are from Baldwin's undated, unpublished memoir of the ACLU's early days, in ACLU papers, box 205, and Cottrell, *Baldwin*, 121. See also Baldwin to Booton Herndon, undated memo, Herndon papers, University of Virginia, box 1. I have capitalized the name of the National ACLU Board throughout so as to distinguish it from the many local boards.

11 Quotations are from Helen Ascher to Baldwin, 6 November 1933, ACLU papers, reel 96, and Morris Ernst, interview with Joe Lash, 7 February 1972, JL, box 49. The claim comes from Baldwin's friend William Butler (interview with Joe Lash, 5 December 1971, JL, box 49) and is supported by the opinion of one of Baldwin's successors, Aryeh Neier, who said that Baldwin's "main concern had been to attract an elite to the organization, people who could speak influentially on behalf of civil liberties" (Neier, *Defending My Enemy*, 74).

12 Morris Ernst, interview with Joe Lash, 7 February 1972, JL, box 49.

13 Quotation is from Baldwin delivering a eulogy for Elizabeth Glendower Evans, 28 January 1938, Evans papers, Schlesinger Library, reel 1.

14 Quotations are from Robert S. Keebler to Baldwin, 16 May 1932, ACLU papers, reel 93, and Benjamin Huebsch to George Leonard, 2 September 1930, Leonard papers, Minnesota Historical Society, box 3. On the ACLU and Bonus Marchers, see Baldwin to Jesse Duke, 1 August 1932; on the offer to defend arrested hunger marchers, see ACLU press release, 1 December 1932, both in ACLU papers, reel 93. On the Pennsylvania efforts, see ACLU papers, reel 104. On California, see Gray, *American Civil Liberties Union of Southern California*.

15 Quotations are from Baldwin, affidavit before Dies Committee, 31 March 1939, reel 169; Forrest Bailey to Clarence Senior, 7 January 1932, reel 92; Baldwin to the National Committee, 18 November 1932, reel 89; William Nunn to Baldwin, 16 March 1931, reel 80; Board minutes, 27 April 1931, reel 79; and Baldwin to Clinton Taft, 31 August 1932, reel 92, all in ACLU papers.

16 Quotation is from Baldwin to *New Republic*, 21 October 1930, ACLU papers, reel 78. The documents on the Gastonia case are on the same reel, or see Klehr, *Heyday*, 29–31, for a summary. On Foster, see press release, 11 October 1930, reel 71, and his resignation, 31 October 1930, reel 78, both in ACLU papers.

17 Quotations are from Evelyn Preston (Baldwin's future wife) to Forrest Bailey, 27 April 1932, and Robert Keebler to Baldwin, 16 May 1932, both in ACLU papers, reel 93. Newspaper clippings on the Kentucky trip are in ACLU papers, reel 91.

18 The quotation is from Baldwin, *Reminiscences*, 238. The details of the mediation attempts are in ACLU papers, reel 92. The legal details are in Walker, *In Defense*, 81–82.

19 Quotations are from the *Buffalo Evening Times*, 6 December 1930, clipping in ACLU papers, reel 72, and excerpts from the Fish committee report, reprinted 8 April 1952, IACLU, box 117.

20 The first two examples were reported by William Keith, 18 January 1932, and Mary D. Brite, 21 January 1932, both in reel 91, but similar examples can be found on almost any reel. On the Moscow gold story, see Baldwin to Austin Lewis, 21 February 1934, and Baldwin to Clinton Taft, 27 February 1934, reel 109. The final quotation is Edward Parsons to Baldwin, 24 August 1934, reel 111. All are in ACLU papers.

21 Quotations are from Baldwin's memoir on the early days of the ACLU, box 205; Forrest Bailey to Clinton Taft, 19 December 1931, reel 83; and Baldwin and Bailey to the Board, 5 January 1932, and to the National Committee, 16 January 1932, reel 89, all in ACLU papers.

22 See Lucille Milner's report, 30 October 1936, and Baldwin to Harry Craven, 12 November 1936, both in ACLU papers, reel 142. On Woollcott, see ACLU papers, reel 127.

23 As quoted by Macdonald, "Defense of Everybody," pt. 2, 57.

24 See Auerbach, "Lawyers and Social Change," 133–69, and Bailey, "Progressive Lawyers," 5. The Baldwin quotation is from his *Reminiscences*, 159.

25 Quotations are from J. V. Stanger to A. L. Wirin, 27 July 1937, reel 154, and Allan Harper to Baldwin, 17 April 1933, reel 97, both in ACLU pa-

pers. Thanks to Baldwin's help, Harper got a job in the Bureau of Indian Affairs.

26 Quotations are from Baldwin speech, 19 February 1934, ACLU papers, reel 105, and as quoted in Lamson, *Baldwin*, 255. A copy of the poll is in AGH, box 2. Murphy, *World War I*, 240–44, talks about the legal realist tradition in the ACLU.

27 Quotations are from Baldwin to Norman Thomas, 16 April 1935, ACLU papers, reel 116; Baldwin, *Reminiscences*, 167–68; and Daniel, *ACLU and the Wagner Act*, 107 (see also 104–19). Daniel suggests that the vote tallies are specious because they included voice votes. He contends that no affiliate supported the Board's position. The tallies, Baldwin to Board, 22 May 1935, are in ACLU papers, reel 116.

28 From 2,700 in 1935 to 3,530 in 1936. The previous years' figures had been 2,500 (1933) and 2,718 (1934). See Appendix 2.

29 On liberals and fascism, see Warren, *Liberals and Communism*, chap. 5.

30 Quotations from Darrow to ACLU, ca. November 1933, and Mary Gawthorpe to Benjamin Huebsch, 29 November 1933, both in ACLU papers, reel 97.

31 There are two schools of thought on the People's Front. The first holds that the Communists manipulated it and duped noncommunists into supporting it. It emphasizes connections between the CPUSA and Moscow and implies that the Communists' main job in the United States was spying for the Soviet Union. The second argues that the People's Front was a legitimate shared enterprise that went sour at the end. My views are much closer to the latter view than the former, with modifications. See my *Long War*, chaps. 5 and 7. A good example of the former position is Klehr, Haynes, and Igorevich, *Secret World*, and Klehr, *Heyday*.

32 Quotations are from Baldwin's affidavit before the Dies Committee, 31 March 1938, ACLU papers, reel 169; Statement on the Attitude of the American Civil Liberties Union to Current Issues of Civil Rights, March 1937, copy in Leonard papers, Minnesota Historical Society, box 4; and Baldwin's interview in James, *People's Lawyers*, 8.

33 Quotations are from Baldwin to John Temple Graves II, 23 January 1940, ACLU papers, reel 185; Baldwin, *Reminiscences*, 158; and Washington committee minutes, 1 November 1937, ACLU papers, reel 150.

34 Quotation is from Baldwin's memo on Ernst, March 1974, RNB, box 6. See also Baldwin, *Reminiscences*, 29, and Fraenkel, *Oral History*, 59. MLE, boxes 123 and 124, contain correspondence between Ernst and New Deal officials.

35 Quotation is from "Legal Left." On the NLG, see Rabinowitz, *Unrepen-*

tant Leftist, 168–70; Auerbach, *Unequal Justice*, 198–203; Bailey, "Case of the National Lawyers Guild," 130–33; and Weinberg and Fassler, *Historical Sketch of the National Lawyers Guild*. The Board approved Ernst's request to use the mailing list on 7 December 1936, ACLU papers, reel 128.

36 Baldwin to Ira Latimer, 25 March 1937, ACLU papers, reel 151. See discussions of public relations tactics in letters from Baldwin to Roger Riis, 2 April 1936, ACLU papers, reel 128; Riis to Baldwin, 4 May 1939, RWR, ACLU files; and Raymond Wise to Baldwin, 11 August 1939, ACLU papers, reel 169.

37 Administration office of New York World's Fair to Baldwin, 26 July 1939, ACLU papers, reel 171. On *Pins and Needles*, see Joan Hopkinson, telegram to Baldwin, 12 May 1938, and CCLC financial memo, 1938, both in ACLU papers, reel 164.

38 H. Williams to Baldwin, 26 January 1938, ACLU papers, reel 165.

39 On the statements, see Lamson, *Baldwin*, 190–92. The statements haunted the ACLU even decades later. See Norman Dorsen's quotation in Garey, *Defending Everybody*, 91.

40 Isserman's Freedom of Information Act file contains a 27 December 1949 report that described him as closely affiliated with the CPUSA, so close "it matters little whether he carries a Communist Party membership card." See National Lawyers Guild papers, Bancroft Library, series 13, box 68. Unlike Isserman, whose Party membership was secret, Flynn informed her fellow ACLU officers when she joined the Party in the late 1930s. Flynn's complaint was expressed in a letter to "Friends," 4 February 1939, ACLU papers, reel 168.

41 Quotations are from Baldwin to Harry Ward, 17 July 1938, RNB, box 8, and Seymour to Baldwin, 10 May 1939, ACLU papers, reel 167. In accepting his Board membership, Childs declared, "I always thought your organization needed to be weighed with dodos" (Childs to Baldwin, 24 May 1937, ACLU papers, reel 142).

42 The first two quotations are from Baldwin, *Reminiscences*, 116. The others are from Baldwin's 29 April 1937 memo and Edward Tittman's 27 March 1937 letter to Baldwin, both in ACLU papers, reel 142.

43 The first two quotations are from Baldwin, *Reminiscences*, 197. The others are from Baldwin to Robert Marshall, 24 March 1937, and Board minutes, 27 December 1937, both in ACLU papers, reel 150. On the same reel, Maurice Wilsie, 4 June 1937, conveys the list.

44 The first quotation comes from an unsigned memo to Baldwin paraphrasing Morris Ernst's recommendations, 4 January [1938], ACLU

papers, reel 153. Over it, Baldwin scrawled "no." The second quotation comes from William Fennell to Ernst, 18 May 1938, MLE, box 123. The final quotation comes from Macdonald, "Defense of Everybody," pt. 2, 48.

45 Baldwin, *Reminiscences*, 162.

46 In *Modern Social Movements*, William Cameron notes that movements "modeled after business corporations tend to hold meetings like those of executive boards" (88), including most of the processes the Union codified in the 1930s. On Milner, see her *Education*.

47 On the Socialist Party of the United States in the 1930s, see Warren, *Alternative Vision*. On the CPUSA, see Klehr, *Heyday*, and Ottanelli, *Communist Party*.

48 Walker, *In Defense*, 121.

49 Quotations are from Thomas to Corliss Lamont, 6 April 1934, reel 109; Holmes to Baldwin, 20 February 1934, reel 105; and Osmond Fraenkel to Thomas, 15 December 1939, reel 168, all in ACLU papers. The details may be found in ACLU papers, reels 105 and 109, and NT, reel 56.

50 On the anti-Stalinists, see Wald, *New York Intellectuals*, pts. 1 and 2. On disillusionment amongst liberals, see Kutulas, *Long War*, chap. 5, and Warren, *Liberals and Communism*, chap. 9. On right-wing anticommunists, see Powers, *Not without Honor*. On the Dies Committee, see Goodman, *Committee*, 24–58.

51 On America First charges, see Baldwin to editor, 10 October 1934, ACLU papers, reel 109. On the "brains trust," see clipping from the *Baltimore Morning Sun*, 29 January 1935, ACLU papers, reel 119. On Frankfurter, see "The Happy Hot Dogs," clipping, 4 November 1935, ACLU papers, reel 119. On Ickes and the dinner, see Lippman's column, December 1937, ACLU papers, clipping in reel 147. The quotation is from Baldwin to Lippman, 15 December 1937, ACLU papers, reel 156. On Ickes and Dies, see *New York Times*, 24 November 1938, and Ickes, *Secret Diary*, 506, 529. On Murphy, see Morris Ernst to Murphy, 21 January 1939, Frank papers, Yale University, series 3, box 26. On Frankfurter's Supreme Court hearings, see *New York Times*, 11, 12 January 1939. A memo, "Charges before the Dies Committee regarding the ACLU," 12 December 1938, ACLU papers, reel 169, is a complete cataloging of accusations leveled by Dies's witnesses. See also Simmons, "American Civil Liberties Union and the Dies Committee."

52 The quotation is from Baldwin to Arthur Garfield Hays, 20 March 1939, AGH, box 5. The files included communications with New Deal congressmen, with Frankfurter, and with ACLU supporters in the Bureau

of Indian Affairs. Approval ratings are from Heineman, "Media Bias," 38. Disapproval ratings are from Britt and Menefee, "Has Mr. Dies the Floor?" On Roosevelt and Dies, see Polenberg, "Roosevelt and Civil Rights," 165.

53 Quotations are from Board statement, 21 December 1936, ACLU papers, reel 147; Baldwin to Arthur Garfield Hays, 20 January 1937, AGH, box 4; Summons and Complaint, ACLU against the *American Mercury* and Harold Lord Varney, n.d., ACLU papers, reel 147; Flynn's postcard vote on the statement, n.d., and Roger Riis to Baldwin, 13 July 1938, both in ACLU papers, reel 156. The Varney article, "The Civil Liberties Union," appeared in the *American Mercury*, December 1936, 385–99. The Mencken article and letter appeared in the *American Mercury*, October 1938, 182–90.

54 W. M. N. Leonard of the Texas affiliate to the ACLU, 16 June 1938, ACLU papers, reel 166. There are similar complaints in ACLU papers, reel 178, including some resignations.

55 Quotations are from Jerome Britchey to Sol Alper, 17 April 1939, ACLU papers, reel 169; Board minutes, 28 November 1938, ACLU Board series, reel 7; Hays telegram to Dies, 22 August 1939, and Baldwin's affidavit, 31 March 1939, both in ACLU papers, reel 169.

56 Quotations are from Morris Moskin to Arthur Garfield Hays, 18 January 1938, AGH, box 4, and Holmes's statement, 28 October 1939, RWR, ACLU files.

57 Quotations are from Holmes to Harry Ward, 6 February 1938, and to Lucille Milner, 8 April 1938, both in JHH, container 185; Baldwin to Harry Ward, 12 July 1938, RNB, box 8; and Harry Ward to Alexander Meiklejohn, 16 May 1937, AJM, box 30. Much later, Baldwin claimed that Van Kleeck was acting on Communist Party orders. See his October 1976 memo in RNB, box 15.

58 Quotations are from dissenting opinion of Ward, 17 June 1938, Van Kleeck papers, Smith College, box 36; Holmes to Riis, 8 February, 2 March 1938, both in JHH, container 185; Policies Concerning the Civil Rights of Labor Relations, August 1938, Leonard papers, Minnesota Historical Society, box 4; and Walker, *In Defense*, 103. Lamson assesses that Baldwin later retold the story so as to separate himself from Ward even though at the time both believed Ford's actions were coercive. See Lamson, *Baldwin*, 217–18.

59 Holmes to Baldwin, 28 September 1938, JHH, container 186. See Kutulas, *Long War*, 152–54, on anti-Stalinists' views of the People's Front; see 126–29 on the *Partisan Review*; on Hook, see 154–55.

60 In his memoir Hook says he, Frank Trager (a Socialist), Ferdinand Lund-
berg, and John Dewey founded the CCF. See Hook, *Out of Step*, 259–64.
Lyons claims he wrote the CCF's manifesto and quotes parts of it in his
Red Decade, 343–44. On the significance of the CCF's founding statement, see Adler and Paterson, "Red Fascism," and Kutulas, "'Totalitarianism' Transformed."

61 Quotations are from Norman Thomas to Board, 6 March 1939, NT, reel
56, and minutes of special meeting, 6 March 1939, ACLU Board series,
reel 7. The original vote (23 January 1939) was 8 to 4 in favor; the final
vote was 17 to 6 against.

62 See NLG minutes beginning 10 February and carrying over to 12 Feb-
ruary, National Lawyers Guild papers, Bancroft Library, series 1, box 1.
Ernst, ACLU Board member Osmond Fraenkel, Minneapolis/St. Paul
ACLU correspondent George B. Leonard, and Philadelphia affiliate ac-
tivist Alexander Frey were all part of the discussion, with all opposing
Ernst.

63 See documents in ACLU papers, reel 171. For background on the group,
see Kutulas, *Long War*, 154–55.

64 Macdonald, "Defense of Everybody," pt. 2, 47.

CHAPTER 2

1 Taft, *Fifteen Years*.

2 Quotation is from Baldwin, *Reminiscences*, 191. On Baldwin's attitude,
see Morris Ernst's interview with Joe Lash, 7 February 1972, JL, box 49.

3 Knutson, "American Civil Liberties Union of Northern California,"
14–21.

4 Quotations are from Baldwin to the National Committee, 7 February
1929, reel 71, and Forrest Bailey to Carl Brannin, 29 August 1931, reel 86.
W. Ellison Chalmers to Forrest Bailey, 15 March 1931, reel 56, reports on
the Madison group. "Suggested By-Laws for Local Committees," April
1930, reel 77, spells out expectations. The statistics are taken from affiliate questionnaires, 1936, reel 129. All are in ACLU papers.

5 Quotations are from Caroline Parker to Forrest Bailey, 28 December
1931, reel 84; Allan Harper, Memo #3—Finances, ca. October 1931, reel
85; and Baldwin to Walter Nelson, 11 January 1932, reel 94, all in ACLU
papers. On the St. Louis problem, see Richard C. Bland to Baldwin, 8
February 1933, ACLU papers, reel 103.

6 Baldwin to Joe Lash, 21 October 1971, JL, box 49.

7 Baldwin to W. G. Nowell, 14 June 1930, offers his criticism. Nowell replied on 27 June 1930, resigning. Harper to Baldwin, 28 October 1930,

confesses disappointment. All are in ACLU papers, reel 78. Harper would later go on to a New Deal job, largely due to Baldwin's string pulling.

8 Quotations are from David Niles to John Codman, summer 1933; Myriam Sieve to CLUM, fall 1933; and Niles to Codman, 13 November 1933, all in CLUM papers, box 1.

9 Latimer to Baldwin, 12 February 1933, ACLU papers, reel 104. See Baldwin to "friends" on the offer to pay a secretary to run an Atlanta group, 22 July 1931, ACLU papers, reel 84.

10 Quotations are from Baldwin to Ernest Besig, 14 November 1938, ACLU papers, reel 163, and George Leonard to Baldwin, 12 January 1933, Leonard papers, Minnesota Historical Society, box 3.

11 Quotations are from Parker-Bennett to Baldwin, 9 November 1930, and Baldwin's reply, 13 November 1930, both in ACLU papers, reel 79. The last two are from Carl Brannin to Baldwin, 15 July 1931, ACLU papers, reel 86. The rest of the details are in those two reels.

12 Quotation is from Lewis to Baldwin, 15 December 1933; see Baldwin's reply, 18 December 1933, both in ACLU papers, reel 102.

13 The first quotation is from Baldwin to Dorothy Detzer, 3 November 1937. The next two are from Clinton Taft to Baldwin, 16 November 1937. All are in ACLU papers, reel 150.

14 Most of my information on the Stromberg case comes from Stromberg's niece, Judy Branfman, who is working on a documentary film on the subject, tentatively titled "The Land of Orange Groves and Jails." I was able to preview the film and hear Branfman discuss it at a Western Association of Women Historians conference in Berkeley, California, on 7 June 2003. The quotation from the law comes from American Civil Liberties Union, *California Red Flag Case*, 4. The quotation from Chief Justice Charles Evans Hughes's opinion is cited at <www.aclumontana. org>. Baldwin's response is in Walker, *In Defense*, 96.

15 For more background, see Beck and Williams, *California*, 392–94.

16 Quotations are from Taft's third-person summary of his experience, June 1930, and Taft to Baldwin, 5 May 1930, both in ACLU papers, reel 76. On financial arrangements, see Baldwin to R. W. Henderson, 8 May 1930, ibid.

17 Baldwin to Gallagher, 10 September 1930; Gallagher to Kathryn Fenn, 2 September 1930 (my emphasis); and Lucille Milner [?] to Fenn, 10 September 1930, all in ACLU papers, reel 71. On the suit, see press releases, 20 March, 10 May 1930, both in ACLU papers, reel 74.

18 Besig, telegram to Wirin, 9 June 1934, ACLU papers, reel 111, retells his experience. SCACLU executive committee to Baldwin and the ACLU, tele-

gram dated 25 January 1934, ACLU papers, reel 111, describes Wirin's. The other quotations come from Harry Ward et al. to Perkins, Wallace, and Wagner, 12 May 1934, reel 280, and Wirin to Clinton Taft, 26 May 1934, reel 111, both in ACLU papers. A good source on both California strikes is Gray, *American Civil Liberties Union of Southern California*. On Glassford, see Loftis, *Witnesses*, 78–79.

19 Quotation is from L. M. Wolf to Baldwin, 21 January 1931, ACLU papers, reel 84. Background on Gallagher comes from introductory biographical materials in Gallagher papers, Southern California Library for Social Studies and Research. On Wirin, see undated notes from an unattributed interview with him, SCACLU papers, box 70. On Besig, see the *San Francisco Examiner*, 18 October 1970.

20 See, for example, Mary Hutchinson to Baldwin, 16 February 1932, ACLU papers, reel 92.

21 The first two quotations are from Baldwin to Taft, 22 February 1935. The third is from Baldwin to Taft, 18 April 1935. All are in ACLU papers, reel 123. The final quotation is from McWilliams, *Honorable in All Things*, 68.

22 Quotation is from George Hedley to Baldwin, 8 February 1935, ACLU papers, reel 123. Financial information is from Knutson, "American Civil Liberties Union of Northern California," 153. The NCACLU's take was approximately $6.00 for each member, $1.00 more per member than the national ACLU raised that year.

23 Schwartz, *From West to East*, 207.

24 Meyer Baylin, a Party organizer, recalls breaking up a few SCACLU meetings in the early 1930s. See Baylin, *Oral History*, 41, 43. I have seen no other references.

25 Quotations are from Al Sessions of the Kern County Union, 17 April 1935, ACLU papers, reel 114; Clinton Taft, paraphrasing Baldwin, to Baldwin, 8 December 1939, ACLU papers, reel 187; and Baldwin, *Reminiscences*, 183, 468.

26 Besig to Baldwin, 25 July 1935, NCACLU papers, box 4.

27 Winter to A. L. Wirin (temporarily affiliated with the national organization), 21 August 1934, ACLU papers, reel 111. In the margin next to her request, Wirin penciled in "NO!," as did Baldwin. A typical letter from Socialist Lillian Symes is hers to Wirin, 8 August 1934, also in ACLU papers, reel 111. On Trotskyist Herbert Solow, see his letter to Baldwin, 22 June 1935, ACLU papers, reel 123. Myron Brinig, a San Francisco poet involved in these early struggles, wrote a poem that contained the

line "Ella is hella," a conclusion many would reach. See Brinig to Marie Short, 8 June 1936, Short papers, Bancroft Library, box 1.

28 Quotations are from Baldwin, *Reminiscences*, 185, and Winter to A. L. Wirin, 8 October 1934; Baldwin to Lillian Symes, 22 October 1934; and Baldwin to Williams, 9 October 1934, ACLU papers, reel 111.

29 Most of the documents are in ACLU papers, reel 123.

30 Examples of local Communist complaints are Richard Bransten to Baldwin, 9 January, 27 March 1935, and Winter to Baldwin, 2 January 1935, ACLU papers, reel 123. Petition, late 1935, is in ACLU papers, reel 123. The 1938 complaints, from Harold Chapman Brown, are in ACLU papers, reel 163. Baldwin's response was in a letter to Brown, 3 May 1938, ACLU papers, reel 163. The NCACLU's response, from which the final quotation was taken, was Besig to Lucille Milner, 16 August 1938, NCACLU papers, box 4.

31 Quotations are from Ira Latimer to Baldwin, 11 October 1937, reel 151, and Lucille Milner to Gus Solomon, 24 September 1935, reel 126. Solomon to Baldwin, 9 September 1935, reel 126, links affiliate independence with freedom not to cooperate with fronts. All are in ACLU papers.

32 Quotations are from Bond to Milner, 6 January 1941, paraphrasing Milner; Milner to Quincy Howe, 14 March 1941; Fletcher Parker to Milner, 24 April 1941; Kimball to Bingham, 22 September 1941; Kimball to ACLU, 22 September 1941; and Milner to Kimball, 2 October 1941, all in ACLU papers, reel 199.

33 Quotations are from Baldwin to Katherine Gay, 17 May 1935, reel 125, and Baldwin to David Ziskind, 20 September 1937 (two quotations), and Ziskind to Baldwin, 4 October 1937, both in reel 150. The full story is in reel 150. All are in ACLU papers.

34 Quotations are from Ira Latimer, testimony before the Subversive Activities Control Board, 5 May 1954, 1233, transcript in IL, box 8; Lucille Milner to Archey Bell, 30 July 1937, ACLU papers, reel 153; and Frederick Ballard to Baldwin, 20 October 1937, ACLU papers, reel 150. On New Jersey, see ACLU papers, reel 153. On Washington and New York, see ACLU papers, reels 137 and 103, respectively.

35 Quotations are from Baldwin to secretaries of local committees, 22 August 1935; Ernest Besig to Baldwin, 17 October 1935; Baldwin to secretaries, 22 August 1935; and Alexander Meiklejohn to Baldwin, 18 September 1935, all in ACLU papers, reel 115. The NCACLU, the SCACLU, the CCLC, and the Erie County Civil Liberties Union objected to the dues

change. The NCACLU and the New York City Committee objected to the front statement. All the documents and bylaws drafts are in ACLU papers, reel 115.

36 Quotations are from Gus Solomon to Baldwin, 4 February 1936, ACLU papers, reel 139; Ira Latimer to Baldwin, 11 March 1937, and Irving Clark to Baldwin, 16 January 1936, both in ACLU papers, reel 140; and Besig to Mary Hutchinson, 8 January 1936, NCACLU papers, box 4.

37 Quotations are from Latimer to *Chicago Tribune*, 1 September 1948, IL, box 6, and Latimer to Baldwin, 18 March 1936, ACLU papers, reel 137. See also Latimer to Baldwin, 21 December 1936, ACLU papers, reel 137. Latimer's recollection of being approached by the CPUSA is in his testimony before the Subversive Activities Control Board, 20 May 1954, transcript in IL, box 8. The local board member in question was Tom McKenna, whom another CCLC person described as "a Stalinist functionary" (Leon M. Despres, tape sent to author, 22 February 2003).

38 Quotations are from CCLC minutes, 6 November 1937, and Latimer to Baldwin, 13 January 1937, both in reel 151; Latimer to Lucille Milner, 19 November 1937, reel 152; Latimer to Baldwin, 8 January 1937, reel 151, all in ACLU papers; and Latimer's testimony before the Committee on Character and Fitness, 22 December 1954, IL, box 8.

39 Quotations are from Leon M. Despres, tape to author, 22 February 2003, and Baldwin, *Reminiscences*, 186. See Latimer to Baldwin, 26 July 1937, reel 151, and CCLC minutes, 21 March, 26 April, and 3 October 1939, reel 175, all in ACLU papers.

40 Quotations are from Baldwin's memo on Wirin, August 1956, ACLU papers, box 457; Hays to Wirin, 20 January 1933, AGH, box 2; and A. A. Heist in undated notes, SCACLU papers, box 70. Baldwin to Latimer, 27 July 1937, ACLU papers, reel 151, points out the comparative salaries.

41 Lucille Milner to Gilman, 22 March 1937, ACLU papers, reel 152.

42 Baldwin to Walter Nelson, 9 October 1937, ACLU papers, reel 152.

43 See Besig to Baldwin, 21 July 1939, reel 175, and Robert Stripling of HUAC to Besig, 22 December 1938, and Besig's affidavit, 30 December 1938, reel 169, all in ACLU papers.

44 Samuel Angoff to Baldwin, 9 November 1937, ACLU papers, reel 152.

CHAPTER 3

1 As quoted in Cottrell, *Baldwin*, 350.

2 Quotations are from Baldwin's memo to Alan Reitman, 21 December 1951, RNB, box 2; Lewy, *Cause That Failed*, 145; and Baldwin as cited in Lamson, *Baldwin*, 201.

3 All quotations are from Hook's letter to Baldwin, 27 September 1939, ACLU papers, reel 168. Follow the debate in ACLU papers, reel 168. Hook finally resigned on 4 December 1939. His intransigence was legendary. See the papers in the "Red Totalitarianism" folder in Kirchwey papers, Schlesinger Library, box 9.

4 Quotations are from Holmes's statement, 26 October 1939, and Thomas to Osmond Fraenkel, 19 December 1939 (on Hook), reel 167, and Hook to Baldwin, 18 October 1939, reel 168, all in ACLU papers.

5 Ward's testimony is in U.S. Congress, House Special Committee on Un-American Activities, *Investigations*, 6231–330. The league changed its name in 1937. The response is Jerome Britchey's to Morris Ernst and Arthur Garfield Hays, 31 October 1939, AGH, box 5.

6 Quotations are from Baldwin, manuscript draft on the early ACLU, in ACLU papers, box 205; Morris Ernst to Ward, 13 October 1939, MLE, box 404; and William Spofford paraphrasing Thomas, in a letter to Baldwin, 4 December 1939, and Roger Riis to Baldwin, 20 October 1939, both in ACLU papers, reel 168. On that same reel are other letters. The final quotation is from William Spofford to Baldwin, 4 December 1939, ACLU papers, reel 168.

7 The first quotation is from William Spofford to Baldwin, 14 October [1939], Van Kleeck papers, Smith College, box 36, and the others are from an unsigned, undated report on Thomas, ACLU papers, reel 168. On the Ward resolution, see Board minutes, 14 December 1939, ACLU Board series, reel 7. On the Thomas matter, see Board minutes, 29 January 1940, ACLU Board series, reel 8.

8 Quotations are from de Silver's letters to Thomas, 5 December 1939, NT, reel 9, and to Baldwin, 6 December 1939, ACLU papers, reel 180.

9 Quotations are from Baldwin's conversation with Alan Westin, 6 December 1978, ACLU papers, box 206, and "A Memo on Elizabeth Gurley Flynn," March 1974, Lamson papers, Mudd Library, box 1.

10 Quotations are from Fraenkel, *Oral History*, 59, and Milner's 22 March 1972 interview with Joe Lash, JL, box 49. The transcription of Fraenkel's comment reads "fix," but "fits" makes more sense.

11 Quotations are from Holmes statement, 28 October 1939, RWR, ACLU files; Ernst to Holmes, 4 January 1940, MLE, box 405; and Riis to Raymond Wise, 30 November 1939, MLE, box 403.

12 See U.S. Congress, House Special Committee on Un-American Activities, *Investigations*, 6308–9.

13 The first quotation is from Dies, "More Snakes Than I Can Kill," 18. The next two come from Baldwin to Gardner Jackson, 16 December 1939,

reel 169, and Ernst to Baldwin, 1 March 1940, reel 182 (my emphasis), both in ACLU papers. The final one is from Ernst to Lamont, 12 January 1940, MLE, box 405.

14 Quotations are from Lamont in a 1971 interview conducted by Helen C. Camp in *Iron*, 154, and Ernst to Frank, 28 October 1939, MLE, box 403. There are two other letters from Ernst to Frank, dated 26 and 27 October 1939, in MLE, box 411. Telegrams in MLE, box 404, show Ernst reserving the room for the party, suggesting it occurred at his instigation.

15 Camp, *Iron*, 154; report dated 4 March 1943 and contained in Isserman's Freedom of Information Act file, copy in National Lawyers Guild papers, Bancroft Library, series 13, box 68.

16 Lamont, from his introduction to *Trial of Flynn*, 21, and Isserman, *Past Is Prologue*, 7.

17 Quotations are from Jackson to Ernst, 28 November 1939, Jackson papers, Roosevelt Library, container 3, and Holmes to Baldwin, 2 April 1940, JHH, container 187. See also Lewis to CLUM, 9 February 1940, ACLU papers, reel 182, and Ackland to Clinton Taft, 12 April 1940, SCACLU papers, box 52.

18 Quotations are from Simmons, "American Civil Liberties Union and the Dies Committee," 197, and Walker, *In Defense*, 129. See also Lewy, *Cause That Failed*, 149, and O'Reilly, *Hoover and the Un-Americans*, 182.

19 Quotations are from Gardner Jackson, paraphrasing Ray Wise in a letter to the Board, 25 December 1939, Jackson papers, Roosevelt Library, container 3; Riis to Baldwin, 20 December 1939, RWR, ACLU files; and Baldwin to Maury Maverick, 15 January 1940, ACLU papers, reel 190. A draft of the original Dies report dated 14 December 1939 is in ACLU papers, reel 169.

20 Hays to Gardner Jackson, 26 December 1939, AGH, box 42; Lamont to Holmes, 17 May 1940, ACLU papers, reel 180; Jackson to Hays, 4 January 1940, Jackson papers, Roosevelt Library, container 3.

21 Quotations are from Ray Wise to Baldwin, 16 December 1939, reel 169, and Mary Van Kleeck to Lucille Milner, 6 January 1940, reel 182. The revised text, dated 8 January 1940, is in reel 182. All are in ACLU papers.

22 All quotations are from Holmes to Baldwin, 3 January 1940, AGH, box 44.

23 The first quotation comes from Baldwin to Henry Dana, 17 May 1940, ACLU papers, reel 180. The others are from Memo to Create a More Harmonious Board, n.d., and Thomas's response to Baldwin, 31 January 1940, both in NT, reel 56.

24 Board minutes, 18 January 1940, ACLU Board series, reel 8. The full resolution text may be found in Lamont, *Trial of Flynn*, 42–43.

25 On Baldwin's secret authorship, see Baldwin to Mary Sterling McAuliffe, 6 March 1972, RNB, box 6, and to Morris Ernst (who drafted the 1939 version of the resolution), 30 January 1940, ACLU papers, reel 180. Ward's ruling and the other measure are in Board minutes, 18, 29 January 1940. The final quotation is from Board minutes, 22 January 1940. At the 5 February annual meeting there were 8 votes for the resolution present and 16 by proxy. All Board minutes are in ACLU Board series, reel 8. The anticommunists' pressures on Baldwin are in Holmes to Baldwin, 19 January 1940, ACLU papers, reel 192, and Thomas to Dorothy Bromley, Ernst, Holmes, Roger Riis, and John Finerty, 19 January 1940, RWR, ACLU files.

26 Quotations are from press release, 5 February 1940, ACLU Board series, reel 8; the Philadelphia ACLU's newsletter, 25 April 1940, ACLU papers, reel 90; the New Jersey Civil Liberties Union's resolution, n.d., ACLU papers, reel 189; *Open Forum*, 23 March 1940, 1; and Edward Parsons to Baldwin, 30 January 1940, ACLU papers, reel 192.

27 Quotations are from Baldwin to Ira Latimer, 20 April 1940, ACLU papers, reel 188; to Ernest Besig, 13 February 1940, NCACLU papers, box 2; and Corliss Lamont to Patrick Malin (Baldwin's successor), 20 June 1951, SCACLU papers, box 52. See Holmes's report on his visit to Philadelphia, 17 April 1940, and to Cleveland, 1 May 1940, both in JHH, container 187. His comment on the former visit was that "you don't make immediate converts."

28 Quotations are from Alice Ware to Elizabeth Gurley Flynn, 15 March 1940, and Alice Venderlaan to Ernest Besig, 20 April 1940, Flynn papers, Tamiment Library, box 4, and Mary Ganthorpe to Baldwin, 22 February 1940, ACLU papers, reel 180.

29 All quotations except the last are from Baldwin to Holmes, 15 March 1940, ACLU papers, reel 180. The last is from Holmes to Lucille Milner, 21 March 1940, JHH, container 187.

30 Riis to Baldwin, 28 March 1940, RWR, ACLU files. Lucille Milner remembered that the mail ran 2 to 1 against the measure; see her *Education*, 266.

31 Quotations are from Holmes's statement upon being elected chairman of the Board, 26 February 1940, ACLU Board series, reel 8, and statement by Riis, 22 April 1940, and Holmes to Baldwin, 19 March 1940, both in ACLU papers, reel 180.

32 The quotations are from Holmes's statement, 26 February 1940, ACLU
Board series, reel 8; Thomas to Osmond Fraenkel, 19 December 1939,
NT, reel 56; Hays, *City Lawyer*, 229; Holmes to de Silver, quoting her
letter to him, 21 February 1940, JHH, container 187; and Baldwin to
Holmes, 12 March 1940, ACLU papers, reel 180. On Baldwin and Flynn,
see Rosalind Baxandall's introduction to *Words on Fire*, 41–42. Because
I was unable to confirm this information anywhere else, I checked with
Baxandall, who told me in a 22 January 2003 e-mail that Flynn's niece
and three or four Party members told her Flynn and Baldwin were lovers. In that same e-mail, she offered her opinion of Baldwin's motives.
HUAC's unpublished 1955 report on the ACLU, p. 20 (ACLU papers, box
609), suggests that financial need rather than principle led the Union to
consider expelling Flynn.

33 Quotations are from Ernst to Holmes, 16 March 1940, MLE, box 405;
Holmes to Riis, 19 March 1940, JHH, container 187; and George West to
Holmes and John Sayre, 25 April 1940, Flynn papers, Tamiment Library,
box 5. The compromise resolution lost by a 6 to 5 vote, with 7 not voting;
see memo to the National Committee, June 1940 in ACLU papers, vol. 12
(1975).

34 Quotations are from Holmes to Riis, 19 March 1940, JHH, container 187,
and to Baldwin, 8 May 1940, ACLU papers, reel 180. On resignations, see
Holmes to Baldwin, 18 March 1940, JHH, container 187.

35 Quotations are from Riis to William Allen White, 4 November 1952, MP,
box 12; Fraenkel, *Oral History*, 56; and William Spofford to Flynn, 9 September 1940, Van Kleeck papers, Smith College, box 19. A transcript of
the proceedings is in Lamont, *Trial of Flynn*.

36 Quotations are from Baldwin to Flynn, 18 August [1940], Flynn papers,
Tamiment Library, box 5, and Herbert Levy to Pat Malin, 11 March 1953,
ACLU papers, box 613. Baldwin later told Helen Camp that he put Flynn
in a taxi and kissed her goodnight; see Camp, *Iron*, 164. This contradicts
Flynn's version, contained in a letter to the editor of the *People's World*,
13 May 1940; in Lamson, *Baldwin*, 235–36, Baldwin contradicts himself
and claims he took Flynn to the hearing but never saw her again afterward. The National Committee endorsed the Flynn expulsion by a majority of one, 26 of 51 members voting yes.

37 Quotations are from William Spofford to Flynn, 9 May 1940, box 19, and
Van Kleeck to Flynn, 21 March 1940, box 36, both in Van Kleeck papers,
Smith College, and Baldwin to Daniel Lerner, 18 September 1940, ACLU
papers, reel 203. The outcome is reported in Board minutes, 24 June
1940, ACLU Board series, reel 8.

38 Quotations are from Holmes to Riis, 15 March 1940, JHH, container 187, and Board minutes, 18 March 1940, ACLU papers, reel 182. See Appendix 2 for numbers. Numbers come from ACLU annual reports, but the 1939 and 1940 reports are internally inconsistent.

39 Quotations are from Baldwin's interview with James in *People's Lawyers*, 9, and Freeman to Floyd Dell, 3 June 1951, in Dell-Freeman folders, Dell papers, Newberry Library. The *Survey Graphic* article is Weybright, "Communists and Civil Liberties," 290.

40 Quotations are from Roger Riis to Baldwin, 20 January 1940, RWR, ACLU file; Edward Parsons to Baldwin, 30 January 1940, ACLU papers, reel 192; and Henry Pratt Fairchild to Riis, 25 March 1940, RWR, ACLU file.

41 Steele, "Fear of the Mob," 74; Walker, *In Defense*, 133; Wright, "ACLU," 96.

42 Quotations are from Milner to Ernst, 4 November 1940, MLE, box 403; Membership Committee report, 4 October 1940, ACLU papers, reel 180; Flynn, "Why I Won't Resign," 11; and Childs to Oliver Holden, 5 April 1940, ACLU papers, reel 180. Milner to Ernst, 14 March 1941, MLE, box 403, reports the success of his drive.

43 Both quotations come from Bingham to Holmes, 27 December 1940, ACLU papers, reel 193. The committee's report, 14 March 1941, is on the same reel. My ideas about organizational cultures come from Freytag, "Organizational Culture."

44 Quotation is from Urofsky, "Roosevelt Court," 73. On external changes, see Foner, *Story of American Freedom*, 216; Milkis, "Roosevelt," 34–35; Plotke, *Building a Democratic Political Order*, 168–80; and Milkman, *P.M.*, 2.

45 Quotations are from Holmes to Baldwin, 30 December 1940; Morris Ernst memo, 27 May 1941; and Eduard Lindeman memo, 30 October 1941, all in ACLU papers, reel 193, and Rice to Ernst, 10 November 1941, MLE, box 137.

46 Quotations are from Abraham Isserman, paraphrasing Ernst, to the Board, 28 February 1940, MLE, box 411, and Baldwin, *Reminiscences*, 129. Ernst's proposal is in ACLU papers, reel 182. Baldwin reported the outcome in a letter to the National Committee and affiliates, 28 March 1941, ACLU papers, reel 199. For more on Ernst and disclosure, see Simmons, "Morris Ernst and Disclosure," 15–30. Ernst's ideas would later influence the Mundt-Nixon bill and the McCarran Act.

47 Baldwin to Lloyd Garrison, 26 February, 18 March 1940, and to Ross, 28 March 1940, all in ACLU papers, reel 179. Ross seems to have been the fourth choice behind Garrison, William A. White, and Zechariah

Chafee. Correspondence between Ross and Baldwin on his other activities in Ross papers, State Historical Society of Wisconsin, box 24, illustrates Baldwin's displeasure with Ross's positions.

48 See Board minutes, 7, 28 October 1940, ACLU Board series, reel 8.

49 Quotations are from William Spofford to Baldwin, 27 January 1941, ACLU papers, reel 193. Both Isserman's letter of resignation, 25 February 1941, and a later summary of his ACLU activities are in National Lawyers Guild papers, Bancroft Library, series 13, box 68.

50 The first two quotations are from Baldwin to Corliss Lamont, 27 March 1941; the last is from Lamont to Baldwin, 26 March 1941. See also Lynd to Baldwin, 8, 14, 27 February 1941, all in ACLU papers, reel 203.

51 Quotations are from Flynn, as cited in a letter from Lucille Milner to the editor of the *Sunday Worker*, 2 July 1941, ACLU papers, reel 197; Baldwin to Minor, 14 June 1940, ACLU papers, reel 185; Baldwin to Fred J. Sisson, 17 September 1940, ACLU papers, reel 182; and Walker, *In Defense*, 127. On the Rapp-Coudert hearings, see Walker, *In Defense*, 125. On the Smith Act see OKF, 1 December 1954, 1. On minority parties on the ballot, see, for instance, E. A. Ross et al. to Robert Jackson, 31 July 1940, ACLU papers, reel 183. Holmes to L. L. Coryell, 11 May 1942, JHH, container 196, features a disclaimer.

52 Sidney Hollander Jr. of the Maryland Civil Liberties Committee to Baldwin, 23 February 1941, ACLU papers, reel 200. On other events, see CCLC minutes, 30 January 1940, ACLU papers, reel 188; *Open Forum*, 9 March 1940, 1–2; and New England Conference on Civil Liberties, 27 January 1940, ACLU papers, reel 189.

53 The Denver quotation is from Baldwin to Orville Poland, 22 April 1941, ACLU papers, reel 200. The others are from Alfred Baker Lewis to Baldwin, 11 April 1940, ACLU papers, reel 182, and Walker, *In Defense*, 127. On Eleanor Roosevelt's visit, see CCLC minutes, 23 January, 6, 13 February, 19 March 1940, ACLU papers, reel 188. On the Denver situation, see a memo from several members of the group to Baldwin, 11 October 1941, and related documents in ACLU papers, reel 199. ACLU papers, reels 182, 189, and 190 contain other branch actions during 1940–41.

54 Quotations are from Russell Chase to Baldwin, 2 December 1941, Chase papers, Western Reserve Historical Society Library, box 1; Baldwin to Carl Mullen, 15 June 1940, ACLU papers, reel 188; Holmes to E. Ryland, 23 April 1941, JHH, container 192; and Baldwin to Holmes, 6 May 1941, ACLU papers, reel 199. The New York quotations are from Baldwin to Eileen Tallman, 9 April 1940; Baldwin's memo to Lucille Milner, 22 May 1940; and Milner to E. Lowenthal, 27 May 1940, all in ACLU papers, reel

189. On the Chicago group, see the exchange between Baldwin and Ira Latimer beginning 11 December 1939, ACLU papers, reel 176.

55 See letters from Boas (11 April 1941) and Rautenstrauch (14 April 1941) to Baldwin. Baldwin's description of the independence of the New Jersey group, followed immediately by his request, is in his letter to Nathaniel Foster, 3 June 1941. Foster to Baldwin, 3 June 1941, raises the previous year's forced resignation. All are in ACLU papers, reel 200.

56 Baldwin to local committees, 30 October 1940, ACLU papers, reel 187. On the national office's failures, see Besig to Baldwin, 6 August 1941, and Clinton Taft of the SCACLU to Lucille Milner, 2 August 1941, both in ACLU papers, reel 199, and Ida Epstein to Agnes Inglis, 13 August 1941, Inglis papers, Labadie Collection, box 1.

57 Quotations are from Holmes to Dilworth Lupton, 15 December 1941, JHH, container 195; Board minutes, 20 October 1941, ACLU papers, reel 192; CLUM, Memo to the Board regarding relationships with affiliates, 12 September 1941, ACLU papers, reel 192; and Margaret Bennett Porter reporting the Colorado vote to the Board, 21 October 1941, ACLU papers, reel 192. The final quotation is from Anne Paulsen to Lucille Milner, 9 October 1941, CLUM papers, box 3.

58 See ACLU papers, reel 186. The Supreme Court expanded its definition of religious freedom and ruled against mandatory flag salutes during these years. See Urofsky, "Roosevelt Court," 86.

59 Quotation is from Arthur Garfield Hays to the ACLU, 26 June 1941, AGH, box 8. All documents are in ACLU papers, reel 193. On the issue of Communism, see Schrecker, *Many Are the Crimes*, 101.

CHAPTER 4

1 Baldwin to Arthur Garfield Hays, 8 January 1943, AGH, box 12, and Ernst to John Haynes Holmes, 25 February 1943, MLE, box 404.

2 Quotations are from Milner to Anne Paulsen of the CLUM, 24 October 1941, reel 200, and Baldwin to Whitney North Seymour, 20 October 1941, and Hays to Baldwin, 3 November 1941, reel 194, all in ACLU papers.

3 Quotations are from Edward Ross to Franklin Collier Jr., 24 July 1940, reel 206, and Stimson to Baldwin, 11 September 1940, reel 181, both in ACLU papers. On conscription policy, see Board minutes, 15, 22 July 1940, ACLU Board series, reel 8. On the network, see conference minutes, 26 September 1940, ACLU papers, reel 181.

4 Collier originally resigned in a letter to E. A. Ross, 1 August 1940, but the quotation is from his letter to Baldwin, 26 April 1941, both in ACLU papers, reel 206. Apparently Ross failed to pass on his resignation to the

national office. The next quotation, Thomas to Baldwin, 14 November 1940, comes from NT, reel 56. The final quote comes from Macdonald, "Defense of Everybody," pt. 2, 53.

5 Steele, *Free Speech*, 1; Warren, *Noble Abstractions*, 3, 8. See also Perrett, *Days of Sadness*, chap. 29; Steele, "Fear of the Mob," 75; and Gary, *Nervous Liberals*, 76.

6 Quotations are from Baldwin, "Liberty in War Time"; Baldwin to local committees, 10 February 1942, ACLU papers, reel 203; Holmes to Baldwin, 14 December 1942, JHH, container 199; and Baldwin to Lucille Milner, 31 March 1944, ACLU papers, reel 234. The annual report was American Civil Liberties Union, *Freedom in Wartime*.

7 Thomas to ACLU, 8 October 1942, NT, reel 56.

8 Niebuhr, "The Limits of Liberty," defined the categories in quotation marks (quotation from 86), to which Baldwin responded with "Liberty in Wartime." On the subject more generally, see Purcell, *Crisis of Democratic Theory*, 235, and Steele, *Free Speech*.

9 Gary, *Nervous Liberals*, 7; Ernst to Holmes, 3 June 1943, AGH, box 12.

10 Quotations are from Board minutes, 15 December 1941, ACLU Board series, reel 9; Fraenkel, *Oral History*, 56; Holmes to Ernst, 16 February 1942, JHH, container 195 (on Ernst and Hays); Baldwin paraphrasing Hays in Baldwin, *Reminiscences*, 168; and Fraenkel paraphrasing Thomas in OKF, 30 July 1942, 8.

11 OKF, 12 October 1942, 10; Ernst to Holmes, 14 April 1942, ACLU papers, reel 203; Ernst to Holmes, 3 June 1943, MLE, box 404; Holmes's statement, ca. April 1942, ACLU papers, reel 203.

12 Quotations are from Ernst to Holmes, 3 June, 2 February 1943, MLE, box 404; OKF, 12 October 1942, 10; and Ernst to Holmes, 3 June 1943, MLE, box 404.

13 All the quotations come from the notes on the special meeting, 12 October 1942, ACLU papers, reel 203, or OKF, 12 October 1942, 10.

14 Thomas's letter to Baldwin, 10 November 1942; Holmes's 15 November 1942 response; and Hays's 16 November 1942 reply are in ACLU papers, reel 203. OKF, 20 November 1942, 13 describes the lunch.

15 See Seymour to Baldwin, 10 April 1941, and Seymour's April 1941 statement, both in ACLU papers, reel 203.

16 The first quotation is from Board regulations, July 1943, ACLU Board series, reel 22. The rest are from Childs to Baldwin, 1 June 1942, ACLU papers, reel 203. The Board approved the trial period on 3 June 1942, ACLU Board series, reel 9; 1943–44 bylaw revisions are in ACLU Board series, reel 22.

17 For more, see Irons, *Justice*, 64–74.

18 The letter, 30 March 1942, is in ACLU Board series, reel 22 (my emphasis). Board discussions about the original, 23 March 1942, are in ACLU Board series, reel 9.

19 The referendum and vote tallies, all dated 22 May 1942, are in ACLU Board series, box 22. Board discussions, 16, 23 March, 6 April 1942, are in ACLU Board series, reel 9. The final quotation is from Felix Morley to the ACLU, 16 June 1942, AGH, box 10.

20 Quotation is from Osmond Fraenkel's characterization of Whitney Seymour, OKF, 22 June 1942, 6. On internment policy, see Drinnon, *Keeper*, 3–10.

21 Quotations are from E. A. Ross to Baldwin, 26 August 1942, ACLU papers, reel 203; ACLU press release, quoting a letter to WRA head Dillon S. Myer signed by Holmes, Hays, and Baldwin, 8 October 1942, ACLU Board series, reel 9; OKF, 26 October 1942, 12; and Baldwin to Norman Thomas, 20 March 1944, ACLU papers, reel 224.

22 Quotations are from Meiklejohn to Ernest Besig, 10 September, 4 August 1942, and Ernest Besig to Gloria Waldron, 27 July 1944, NCACLU papers, box 28. On Myer and Baldwin, see Myer, *Uprooted Americans*, xix.

23 Quotations are from Holmes to Baldwin, 27 August 1942, ACLU papers, reel 203, and Meiklejohn to Lucille Milner, 17 October [1944], ELP, box 1.

24 "Tuna Lake" is Arthur Garfield Hays's mistake; see his letter to Baldwin, 27 March 1946, ACLU papers, reel 234. On distances, see A. L. Wirin [?] to Baldwin, 15 September 1944, NCACLU papers, box 28. As late as 1947, the SCACLU chastised the office for using "Jap"; see A. L. Wirin to Cliff Forster, 29 April 1947, ACLU papers, reel 243. Board minutes, 17 September 1942, ACLU Board series, reel 9, notes the correct term. Board minutes, 1 November 1943, ACLU Board series, reel 9, refers test cases to the Seditious Cases Committee.

25 Quotations are from Baldwin to the editor of the *New Republic*, 10 April 1944, reel 223, and Ernest Besig to Baldwin, 20 October 1945, reel 230, both in ACLU papers. On the JACL, see Yoo, *Growing Up Nisei*, 140–47, and Daniels, *Prisoners without Trial*, 20–21. The 1999 documentary film by Emiko Omori, *Rabbit in the Moon*, offers a scathing Nisei view of the JACL. One JACL activist, Saburo Kido, later joined the National Committee.

26 Baldwin memo, 11 April 1944, of a phone conversation with Dillon Myer, reel 224, and Baldwin to Wirin, 27 March 1944, reel 223. Baldwin

to Wirin, 6 March 1944, reel 223, talks about the value of soldiers' families as test cases. All are in ACLU papers.

27 On Hirabayashi, quotations are from Mary Farquharson to Baldwin, 14 May 1942, reel 214, and Memo on the Court Cases, September 1942, reel 211, both in ACLU papers. On Endo, see her attorney's report on her background to the ACLU, 16 September 1942, reel 213, and Forster to Wirin, 19 March, 9 December 1943, reels 218 and 224, on who will defend her; all are in ACLU papers. On Korematsu, quotations are from Baldwin to Besig, 8 May 1942, NCACLU papers, box 4, and Baldwin to Besig, 2 June 1944, ACLU papers, reel 223. Also see Besig's report to Baldwin, 10 June 1942, NCACLU papers, box 4. On the Yasui decision, see Board minutes, 23 November 1942, ACLU Board series, reel 9. Irons, *Justice*, includes details on all four cases.

28 The quotation comes from Irons's interview with Besig, 12 January 1982, and is quoted in Irons, *Justice*, 360. Irons's assessment is on p. 254 of the same source. See also viii.

29 Steele, *Free Speech*, is a good source on all of these movements, as is Ribuffo, *Old Christian Right*.

30 Quotations are from memo on the clear-and-present-danger test, 30 April 1942, ACLU papers, reel 217, and Morris Ernst to Baldwin, 13 May 1942, AGH, box 10. ACLU memo, 30 April 1942, ACLU papers, reel 217, declares that the ACLU did not accept the test "in principle," although Baldwin told the Justice Department otherwise; see 27 April 1942, ACLU papers, reel 217. On the government's position, see Steele, *Free Speech*, 151–56.

31 The first quotation is from an ACLU press release, 15 April 1942, ACLU Board series, reel 9; see also Board minutes, 12, 19 January 1942, on meetings with Biddle. On Kirchwey, see documents in ACLU papers, reel 203, and Kirchwey papers, Schlesinger Library, box 13. Canby to Baldwin, 22 April 1942, and Perry to Baldwin, 18 April 1942, are in ACLU papers, reel 216. Background on the post office actions may be found in Steele, *Free Speech*, 163–66.

32 Quotations are from "Muzzling the Fascists" and Ernst to Baldwin, 13 May 1942, ACLU papers, reel 225.

33 The committee was formed 11 May 1942; see Board minutes, ACLU papers, reel 203. For examples of a disproportionate number of "no action" recommendations, see Board minutes, 24 May, 12 July 1943, ACLU Board series, reel 9.

34 The report, dated 3 July 1942 and signed by Hays, Whitney North Seymour, Osmond Fraenkel, and John Finerty, is in ACLU Board series, reel

22. On the cases themselves, see Steele, *Free Speech*, 223–33; Ribuffo, *Old Christian Right*, 188–96; Perrett, *Days of Sadness*, 360–62; MacDonnell, *Insidious Foes*; and Polenberg, *War and Society*, 48.

35 Quotations are from Holmes to Baldwin, 11 August 1942, reel 203; Baldwin to Edward Tittman, 5 October 1942, reel 216; Baldwin to Holmes, 11 August 1942, reel 203; memo on meeting of Seditious Cases Committee, 19 August 1942, reel 216, all in ACLU papers; Board minutes, 28 September 1942, ACLU Board series, reel 9; and OKF, 4 January 1943, 14.

36 Quotations are from Morris Ernst to John Haynes Holmes, 2 February 1943, MLE, box 404; Whitney Seymour, statement on behalf of the Board majority, 29 January 1943, ACLU Board series, reel 22; Committee on Seditious Cases minutes, 2 December 1942, ACLU papers, reel 216; and Frederick Schuman to Hays and Baldwin, 15 April 1942, ACLU papers, reel 203. See the statement that accompanied the referendum, 28 January 1943, ACLU Board series, reel 22, and the vote report, 11 March 1943, ACLU papers, reel 238. Corliss Lamont to Baldwin, 24 October 1942, ACLU papers, reel 203, implied that Baldwin played fast and loose with the original letter.

37 Quotations are from Board minutes, 19 October 1942, ACLU Board series, reel 9; Baldwin, in Lamson, *Baldwin*, 240; Board minutes, 9 November 1942, ACLU Board series, reel 9; Baldwin to Holmes, 9 December 1942, ACLU papers, reel 203 (two quotations); and Thomas to Holmes, 14 November 1942, and Fraenkel to Baldwin, 10 November 1942, both in ACLU papers, reel 203.

38 Quotations are from Ralph Barton Perry to Baldwin, 18 April 1942, ACLU papers, reel 215, and Baldwin to Arthur Garfield Hays, 16 July 1942, AGH, box 10.

39 Lamont to Holmes, 27 May 1943, and Baldwin to Holmes, 1 May 1943, both in ACLU papers, reel 210. Board vote, 24 May 1943, is in ACLU Board series, reel 9.

40 Quotations are from Baldwin to Daniel Lyons, 9 June 1943; Osmond Fraenkel to Baldwin, 8 June 1943; and Baldwin to signers of the Stephan petition, 21 May 1943, all in reel 287. The original letter is Baldwin to assorted recipients, 28 April 1943, reel 286. See also Baldwin, telegram to ACLU secretary Sally Avitabile, 2 July 1943, and Baldwin's later memo on Max Stephan, March 1951, both in reel 287, which concedes nothing. All are in ACLU papers.

41 Quotations are from Holmes to Whitney North Seymour, 25 May 1943, JHH, container 199; Joe Lash's notes on a conversation with Lamont, 28 September 1972, JL, box 49; Baldwin to Lamont, 9 June 1943, ACLU

papers, reel 210; and Holmes paraphrasing Baldwin in a letter to John Finerty, 3 June 1943, JHH, container 199. For more, see Holmes's handwritten notes on the chronology, JHH, container 199, and ACLU papers, reel 287.

42 The first quotation is cited in Cottrell, *Baldwin*, 306. The second is from Joe Lash's interview with Baldwin, 21 October 1971, JL, box 49. The third and fourth come from Macdonald, "Defense of Everybody," pt. 2, 30. On the tense office situation, see Cottrell, *Baldwin*, 305–6.

43 Quotations are from Baldwin to Mary E. Bulkley, 9 September [1942], RNB, box 4; Baldwin quoting Milner in his memo on cooperation, August 1944, ACLU papers, reel 288; and Milner, *Education*, 301. See Milner, *Education*, 298–307, for her version of the fights. Baldwin, *Reminiscences*, 156, offers another view. Baldwin's August 1944 memo gives an overall impression of pettiness rather than legitimate complaints. I can find nothing in the ACLU papers or Baldwin's personal papers to confirm anything more than a friendship with Milner. Cottrell's evidence in *Baldwin*, 304, is based on one secretary's opinion.

44 All quotations except the first come from a memo of the conversation with Milner, Benjamin Huebsch, and Richard Childs, 15 June 1945, ACLU papers, reel 288. The first is from Joe Lash's memo on his talk with Milner, 22 March 1972, JL, box 49.

45 Plotke, *Building a Democratic Political Order*, 299.

46 Macdonald, "Defense of Everybody," pt. 2, 53.

CHAPTER 5

1 More on this incident appears later in this chapter; see also Kutulas, "In Quest of Autonomy."

2 Quotations are from Baldwin to Besig, 8 January 1943, and Herbert Carrasco to Besig, 14 January 1943, NCACLU papers, box 4; Betty Sanger to Baldwin, 29 November 1945, ACLU papers, reel 231; and Besig to Edward Parsons, 13 January 1943, ELP, box 1.

3 Baldwin to local committees, 10 February, 3 October 1942, ACLU papers, reel 203.

4 Quotations are from CLUM minutes, 16 June 1942, CLUM papers, box 4; Besig to Baldwin, 8 July 1942, ACLU papers, reel 213; and CLUM recommendations on policy, 13 March 1943, CLUM papers, box 5. On the decision not to extend the vote, see Board minutes, 3 June 1942, ACLU Board series, reel 9.

5 The first quotation is from Besig to Norman Thomas, 10 July 1942, NCACLU papers, box 28. The second and third are from OKF, 13 July

1942, 7. The fourth and fifth are from Forster to Besig, 6, 10 July 1942, NCACLU papers, box 56.

6 Quotations are from Baldwin to Edward Parsons, 14 December 1943, AJM, box 4; NCACLU statement, n.d., ELP, box 15; and Meiklejohn to Besig, 28 April 1943, NCACLU papers, box 2.

7 The first two quotations come from Cliff Forster to Osmond Fraenkel, 31 May 1944, ACLU papers, reel 224. The last is from Meiklejohn to Holmes, 27 December [1943], ELP, box 3.

8 McWilliams, *Honorable in All Things*, 187; Okrand, *Forty Years*, 118.

9 Quotations are from *San Francisco Examiner*, 23 January 1989, and Lily Yorozu to Farquharson, 9 June 1942, Farquharson papers, University of Washington Library, box 1. Besig and Korematsu's sometimes poignant correspondence is in NCACLU papers, box 56.

10 Quotations are from Parsons to Baldwin, 11 October 1945, ACLU papers, reel 230; Meiklejohn to Lucille Milner, 17 October 1944, ELP, box 1; and Besig to Meiklejohn, 4 September 1945, Collins papers, Bancroft Library, box 21.

11 Quotations are from John Haynes Holmes to Baldwin, 31 August 1943, reel 213; A. L. Wirin to Baldwin, 15 October 1943, reel 217; Besig to Holmes, 23 March 1943, reel 213, all in ACLU papers; Parsons to Holmes and Baldwin, 10 December 1943, AJM, box 23; and Besig to Meiklejohn, 30 June 1943, NCACLU papers, box 2.

12 Holmes to Baldwin, 19 April 1943, JHH, container 199.

13 Quotations are from Parsons to William Spofford, 1 February 1946, ELP, box 4; Besig to Baldwin, 22 January 1943, reel 213, and Baldwin to Holmes, 10 August 1943, reel 210, both in ACLU papers; Meiklejohn to Besig, 10 September 1942, NCACLU papers, box 28; and Thomas to Besig, 21 November 1942, NT, reel 56.

14 Quotations are from Statement on Relations with the Northern California Branch, 10 December 1943, ACLU Board series, reel 22; Parsons to NCACLU, 25 March 1943, NCACLU papers, box 2; and Parsons to Holmes, 3 December 1943, ACLU papers, reel 213. See also Seymour to NCACLU, 3 February 1943, NCACLU papers, box 2, and Baldwin to Holmes, 10 January 1944, ACLU papers, reel 213.

15 A good summary of Baldwin's attitudes is in Drinnon, *Keeper*, 124–25.

16 The details are in U.S. Department of the Interior, *Impounded People*, 63–71, and Collins, *Native American Aliens*, 48.

17 Quotations are from Baldwin memo, 11 April 1944, reel 224; Besig to Baldwin, 7 June 1944, and Baldwin memo, 14 July 1944, reel 223, all in ACLU papers; and Besig to Cliff Forster, 30 August 1944, NCACLU papers,

box 28. See also Baldwin, Tule Lake memo, 14 July 1944, ACLU papers, reel 223; *NCACLU News*, August 1944, 1; and Myer to Baldwin, 17 August 1944, ACLU papers, reel 224, for the versions of the participants.

18 Board minutes, 7 August, 11 September 1944, ACLU Board series, reel 10. On the brutalization of segregees, see Drinnon, *Keeper*, chap. 6. Footage of the beatings can be seen in Omori, *Rabbit in the Moon*.

19 The first quotation is from Cliff Forster to Wirin, 12 September 1944, NCACLU papers, box 28. The others are from Baldwin to Meiklejohn, 29 September 1944, and Wirin to Baldwin, 13 September 1944, both in ACLU papers, reel 223.

20 The best secondary source explaining renunciation is Collins, *Native American Aliens*. See also Christgau, "Collins versus the World."

21 Quotations are from Edward Ennis to Cliff Forster, 23 July 1945, reel 230, and Wirin to Besig, 8 February 1945, and Wirin's memo for Baldwin and Osmond Fraenkel, 13 May 1946, reel 238, all in ACLU papers. The initial decision was made by the Board on 28 February 1944; see ACLU papers, reel 226. The committee formed on 24 September 1945 and made its report on 8 October 1945; see ACLU Board series, reel 10. The decision to postpone was explained in Wirin to Forster, 30 October 1946, ACLU papers, reel 233. The California Alien Land Law prevented Japanese nationals from owning agricultural land.

22 Quotations are from Besig to Baldwin, 27 June 1945, ACLU papers, reel 230; Collins, statement draft, n.d., Collins Papers, Bancroft Library, box 21; Baldwin to Saburo Kido, 18 March 1946, ACLU papers, reel 230; and Sachiye Uyemaruko on a form letter, ca. April 1946, Collins papers, box 21. Besig's doubts were expressed in letters to Alexander Meiklejohn, 4 September 1945, Collins papers, box 21, and to Baldwin, 6 October 1945, ACLU papers, reel 230.

23 Quotations are from Wirin to Baldwin, 22 October 1945, reel 230; Besig to Jobu Yasum, 2 January 1946, and to Wirin, 9 February 1946, reel 238, all in ACLU papers; and Harry Uchida to Tex [Nakamira], 21 February 1946, Collins papers, Bancroft Library, box 2.

24 Quotation is from Hays to Baldwin, 26 November 1947, AGH, box 14. On the threat of a suit, see Wirin to Parsons, 4 April 1946, ACLU papers, reel 234. On the national office's opinion of Wirin, see Arthur Garfield Hays to Baldwin, 26 November 1947, and Baldwin to Hays, 3 December 1947, both in AGH, box 14. On financial arrangements between Wirin and the SCACLU, see the documents in ACLU papers, reel 208.

25 Quotation is from Baldwin to A. A. Heist, 8 May 1946, ACLU papers, reel 234. The resolution, 10 April 1946, is in ACLU Board series, reel 22.

26 Quotations are from Collins, 31 March 1972 interview, cited in Collins, *Native American Aliens*, 115, and Besig to the Board, 11 March 1946, Collins Papers, Bancroft Library, box 21. Collins was known for his "shotgun" style of argument; see Irons, *Justice*, 117. On the individual renunciant cases, see Collins, *Native American Aliens*, 134–38.

27 Quotations are from Baldwin to Holmes, 10 August 1943, reel 210; SCACLU board minutes, 15 February 1943, reel 217; Edward Allen to Baldwin, 20 December 1942, reel 214; C. I. Claflin to Baldwin, 3 December 1942, reel 209; and Baldwin to Edward Parsons, 22 August 1944, reel 224, all in ACLU papers.

28 The first quotation is from Alexander Meiklejohn to the NCACLU, 15 February 1944, AJM, box 47. The four large branches were the NCACLU, the SCACLU, the CLUM, and the CCLC. The other quotations are from Albert Sprague Coolidge to Baldwin, 7 June 1942, ACLU papers, reel 203, and CLUM recommendations, 13 March 1943, CLUM papers, box 5.

29 The Denver quotations are from Margaret Bennet Porter to Russell Chase, 10 February 1942, Chase Papers, Western Reserve Historical Society Library, box 1, and Porter to Baldwin, 8 June 1942, ACLU papers, reel 208. The Cleveland quotations are from a P.S. on a copy of a letter that Baldwin wrote to Chase and forwarded to John Haynes Holmes, 16 December 1941, and Chase to Baldwin, 22 December 1941, reel 201, and Bill Thomas to Baldwin, 5 May 1942, reel 203, all in ACLU papers. The Erie County quotations are from Minutes, Erie County Civil Liberties Committee, 14 December 1944, ACLU papers, reel 214. ACLU papers, reel 208, contains the full set of documents on the temporary end of the Denver group.

30 The first quotation is from Meiklejohn to the NCACLU, 15 February 1944, AJM, box 47 (emphasis in original); a copy of the 3 March 1944 petition is also in AJM, box 47. On consultations amongst the branches, see Besig to Clinton Taft, 22 January 1944, SCACLU papers, box 52. The temporary arrangement is spelled out in Baldwin to affiliates, 17 February 1944, NCACLU papers, box 4.

31 The first two quotations are from Holmes to John Paul Jones, 11 April 1944, JHH, container 204. The report, dated 13 July 1944, is in ACLU Board series, reel 22. Besig's complaint to Baldwin, 3 May 1944, is in NCACLU papers, box 4.

32 The quotations are from the pro argument in the packet of material sent to Board and National Committee members, 27 October 1944, ACLU Board series, reel 22, and American Civil Liberties Union, *Liberty on the Home Front*, 58–59. The Board discussion occurred on 25 September

1944, and the vote was announced on 20 November 1944; both are in ACLU Board series, reel 10.

33 Quotations are from Coolidge to members, 27 April 1942, Chafee papers, Harvard Archives, box 3, and Baldwin to Coolidge, 15 June 1943, and to Howard Penley, 26 May 1943, ACLU papers, reel 214 (last two). See also Coolidge to Baldwin, 13 June 1943, ACLU papers, reel 214. On Luscomb and the war years, see Strom, *Political Woman*, chap. 6.

34 The quotations come from William Rodriguez to the ACLU, 25 April 1945, ACLU papers, reel 230; *Official Report of the Proceedings before the Subversive Activities Control Board*, 20 May 1954, 958 and 957, IL, box 8; and Leon M. Despres tape to author, 22 February 2003. Background on Latimer may be found in his *Chicago Tribune* obituary, 17 February 1985.

35 Baldwin to Latimer, 1 February 1943, reel 216. Latimer's claims are in letters to Cliff Forster, 13 November 1942, and to Baldwin, 16 December 1942, 5 February 1943, reel 216, and 9 December 1942, reel 217. All are in ACLU papers.

36 The first and last three quotations are from Latimer to Baldwin, 6 January 1942, ACLU papers, reel 217. The second and third quotations are from Baldwin to Homer Jack, 13 December 1945, ACLU papers, reel 231. Latimer to Baldwin, 6 January 1943, ACLU papers, reel 217, explains about the Bundists. Baldwin to Edgar Bernhard, 26 September 1942, ACLU papers, reel 216, expresses his concern that the CCLC "explore every single case of whatever character." The Dilling debate is in CCLC minutes, 6, 13, 20 October 1942, IL, box 3. The material on the Summers case is in ACLU papers, reel 226.

37 Quotations are from Baldwin to Latimer, 16 September 1943, and CCLC minutes, 20 July 1943, reel 214, and the CCLC's annual report for 1943, reel 220, all in ACLU papers; Edward Porter to Latimer, 8 July 1944, IL, box 4; CCLC executive board minutes, 16 May 1944, and Baldwin to John Lapp, 18 May 1944, both in ACLU papers, reel 220.

38 Quotations are from Edward Porter to John Foley, 19 September 1944, IL, box 4; Frank McCulloch to Baldwin, 24 January 1944, ACLU papers, reel 220; and Lapp to Baldwin, 15 January 1945, and Baldwin, memo for the Board, 16 February 1945, ACLU papers, reel 230. Regarding Communism, see John Haynes Holmes to Baldwin, 6 March 1945, JHH, container 209.

39 See the *Chicago Defender* clippings in ACLU papers, reel 235.

40 The quotation and information on Wain are in Baldwin memo, 15 March 1945, ACLU papers, reel 230. For Board actions, see minutes for

8 January, 2, 16 April 1945, as well as press release, 27 April 1945, all in ACLU Board series, reel 10. There is a copy of Wain's letter to Baldwin, 23 February 1945, in NCACLU papers, box 16.

41 Quotations are from Baldwin to Latimer, 15 November 1947, and to John Lapp, 14 October 1947, ACLU papers, reel 241. On the CRC, see Horne, *Communist Front?* On Latimer, see Committee on Character and Fitness, First Appellate Court District of Illinois, *Hearings*, 22 December 1954, IL, box 8. On the CCLC, see its minutes, 17 April, 26 June 1945, IL, box 4, and 7 May 1946, IL, box 5. Latimer's obituary is in the *Chicago Tribune*, 17 February 1985. Latimer later testified before several anticommunist committees and had his fitness investigated by the Illinois State Bar.

42 Quotations are from the statement of the Chicago Division of the ACLU on its relationship with the national organization, 9 June 1950, box 117, and Ed Meyerding to George Rundquist, 5 January 1955, box 116, IACLU; Edward Potter to ACLU, 8 May 1946, and John Haynes Holmes to Irving Flamm, 16 April 1946, ACLU papers, reel 234.

43 Quotations are from Paul C. Thomas to Arthur Garfield Hays, 6 October 1942, and Thomas to Baldwin, 12 October 1942, reel 214, and Philip McNairy to Milner, 27 February 1945, reel 231. On branch size, see Mary Babcock Abbott to Milner, 16 June 1945, and Milner to Abbott, 25 June 1945, reel 231. On the 1943 takeover concern, see Abbott to Milner, 2 November 1943, reel 214. All are in ACLU papers.

44 Parsons to Holmes and Baldwin, ca. 30 November 1943, ELP, box 1.

CHAPTER 6

1 All materials, including a clipping of the article, which appeared in *New Masses*, are in ACLU papers, reel 245. The quotation is from a letter from Cliff Forster to Baldwin, 16 May 1947.

2 See Baldwin memo, 27 December 1947, ACLU papers, box 76, and Report on Future Policies and Activities, 16 March 1949, MLE, box 402.

3 Quotations are from J. B. Aronoff to ACLU, 26 March 1946; H. A. Overstreet to Baldwin, 30 January 1946; and Douglas Rodewald to ACLU, 2 September 1946, all in ACLU papers, reel 235. See also letters from Samuel Wasserman, 29 January 1946, and Dr. and Mrs. Robert Citron, 24 January 1946, ibid.

4 Quotations are from Cliff Forster to John Saltonstall Jr., 21 May 1947, ACLU papers, box 476, and Baldwin to Louis Adamic, 24 April 1946, ACLU papers, reel 239, where there are several similar letters. On the CRC, see Horne, *Communist Front?*

5 Quotations are from Schlesinger to Baldwin, 18 April 1946, reel 239, and Baldwin to A. A. Heist, 30 March 1947, reel 241. More cooperative was Dean John Day of Topeka, who received a letter from Baldwin and dropped his CRC connection. See their exchange in reel 256. On Houston, see his 1948 exchange with Baldwin and letter of resignation, 21 June 1948, reel 256. All are in ACLU papers.

6 Baldwin interview with Joe Lash, 21 October 1971, JL, box 49.

7 Quotation is from McAuliffe, *Crisis on the Left*, 107. On liberal anticommunism, see McAuliffe, *Crisis on the Left*; Pells, *Liberal Mind*; and Schrecker, *Many Are the Crimes*. On the ex-radicals, see Wald, *New York Intellectuals*; Cooney, *Rise of the New York Intellectuals*; and Jumonville, *Critical Crossings*.

8 Quotations are from Florence Isbell, as cited in Cottrell, *Baldwin*, 304; Walker, *In Defense*, 205; and Ernst in an interview with Joe Lash, 7 February 1972, JL, box 49. On salary negotiations, see Holmes to William Northrup, 4 January 1949, JHH, container 223. On Baldwin's postwar activities, see Cottrell, *Baldwin*, 313–20.

9 Fly to Holmes, 9 July 1946, reel 234; to Baldwin, 26 November 1947, reel 241; and Holmes to Baldwin, 8 June 1949, reel 260, all in ACLU papers.

10 Baldwin to Edna Walls, 20 December 1946, ACLU papers, reel 241.

11 Quotations are from Edward Allen to Thomas, 17 November 1951, NT, reel 56, and Merle Curti to Pat Malin, 30 June 1953, ACLU papers, box 394. On the public relations aspects, see Academic Freedom Committee minutes, 8 December 1953, ACLU papers, box 78.

12 Quotations are from Hamby, *Beyond*, 171; Board minutes, 3 November 1947, ACLU Board series, reel 11; and Baldwin, *Reminiscences*, 254. See documents and Board minutes for 1947 and 1948, ACLU Board series, reels 11 and 22.

13 Quotations are from Pells, *Liberal Mind*, 267; Ernst's draft of a memo on the ACLU's approach to the loyalty problem, 20 October 1947, MLE, box 10 (two quotations); Ernst to Peyton Ford, 9 October 1947, MLE, box 410; Fly's report to the Board, 12 July 1948, ACLU papers, reel 251; and Cliff Forster, memo on Washington trip, 24 April 1947, ACLU papers, reel 242. See also Board minutes for 16 June 1947, ACLU papers, reel 241.

14 Press release, 12 April 1947, ACLU papers, reel 243; Board minutes, 19 May, 2, 14 July 1947, ACLU Board series, reel 10; Forster's memo, 24 April 1947, ACLU papers, reel 242; Forster to Besig (quotation), 16 December 1948, ACLU papers, reel 253. Final anecdote told by Corliss Lamont to Joe Lash, 28 September 1972, JL, box 49.

15 Both the majority and minority reports, January 1948, are in ACLU papers, reel 251. The relevant Board minutes, 24 November 1947 and 19 January 1948, are in ACLU Board series, reels 10 and 11.

16 Quotations are from OKF, 12 February 1955, 70; Board minutes, 24 October 1949, 25 June 1951, ACLU Board series, reel 12; and Alan Reitman to the Board, 17 January 1952, SCACLU papers, box 60. On the picketing, see Board minutes, 10 October 1949, ACLU Board series, reel 12.

17 Quotations are from Herbert Levy to Due Process Committee, 3 November 1952, ACLU Board series, reel 23; Chicago Division minutes, 25 June 1952, IACLU, box 104; New Haven Civil Liberties Council to President Truman, 23 November 1952, AJM, box 48; and Baldwin to Aubrey Williams, 22 December 1952, ACLU papers, box 203. On branch responses, see Chapter 7. Osmond Fraenkel notes the left attack in OKF, 28 May 1952, 40.

18 On Bridges, see Board minutes, 7 November, 19 December 1949, 12 June, 28 August 1950, reel 12, and minutes 20 April 1953, reel 13, all in ACLU Board series. On passports, see Pat Malin to Passport Committee, 28 November 1951, and Merlyn Pitzele to Malin, 19 November 1951, NT, reel 56. On Mundt-Nixon, see Ernst's article in *New Leader*, 15 May 1948, clipping in ACLU papers, reel 255.

19 Quotations are from Ennis's statement on the Emergency Detention Provisions of the McCarran Act, summer 1950, ACLU papers, reel 273; minutes, 30 October 1950, ACLU Board series, reel 12; and John Finerty's Clear and Present Danger statement, 21 April 1949, ACLU papers, reel 260. On the confusion of even the redrafted clear-and-present-danger reports, see Rice to Cliff Forster, 1 December 1948, ACLU papers, reel 251. Rice was best known as an author but trained as an attorney.

20 Quotations are from Gellhorn to Baldwin, 29 April 1948, ACLU papers, reel 255; Ernst to Elsie Harper, 12 May 1948, MLE, box 411; and Ernst to Forster, 8 January 1948, and Forster to Ernst, 29 January 1948, both in ACLU papers, reel 255. The congressional quotations are from U.S. Congress, House of Representatives, Committee on Un-American Activities, *Hearings*, Nixon on 225 and Hays on 229. MLE, box 115, contains correspondence between Nixon and Ernst, including Nixon's 12 July 1956 letter declining the use of Ernst's house.

21 Quotations are from Forster's memo on HUAC, 25 March 1948, and Holmes to Nixon, 11 October 1948, reel 253, and John Finerty to Baldwin, 20 February 1948, reel 255, all in ACLU papers. The ACLU's statement, 20 January 1947, is in ACLU Board series, reel 22. Ernst's memo

and Hays's opposition, both 18 February 1948, are in ACLU papers, reel 251. The protest came from Harry Paxton to ACLU, 25 April 1949, circulated by Baldwin to the Board, 12 May 1949, ACLU Board series, reel 22.

22 Quotations are from Davis Hobbs to Pat Malin, 10 March 1952, ACLU papers, box 354; Board minutes, 9 February 1948, ACLU Board series, reel 11; Baldwin to Booton Herndon, undated memo, Herndon papers, University of Virginia, box 1; Neier, *Taking Liberties*, 133; and American Civil Liberties Union, *We Hold These Truths*, 11. On the amicus briefs, see the exchange between Ernest Besig and A. A. Heist, 4, 7 March 1949, NCACLU papers, box 3.

23 George Rundquist to A. A. Heist, 16 October 1951, ACLU papers, box 457.

24 A. A. Heist quoting an unnamed famous New Yorker, 13 October 1947, SCACLU papers, box 52. On the turnover, see Board minutes, 6 March 1950, ACLU Board series, reel 12. That would mean close to 1,000 people failed to renew their memberships.

25 Quotations are from Jay Lavenson to Patrick Malin, 18 November 1953, ACLU papers, box 354; Board minutes, 26 June 1950, ACLU papers, reel 269; and Lavenson to Malin and Thomas to Edward Allen, 28 June 1951, NT, reel 56.

26 Quotations are from OKF, 28 August 1950, 31 May 1952, 30, 36, and Herbert Levy to Norman Cousins, 11 July 1952, ACLU papers, box 872.

27 Pitzele's review appeared in the *New Leader*, 16 June 1952, 15–18. The Lamont quotation is from Pitzele's notes on the 15 May 1952 meeting, MP, box 24, as is Pitzele's recollection about the meeting. His apology, 22 May 1952, is in MP, box 23. His observation to legionnaire Karl Baarslag is in a letter dated 27 June 1952, MP, box 12. His comment to Thomas, 1 October 1952, is in MLE, box 409. The official minutes of the special meeting, 15 May 1952, are in ACLU Board series, reel 12. The word "rampage" is Osmond Fraenkel's, taken from a diary entry, 15 May 1952, OKF, 39. Baldwin recalled the measure against public personal critiques in a letter to A. R. [Alan Reitman?], 6 June 1952, NT, reel 56.

28 Quotations are from the special committee's report on the book, 14 July 1952, reel 23, and Board minutes, 21 July 1952, reel 12, both in ACLU Board series, and Edward Bernays to Alan Reitman, 10 October 1952, NT, reel 56.

29 Quotations are from OKF, 6 October 1952, 44; Thomas to the Board, 2 October 1952, NT, reel 56; and OKF, 5 October 1952, 44. See Board minutes, 23 June, 21 July, 6 October 1952, ACLU Board series, reel 12. Pitzele did not vote on any of the nominations.

30 Quotations are from Varian Fry to Baldwin, 26 October 1951; Baldwin to Fry, 25 October 1951; and George Rundquist to Myron Tripp, 5 June 1951, all in ACLU papers, box 15. Lamont, "ACLU and the FBI," talks about how the ACLU consulted the FBI about him.

31 The quotations are from Memo from Herbert Levy to Pat Malin, 18 January 1951, ACLU papers, box 15; Holmes to Benjamin Huebsch, 6 December 1944, JHH, container 209; Baldwin to the Board, 11 February 1948, ACLU papers, reel 251; Lamont's memo on the events of 1948, October 1948, MP, box 23 (two quotations); and Lamont to Ernest Angell, 26 September 1952, ACLU papers, box 15 (last two quotations). Votes were reported in a memo with no date titled "Results of Election, 1948," ACLU papers, reel 256. There is an entire folder in ACLU papers, box 15, devoted to Lamont.

32 Lamont to Pat Malin, 20 June 1951, SCACLU papers, box 52.

33 See Baldwin's manuscript on the early ACLU, p. 33, in ACLU papers, box 205.

34 Board minutes, 26 January 1948, ACLU Board series, reel 11.

35 Quotations are from Monroe, *Safeguarding Civil Liberties*, 97; Lucille Milner interview with Joe Lash, 22 March 1972, JL, box 49; and Garey, *Defending Everybody*, 133. Aryeh Neier seconded Monroe's assessment in *Defending My Enemy*, 74. Garey, *Defending Everybody*, 133, quotes Alan Reitman's recollection that when Baldwin hired him in 1949 to be the Union's publicity director, he was the fifteenth director in two years.

36 Quotations are from Allen to George Rundquist, 30 August 1950, ACLU papers, box 471, and Heist to Besig, 18 February 1949, NCACLU papers, box 3. See also Besig to Baldwin, 12 July 1947, NCACLU papers, box 4. In 1950, for instance, Americans for Democratic Action had 123 branches, a membership of 35,000, and a budget of $240,000, compared with the Union's 17 affiliates, 9,355 members, and $67,818 budget; figures are from Gillon, *Politics and Vision*, 57–58.

37 Quotations are from Baldwin to Besig, 14 July 1947, NCACLU papers, box 4, and Baldwin's penciled note on a letter from Besig, 30 July 1947, ACLU papers, box 456. On the implication that it was the affiliates' responsibility if the office forgot to consult them, see Besig to Baldwin, 5 December 1947, NCACLU papers, box 4.

38 Quotations are from Besig to Baldwin, 26 March 1948; Baldwin to Heist, 7 September 1948; and Besig to Baldwin, 12 May 1948, all in NCACLU papers, box 4; Baldwin to Mary Farquharson, 16 March 1948, ACLU papers, reel 251; and Besig to Milton Bentz, 2 September 1948, box 4, and to Elisabeth Roitman, 28 October 1948, box 16, both in NCACLU papers.

In NCACLU papers, box 4, there is a copy of the tentative program and Holmes's 12 November 1948 letter canceling the conference.

39 Quotations are from Ernest Besig to George Rundquist, 16 February 1951, ACLU papers, box 454; Board minutes, 7 June 1948, ACLU Board series, reel 11; John Haynes Holmes to William Johnson, 14 June 1948, ACLU papers, box 394 (see copy of the same letter to Edward Parsons, 14 June 1948, in ELP, box 4); and Board minutes, 24 May 1948, ACLU Board series, reel 11.

40 Quotations are from Lee to Milton Bentz, 31 December 1948; Marjorie Hanson Matson to Baldwin, 6 August 1948; and M. Huyett Sangree to Holmes, 2 July 1948, all in ACLU papers, box 394; Board minutes, 20 December 1948, ACLU Board series, reel 11; and Baldwin to Besig, 26 January 1949, paraphrasing Besig's characterization (emphasis in original), ACLU papers, box 394. Box 394 contains individual affiliate reports on voting where not already designated. The fourth affiliate to reject the resolution was St. Louis.

41 The first quotation is from Besig to Milton Bentz, 2 September 1948, NCACLU papers, box 4. All others are from OKF, 19 March 1949, 19.

42 The first two quotations are from Board minutes, 20 December 1948, ACLU Board series, reel 11, and Baldwin's memo on the ACLU's program, 28 December 1948, ACLU papers, reel 251. All other quotations are from Policy Planning Committee Report, 14 March 1949, RNB, box 2.

43 Both quotations come from letters from Holmes to Ernst, 5, 4 April 1949, JHH, container 223. The salary ultimately offered Baldwin's successor was $10,000 per year. Baldwin continued to draw an income from the ACLU, formalized in 1955 at $3,000 a year for the rest of his life. See Walter Frank to assorted ACLU officers, 2 June 1955, MLE, box 409.

44 Quotations are from Garey, *Defending Everybody*, 133; Holmes to Baldwin, 10 November 1949, JHH, container 232; Baldwin to Mary McAuliffe, 6 March 1972, RNB, box 6 (three quotations); George Rundquist to A. A. Heist, 11 October 1951, 25 January, 3 March 1950, ACLU papers, box 457; and Macdonald, "Defense of Everybody," pt. 2, 30.

45 Quotations are from Osmond Fraenkel paraphrasing Childs, OKF, 28 April 1949, 20; Besig to Baldwin, 2 September 1949, NCACLU papers, box 4; and Baldwin's memo on affiliates, 24 March 1949, ACLU Board series, reel 22.

46 Quotations are from Holmes to Childs, 19 May 1949, JHH, container 223; Board minutes, 9 May 1949, ACLU Board series, reel 12; and affiliate protests, the first from SCACLU and the second from Erie County, reported to the Board on 20 September 1949, ACLU Board series, reel

22. Board minutes, 26 September 1949, ACLU Board series, reel 12, has the Board's vote. On the Iowa meeting, see minutes, March 1950, ACLU papers, box 471, and Board minutes, 20 March 1950, ACLU Board series, reel 12.

47 Quotations are from Monroe, *Safeguarding Civil Liberties*, 124; Malin to James Caldwell, 3 August 1956, NCACLU papers, box 1; and George Rundquist describing Malin's attitude to A. A. Heist, 3 March 1950, ACLU papers, reel 269. The NCACLU minutes for 22 June 1950 note that Malin was already promoting the idea, but most affiliates were not fully integrated into the national organization until several years later. See NCACLU papers, box 47.

48 Quotations come from Board minutes, 16 April 1951, ACLU Board series, reel 23, and OKF, 10 May 1951, 35. See American Civil Liberties Union, *We Hold These Truths*, 12–13, on the program.

49 Quotations are from Heist to Besig, 18 April 1951, NCACLU papers, box 16; Malin to Jerome McNair et al., 3 July 1951, ACLU papers, box 322; Besig to Meiklejohn, 16 July 1951, AJM, box 4; and Malin to McNair et al. paraphrasing an SCACLU letter of protest, 3 July 1951, ACLU papers, box 322.

50 Quotations are from Board minutes, 29 March 1954, ACLU Board series, reel 13; Baldwin, memo for Malin, June 1951, RNB, box 2; and Baldwin to Norman Thomas, 25 August 1953, NT, reel 56. On Malin's role, see Board minutes, 29 June 1953, ACLU Board series, reel 13.

51 The first two quotations come from Affiliates' Conference Minutes, March 1955, ACLU Board series, reel 29. The rest are from Ernst to Louis Galantiere, 29 August 1961, MLE, box 566; Ferman's letter to the *Civil Liberties Review* 4 (March/April 1978): 5; FBI memo cited by Neier, *Taking Liberties*, 142; and FBI memo cited in Walker, *In Defense*, 333. On Malin and Ferman, see also Neier, "Adhering to Principle," 29. On Ferman and McCarthy, see Morgan, *One Man*, 263.

52 Quotations are from Ed Meyerding to Malin, 30 November 1954, ACLU Board series, reel 23; Holmes to Malin, 12 May 1950, JHH, container 232; and Macdonald, "Defense of Everybody," pt. 2, 58.

53 Aubrey Williams to Alexander Meiklejohn, 23 September 1953, ACLU papers, box 394. ACLU papers, box 354, contains letters of complaints addressed to the Union in the early 1950s.

54 Walker, *In Defense*, 195. See also McAuliffe, *Crisis on the Left*, 91; Goldstein, *Political Repression*, 368; Schrecker, *Many Are the Crimes*, 411; and Markmann, *Noblest Cry*, 171–72.

CHAPTER 7

1 Quotations are from Frances and Allen Graces to ACLU, 4 November 1949, ACLU papers, box 508. For more history on the Seattle group, see Honig and Brenner, *On Freedom's Frontier*, 27–28.

2 All numbers come from a listing of national and local membership, 30 June 1951, ACLU Board series, reel 23.

3 Ray to Ernest Besig, 16 January 1953, NCACLU papers, box 6. Her assessment parallels what sociologists would define as "institutionalization" (Roche and Sachs, "Bureaucrat and Enthusiast," 379).

4 On pursuing cases at the trial stage, see Monroe, *Safeguarding Civil Liberties*, 109, and Ernest Besig to A. A. Heist, 4 March 1949, NCACLU papers, box 3.

5 Quotations are from Charles Stewart Jr. to Baldwin, 22 July 1947, ACLU papers, reel 241; Leon Despres, report following visit to the national organization, 19 March 1949, Despres papers, Chicago Historical Society, box 242; and Chicago Division minutes, 3 January 1952, SCACLU papers, box 45. On the loans, see Board minutes for 18 November, 16 December 1946, 13, 26 January, 28 July 1947, 7 June 1948, all in ACLU Board series, reels 10 and 11. See also George Rundquist to Ed Meyerding, 7 February 1951, ACLU papers, box 323, on Chicago pulling itself together.

6 Quotations are from Baldwin to Will Johnson, 27 December 1948, box 465; Chicago Division minutes, 10 November 1947, reel 241; and Baldwin to Dale Pontius, 21 April 1948, box 465, all in ACLU papers. On the Chicago Division's concern, see their minutes, 11 December 1947, IACLU, box 103.

7 Quotations are from Osler to Jeff Fuller, 28 December 1956, box 324; Baldwin, April 1950 memo on the NCACLU, box 454; and Pat Malin, intraoffice memo to Louis Joughin, 12 June 1956, box 454, all in ACLU papers.

8 Betty Sanger to Kirtley Mather, 15 October 1946; to Baldwin, 15 October 1946; and to Milton Kaufman of the CRC, 11 November 1946, all in CLUM papers, box 6. Kaufman responded (15 October 1946) that "it is not often that the Civil Rights Congress receives any sign of helpful interest from ACLU branches."

9 On Faxon, see George Rundquist to Luther MacNair, 17 April 1953, CLUM papers, box 11. The first three quotations come from that letter; the next two are from Levy to Grier Bartol, 27 November 1951, ACLU papers, box 476; and the final quote is from Luscomb to Kirtley Mather, 11 May 1954, Luscomb papers, Schlesinger Library, box 18.

10 Quotations are from A. A. Heist to Luther MacNair, 20 February 1951,

box 10, and Jeff Fuller to MacNair, 23 January 1953, box 11, CLUM papers; Booton Herndon in a piece by Roger Baldwin, "The Lawyer You Didn't Know You Had" (1961), clipping in Milligan papers, Iliff School of Theology, series 6; and Charles Graham to George Rundquist, 13 February 1951, ACLU papers, box 459.

11 Quotations are from Sanger to Baldwin, 21 January 1947, ACLU papers, box 476; Luscomb to Jerry O'Connell, 2 May 1950, Luscomb papers, Schlesinger Library, box 9; Heist to Baldwin, 24 July 1947, ACLU papers, box 456; and Luscomb to Albert Sprague Coolidge, 24 April 1950, Luscomb papers, Schlesinger Library, box 18.

12 Quotations are from John Stockham to Baldwin, 24 July 1946; statement read by Stockham at Smith's St. Louis meeting, 29 May 1946; and Baldwin to Stockham, 27 May, 13 June 1946, all in ACLU papers, reel 237.

13 Quotations are from Baldwin to Homer Jack, 19 February 1946; Smith to Baldwin, 14 April 1946 (two quotations);Baldwin to Smith, 18 February 1946; Baldwin, memo for files, 4 April 1946; and Charles Liebman to Baldwin, 14 June 1946, all in ACLU papers, reel 237.

14 Quotations are from Despres to Richard A. Meyer, 6 January 1947, Despres papers, Chicago Historical Society, box 242; and Board minutes, 8 November 1946, ACLU Board series, reel 10. For more on the case, see Ribuffo, *Old Christian Right*, 216–23, and Walker, *In Defense*, 229.

15 Quotations are from Taft to Baldwin, 5 January 1946, ACLU papers, reel 233; Sigmund Groch, memo of Smith's public meeting, 28 November 1945, SCACLU papers, box 44; and Board minutes, 4 February 1946, ACLU papers, reel 236. For information on the Mobilization for Democracy, see Sitton, "Direct Democracy versus Free Speech," 289–92. There is a copy of Taft's tribute in ACLU papers, reel 237.

16 Quotations are from Board minutes, 4 February 1946, ACLU Board series, reel 10; Taft to Baldwin, 20 March 1946, ACLU papers, reel 236; and Baldwin to A. A. Heist, 12 November 1945, ACLU papers, reel 233. Heist's defense of McWilliams, 7 February 1946, is in ACLU papers, reel 234. McWilliams also served on the ACLU National Committee through 1948, where, apparently, his *Who's Who* status outranked his political volatility.

17 Quotations are from Baldwin to McWilliams, 6 May 1946, reel 234, and McWilliams to Baldwin, 11 May, 22 January 1946, reel 233, all in ACLU papers; John Haynes Holmes to Edwin Ryland, 30 January 1946, JHH, container 213; and Edward Ryland to Holmes, "confidential," 6 February 1946, ACLU papers, reel 234.

18 Quotations are from A. L. Wirin to Ernst, 11 April 1952, MLE, box 407;

A. A. Heist to the CLUM, 22 June 1948, CLUM papers, box 7; and Heist to Herbert Levy, 22 June 1949, ACLU papers, reel 261.

19 Quotations are from Luscomb to Albert Sprague Coolidge, 24 April 1950, Luscomb papers, Schlesinger Library, box 18; Homer Jack in American Civil Liberties Union Branch of Illinois minutes, 11 February 1954, IACLU, box 104; Minutes of the St. Louis Civil Liberties Committee, 23 February 1954, SCACLU papers, box 47; Besig to Luther MacNair, 21 May 1951, NCACLU papers, box 16; Ed Meyerding to George Rundquist, 22 April 1952, IACLU, box 115; Neier, "Adhering to Principle," 26; and Luscomb to Coolidge, 24 April 1950, Luscomb papers, Schlesinger Library, box 18.

20 Quotations are from Besig to Baldwin, 29 March 1948, NCACLU papers, box 4 (my emphasis), and Heist to Baldwin, 3 October 1947, ACLU papers, reel 243.

21 Quotations are from Board minutes, 12 May 1947, ACLU Board series, reel 11; Besig to Baldwin, 23 July 1947, ACLU papers, reel 241 (emphasis in original); Wirin to Cliff Forster, 12 June 1947, ACLU papers, box 456; Board minutes, 8 September 1947, ACLU Board series, reel 10; Frederick Robin to Besig, 8 August 1947, ACLU papers, box 456; Board minutes, 30 June 1947, ACLU Board series, reel 10; and Heist to Baldwin, 14 July 1947, ACLU papers, reel 241. On the divergent votes, see office to Board, 26 April 1951, ACLU Board series, reel 23.

22 Quotations are from Heist to Baldwin, 3 October 1947, ACLU papers, reel 241; to the CLUM, 22 October 1947, and to Elisabeth Roitman, 11 June 1948, 18 February 1949, CLUM papers, boxes 7 and 8; Board minutes, 19 January 1948, ACLU Board series, reel 11; Frederick Robin to Cliff Forster, memo dated 29 March 1947, ACLU papers, box 456; and George Rundquist to Donald Paterson, 3 April 1953, NCACLU papers, box 1.

23 The first exchange is from Baldwin to Heist, 21 December 1948, and Heist to Baldwin, 23 December 1948, reel 251. The other quotations are from Baldwin to Malin, 22 July 1950, box 457; Malin to Gloria Gantz, 1 August 1951, box 322; and Heist to George Rundquist, 4 May 1950, box 457. All are in ACLU papers.

24 Heist to Besig, 7 March 1949, NCACLU papers, box 3.

25 Quotations are from Edward Spiegel to Besig, 22 June 1948, NCACLU papers, box 16, and Mary Farquharson to Baldwin, 13 March 1948, ACLU papers, box 508.

26 Quotations are from Heist to Baldwin, 2 March 1948, and Baldwin to

Heist, 26 February 1948, NCACLU papers, box 4, and special Board minutes, 28 April 1949, ACLU Board series, reel 11.

27 Special Board minutes, 28 April 1949, and Board minutes, 5 June 1949, both in ACLU Board series, reel 11.

28 Quotations are from Board minutes, 20 March 1950, ACLU Board series, reel 12, and Heist to Edward Allen, 20 June 1951, SCACLU papers, box 52. The minutes of the Iowa Civil Liberties Union, March 1950, ACLU papers, box 471, list the recommendations and Board minutes; minutes from 20 March and 3 April 1950, ACLU Board series, reel 12, show the Board's reaction.

29 Quotations are from Jerome MacNair to Rundquist, 16 June 1952, box 322, and Besig to Rundquist, 2 January 1951, box 454. On the CLUM, see CLUM minutes, 11 February 1952, box 476. All are in ACLU papers.

30 Quotations are from committee on members and affiliates to Board, 10 April 1951, MP, box 11, and Board minutes, 16 April 1951, ACLU Board series, reel 23. On voting arrangements, see Malin to Luther MacNair et al., 3 July 1951, ACLU papers, box 322.

31 Quotations are from A. A. Heist to Rundquist, 29 May 1951, ACLU papers, box 457; Heist to Malin, 22 September 1951, NCACLU papers, box 4; Edward Allen to Ernest Angell, 18 June 1951, IACLU, box 115 (two quotations); and Rundquist to Allen, 2 June 1951, ACLU papers, box 471 (two quotations).

32 The text is in bylaws copies from the early 1950s in ACLU Board series, reel 23 (my emphasis). The opinion, prepared by Harold Sherman, 12 May 1951, is in NCACLU papers, box 3. Herbert M. Levy, hardly the Union's most liberal officer, challenged the provision in a letter to William Fitelson, 20 June 1951, NCACLU papers, box 3. The final quotations are from Malin to Luther MacNair et al., 3 July 1951, ACLU papers, box 322.

33 Board minutes, 27 April 1953, ACLU Board series, reel 13.

34 Quotations are from Mary Farquharson to Baldwin, 13 March 1948, ACLU papers, reel 251, and Healey and Isserman, *California Red*, 147. On Monroe, see *Safeguarding Civil Liberties*, x, 136; on the size of the SCACLU, see Healey and Isserman, *California Red*, 147. The 1949 report is cited in an internal FBI memo from A. H. Belmont to L. V. Boardman, 10 December 1955, Freedom of Information Act documents on the American Civil Liberties Union.

35 Both early quotations are from *Open Forum*, 23 July 1949, 1. On the radio program, see *Open Forum*, 19 January 1952, 2. On the Hollywood inquiry,

see Board minutes, 27 April, 15 June 1953, ACLU Board series, reel 13. On the legal strategy, see Monroe, *Safeguarding Civil Liberties*, 109. On Operation Abolition, as it was called, see Simmons, "Origins of the Campaign to Abolish HUAC" (quotation from 149), and documents in SCACLU papers, box 92. The decision to prioritize abolishing HUAC was made at the 1960 Biennial Conference; see minutes, April 1960, ACLU Board series, reel 29.

36 Quotation is from Edward Parsons to Holmes, 25 October 1948, ACLU papers, box 454. On loyalty cases, see Knutson, "American Civil Liberties Union of Northern California," 106, and Hiram Bingham to Ernest Angell, 19 June 1951, ACLU papers, box 454. Compare with the brief in the ACLU's 1953–54 annual report, 30. On the loyalty oath controversy, see Northern California Branch of the American Civil Liberties Union, *Crisis at the University of California*. On the Tenney Committee, see Parsons's statement, 1 April 1948, ELP, box 15, and the NCACLU's August 1953 policy statement, ACLU Board series, reel 23. Freedom of Information Act files reveal that the government kept tabs on the NCACLU.

37 On the CLUM, see Board minutes, 18 August, 6, 20 October 1947, ACLU Board series, reel 10. On the Chicago group, see Chicago Division minutes, 6 November 1947, IACLU, box 103. On Maryland, see Meyerding to Malin, 17 February 1953 (quotations), and George Rundquist to Meyerding, 20 February 1953, IACLU, box 116. See also Maryland board minutes, 10 February 1953, SCACLU papers, box 46.

38 Quotations are from CLUM executive committee minutes, 1 December 1952, box 46, and SCACLU board minutes, 5 May 1952, box 457, both in SCACLU papers; New Haven Civil Liberties Council's letter to Truman, 23 November 1952, AJM, box 48; and Board minutes, 1 December 1952, ACLU Board series, reel 12.

39 Quotations are from Holmes to Walter Gellhorn, 16 February 1950, JHH, container 232, and Baldwin to A. S. Coolidge, 2 December 1949, box 476, and Rundquist to A. K. Chalmers, 12 December 1952, box 324, ACLU papers. There are a number of exchanges between CLUM personnel and headquarters debating matters of autonomy and politics, in ACLU papers, reel 251.

40 Herbert Levy to Grier Bartol, 27 November 1951, ACLU papers, box 476. On the matter, see CLUM papers, box 10, particularly executive committee minutes, 12 January 1951; general committee minutes, 17 May 1951; and Luscomb's statement, 17 January 1951.

41 Quotations are from Ray to Besig, addendum to 18 September 1953 letter, NCACLU papers, box 16, and Malin to Farquharson, 13 July 1955,

Farquharson papers, University of Washington Library, box 3. The details of the story can be found in ACLU papers, box 328. Ray's letter to Thomas, 7 February 1954, is in NT, reel 57.

42 Quotations are from Allan Hart to Rundquist, 30 November 1951, and Fuller to Ruth Haefner, 16 March 1955, box 327, and Reverend Franklin Smith to Fuller, 17 June 1954, box 326, all in ACLU papers.

43 Quotation is from Malin to Wolf, 13 October 1953, ACLU papers, box 324. The rest of the details are there as well.

44 Quotations are from Rundquist to Sheldon Rahn, 6 April 1953, ACLU papers, box 477, and Levy to Ed Meyerding, 7 August 1952, IACLU, box 116. Lamont, *Yes to Life*, 140–41, notes that Malin himself ran Lamont's name past J. Edgar Hoover. Gentry, *Hoover*, 439–40, confirms the practice, which is evident in Freedom of Information Act files as well.

45 Quotations are from William Sanborn to Fuller, 13 July 1955, ACLU papers, box 324, and Robert Halbeisen to Thomas, 22 February 1957, and Louis Joughin to Halbeisen, 27 February 1957, both in NT, reel 57. ACLU papers, boxes 324 and 328, contain the saga of the Detroit/Michigan affiliate.

46 Quotations are from Fuller, memo to Malin, 27 August 1954, ACLU papers, box 324, and Levy to the editors of *Civil Liberties Review* 4 (March/April 1978): 4. On Levy, see Malin to Ernest Besig, 2 June 1952, ACLU papers, box 454.

47 Quotations are from Alan Reitman to Malin, 23 November 1954, box 859, and Jeff Fuller to Philip Houtz, 14 October 1954, box 323, both in ACLU papers, and OKF, 6 June 1955, 71. See also Rundquist to William Reynard, 7 November 1952, box 323, and 6 November 1952, box 859, and Reitman to Lindsey Waldon, 6 November 1952, box 459, all in ACLU papers. On information from the FBI, see Reitman to Malin, 23 November 1954, box 859, and 30 June 1955, box 613, both in ACLU papers.

48 Quotations are from Leonard Boudin's interview in James, *People's Lawyers*, 19; Norman Thomas to Ann Ray, 28 January 1954, NT, reel 57; and Alan Reitman, staff memo, 18 December 1953, ACLU papers, box 78. McWilliams talks about the impact of his ECLC affiliation with the ACLU in *Honorable in All Things*, 475. Reitman's memo reads like it was composed by a private investigator spying on someone.

49 The quotation is from *New York Times*, 4 August 1977. On Ferman's more personal motivation, see Neier, "Adhering to Principle," 28.

50 Quotations are from Rundquist to Walter Bergman, 10 June 1952, ACLU papers, box 477, and memo cited in Donner, *Age of Surveillance*, 145.

51 Quotation is from letter, 5 October 1953, NCACLU papers, box 16.
52 Betty Sanger to Baldwin, 8 November 1945, ACLU papers, reel 231.

CHAPTER 8

1 Liptak, "ACLU Board Split" (quotation).
2 Quotations are from Garey, *Defending Everybody*, 135; Holmes to Merlyn Pitzele, 9 April 1947, MP, box 11; and an unnamed director quoted in Macdonald, "Defense of Everybody," pt. 2, 39.
3 Quotations are from Rundquist to Luther MacNair, 17 April 1953, and to Thornton Merriam, 19 February 1952, ACLU papers, box 324; Macdonald, "Defense of Everybody," pt. 1, 36; and A. A. Heist to Besig, 7 March 1949, NCACLU papers, box 3.
4 Quotations are from Board minutes, 26 June 1950, reel 269, and Heist to Baldwin, 29 October 1951, box 322, both in ACLU papers.
5 Quotations are from Dan James, "Who Are the Civil Libertarians," *New Leader*, 30 June 1952, 12; Louis Joughin to Edward Meyerding, 3 July 1952, IACLU, box 116; and Thomas to Malin, 30 October 1952, NT, reel 56. For a conservative's view of the American Legion resolution, see Donohue, *Politics of the American Civil Liberties Union*, 182–83.
6 Quotations are from Thomas to Patrick Malin, 30 October 1952, NT, reel 56; minutes of the Membership and Affiliates Committee, 2 November 1952, copy in Minnesota Civil Liberties Union papers, Minnesota Historical Society, box 1 (two quotations); and OKF, 14 April 1953, 45.
7 On the bureaucratic bottleneck, see minutes for February through April 1953 in ACLU Board series, reel 13, and George Rundquist to Spencer Coxe, 7 January 1953, ACLU papers, box 500. On budget problems, see Malin to Budget and Office Management Committee, 18 December 1952, reel 23, and Board minutes, 27 April 1953, reel 13, both in ACLU Board series.
8 The first three quotations are from Norman Thomas to Patrick Malin, 30 October 1952, NT, reel 56. The others are from Fitelson to Patrick Malin, 25 February 1953, Oxnam papers, Library of Congress, HUAC file.
9 The Pitzele motion was debated on 17 March 1953, and the final debate took place on 15 April 1953; see ACLU Board series, reel 13. Morris Ernst, Dorothy Dunbar Bromley, Norman Thomas, Elmer Rice, Merlyn Pitzele, and Richard Childs each submitted a statement on the CPUSA. All are in ACLU Board series, reel 23.
10 The evolution of the three statements, originally six, may be traced by consulting Board minutes between January and April 1953, ACLU Board series, reel 13.

11 Quotations are from Baldwin to Mary McAuliffe, 6 March 1972, RNB, box 6; OKF, 15 April 1953, 45; Lamont to Alexander Meiklejohn, 30 March 1953, AJM, box 18; Lamont to Thomas, 16 October 1952, NT, reel 56; and Lamont to all affiliates, 11 September 1953, AJM, box 48.

12 The first quotation is from Board minutes, 4 May 1953, ACLU Board series, reel 13 (my emphasis). SCACLU minutes put the word "advice" in quotation marks; see minutes, 23 June 1953, copy in CLUM papers, box 11. The other quotations are from the office copy of Lamont to Fellow Members of the ACLU, 4 June 1953, ACLU papers, box 294.

13 Quotations are from Board agenda, 15 June 1953, ACLU Board series, reel 13; Rhoda Truax Aldrich to George Rundquist, 9 April 1953, ACLU papers, box 324; Edward Allen of Iowa to assorted affiliates, 25 May 1953, NCACLU papers, box 2; Howard K. Beale to Thomas, 28 June 1953, NT, reel 56; and Besig to Alexander Meiklejohn, 19 May 1953, AJM, box 4.

14 Quotations are from Malin to the National Committee and affiliates, 14 July 1953, ACLU Board series, reel 23; OKF, 23 September 1953, 47; Angell's statement, 1 September 1953, copy in NT, reel 56; and Lamont's telegram to affiliates, 11 September 1953, AJM, box 48. The Board approved Angell's statement in theory but not its text.

15 The quotations are from Lamont to Alexander Meiklejohn, 30 March 1953, AJM, box 18; Ann Ray to Ernest Besig, 18 September 1953, NCACLU papers, box 16; Lamont to Besig, 7 October 1953, AJM, box 18; and Board minutes, 5 October 1953, ACLU Board series, reel 13. On the Board's decision, see report, 29 October 1953, ACLU Board series, reel 23.

16 Tallies are reported in Malin to the Board, 16 October 1953, ACLU Board series, reel 29. The final vote was 18,995 for the statements, 21,271 against (14,320 were affiliate votes), and 1,554 abstentions. Only 69 percent of the National Committee voted. The quotations are from Eason Monroe's notes on the statements for the biennial conference, ca. February 1954, SCACLU papers, box 52.

17 Quotations are from Garey, *Defending Everybody*, 135; OKF, 29 October 1953, 50, describing William Fitelson; and Malin to Board, 16 October 1953, ACLU Board series, reel 29.

18 Quotations are from Board minutes, 19 October 1953, ACLU Board series, reel 13; Besig to Alexander Meiklejohn, 20 October 1953, AJM, box 4; and Chicago Division minutes, 15, 22 October 1953, IACLU, box 104.

19 Quotations are from Corliss Lamont to Meiklejohn, 17 November 1953, AJM, box 18; Besig to Meiklejohn, 20 November 1953, AJM, box 4; and Meiklejohn to Besig, ca. November 1953, NCACLU papers, box 2.

20 Quotations are from Lamont to John Finerty, 1 December 1953, Finerty papers, University of Oregon Library, box 13; Lamont to the National Committee and affiliates, 22 January 1954, ACLU Board series, reel 23; and Chicago minutes, 12 November 1953, box 104, and Edward Allen to Ed Meyerding, 19 November 1953, box 114, both in IACLU. See Lamont to Meiklejohn, 17 November 1953, AJM, box 18, on his suspicion he would not be renominated.

21 Quotations are from Malin to Board, 13 November 1953, ACLU Board series, reel 23. In AJM, box 4, see Malin's letter postponing the conference, 6 November 1953, and his letter after he returned from Florida, 27 December 1953.

22 Quotations are from Holmes to Malin, 17 November 1953, ACLU papers, box 15; OKF, 29 October 1953, 50; Thomas to Holmes, 18 November 1953, and White to Thomas, 3 November 1953, NT, reel 56; Holmes to Malin, 28 June 1955, ACLU papers, box 15; and OKF, 17 November 1953, 50. Seymour's resignation is in Seymour to Ernest Angell, 4 November 1953, NT, reel 56. Votes on Lamont are in 2, 16 November 1953 meetings, ACLU Board series, reel 13.

23 The first two quotations are from White to Thomas, 3 November 1953, NT, reel 56. The last is from Thomas to ACLU Board, 26 October 1953, MP, box 12.

24 All quotations except the first and last come from Board minutes, 30 November 1953, ACLU Board series, reel 13. The first is from Besig to Lamont, 14 September 1953, NCACLU papers, box 2. The last is from Aubrey Williams to Malin, 12 February 1954, NT, reel 57.

25 Quotations are from Alexander Meiklejohn to "friends," 21 January 1954, ACLU Board series, reel 29; Ann Ray to Besig, P.S. dated 4 November, NCACLU papers, box 16; and Wolfgang Homberger to ACLU, 16 January 1954, box 322, and Lynd to Malin, 14 November 1953, box 203, both in ACLU papers. ACLU, box 322, contains other dues-withholding responses besides Homberger's, as does CLUM papers, box 11.

26 The quotations are from OKF, 14 February 1954, 56, 57, and the Graham statement in ACLU Board series, reel 23. Full conference minutes are in ACLU Board series, reel 29. Perhaps the proceedings worked in favor of the branches so easily because, as Howard Beale noted, the Board was "so completely autocratic" that members "did not even bother to come to the meetings." See Beale to Thomas, 28 May 1954, NT, reel 57.

27 Quotations are from Chicago minutes, 18 February 1954, IACLU, box 104; Alexander Meiklejohn to "friends," 21 January 1954, ACLU Board series, reel 29; Proposed Amendments to the Constitution and By-Laws,

19 April 1954, copy in IACLU, box 118; *NCACLU News*, March 1954, 1; biennial conference minutes, February 1954, copy in IACLU, box 118; and CLUM minutes, 5 March 1954, SCACLU papers, box 46.

28 Quotations are from Fly to friends, 2 March 1954 (two quotations); Thomas to Ann Ray, 28 January 1954; Fly to friends and Thomas to "colleagues," 4 March 1954; and Fly to friends and William L. White to Thomas, 3 November 1953, all in NT, reels 56 and 57.

29 Statement, early March 1954, ACLU Board series, reel 23.

30 Malin to the Board, 12 March 1954, ACLU Board series, reel 23 (emphasis in original).

31 For a firsthand look at how the meeting went, see OKF, 15 March 1954, 59. The White and Finerty letters, both late March 1954, are in ACLU Board series, reel 23.

32 Quotations are from Besig to Malin, 18 March 1954, and to the Board, 10 April 1954, box 5; Beale to Besig, 31 March 1954, box 2; R. B. Brooks to the Board, 27 April 1954, box 2; Besig to Malin, 18 March 1954, box 2, all in NCACLU papers; and Beale to Norman Thomas, 28 May 1954, NT, reel 57. Beale to Malin, 31 March 1954, ACLU papers, box 394, suggests Beale did not blame Malin. Clore Warne to Malin, 24 March 1954, ACLU papers, box 394, and Mary Leue to Norman Thomas, 10 April 1954, NT, reel 57, protest the lack of democracy.

33 Malin's warnings are from Board minutes, 29 March 1954, ACLU Board series, reel 13, and Public Relations Committee minutes, 1 April 1953, SCACLU papers, box 60. The next quotations are from OKF, 17 March 1954, 59; Malin to the Board, 18 March 1954, ACLU Board series, reel 23; and OKF, 29 March 1954, 60. The last two are from Thomas to Howard Beale, 14 June 1954, and Thomas to William Fitelson, 16 March 1954, both in NT, reel 57. The *World Telegram* clipping is in ACLU Board series, box 23; the *Post* clipping is in IACLU, box 118.

34 Quotations are from John C. Holt to Malin, 29 May 1954, and Mary Leue to Thomas, 10 April 1954, NT, reel 57; Howard Beale to Malin, 31 March 1954, box 394, and Public Relations Committee minutes, 3 December 1953, box 78, both in ACLU papers; and OKF, 29 March 1954, 60. Ernest Besig to Malin, 18 March 1954, NCACLU papers, box 2, also uses the phrase "broke faith." The revised budget was discussed at the next Board meeting after the Thomas resolution passed; see 22 March 1954, ACLU Board series, reel 23. The year before, the ACLU had added 7,000 new members. In 1954, it would add only 1,100.

35 All quotations are from OKF, 8 July 1954, 63. Statements dated 9 July 1954 are in ACLU Board series, reel 23. The Board vote, 2 August 1954,

is in ACLU Board series, reel 13. See ACLU Board series, reel 13, for the NCACLU's 22 November 1954 request for a referendum and the Board's response that, by constitutional definition, not enough members asked for a referendum to hold one. The final quotation is from Walker, *In Defense*, 208.

36 Quotations are from Malin to the Budget and Office Management Committee and the membership and Affiliates Committee, 25 August 1954, ACLU Board series, reel 23; SCACLU minutes, 7 July 1954, ACLU papers, box 457; OKF, 9 September 1954, 64; and Besig to James Perlman, 6 December 1954, ACLU papers, box 322.

37 The first quotations come from Clyde W. Summers to Ernest Besig, 11 February 1955, NCACLU papers, box 1. All other quotations except the last two come from Meyerding's letter, 30 November 1954, ACLU Board series, reel 23. The final two come from Board minutes, 17, 31 January 1955, ACLU Board series, reel 14.

38 Quotations come from Louis Joughin to Malin, 17 March 1955, ACLU papers, box 401, and Board minutes, 14 March 1955, ACLU Board series, reel 14. Joughin's letter provided a corrective to the too-positive version the Board heard reported.

39 The quotations are from "Survey of National Office Organizations and Procedures and its Relations with the Affiliates" (sometimes called the Cresap Report), 1955, V-22, V-3, II-3, and II-5, IACLU, box 101.

40 Quotations are from St. Louis Committee minutes, 23 February 1954, SCACLU papers, box 47; *NCACLU News*, January 1955, 2; and Sonia Osler to Jeff Fuller, 28 December 1956, box 324, and Besig to Fuller, 31 December 1954, box 328, both in ACLU papers.

41 Louis Joughin to Malin, 16 December 1955, ACLU papers, box 613. See also Chicago Conference on Affiliates, 12, 13 March 1955, reel 29, and financial documents of the period, reel 23, both in ACLU Board series.

42 Quotations are from Leon Despres, report on a national meeting of the ACLU, March 1949, Despres papers, Chicago Historical Society, box 242; Board minutes, 21 November 1955, ACLU Board series, reel 14; and Forster to Baldwin, August 1951, RNB, box 2. On directors' dissatisfaction with staff, see, for example, OKF, 24 June 1957, 93. On the Christmas party, see OKF, 22 December 1950, 33.

43 Quotations are from Burt Neuborne as cited in Garey, *Defending Everybody*, 134; Louis Joughin to Malin, 16 December 1955, ACLU papers, box 613; and Baldwin to Ernest Angell, 7 July 1951, RNB, box 2.

44 Quotations are from Malin to constitutional committee, 14 February 1956, ACLU Board series, reel 29, and staff statement, 1 March 1956,

copy in NCACLU papers, box 1. On the HUAC report, see Malin to Francis Walter, 10 December 1955, ACLU papers, box 609. Both Ernest Besig and Osmond Fraenkel used the word "bombshell." See *NCACLU News*, April 1956, 4, and OKF, 2 March 1956, 78.

45 Quotations are from OKF, 1 March 1956, 77, and Board minutes, 5 March 1956, ACLU Board series, reel 14. Malin really did seem to be invisible. A 1968 story the Union paid A. F. Mahan to write failed to mention Malin at all; Mahan's history moved from Baldwin to John de Pemberton, Malin's successor. See ACLU Board series, reel 29.

46 OKF, 25 June 1956, 81. Board minutes throughout the second half of the year include discussions of the constitution; see ACLU Board series, reel 14. The texts of the final choice (designated C) and two alternatives are attached to Malin to corporation, 15 October 1956, and his report of the vote is 22 December 1956, both in ACLU papers, box 395.

47 Late 1950s financial documents are in ACLU Board series, reel 23. The annual percentage really determined a branch's ability to function. In 1954 the Minnesota affiliate got back only 18 percent of what it raised, barely $600. Four years later it got back 80 percent, close to $3,000. See Richter, *Reflections*, 53.

48 Quotations are from Ernst's conversation with Joe Lash, 7 February 1972, JL, box 49, and OKF, 4 March 1957, 89. Ernst left the Board in 1960.

49 From an FBI memo by Louis B. Nichols, 20 August 1956, cited in Neier, *Taking Liberties*, 141.

50 All quotations are from HUAC, "A Study and Report of the American Civil Liberties Union," 1, 2, copy in ACLU papers, box 609. See also Malin's long response (fifty pages) to Francis Walter, 10 December 1955, ibid. One of the more controversial parts of the report is the allegation that the ACLU expelled Elizabeth Gurley Flynn to satisfy big contributor Margaret de Silver. Malin evades commenting on the charge; see HUAC report, 17, and Malin's memo, 36. On the FBI and the ACLU, see O'Reilly, *Hoover and the Un-Americans*, 190–91.

51 Quotation is from an unnamed leader in a memo from Roger Baldwin to the Board, 1964, appendix to "The ACLU—Today and Tomorrow," ACLU Board series, reel 29. On the later 1950s, see Markmann, *Noblest Cry*, and Walker, *In Defense*, although the latter source tends to skip the later 1950s altogether. On Oswald, see OKF, 2 December 1963, 184.

52 Quotation is from a chapter title in Garey, *Defending Everybody*, 143.

53 Quotation is from 1957–60 Constitutional Committee to Board, National Committee and Affiliates, 31 March 1960, ACLU Board series, reel

29. On amicus cases, see Mel Wulf in James, *People's Lawyers*, 30. On the financial crisis, see John de Pemberton's memo, 15 June 1962, ACLU Board series, reel 29.

54 Quotations are from Board minutes, 10 October 1955, reel 14, and Special Board Committee on Biennial Conference Recommendations, 29 March 1956, reel 23, both in ACLU Board series, and Marshall to Elmer Rice, 18 June 1954, Rice papers, Harvard Theater Library, box 2.

55 Quotations are from OKF, 15 July, 2 December 1957, 93, 97; Markmann, *Noblest Cry*, 264; Summary Report of 1964 Biennial Conference, 9 July 1964, 14, ACLU Board series, reel 29; OKF, 12 August 1963, 23 June 1964, 178, 195; and Ernst to Lewis Galantiere, 29 August 1961, MLE, box 566.

56 All quotations are from OKF, 17 August 1959, 4 January 1962, 6 March 1961, 120, 154, 143. On Speiser, see O'Reilly, *Hoover and the Un-Americans*, 192. On Wulf, see his oral history in James, *People's Lawyers*, 28.

57 Quotations are from ACLU Public Relations Committee Minutes, 16 January 1957, as cited in Morgan, *One Man*, 23; OKF, 23 June 1964, 204; Morgan, *One Man*, 3; Neier, *Taking Liberties*, 44; OKF, 23 June 1964, 204; and Walker, *In Defense*, 267.

58 Wulf in James, *People's Lawyers*, 28. On Morgan, see his *One Man* and Garey, *Defending Everybody*, 145.

59 Pemberton's quotations come from his speech, "ACLU at the Crossroads," summarized in Report of the 1968 Biennial Conference, ACLU Board series, reel 29. The others are from Malin to corporation members, 25 January 1954, ACLU Board series, reel 29; Garey, *Defending Everybody*, 135; and Fraenkel, *Oral History*, 132.

60 Morgan, *One Man*, 139. On the case, see Walker, *In Defense*, 271. On the problem of partisanship, see OKF, 11 July 1967, pt. 2, 37.

61 Quotations are from OKF, 2 March 1968, pt. 2, 50, and Walker, *In Defense*, 285, 315. On the ACLU and the Spock case, see Mitford, *Trial of Dr. Spock*, 269–72. The new governance system is outlined in the 1968 Biennial Conference summary, 102–10, ACLU Board series, reel 29.

62 The first quotation and the membership figures are from Neier, *Defending My Enemy*, 77 (quotation), 78 (figures). The two other quotations are Ernst to Baldwin, 31 December, 7 November 1973, MLE, box 886. See also Lukas, "ACLU," 18, and Morgan, *One Man*, 264–65. On Neier's style and programs, see Walker, *In Defense*, 314–17, and Stern, "Civil Liberties Units Expanding," 52.

63 Wulf in James, *People's Lawyers*, 29; Ed Ennis to the Executive Committee, 28 December 1973, RNB, box 6.

64 Fraenkel to the Board, 23 January 1974, RNB, box 6; Fraenkel in the *New*

York Times, 22 June 1976; Baldwin to the Board, 26 March 1976, RNB, box 6. The inscription on the citation is quoted in Cottrell, *Baldwin*, 388.

65 Quotations are from Neier, as cited in Marro, "ACLU Aides Fear Effects," and Neier, as cited in Lukas, "ACLU," 26. "Utilitarian calculus" comes from Gibson and Bingham, *Civil Liberties and Nazis*, chap. 4, which focuses on the ACLU.

66 On Skokie, see Neier, *Defending My Enemy*, 78 (statistics).

67 Walker, *In Defense*, 370–71. The exact favorable percentage was 47. The Union's website is <www.aclu.org>.

68 Macdonald, "Defense of Everybody," pt. 1, 35.

AFTERWORD

1 As quoted in Gustav Niebuhr, "U.S. 'Secular' Groups Set Tone for Terror Attacks, Falwell Says," *New York Times*, 14 September 2001.

2 Robin Toner, "Some Foresee a Sea Change in Attitudes on Freedoms," *New York Times*, 15 September 2001.

3 To learn more about the ACLU's responses to 9/11, check <www.aclu. org>.

4 "Justice Admits FBI Keeping Tabs on ACLU, Greenpeace," *Minneapolis Star-Tribune*, 8 July 2005.

5 On the "Safe and Free" campaign, see *Civil Liberties*, Fall 2002, 7, from which the quotation is drawn. On the freedom campaigns, see *Civil Liberties*, Winter 2005, 2–3.

6 Compare the 1939 poll in Britt and Menefee, "Did Publicity Influence Public Opinion?," with two recent polls at <www.lexis-nexis.com>, one conducted 16 March–4 April 2004 and the other conducted 16–17 February 2004.

7 As quoted in *Time* magazine's cover story, "The Twenty-Five Most Influential Hispanics in America," 22 August 2005, 49.

BIBLIOGRAPHY

MANUSCRIPT SOURCES

Astor and Lennox Collection, New York Public Library, New York, New York
    Norman Thomas papers (microfilm)
Bancroft Library, University of California, Berkeley
    Wayne M. Collins papers
    National Lawyers Guild papers
    Edward Lambe Parsons papers
    Marie Short papers
California Historical Society, San Francisco
    Northern California Branch of the American Civil Liberties Union papers
Chicago Historical Society, Chicago, Illinois
    Leon M. Despres papers
    Ira Latimer papers
Harvard Archives, Harvard University, Cambridge, Massachusetts
    Zechariah Chafee Jr. papers
Harvard Theater Library, Harvard University, Cambridge, Massachusetts
    Elmer Rice papers
Iliff School of Theology, Ira J. Taylor Library, Denver, Colorado
    Charles S. Milligan papers
Labadie Collection, University of Michigan Library, Ann Arbor
    Agnes Inglis papers
Library of Congress, Washington, D.C.
    John Haynes Holmes papers
    Benjamin Huebsch papers
    G. Bromley Oxnam papers
    Roger William Riis papers
Massachusetts Historical Society, Boston
    Civil Liberties Union of Massachusetts papers

Minnesota Historical Society, St. Paul
  George B. Leonard papers
  Minnesota Civil Liberties Union papers
Seeley G. Mudd Manuscript Library, Princeton University, Princeton,
    New Jersey
  American Civil Liberties Union Board papers
  American Civil Liberties Union papers
  Roger Nash Baldwin papers
  Osmond K. Fraenkel diaries
  Arthur Garfield Hays papers
  Peggy Lamson papers
Newberry Library, Chicago, Illinois
  Floyd Dell papers
Harry Ransom Humanities Research Center, University of Texas, Austin
  Morris Ernst papers
Franklin D. Roosevelt Library, Hyde Park, New York
  Gardner Jackson papers
  Joseph Lash papers
Schlesinger Library, Radcliffe Center for Advanced Studies, Harvard
    University, Cambridge, Massachusetts
  Dorothy Dunbar Bromley papers
  Mary Ware Dennett papers
  Elizabeth Glendower Evans papers
  Freda Kirchwey papers
  Florence Luscomb papers
Smith College, Sophia Smith Collection, Northampton, Massachusetts
  Helen Tufts Bailie papers
  Dorothy Kenyon papers
  Jessie O'Connor papers
  Mary Van Kleeck papers
Southern California Library for Social Studies and Research,
    Los Angeles
  Civil Rights Congress of Los Angeles papers
  Leo Gallagher papers
State Historical Society of Wisconsin, Madison
  Americans for Democratic Action collection
  Howard Beale papers
  Alexander J. Meiklejohn papers
  Merlyn Pitzele papers
  Edward A. Ross papers

Richard Rovere papers

James Wechsler papers

Swarthmore Peace Collection, Swarthmore College, Swarthmore,
Pennsylvania

L. Hollingsworth Wood papers

Tamiment Library, New York University, New York, New York

American Committee for Cultural Freedom papers

Elizabeth Gurley Flynn papers

University of Chicago, Chicago, Ill.

American Civil Liberties Union branch of Illinois papers

University of Oregon Library, Eugene

John Finerty papers

Eugene Lyons papers

University of Virginia, Special Collections, Alderman Library,
Charlottesville

Walter Frank papers

Booton Herndon papers

University of Washington Library, Special Collections, Seattle

American Civil Liberties Union of Washington papers

Arthur Barnett papers

Mary Farquharson papers

Western Reserve Historical Society Library, Cleveland, Ohio

Russell Chase papers

Yale University, New Haven, Connecticut

Jerome Frank papers

Charles E. Young Library, Special Collections, University of California,
Los Angeles

Carey McWilliams papers

Southern California Branch of the American Civil Liberties Union
papers

GOVERNMENT DOCUMENTS

Freedom of Information Act documents on the American Civil Liberties
Union, Federal Bureau of Investigation, Washington, D.C.

Freedom of Information Act documents on James L. Fly, Federal Bureau of
Investigation, Washington, D.C.

U.S. Congress. House of Representatives. Committee on Un-American
Activities. *Hearings on Proposed Legislation to Curb or Control the
Communist Party of the United States.* 80th Cong., 2nd sess., 1948.
Washington, D.C.: Government Printing Office, 1948.

——. House Special Committee on Un-American Activities.
Investigations of Un-American Activities in the United States. Vol. 10. 76th
Cong., 2nd sess., 1939. Washington, D.C.: Government Printing Office,
1939.

U.S. Department of the Interior. War Relocation Authority. *Impounded
People: Japanese Americans in the Relocation Centers.* Washington, D.C.:
Government Printing Office, 1946.

MEMOIRS, DIARIES, AUTOBIOGRAPHIES, ORAL HISTORIES,
AND PUBLISHED LETTERS

Baldwin, Roger Nash. *The Reminiscences of Roger Baldwin, 1953/54.*
New York: Columbia University Oral History Research Office,
1972.

Baylin, Meyer. *Oral History.* Interview by Ernest Besig. Berkeley, Calif.:
Bancroft Library, 1993.

Despres, Leon M. *History with the ACLU.* Tape made and sent to author,
2 February 2003.

Fraenkel, Osmond K. *Oral History.* Interview by Mark Bloom, 1974.
Sanford, N.C.: Microfilming Corporation of America, 1979.

Hays, Arthur Garfield. *City Lawyer: The Autobiography of a Law Practice.*
New York: Simon and Schuster, 1942.

Healey, Dorothy Ray, and Maurice Isserman. *California Red: A Life in
the American Communist Party.* Urbana: University of Illinois Press,
1993.

Hook, Sidney. *Out of Step: An Unquiet Life in the Twentieth Century.* New
York: Harper and Row, 1987.

Ickes, Harold. *The Secret Diary of Harold Ickes.* New York: Simon and
Schuster, 1953.

Isserman, Abraham J. *The Past Is Prologue: Crisis in the American Civil
Liberties Union.* New York: privately published, 1977.

Lamont, Corliss. *Yes to Life: Memoirs of Corliss Lamont.* New York: Horizon
Press, 1981.

McWilliams, Carey. *Honorable in All Things: An Oral History.* Interview by
Joel Gardner. Los Angeles: UCLA Oral History Center, 1982.

Milner, Lucille. *Education of an American Liberal: An Autobiography.* New
York: Horizon Press, 1954.

Monroe, Eason. *Safeguarding Civil Liberties: An Oral History.* Interview by
Joel Gardner. Los Angeles: UCLA Oral History Center, 1974.

Morgan, Charles, Jr. *One Man, One Voice.* New York: Holt, Rinehart and
Winston, 1979.

Neier, Aryeh. *Taking Liberties: Four Decades in the Struggle for Rights.* New York: Public Affairs, 2003.

Okrand, Fred. *Forty Years Defending the Constitution: An Oral History.* Interview by Michael Balter. Los Angeles: UCLA Oral History Center, 1984.

Rabinowitz, Victor. *Unrepentant Leftist: A Lawyer's Memoir.* Urbana: University of Illinois Press, 1996.

OTHER PRIMARY SOURCES

"A.B.A. Rival." *Time*, 18 January, 1 March 1937, 50–51, 43.

American Civil Liberties Union. *The California Red Flag Case.* New York: ACLU, 1930.

———. *Freedom in Wartime.* New York: ACLU, 1943.

———. *Liberty on the Home Front.* New York: ACLU, 1945.

———. *We Hold These Truths . . . Freedom, Justice, Equality.* New York: ACLU, 1953.

American Civil Liberties Union Board Papers. Glen Rock, N.J.: Microfilming Corporation of America, 1976. Microfilm.

American Civil Liberties Union Papers. Wilmington, Del.: Scholarly Resources, 1996. Microfilm.

Baldwin, Roger. "Liberty in War Time." *Nation*, 7 February 1942, 175.

Bernhard, Edgar, Ira Latimer, and Harvey O'Connor. *The Pursuit of Freedom: A History of Civil Liberty in Illinois, 1787–1942.* Chicago: Chicago Civil Liberties Committee, 1942.

Britt, Steuart Henderson, and Selden C. Menefee. "Did the Publicity of the Dies Committee in 1938 Influence Public Opinion?" *Public Opinion Quarterly* 3 (July 1939): 449–57.

———. "Has Mr. Dies the Floor?" *New Republic*, 8 March 1939, 125–27.

Dies, Martin. "More Snakes Than I Can Kill." Pt. 2. *Liberty Magazine*, 27 January 1940, 17–22.

Flynn, Elizabeth Gurley. "Why I Won't Resign from the ACLU." *New Masses*, 19 March 1940.

James, Marquis. "Morris L. Ernst." *Scribner's Magazine*, July 1938, 7–11, 57–58.

Lamont, Corliss. "The ACLU and the FBI: A Statement." *Rights*, September/October 1977, 16.

———, ed. *Trial of Elizabeth Gurley Flynn.* New York: Horizon Press, 1968.

"The Legal Left." *Time*, 7 March 1938, 16.

Lukas, J. Anthony. "The ACLU against Itself." *New York Times Magazine*, 9 July 1978, 9–11, 18, 20, 26–29.

Lyons, Eugene. *The Red Decade: The Stalinist Penetration of America.* Indianapolis: Bobbs-Merrill, 1941. Reprinted as *The Red Decade: The Classic Work on Communism in America during the 1930s.* New Rochelle, N.Y.: Arlington House, 1970.

Mencken, H. L. "The American Civil Liberties Union." *American Mercury,* October 1938, 182–90.

Miller, Merle. *The Judges and the Judged.* Garden City, N.Y.: Doubleday, 1952.

"Muzzling the Fascists." *New Republic,* 6 April 1942, 446.

National Association for the Advancement of Colored People Papers. Frederick, Md.: University Publications of America, 1987. Microfilm.

Niebuhr, Reinhold. "The Limits of Liberty." *Nation,* 24 January 1942, 86–88.

Northern California Branch of the American Civil Liberties Union. *Crisis at the University of California: A Further Statement to the People of California.* San Francisco: ACLU, 1950.

Stern, Michael. "Civil Liberties Units Expanding." *New York Times,* 22 December 1968.

Stone, I. F. *The Truman Era, 1945–1952: A Nonconformist History of Our Times.* 1953. Reprint, Boston: Little, Brown, 1972.

Taft, Clinton J. *Fifteen Years on Freedom's Front.* Los Angeles: SCACLU, 1939.

Varney, Harold Lord. "The Civil Liberties Union." *American Mercury,* December 1936, 385–99.

Weybright, Victor. "Communists and Civil Liberties." *Survey Graphic,* May 1940, 290–93.

SECONDARY SOURCES

Adler, Les K., and Thomas G. Paterson. "Red Fascism: The Merger of Nazi Germany and Soviet Russia in the American Image of Totalitarianism, 1930's–1950's." *American Historical Review* 75 (April 1970): 1046–64.

Alpers, Benjamin L. *Dictators, Democracy, and American Popular Culture: Envisioning the Totalitarian Enemy, 1920s–1950s.* Chapel Hill: University of North Carolina Press, 2003.

Auerbach, Jerold S. "The Depression Decade." In *The Pulse of Freedom: American Liberties, 1920–1970s,* edited by Alan Reitman, 65–104. New York: Norton, 1975.

———. "Lawyers and Social Change in the Depression Decade." In *The New Deal: The National Level,* edited by John Braeman, Robert Bremmer, and David Brody, 133–69. Vol 1 of *The New Deal*. Columbus: Ohio State University Press, 1975.

———. *Unequal Justice: Lawyers and Social Change in Modern America.* New York: Oxford University Press, 1976.

Bailey, Percival R. "The Case of the National Lawyers Guild, 1939–1958." In *Beyond the Hiss Case: The FBI, Congress, and the Cold War*, edited by Athan Theoharis, 129–75. Philadelphia: Temple University Press, 1982.

———. "Progressive Lawyers: A History of the National Lawyers Guild, 1936–1958." Ph.D. diss, Rutgers University, 1979.

Baxandall, Rosalyn Fraad. *Words on Fire: The Life and Writing of Elizabeth Gurley Flynn*. New Brunswick: Rutgers University Press, 1978.

Beck, Warren A., and David A. Williams. *California: A History of the Golden State*. Garden City, N.Y.: Doubleday, 1972.

Brinkley, Alan. *The End of Reform: New Deal Liberalism in Recession and War*. New York: Knopf, 1995.

Cameron, William Bruce. *Modern Social Movements: A Sociological Outline*. New York: Random House, 1966.

Camp, Helen C. *Iron in Her Soul: Elizabeth Gurley Flynn and the American Left*. Pullman: Washington State University Press, 1995.

Christgau, John. "Collins versus the World: The Fight to Restore Citizenship to Japanese American Renunciants of World War II." *Pacific Historical Review* 54 (February 1985): 1–31.

Cohen, Lizabeth. *A Consumers' Republic: The Politics of Mass Consumption in Postwar America*. New York: Vintage, 2004.

———. *Making a New Deal: Industrial Workers in Chicago, 1919–1939*. New York: Cambridge University Press, 1990.

Collins, Donald E. *Native American Aliens: Disloyalty and the Renunciation of Citizenship by Japanese Americans during World War II*. Westport, N.Y.: Greenwood Press, 1985.

Cooney, Terry A. *The Rise of the New York Intellectuals*. Madison: University of Wisconsin Press, 1986.

Cottrell, Robert C. *Roger Nash Baldwin and the American Civil Liberties Union*. New York: Columbia University Press, 2000.

———. "Roger Nash Baldwin, the National Civil Liberties Bureau and Military Intelligence during World War I." *Historian* 60 (Fall 1997): 87–106.

Crunden, Robert Morse. *Ministers of Reform: The Progressives' Achievement in American Civilization, 1889–1920*. New York: Basic Books, 1982.

Daniel, Cletus E. *The ACLU and the Wagner Act*. Ithaca: New York State School of Industrial and Labor Relations, 1980.

Daniels, Roger. *Prisoners without Trial: Japanese Americans in World War II*. New York: Hill and Wang, 1993.

Denning, Michael. *The Cultural Front: The Laboring of American Culture in the 20th Century*. New York: Verso, 1996.

Donner, Frank J. *The Age of Surveillance: The Aims and Methods of America's Political Intelligence System*. New York: Random House, 1980, 1981.

Donohue, Kathleen G. *Freedom from Want: American Liberalism and the Idea of the Consumer*. Baltimore: Johns Hopkins University Press, 2003.

Donohue, William A. *The Politics of the American Civil Liberties Union*. New Brunswick: Transaction, 1985.

———. *Twilight of Liberty: The Legacy of the ACLU*. New Brunswick: Transaction, 1994.

Drinnon, Richard. *Keeper of Concentration Camps: Dillon S. Myer and American Racism*. Berkeley: University of California Press, 1987.

Foner, Eric. *The Story of American Freedom*. New York: Norton, 1998.

Freytag, Walter R. "Organizational Culture." In *Psychology in Organizations: Integrating Science and Practice*, edited by Kevin R. Murphy and Frank E Saal, 179–96. Hillsdale, N.J.: Lawrence Erlbaum Associates, 1990.

Garey, Diane. *Defending Everybody: A History of the American Civil Liberties Union*. New York: TV Books, 1998.

Gary, Brett. *The Nervous Liberals: Propaganda Anxieties from World War I to the Cold War*. New York: Columbia University Press, 1999.

Gentry, Curt. *J. Edgar Hoover: The Man and the Secrets*. New York: London, 1991.

Gibson, James L., and Richard Bingham. *Civil Liberties and Nazis: The Skokie Free Speech Controversy*. New York: Praeger, 1985.

Gillon, Steven M. *Politics and Vision: The ADA and American Liberalism, 1947–1985*. New York: Oxford University Press, 1987.

Goldstein, Robert Justin. *Political Repression in Modern America: From 1870 to the Present*. Cambridge: G. K. Hall and Co., 1978.

Goodman, Walter. *The Committee: The Extraordinary Career of the House Committee on Un-American Activities*. New York: Farrar, Straus and Giroux, 1968.

Graber, Mark A. *Transforming Free Speech: The Ambiguous Legacy of Civil Libertarianism*. Berkeley: University of California Press, 1991.

Grant, George. *Trial and Error: The American Civil Liberties Union and Its Impact on Your Family*. Brentwood, Tenn.: Wolgemuth and Hyatt, 1989.

Gray, James. *The American Civil Liberties Union of Southern California and Imperial Valley Agricultural Labor Disturbances, 1930, 1934*. San Francisco: R and E Research Associates, 1977.

Hamby, Alonzo L. *Beyond the New Deal: Harry S. Truman and American Liberalism*. New York: Columbia University Press, 1973.

Heineman, Kenneth. "Media Bias in Coverage of the Dies Committee on Un-American Activities, 1938-1940." *Historian* 55 (Fall 1992): 37-52.

Honig, Douglas, and Laura Brenner. *On Freedom's Frontier: The First Fifty Years of the American Civil Liberties Union in Washington State*. Seattle: American Civil Liberties Union of Washington Press, 1987.

Horne, Gerald. *Communist Front? The Civil Rights Congress, 1946-1956*. Rutherford, N.J.: Associated University Presses, 1988.

Irons, Peter. *Justice at War*. New York: Oxford University Press, 1983.

Isserman, Maurice, and Michael Kazin. *America Divided: The Civil War of the 1960s*. New York: Oxford University Press, 2000.

Jacoby, Russell. *The Last Intellectuals: American Culture in the Age of Academe*. New York: Basic Books, 1987.

James, Marlise. *The People's Lawyers*. New York: Holt, Rinehart and Winston, 1973.

Johnson, Donald. *The Challenge to America's Freedoms*. Lexington: University of Kentucky Press, 1963.

Jumonville, Neil. *Critical Crossings: The New York Intellectuals in Postwar America*. Berkeley: University of California Press, 1991.

Keller, William W. *The Liberals and J. Edgar Hoover: Rise and Fall of a Domestic Intelligence State*. Princeton: Princeton University Press, 1989.

Klehr, Harvey. *The Heyday of American Communism: The Depression Decade*. New York: Basic Books, 1984.

Klehr, Harvey, John Earl Haynes, and Fridrikh Igorevich Firsov. *The Secret World of American Communism*. New Haven: Yale University Press, 1995.

Knutson, Robert Logan. "The American Civil Liberties Union of Northern California." M.A. thesis, University of California at Berkeley, 1950.

Kornhauser, William. "Social Bases of Political Commitment: A Study of Liberals and Radicals." In *Social and Political Movements*, edited by Gary B. Rush and R. Serge Denisoff, 299-313. New York: Appleton-Century-Crofts, 1971.

Kutler, Stanley I. *The American Inquisition: Justice and Injustice in the Cold War*. New York: Hill and Wang, 1982.

Kutulas, Judy. "In Quest of Autonomy: The Northern California Affiliate of the American Civil Liberties Union and World War II." *Pacific Historical Review* 67 (May 1998): 201-31.

———. *The Long War: The Intellectual People's Front and Anti-Stalinism, 1930–1940*. Durham: Duke University Press, 1995.

———. "'Totalitarianism' Transformed: The Mainstreaming of Anti-Communism." *Mid-America* 77 (Winter 1995): 71–88.

Lamson, Peggy. *Roger Baldwin: Founder of the American Civil Liberties Union*. Boston: Houghton Mifflin, 1976.

Lewy, Guenther. *The Cause That Failed: Communism in American Political Life*. New York: Oxford University Press, 1990.

Lieven, Anatol. *America Right or Wrong: An Anatomy of American Nationalism*. New York: Oxford University Press, 2004.

Liptak, Adam. "ACLU Board Is Split over Using Watch Lists." *New York Times*, 31 July 2004.

Loftis, Anne. *Witnesses to the Struggle: Imaging the 1930s California Labor Movement*. Reno: University of Nevada Press, 1998.

Macdonald, Dwight. "The Defense of Everybody." *New Yorker*, 11, 18 July 1953, 30–55, 29–59.

MacDonnell, Francis. *Insidious Foes: The Axis Fifth Column and the American Home Front*. New York: Oxford University Press, 1995.

Markmann, Charles Lam. *The Noblest Cry: A History of the American Civil Liberties Union*. New York: St. Martin's Press, 1965.

Marro, Anthony. "ACLU Aides Fear Effects of Former FBI Ties." *New York Times*, 15 August 1977.

Mattson, Kevin. *Intellectuals in Action: The Origins of the New Left and Radical Liberalism, 1945–1970*. University Park: Pennsylvania State University Press, 2002.

McAuliffe, Mary S. *Crisis on the Left: Cold War Politics and American Liberals, 1947–1954*. Amherst: University of Massachusetts Press, 1978.

McIlhany, William H., II. *The ACLU on Trial*. New Rochelle, N.Y.: Arlington House, 1976.

Milkis, Sidney M. "Franklin D. Roosevelt, the Economic Constitutional Order and the New Politics of Presidential Leadership." In *The New Deal and the Triumph of Liberalism*, edited by Sidney M. Milkis and Jerome M. Mileur, 31–72. Amherst: University of Massachusetts Press, 2002.

Milkman, Paul. *P.M.: A New Deal in Journalism, 1940–1948*. New Brunswick: Rutgers University Press, 1997.

Mills, C. Wright. *White Collar: The American Middle Classes*. New York: Oxford University Press, 1956.

Mitford, Jessica. *The Trial of Dr. Spock, the Reverend William Sloan Coffin, Jr., Michael Ferber, Mitchell Goodman, and Marcus Raskin*. New York: Knopf, 1969.

Murphy, Paul L. *The Meaning of Freedom of Speech: First Amendment Freedoms from Wilson to FDR*. Westport, N.Y.: Greenwood Press, 1972.

———. *World War I and the Origin of Civil Liberties in the United States*. New York: Norton, 1979.

Myer, Dillon S. *Uprooted Americans: The Japanese Americans and the War Relocation Authority during World War II*. Tucson: University of Arizona Press, 1971.

Neier, Aryeh. "Adhering to Principle: Lessons from the 1950s." *Civil Liberties Review* 4 (November/December 1977): 26–32.

———. *Defending My Enemy: American Nazis, the Skokie Case, and the Risks of Freedom*. New York: E. P. Dutton, 1979.

Omori, Emiko. *Rabbit in the Moon*. San Francisco: Wabi-Sabi Production, 1999.

O'Reilly, Kenneth. *Hoover and the Un-Americans: The FBI, HUAC, and the Red Menace*. Philadelphia: Temple University Press, 1983.

Ottanelli, Frasier M. *The Communist Party of the United States: From the Depression to World War II*. New Brunswick: Rutgers University Press, 1991.

Pells, Richard. *The Liberal Mind in a Conservative Age: American Intellectuals in the 1940s and 1950s*. New York: Harper and Row, 1985.

———. *Radical Visions and American Dreams: Culture and Social Thought in the Depression Years*. 1973. Reprint, Middletown, Conn.: Wesleyan University Press, 1984.

Perrett, Geoffrey. *Days of Sadness, Years of Triumph: The American People, 1939–1945*. Madison: University of Wisconsin Press, 1973.

Plotke, David. *Building a Democratic Political Order: Reshaping American Liberalism in the 1930s and 1940s*. New York: Cambridge University Press, 1996.

Polenberg, Richard. *Fighting Faiths: The Abrams Case, the Supreme Court and Free Speech*. New York: Viking Press, 1987.

———. "Franklin Roosevelt and Civil Rights: The Case of the Dies Committee." *Historian* 30 (Summer 1968): 165–78.

———. *War and Society: The United States, 1941–1945*. New York: Lippincott, 1972.

Powers, Richard Gid. *Not without Honor: The History of American Anticommunism*. New York: Free Press, 1995.

———. *Secrecy and Power: The Life of J. Edgar Hoover*. New York: Free Press, 1987.

Purcell, Edward A., Jr. *The Crisis of Democratic Theory: Scientific Naturalism and the Problem of Value*. Lexington: University Press of Kentucky, 1973.

Reitman, Alan, ed. *The Pulse of Freedom: American Liberties, 1920–1970s*. New York: Norton, 1975.

Ribuffo, Leo P. *The Old Christian Right: The Protestant Far Right from the Great Depression to the Cold War*. Philadelphia: Temple University Press, 1983.

Richter, Patricia. *Reflections in Time: A History of the Minnesota Civil Liberties Union, 1952–1972*. Burnsville, Minn.: Friends of the Bill of Rights Foundation, 1996.

Roche, John P., and Stephen Sachs. "The Bureaucrat and the Enthusiast: An Exploration of the Leadership of Social Movements." In *Social and Political Movements*, edited by Gary B. Rush and R. Serge Denisoff, 373–80. New York: Appleton-Century-Crofts, 1971.

Schrecker, Ellen. *Many Are the Crimes: McCarthyism in America*. Boston: Little, Brown, 1998.

Schulman, Bruce J. *The Seventies: The Great Shift in American Culture, Society and Politics*. New York: Free Press, 2001.

Schwartz, Stephen. *From West to East: California and the Making of the American Mind*. New York: Free Press, 1998.

Simmons, Jerold. "The American Civil Liberties Union and the Dies Committee, 1938–1940." *Harvard Civil Rights/Civil Liberties Law Review* 17 (Spring 1982): 183–207.

———. "Morris Ernst and Disclosure: One Liberal's Quest for a Solution to the Problem of Domestic Communism, 1939–1949." *Mid-America* 71 (January 1989): 15–30.

———. "The Origins of the Campaign to Abolish HUAC, 1956–1961: The California Connection." *Southern California Quarterly* 64 (Summer 1982): 141–57.

Sitton, Tom. "Direct Democracy versus Free Speech: Gerald L. K. Smith and the Recall Election of 1946 in Los Angeles." *Pacific Historical Review* 57 (August 1988): 285–304.

Skocpol, Theda. "The Legacies of New Deal Liberalism." In *Liberalism Reconsidered*, edited by Douglas MacLean and Claudia Mills, 87–104. Totowa, N.J.: Rowman and Allanheld, 1983.

Steele, Richard W. "Fear of the Mob and Faith in Government in Free Speech Discourse, 1919–1941." *American Journal of Legal History* 38 (January 1994): 55–83.

———. *Free Speech in the Good War*. New York: St. Martin's Press, 1999.

Strom, Sharon Hartman. *Political Woman: Florence Luscomb and the Legacy of Radical Reform*. Philadelphia: Temple University Press, 2001.

Theoharis, Athan, and John Cox. *The Boss: J. Edgar Hoover and the Great American Inquisition*. Philadelphia: Temple University Press, 1988.

Urofsjy, Melvin. "The Roosevelt Court." In *The Achievements of American Liberalism: The New Deal and Its Legacies*, edited by William Chafe, 62–98. New York: Columbia University Press, 2003.

Wald, Alan M. *Exiles from a Future Time: The Forging of the Mid-Twentieth-Century Literary Left*. Chapel Hill: University of North Carolina Press, 2002.

———. *The New York Intellectuals: The Rise and Decline of the Anti-Stalinist Left from the 1930s to the 1980s*. Chapel Hill: University of North Carolina Press, 1987.

Walker, Samuel. *In Defense of American Liberties: A History of the ACLU*. New York: Oxford University Press, 1990.

Wang, Jessica. *American Science in an Age of Anxiety: Scientists, Anticommunism, and the Cold War*. Chapel Hill: University of North Carolina Press, 1999.

Warren, Frank A. *An Alternative Vision: The Socialist Party in the 1930s*. Bloomington: Indiana University Press, 1975.

———. *Liberals and Communism: The "Red Decade" Revisited*. New York: Columbia University Press, 1966, 1993.

———. *Noble Abstractions: American Liberal Intellectuals and World War II*. Columbus: Ohio State University Press, 1999.

Weber, Max. *The Protestant Ethic and the Spirit of Capitalism*. Translated by Talcott Parsons. New York: Scribner, 1958.

———. *The Theory of Social and Economic Organization*. Translated by A. M. Henderson and Talcott Parsons. 1947. Reprint, New York: Free Press, 1968.

Weinberg, Doron, and Marty Fassler. *A Historical Sketch of the National Lawyers Guild in American Politics, 1936–1968*. New York: National Lawyers Guild, n.d.

Wright, Brian R. "The ACLU: Between Politics and Principle: A Study of a Pressure Group during Wartime." Ph.D. diss, Princeton University, 1975.

Yoo, David. *Growing Up Nisei: Race, Generation, and Culture among Japanese Americans of California, 1924–1949*. Urbana: University of Illinois Press, 2000.

INDEX

Absolutists, 93, 95, 99, 104, 105, 106, 114, 137

Academic freedom, 83, 141, 173

Activist judges, 219

African Americans, 10, 137, 138, 171

Agricultural and Cannery Workers Industrial Union, 55

Allen, Edward, 153

Allies, 81, 93, 103

American Civil Liberties Union (ACLU), affiliates

—after World War II: membership recruitment by, 139–40; resenting Baldwin, 140; wanting action on the Rosenberg case, 145; wanting power, 153–54; anger of over 1940 resolution, 155–56; courted by Malin, 157–62; six small new, 159; in postwar California, 161–62; focus of, 163–88; few paid directors or attorneys in, 165; distrusting Baldwin, 169; 1950 Des Moines convention of, 176; wary about merging, 177; gaining power, 178; disdaining anticommunism, 181, 191; more confrontational, 190; debating security and communism, 192–205; coming into their own, 201, 213; shocked by Board actions, 203–5; speaking out against draft, 215. *See also* Des Moines

—before World War II: in early ACLU, 20; Wagner Act and, 26; struggles/successes of, 42–44; executive boards of, 44; lacking nurturing, 46; difficult personalities and, 46–47; civil liberties and, 50, 52; front groups and, 53–56; rejecting national's rules, 57–58; paying local directors, 61; 1940 resolution hated by, 73–74; hating disenfranchisement, 77–78; field secretaries of, 81; gaining new confidence, 84; unyielding re Communists, 86

—during World War II: Flynn purge and, 77–78, 81, 114; Browder and, 90; discrediting JACL, 101; differences of with national, 113–35; becoming assertive, 114; Baldwin's style and, 114–15; freer due to war, 115; sensitive to internees' plight, 117–18; showdown with national, 118–22, 127–28; excellent wartime work of, 123–26; wanting board liaisons, 127

American Civil Liberties Union, national

—after World War II: rivals of, 137; agenda of, 137, 138; spying on CRC, 138; Hollywood Ten and,

143–44; Communists and, 143–55, 189, 191; second-generation leadership of, 146, 157; postwar weakness of, 161–62; making branches unhappy, 164–88; 1949 annual meeting of, 176; losing to affiliates, 178; and Lattimore and Rosenberg matters, 181; convention system of, 201, 210, 212; dealing with civil rights and Vietnam war, 214–15; wanting neutrality, 215; response of to 9/11, 220; ACLU Freedom Concert, 221. *See also* Working conditions in ACLU

— before World War II: financial challenges of, 21–22; as champion of disenfranchised, 24; ads for, 30; America First and, 35; Henry Ford and, 38–39; snobby toward affiliates, 42–44, 47, 56; volunteers as drones in, 48; Northern California affiliate and, 55; rallying around Baldwin, 57; Nazi-Soviet Pact and, 64; leftists leaving, 72, 79; anticommunists in, 73, 190–91; undemocratic in Flynn purge, 77–78, 81; declining disclosure, 82; opposing draft, 90

— Board of Directors, 20, 26, 48, 64, 66; polarized in 1940s, 64–88; ineffective, 89–90; younger and more liberal, 92–93; wartime factionalism paralyzing, 93; banning free discussion, 96; voting re Japanese Americans, 98; disagreeing on free speech during wartime, 103–4; rejecting change, 115; meetings of chaotic, 140–41; divided over future,

156; stifling affiliates, 158–59, 178; jealous of SCACLU, 180; three anticommunist statements of, 194, 205

— Committees: National, 20, 72–98 passim, 114, 127, 142, 152, 158, 169, 176, 178, 198, 200; Lawyers, 96, 143–44; Membership and Affiliates, 192–205; Nominating, 198–99; Policy, 152; Seditious Cases, 100, 105, 106

— during World War II: supporting World War II, 90; war stance of, 91; response to internment, 97–103; cooperating with JACL, 101; attracted to Hirabayashi case, 102; not intervening in sedition cases, 106; hiding dirty laundry, 108; differing from affiliates, 113–35; filing amicus brief in Korematsu case, 116; standing against deportation and for test cases, 123; withholding financial support, 124; relying on affiliates, 125; conceding frustrations, 126; unable to create successful affiliates, 133–34

American Committee for Cultural Freedom, 4

American Committee for Democracy and Intellectual Freedom, 40, 81

American Committee for the Protection of the Foreign Born, 81

American Jewish Congress, 214

American League against War and Fascism, 28. *See also* American League for Peace and Democracy

American League for Peace and Democracy, 66

American Legion, 139, 192

American Russian Institute, 143

Americans for Democratic Action, 4, 144, 153

Amicus briefs: in Korematsu case, 102; in sedition cases, 106; Hollywood Ten and, 143–44; in Yates case, 144–45; national geared toward, 165; of NCACLU in Smith Act trials, 180–81; Board strategy of, 190; 85 percent of 1960s work, 212; strategy reversed in 1962, 213

Angell, Ernest, 157, 196, 197

Anticommunists: liberal, 2, 138–39; red hunters, 23; decreasing ACLU membership, 35; challenging diversity of ACLU, 64; seeing Ward as danger, 66, 67; accepting definition of totalitarianism, 72–73; removing Flynn and, 76–77, 83, 88; justification for postwar anticommunism, 78; losing ACLU ground, 90; prominent postwar, 138, 163–88; Gerald L. K. Smith and, 169; national subculture of, 191

Antifascism, 26–27, 68, 88

Associated Farmers, 50

Atlanta affiliate, unofficial, 155

Baker, Alfred Lewis, 70

Baldwin, Roger: shaping of ACLU and, 7, 9–10, 18–19; retirement of, 10; reverence toward, 11; management style of, 11, 20, 33, 47; Executive Order 9066 and, 13; upbringing of, 17; effects of World War I on, 17–18; People's Front and, 28, 34; criticized for

radicalism, 30; Dies Committee and, 37–38; views on affiliates of, 43, 44; funding of branches and, 45, 46, 51; California politics and, 50; front groups and, 53, 58; Nazi-Soviet Pact and, 65; anticommunists and, 67; assessing Dies's work, 70–71; separating factions, 72–73; 1940 resolution and, 73–75; Flynn and, 76–77; covering up crises, 78; unable to shape ACLU, 83, 88

— after World War II: MacArthur's invitation and, 136; unequal to ACLU change, 140; chaotic board and, 141; trusted less, 153–54; brazen toward affiliates, 154–76 passim; forced to depart, 156; leaving behind crisis, 156–57; compared to Malin, 208–9; winning Medal of Freedom, 217

— during World War II: Browder and, 90; as liaison to Roosevelt, 91–93; views on Japanese Americans of, 99; challenging internment, 101–2; cooperating with Justice Department, 103; seditious literature and, 104; resentments of, 108–11; wanting nationwide policies, 114; fed up with Besig, 115–16, 121–23; intolerant of democratic reforms, 127–28; fed up with Latimer, 130

Beale, Howard, 203

Beardsley, John, 49

Besig, Ernest, 13, 50–60 passim, 102, 103; and Tule Lake, 113, 120–25; Korematsu and, 117–19; 1940 resolution and, 144; as thorny leader, 157–58; Baldwin's "praises" and, 167; on merging, 177; disgusted by Board, 195–205 passim

Biddle, Francis, 29, 92, 99, 104

Bill of Rights, 19, 42, 173

Blacklisting, 148–49, 168

Board of Directors. *See* American Civil Liberties Union, national, Board of Directors

Boas, Franz, 40

Bond, Frederick Drew, 56

Boston affiliate. *See* Civil Liberties Union of Massachusetts

Branches. *See* American Civil Liberties Union, affiliates

Brawley, Calif., 49, 50

Bridges, Harry, 145

Browder, Earl, 90

Brown v. Board of Education, 213

Budget. *See* Funding

Bureaucracy, 9–11, 24, 105, 112, 151, 164–65, 187

Bureau of Indian Affairs, 25

Burling, John, 103

Bush, George H. W., 217–18

Bush, George W., 15

Bylaws: Section 10(d), 178–79, 201, 203; new, 209, 215

California affiliate, Northern. *See* Northern California Branch of the American Civil Liberties Union

California affiliate, Southern. *See* Southern California Branch of the American Civil Liberties Union

California Agricultural Workers Industrial Union, 49

California Criminal Syndicalism Law, 49, 54, 55

Camps for Japanese Americans. *See* Internment of Japanese Americans

Censorship, 41, 104, 149, 180

Centralia, Wash., 47

Central Valley of California, 49

Chafee, Zechariah, 19, 25

Chicago Civil Liberties Committee (CCLC), 30, 58–59, 84, 85, 127–33, 145, 155, 158, 164, 166, 170, 187

Chicago Defender, 132

Chicago Division ACLU, 164, 165–66, 170, 179, 181, 186–87, 197–98

Childs, Richard, 31, 80, 96, 158, 213

Civil disobedience, 215

Civil liberties: as chic liberal value, 1–2, 41; versus national security, 3, 19, 190; affiliates and, 13; as cornerstone, 19; fascists and, 27; controversial, 40; as membership test, 73; after Flynn debacle, 78–79, 81; defending again, 84; new groups mobilized for, 90; Wilson's handling of, 91; Roosevelt's handling of, 91–92; versus practicalities, 94; during war, 106, 113, 120; renunciation of citizenship does not involve, 123; private cases ruled out, 125; ACLU not unified on, 138; continuing compromises on, 139, 145–46; popularizing, 153; ACLU as coordinator of, 156; national lacking passion for, 164, 169, 181, 186; of communists, 196; under Warren Court, 212; some defenses easier than others, 217; 9/11 and, 219

Civil Liberties Union of Massachusetts (CLUM), 45, 61, 70, 84, 87, 126–32, 155, 167, 168, 175, 177, 181, 182, 195, 201, 215

Civil rights, 41, 212–14

Civil Rights Congress (CRC), 131, 133, 137, 167, 168, 172, 185–86

Clark, Tom, 142–43

Clear-and-present-danger standard, 19, 38, 103–4, 144

Cleveland affiliate, 42, 126, 145, 164, 181

Cold war, 4, 7, 139, 148, 180

College Freedom Tour, 221

Collins, Wayne, 116, 122, 123, 125

Colorado Civil Liberties Union, 87. *See also* Denver Civil Liberties Committee

Combined Federal Campaign, 189

Committee for Cultural Freedom (CCF), 39, 65, 81

Committee on Un-American Activities. *See* HUAC

Common Sense, 80

Communist Party of the United States of America (CPUSA). *See* Communists

Communists, in 1930s, 3–4, 7; organizers of in trouble, 22; intensity of, 24; excluding Soviet opponents, 27; disrupting Socialist rally, 34; Martin Dies and, 35, 37; affiliates talking to, 48; in California, 52, 54; in Chicago, 58–59; Flynn trouble and, 64, 75–77; Isserman and, 69; Flynn's communism and Board, 75–77; under totalitarian rubric, 78–79;

Browder and, 90; and devotion to Allies, 93; Latimer and, 129–32; J. Parnell Thomas, Baldwin, and, 136; influential, 137; seen as totalitarian, 139; ACLU and, 143–55; Smith Act and, 144; affiliates and, 163–65; union rights of, 174; Luscomb and, 182; national suspecting branches of sympathizing with, 186; liberties, security, and, 192–205

Congress of Racial Equality, 214

Conscientious objectors, 90–91, 102

Cottrell, Robert, 110

Coughlin, Father Charles, 104

Daily Worker, 191

Darrow, Clarence, 19, 27

Denver Civil Liberties Committee, 85, 126, 168, 185–87. *See also* Colorado Civil Liberties Union

Depression, the, 8, 21, 23, 24; effect on affiliates of, 44, 45

Desegregation, 213

de Silver, Albert, 18

de Silver, Margaret, 30, 67, 76

Des Moines: 1950 convention in, 176; formula, 177

Detroit affiliate, 42, 44, 45, 62, 155, 183–84, 197

Dies, Martin, 35–37, 68–72, 82

Dies Committee. *See* HUAC

Dilling, Elizabeth, 130

Due process, 97, 107, 119

Dukakis, Michael, 217–18

Emergency Civil Liberties Committee (ECLC), 168, 180, 185–86, 199, 201, 206

Endo, Mitsuyi, 102

Ennis, Edward, 99, 102, 103, 123, 143

Erie County, N.Y., affiliate, 126, 127, 155, 158

Ernst, Morris, 29, 32, 39–40, 68–70, 76, 79–82, 89, 93–94, 104, 105, 138, 140, 142, 144, 145, 146, 147, 156, 160, 172, 180, 201–2, 213, 216

Executive Order 9066, 97–103, 122

Fair Deal, 9, 31

Falwell, Jerry, 219, 221

Farquharson, Mary, 117, 118

Fascists: American, in 1930s, 3–4, 27; rise of, 6; under totalitarian rubric, 78–79; antiwar organizations and, 103; bringing ACLU bad publicity, 137

FBI (Federal Bureau of Investigation): early, 19; viewing ACLU as radical, 23; Ernst alerting, 69; gathering information on Union, 84; loyalty probes and, 143; communist affiliation and, 150–51; advised by Ferman, 160–61; Ferman, Levy, and, 184–87, 211; Malin consulting, 211–12; missing Ferman, 213; 1970s revelations about, 217

Fellow travelers. See Communists

Ferman, Irving, 160–61, 180, 184–87, 211, 213, 217

Fifth Amendment, 194

Finances. See Funding

First Amendment. See Free speech

Fish, Hamilton, 23, 35

Fitelson, William, 191, 193, 203

Fly, James L., 140–43, 201, 203

Flynn, Elizabeth Gurley, 31, 33, 43; expulsion of, 72, 75–78, 80, 83–84, 108, 109; as CRC founder, 137–38, 149, 189; expulsion of rescinded, 216

Ford, Henry, 38, 65, 66

Forster, Cliff, 103, 115, 143, 146

Fourteenth Amendment, 49

Fraenkel, Osmond, 67, 77, 84, 89, 93, 94, 95, 96, 99, 107, 115, 146, 156, 195–216 passim

Frankfurter, Felix, 19, 25, 35

Freedom of Information Act documents, 69, 160, 186, 217

Freeman, Joseph, 79

Free speech, 76, 82, 92–93, 103, 105, 106, 137, 143, 145, 169, 171, 179, 190

Front groups, 62

Fry, Varian, 138

Fuller, Jeffrey, 183–84

Funding, 12, 57, 66, 80, 153, 158–60, 165–66, 177, 193, 201, 204–8, 210, 212

Gallagher, Leo, 49–50, 51, 52, 85; as CRC founder, 137–38

Gellhorn, Walter, 146

German-American Bund, 103, 130

German sympathizers, accused, 120

Glasser, Ira, 219

Glassford, Pellham, 50, 51

Graham, Frank, 200

Graham statement, 202, 203

Guantanamo Bay, 220

Gyllenhaal, Jake, 222

Harper, Allan, 45

Hartford affiliate, 56

Hays, Arthur Garfield, 19, 22, 24,

37, 49, 69, 71, 75, 90, 93, 94, 95, 96, 124, 146–47

Heist, A. A., 153–54, 169, 173–76, 180

Hirabayashi, Gordon, 101–2, 117

Hitler, Adolf, 27, 65

Hollywood Ten, 143

Holmes, John Haynes, 17, 33–39, 66–68, 71, 72, 73, 74, 75, 76, 77, 78, 79, 85, 92, 93, 94, 95, 99, 106, 108–9, 119, 127, 138, 140, 141, 147, 151, 157, 158, 174, 182, 190, 198–99

Hook, Sidney, 39, 40, 65, 83

Hoover, J. Edgar, 19, 82, 99, 160, 180, 187

Houston, Charles, 138

HUAC (House Committee on Un-American Activities), 23, 35, 62, 66, 68, 85, 143, 146–48, 180, 181, 186, 192, 209

Ickes, Harold, 29, 35, 121

International Labor Defense (ILD), 48–49, 50, 51, 53, 54

Internment of Japanese Americans, 97–103; and restrictions for further disloyalty, 113, 120–22; affiliates' response to, 115–16; seen by national as tolerable, 117; affiliates' experts on, 117–18; 1943 strike and, 120; desire to leave United States and, 122; psychological impact of, 125; Wirin understanding pain of, 125

Iowa Civil Liberties Union, 126, 153, 158, 195

Issei, 100, 103, 122

Isserman, Abraham, 30, 34, 69–70, 72, 83, 86

Jackson, Gardner, 70

Japan, postwar, 137

Japanese American Citizens' League (JACL), 101, 120, 123

Japanese Americans, 3–4, 97–103; affiliate-national conflict over, 13, 115; trusting affiliates more, 119; act to remove disloyal, 122; reverse renunciations and, 125. *See also* Internment of Japanese Americans

Judges and the Judged, The, 148–49, 192

Kibei, 120, 122

Kirchwey, Freda, 104

Korematsu, Fred, 13, 102, 115, 116, 117, 128

Labor, organized, 32, 37–38, 85, 114, 137

Lamont, Corliss, 64–71, 93, 108–9, 136–37, 149, 150–51, 186, 195–98, 201

Latimer, Ira, 46, 58–60, 129–33, 137–38, 166, 170, 197–98

Lattimore, Owen, 181

Lawyers' Constitutional Defense Committee, 214

Lee, Alfred, 155

Legal approaches: legal realism, 19; legal remedies preferred, 31, 80; Ernst doing less legal work, 95; to Japanese American internment, 99, 101

Levy, Herbert Monte, 168, 183–85, 213

Levy, Howard, 215

Lewis, Austin, 43–44, 47

Liberal(s): Communism and, 4;

weaknesses of, 5; legal system and, 5–6; as second generation of ACLU, 8; needs versus liberties and, 19; wanting work, 24; appealing to, 41; ACLU respectability and, 59; reacting to ACLU actions, 79, 81; ACLU legitimating opinions of, 89; anticommunist detour and, 90; viewing Roosevelt as one of them, 92; keeping ACLU in mainstream of, 100, 103; viewing ACLU as passé, 111; postwar fence-mending of, 137; Ferman as capitulating, 161; affiliates disagreeing with respectability of, 163–64; Gerald L. K. Smith and, 169; being duped, 201; response to post-9/11 activities by, 220

Lowrie, Kathleen, 184

Loyalty (of Japanese Americans), 98, 100–102, 117; questionnaires for, 120

Loyalty: Truman's crusades regarding, 141–43; tests, oaths, and other measures determining, 161, 169–81 passim, 188, 194, 212

Luscomb, Florence, 168–69, 173, 182

Lynd, Robert, 83, 200

MacArthur, Douglas, 136, 140

Madison affiliate. See Wisconsin affiliate

Malin, Patrick Murphy, 10; as delegator, 157; courting affiliates, 157–62; changing ACLU structure, 176–78, 190; seeking branch patience, 179; Lattimore

and, 181; Ann Ray and, 182–83; tricked by Thomas, 183–84; debate on communism and, 192–205; furious with Lamont, 196–97; upset by strong anticommunism, 202–5; compared to Baldwin, 208–9; wanting to abandon affiliates, 209–20; leaving, 213; compared to Neier, 216

Marshall, Thurgood, 213

Marx, Groucho, 26

Maryland Civil Liberties Committee, 181, 184–85

Massachusetts affiliate. See Civil Liberties Union of Massachusetts

McAuliffe, Mary Sperling, 4

McCarran Act, 146

McCarthy, Joseph, and McCarthyism, 133, 160, 164, 180, 194–95, 196, 212

McCloy, John, 99

McWilliams, Carey, 116–17, 138, 171–72, 185–86

Meiklejohn, Alexander, 99, 100, 116, 118, 119, 127, 198

Membership, 11–12, 14; failure of campaign for, 23; improved prospects for, 24; strong growth of in 1936, 26; competition for, 48; decreasing disgruntlement among, 65; recruitment of during war, 94; slow national growth of postwar, 139, 168; dissatisfied, 148; doubling of under Malin, 159; SCACLU bringing most, 161, 179; affiliate growth of, 163–64, 168; merging of affiliates', 177; 1940 resolution and, 192; affiliates and boom in, 204;

Nixon impeachment and, 216; "card-carrying" cache of, 217–18; increase in since 9/11, 221

Meyerding, Ed, 181, 205–6

"Military necessity," 102, 117

Miller, Merle, 148–50. *See also The Judges and the Judged*

Milner, Lucille, 18, 32–33, 56, 68, 80, 90, 110–11, 126, 134

Minnesota affiliate, 197

Minor, Robert, 84

Mobilization for Democracy, 171

Monroe, Eason, 153, 179

Mooney, Tom, 51

Morgan, Charles, 213, 215

Muir, Jean, 148–49

Mundt, Karl, 146

Mundt-Nixon bill, 145–46

Murphy, Frank, 35

Myer, Dillon S., 99, 121–22

NAACP (National Association for the Advancement of Colored People), 4, 84, 114, 131, 137, 153, 212, 214

Nation, 2, 93, 104, 105, 203

National Committee. *See* American Civil Liberties Union, national, Committees

National Committee on Conscientious Objectors, 90–91

National Federation for Constitutional Liberties, 83

National Labor Relations Board (NLRB), 6, 26, 38, 51

National Lawyers Guild (NLG), 29, 40

Nazis: German, 103; American, 217

Nazi-Soviet Pact, 64, 79

National security versus individual rights, 3, 7, 190

Neier, Aryeh, 147, 173, 216, 217

Nelles, Walter, 18

New Deal, 2–3, 31; liberals and, 3; Second New Deal, 6; requiring bureaucracy, 9; needing bureaucrats, 24; ruled unconstitutional, 29; Martin Dies and, 35–38; ACLU's appeal to New Dealers, 41

New Haven affiliate, 145, 181

New Jersey affiliate, 86

New Leader, 149, 150, 192

New Masses, 149

New Republic, 104, 105

New York City affiliate, 57, 165–66, 186, 203

New York Post, 203

New York Times, 189

New York World Telegram, 189, 203

Nichols, Louis B., 160, 187

Niebuhr, Reinhold, 92

9/11 (11 September 2001), 15, 189, 219–20

1940 resolution, 73–74, 114, 151, 154–55, 159, 177–78, 181, 189, 191, 196, 201, 216

Nisei, 100, 101, 103; draft of, 120; Nationality Act of 1940 and, 122

Nixon, Richard, 146–47, 216

Nominating Committee. *See* American Civil Liberties Union, national, Committees

Non-Partisan Labor Defense, 54

Northern California Branch of the American Civil Liberties Union (NCACLU): squabbling with SCACLU, 47; autonomy, funding, and, 52; relationship

of with radicals, 53–55, 61–62;
1940 resolution and, 74; testing
internment legality, 102; taking Korematsu case to Supreme
Court, 116; in showdown with
national, 118–22; trusted by
Tule Lakers, 123; as linchpin of
revolt, 125–28; wanting vigorous
anti-Loyalty stance, 142; united
with SCACLU over Baldwin, 154;
rejecting 1940 resolution, 155;
fighting with Board, 158; providing ACLU's postwar strength,
161–62; with SCACLU as half
of affiliate membership, 164,
opposed to loyalty tests, 173,
180–81; and peacetime draft,
174; refusing to merge, 177; FBI
given minutes of, 186–87. *See
also* Besig, Ernest; Internment of
Japanese Americans

O'Connor, Harvey, 186
Ohio affiliate, central, 197
Open Forum, 174
Oregon affiliate. *See* Portland, Ore.,
affiliate
Osler, Sonia, 167
Oswald, Lee Harvey, 212

Pacifists, 91, 102
Parker-Bennett, Adele, 47
Parsons, Edward, 119–20, 135
Passports, 145
Patriot Act (USA PATRIOT Act),
219–20
Pemberton, John de, 213, 215,
216
Pennsylvania affiliates, including
Philadelphia and Pittsburgh

branches, 30, 44, 45, 84, 155, 164,
186–87
People's Front: turning radicals
into liberals, 6; prodemocratic,
27–28; aggravating rivalries, 34;
pressure to disassociate from,
36–37; CCF and, 39–40; Baldwin's pressure to associate with,
58; Nazi-Soviet Pact and, 65–66;
Baldwin's disappointment with,
68
People's World, 174–75
Perkins, Frances, 29, 51
Philbrick, Herbert, 67–68
Pitzele, Merlyn, 138, 149, 150,
191–93, 195
PM, 105
Portland, Ore., affiliate, 183
Professionalism, 9, 14, 51, 52, 59,
80–81; among affiliates, 114;
detachment and, 151; not excit-
ing affiliates, 168–69
Public relations, 22, 23, 32, 36, 62,
72–73, 75, 80–81, 101, 118, 123,
145–167 passim, 187, 192, 203–4,
222

Queens, N.Y., affiliate, 154

Race Bias in Housing, 213
Racial matters, 10, 98, 117, 131,
212–13
Radicals: ACLU founders as, 2, 5,
40; reputation of, 14; World War I
producing, 17; affiliates seen as,
52; Malin, affiliates, and, 177;
ACLU's post-9/11 agenda seen as
the work of, 221
Radio, 148, 180
Rapp-Coudert hearings, 84

Ray, Ann, 165, 182
Reagan, Ronald, 217
Relativists, 92–96, 99, 100, 103–7, 114, 115, 137, 221
Religious groups and affiliates, 46
Republicans, 7, 31, 93, 142, 157
Respectability. *See* Professionalism
Rice, Elmer, 146
Riis, Roger, 68, 70, 75, 77
Robbins, Tim, 222
Robeson, Paul, 145
Rockland County, N.Y., 85–86
Rockwell, George Lincoln, 212
Romero, Anthony, 189, 219, 221
Roosevelt, Eleanor, 29, 85
Roosevelt, Franklin D., and Roosevelt administration, 6, 29, 32, 35–36, 71, 79, 97, 101, 119. *See also* New Deal
Rosenberg, Ethel and Julius, 145, 181
Ross, Edward A., 82–83, 99
Rundquist, George, 159, 177, 182, 183–84, 188

St. Louis affiliate, 45, 169, 179
St. Paul affiliate, 134
San Francisco affiliate. *See* Northern California Branch of the American Civil Liberties Union
Sanger, Betty, 168, 182
Schlesinger, Arthur, 138
Scopes, John, 19–20
Seattle affiliate, 47, 58, 62, 102, 117, 163, 175, 182, 186–87, 197, 203
Seymour, Whitney North, 31, 93, 107, 190, 199
Seymour resolution, 107, 119, 120, 126, 128
Silver Shirts, 103

Sinclair, Upton, 42, 43
Skokie, Ill., 217
Smith, Gerald L. K., 103, 137, 169, 170, 171
Smith Act, 144–45, 179, 180
Socialist Party of the United States and Socialists, 17, 20–21, 24, 33, 34, 37, 54, 58–59
Southern California Branch of the American Civil Liberties Union (SCACLU) 13, 30; as only stable affiliate, 42; and campaign to repeal Criminal Syndicalism Law, 43; squabbling with NCACLU, 47; red flag case and, 49; as "nest of communists," 53, 58; handling labor cases, 62; 1940 resolution and, 74; desiring National Committee representation, 87; Japanese Americans and, 116–18; privileged by Baldwin, 122; Wirin's pay and, 124; endorsing representation, 127; opposed to loyalty tests, 142, 173; Rosenberg case and, 145, 181; united with NCACLU over Baldwin, 154; rejecting 1940 resolution, 155; fighting with Board, 158; providing ACLU's postwar strength, 161–64, 179; Gerald L. K. Smith and, 171; preferring left-wing clients, 172, 180; and peacetime draft, 174; merging, 177, 179; working to abolish HUAC, 186; FBI given minutes of, 186–87
Speiser, Lawrence, 213
Spock, Benjamin, 215
Stalin, Josef, 65
Stephan, Max, 108, 109–10

Stimson, Henry, 91
Stromberg, Yetta, 49
Summers, Clyde, 130
Supreme Court, 29, 49, 102, 103,
    116, 144, 170–71, 212

Taft, Clinton J., 42, 49–50, 171
Tenney Committee (of California),
    172, 179–80
Terminello, Father Arthur, 170
Thomas, J. Parnell, 136–37
Thomas, Norman, 17, 33, 34, 38,
    39, 65–67, 72–73, 76, 79, 91, 92,
    95, 139, 141, 148, 149, 152, 182,
    183, 190–92, 201, 204, 213
Totalitarianism, 39, 65, 72–73
Tresca, Carlo, 76
Trotskyists, 54, 130, 144
Truman, Harry, 141–42, 145, 181,
    213
Tule Lake internment camp,
    100, 113–23 passim, 220. See
    also Internment of Japanese
    Americans

United Nations, 194
U.S. Congress, House of Repre-
    sentatives, House Un-American
    Activities Committee. See HUAC
U.S. Department of the Interior, 26
U.S. Justice Department, 26, 90, 99,
    103, 116–19, 123, 125, 142, 144,
    165, 173; Enemy Aliens Division,
    99
Upstate New York affiliate. See Erie
    County, N.Y., affiliate

Van Gerbig, Geraldine, 56–57
Van Kleeck, Mary, 34, 38, 55, 58,
    72, 78

Veterans of Foreign Wars, 23
Vietnam, war in, 214–15, 217

Wagner, Robert, 51
Wagner Labor Relations Act of
    1935, 26
Wahlberg, Edgar, 183–84
Wain, Philip, 132
Walker, Samuel, 14, 140
Wallace, Henry, 51
Ward, Harry F., 18, 28, 38, 44, 58,
    65–66, 68, 73, 75, 76, 137–38
War Relocation Authority (WRA) 98,
    99, 120, 124, 125
Warren, Earl, 212, 217
Washington, D.C., affiliate, 57,
    70
Washington, D.C., office, 160, 180
"Watch lists," 189
White, William L., 190, 199, 202,
    203
Who's Who, 114, 169
Williams, Chester, 54
Williams, Robin, 221
Wilsie, Maurice, 56–57
Wilson, Woodrow, 18, 91
Winter, Ella, 54, 55
Wirin, Abraham Lincoln (A. L.), 50,
    51–52, 60–61, 118, 122, 123–25,
    144, 171, 173, 179–80
Wisconsin affiliate, 44, 58, 179,
    195
Witch hunts, 172, 195
Workers' rights. See Labor,
    organized
Working conditions in ACLU: low
    pay, threatened strikes, and, 140;
    better under Malin, 157, 208; sal-
    ary cuts and, 204, 208, 212; affili-
    ates' pay, 216

Works Progress Administration, 6

World War I, 17; strengthening ACLU, 89

World War II: spurring growth, 6; protecting democracy and, 81; challenges from, 87; making protecting dissident rights hard, 90, 103–4. *See also* Internment of Japanese Americans

Wulf, Mel, 213–16

Yasui, Minoru, 101, 102

Yates case, 144

Young Pioneers, 49